REPUTATION MANAGEMENT

The Key to Successful Public Relations and Corporate Communication

JOHN DOORLEY AND HELIO FRED GARCIA

Illustrated by Julie M. Osborn

To SUSAN,
WHO PROTECTS, DEFENDS,
AND ADVANCES A
POWERFUL REPUTATION.
THANK YOU FOR
YOUR FRIENDSHIP.

Routledge
Taylor & Francis Group
New York London

Routledge is an imprint of the
Taylor & Francis Group, an informa business

Routledge
Taylor & Francis Group
270 Madison Avenue
New York, NY 10016

Routledge
Taylor & Francis Group
2 Park Square
Milton Park, Abingdon
Oxon OX14 4RN

Printed in the United States of America on acid-free paper
10 9 8 7 6 5 4 3 2 1

International Standard Book Number-10: 0-415-97471-2 (Softcover) 0-415-97470-4 (Hardcover)
International Standard Book Number-13: 978-0-415-97471-4 (Softcover) 978-0-415-97470-7 (Hardcover)

Visit the Taylor & Francis Web site at
http://www.taylorandfrancis.com

and the Routledge Web site at
http://www.routledge-ny.com

Contents

Preface

Public Relations: The management of communication between an organization and its publics.

(Hunt and Grunig)[1]

Corporate and organizational communication: The centralized management of communication on behalf of the organization; the function is a critical contributor to an organization's reputation—and thereby its competitiveness, productivity, and financial success.

(Doorley and Garcia)

This book on public relations and corporate and organizational communication is grounded on the simple premise that everything communicators do should be respectful of, if not geared toward, the long-term interests of the organization. Organizations that manage their reputations well benefit not just in so-called soft, feel-good ways, but in quantifiable, bottom-line ways as well. Organizations that ignore the reputational effects of their actions pay the consequences over the long term, as the rash of business scandals since 2002 has shown. And the consequences range from soft, embarrassing ones to dissolution of the organization.

This book is unique because:

⇒ It covers each of the major disciplines in the field of corporate and organizational communication, bridging real-world practice with communication theory and history.

⇒ It covers the field from the perspective of reputation management, and provides a new framework for managing reputation into the future.

⇒ Each chapter was written by someone who has practiced the craft successfully at a high level.

⇒ The authors cite personal experiences, including both successes and failures.

⇒ Each of the chapters includes some history and theory, real-world, how-to information, and the perspective of a practitioner other than the chapter's author. Each chapter concludes with best practices, resources for further study, and questions for further discussion.

It is our hope that this book will help advance the practice of public relations and corporate and organizational communication by helping practitioners and students become more knowledgeable about the history, theory, and practice of their craft. Ours is not a primer—for example, we do not show readers how to write a press release. Our book presumes a basic knowledge of communication theory and practice appropriate to professional communicators, executives, and students at the advanced undergraduate or graduate levels. There are good basic public relations and communication texts on the market. What we have tried to produce is a how-to book, based on solid academic principles and written by leaders from the communication professions—a book that addresses communication problems and opportunities in a thoughtful, thoroughgoing, practical way.

This book is a team project. John and Fred have collaborated on the entire book, and have shared responsibility for drafting individual chapters. John has taken the lead in drafting the chapters on Reputation Management, Employee Communication, Media Relations, and Community Relations. Fred has taken the lead in drafting the chapters on Communication Ethics, Investor Relations, Issues Management, Crisis Management, and Challenges and Opportunities. John wrote the proposal for the book and secured the agreement with the publisher.

> We have also sought the help of several prominent practitioners whose perspectives and experiences complement ours.

We have also sought the help of several prominent practitioners whose perspectives and experiences complement ours. These contributions come in two forms: authorship of individual chapters, and contributions of sidebars or case studies within chapters.

To keep clear who wrote what, the chapters written by John and Fred have no author attribution at the beginning of the chapter; each chapter written by a contributor begins with the contributor's byline.

Illustrations

We had talked with two illustrators whose work has been prominently published in media, including *The New Yorker*. But we thought it would be nice to retain a student, and, long story short, we found Julie Osborn, a graduate student in the Center for Advanced Digital Applications Program in New York University's School of Continuing and Professional Studies. Lucky us! Julie's work, though Jules Pfeiffer-like, is original, sometimes

humorous, always engaging. It was Julie who conceived Mr. ProCom and Ms. ProCom. But then the question became: which person to use with which chapter? Being quite the serious professional communicators ourselves, we pondered the media relations challenges, the looming issues to manage. Should we prepare a crisis communication contingency plan? In the end, we decided to have Ms. ProCom adorn the cover of each of the fourteen chapters. Why? Perhaps because we have a few more male contributors in our book than female; perhaps because women communicators now have a population edge in the PR profession, or perhaps because Fred and John found Ms. ProCom to be better company. In any case, we show them working together here—teamwork, it is called, which entails picking each other up every now and then. And if any of this is upsetting to anyone anywhere—well, we simply have no comment!

Structure of the Book

Chapter 1 includes "The Ten Precepts of Reputation Management," with the tenth stipulating that reputation should be managed like any other asset—that is, in a strategic way. The rest of the chapter includes a new, copyrighted framework for implementing comprehensive reputation management. It is remarkable, but very few organizations approach reputation management in a comprehensive way, as they would any other asset; in fact, most organizations do not know what their reputations are worth. Corporate communication professionals should make it their business to understand the value of reputation, and ways to support, enhance, and measure it. Chapter 1 also includes a discussion of the Pushmi-Pullyu syndrome, whose schizophrenic tug has been felt by every communication professional.

Chapter 2 focuses on ethics. The subject is up front in the book, right where it belongs. The ethical practice of communication is neither an oxymoron nor an afterthought, but should be an integral part of practicing the craft. And it has a tangible effect on reputation. Failure to keep ethical issues always in mind can cause predictable, negative consequences. At New York University's Center for Marketing, whose students are working professionals, Fred used to teach communication ethics in the fall semester and crisis communication in the spring semester. Students invariably wanted to discuss the same case studies in both semesters; they noticed a meaningful overlap in companies with ethical challenges and crises. That led some students to note:

> Chapter 1 also includes a discussion of the Pushmi-Pullyu syndrome, whose schizophrenic tug has been felt by every communication professional.

"Better pay attention during fall or you'll be quite busy in the spring." This chapter includes general principles of communication ethics, the normative standards of behavior embodied in the codes of ethics of major professional organizations, accounts of recent scandals in communication ethics, and two historical sidebars showing that such ethical issues have been part of professional communication for many, many years.

Chapters 3–13 are organized according to the corporate and organizational communication disciplines (for example, media relations, employee communication, and government relations), or around issues or functions that protect reputation (such as corporate responsibility, issues management, and crisis communication). Each of these chapters begins with a true anecdote that reflects the essence of the chapter.

Chapter 14 looks ahead, and frames criteria for the successful practice of public relations and corporate and organizational communication in the future. It also describes ways to enhance the credibility of the communication function among senior leaders. It provides a framework for thinking strategically about the impact of communication, and on assuring that all the organizational communication functions are aligned not only with each other but also with the bigger enterprise.

> Communication is not rocket science, but it is not easy either, and it can make or break an organization, perhaps faster than any other function.

We hope that students and professional communicators will find the personal, anecdotal approach an interesting and informative complement to other books in the field, most of which take a third-person, definitional approach. This book should also be helpful to people—from managers to CEOs—who supervise or work with professional communicators. Communication is not rocket science, but it is not easy either, and it can make or break an organization, perhaps faster than any other function.

Today, those who communicate on behalf of institutions have greater power than ever before, because communication media are more powerful than ever. And professional communicators are under greater pressure to use their power in the right and responsible way to meet the pressing requirements of laws and regulations, corporate and organizational governance, and a more vigilant society. Paradoxically, pressures to compromise the forthrightness standard are also becoming greater in this increasingly competitive and fast-paced world.

In order for organizations to build solid, sustainable reputations and avoid the kinds of scandals that have recently affected so many of them, organizational communication, like organizational performance, must be proficient and ethical, because communication and performance are major components of reputation. An organization must speak to all its constituencies with one voice that is highly trained and true. It is our hope that those with a stake in corporate and organizational communication, as well as students and aspiring communicators, will find in this book sound, ethical communication principles and practices that they can believe in and adhere to over the long term.

You Say Communications … We Say Communication

This is a stylistic point, of course, but some logic can be brought to the discussion. Most academics label their disciplines and their courses as singular. They are professors of communication, and they teach organizational communication, inter-cultural communication, and so on. On the other hand, practitioners most often use the plural, and they work in departments of corporate communications, employee communications, and so on.

We're afraid the academics have it. Communication covers the entire spectrum. It is a discipline, like art or language, and is therefore singular. And to label it and think of it as singular is to help elevate what is too often perceived as tactical—for example, issuing press releases and publishing newsletters.

Most unabridged dictionaries make only a few exceptions to the use of communication as singular. They refer to the various means of sending messages as plural, so that radio, television, telephones, and the Internet are communications media. And they refer to multiple messages as communications. In the 1980s, when Fred headed "communications" for a large investment bank, he was often approached by bankers who wanted to add a phone extension or install a computer. "Communications" sounds like the phone company.

This book will go with logic, and the unabridged dictionaries, and use communication. We will use the plural only in referring to the media, and to the titles of practitioners and the names of their departments, because that is how practitioners usually refer to themselves. Everywhere else, it will be communication.

John Doorley and Helio Fred Garcia

ENDNOTE

1. James E. Grunig, Todd Hunt, *Managing Public Relations*, 1984, Holt, Rinehart and Winston, New York, p. 7.

Acknowledgments

This book would not have been possible without the active support and encouragement of many people in addition to the two primary authors and all of the contributors. We wish to thank all those who have supported us, our work, and the book. We wish in particular to thank our editors at Routledge, Taylor, & Francis Group, Matthew Byrnie and Michele Dimont, for their steady hands in helping us shape a book that would be valuable to both the professional and academic audiences.

We wish also to take a moment, individually, to acknowledge and thank those who have helped each of us in our task.

John Doorley's Acknowledgments

To Carole Doorley, with love and gratitude.

To these executives, former executives, and friends who have done the profession of public relations proud by communicating strategically, ethically, and very successfully over the years. I appreciate your reading the various iterations of the manuscript, the fervent discussions, and the insights Fred and I could not have brought by ourselves.

Albert D. Angel
Mike Atieh
John Baruch
Kenneth P. Berkowitz
Rich Coyle

Randy Poe
Robert Pellet
Richard D. Trabert
Paul Verbinnen

To these communication scholars for their encouragement, editing, and scholarly insights:

Boston College:
Edmund M. Burke

New York University:
William E. Burrows

Purdue University:
Stacey Connaughton

Rutgers University:
David Gibson
Todd Hunt

James Katz
Brent D. Ruben

University of California, Santa Barbara:
Ronald Rice

University of Missouri:
Donald Ranly

Western Michigan University:
Maureen Taylor

To Lisa Ryan and Jim Masuga of Heyman Associates for helping to recruit contributors and coauthors. To Michael Cushny of NYU for sending us Julie Osborn, our illustrator.

To the following family, friends, and colleagues for their logistical, proofreading, and editing support: Carole Doorley, Jonathan Doorley, Nanci Doorley, Clark and Nancy Landale, Madeline Najdzin, Nick Kornick, and Dr. Charles P. Yezbak.

Helio Fred Garcia's Acknowledgments

Much of the content of the chapters I drafted was honed over several decades of advising clients and teaching students, mostly at NYU. I thank those clients and students whose insights and challenges allowed me to grapple with the issues distilled here.

I thank my partners and colleagues at Logos Consulting Group, especially Barbara Greene and Anthony Ewing, for their help framing much of the content, and for their ongoing support and insight.

Elizabeth Jacques did much of the research for Fred's chapters and copyedited much of the manuscript. I thank her for the care she showed in helping make the manuscript more effective.

Investor relations expert Eugene L. Donati played a significant role in assuring that the content of Chapter 8, investor relations, was both accurate and current. He receives my heartfelt thanks for efforts above and beyond the call. I also thank Michael Watts, who heads IR at Gen-Probe, for providing the anecdote that opens the IR chapter.

Lisa Wagner of ArtTech Web designed the graphics in the ethics, issues, crisis, and challenges chapters, and I thank her for helping to make complex ideas easy to grasp.

Finally, I wish to thank the three women in my life: my wife, Laurel Garcia Colvin, and our children, Katie and Juliana Garcia. They tolerated my burying myself in research and writing, and my too-frequent absences, and always welcomed me home.

About the Authors

This book is written and edited from the perspective of communicators who have done it and taught it.

While John Doorley was head of corporate communications at Merck, from 1987 until 2000, the company was on just about everyone's "most admired" list, usually at the top. And while John won't play the rooster taking credit for the dawn, he will accept some credit for the company's accomplishments on the communication front. Before joining Merck, he was the chief speech writer for the CEO of Hoffmann-La Roche Inc. From the academic perspective, John learned a lot over the years as an adjunct at Rutgers University and New York University (NYU). Then, upon joining the full-time Communication Department faculty at Rutgers in the fall of 2001, he developed a course called Organizational Reputation Management, and it is on that subject that he is especially focused. His work in reputation management has been covered in *PR Week* and *O'Dwyer's Public Relations News*, and *PR News* called him a "luminary on reputation management." John moved to NYU in the fall of 2004 when he was retained by Renee Harris of the School of Continuing and Professional Studies to help build the curriculum for the new MS degree in public relations and corporate communication. (The list of courses is much like the list of this book's chapters.) When the program was launched at NYU in September 2005, John was named clinical assistant professor and academic director. He holds a bachelor of science degree in biology from St. Vincent College and a master of arts in journalism from NYU. John has won numerous writing awards, has been recognized by the New Jersey Governor's Office for his pro bono work with pediatric cancer patients, and recently received the Award For Outstanding Service from NYU's School of Continuing and Professional Studies. John can be reached at johndoorley@aol.com.

Helio Fred Garcia started in public relations in 1980 and has focused increasingly on high-stakes challenges that directly affect reputation and competitiveness. In the 1980s, Fred worked at leading public relations firms, and was head of public relations for the global investment bank CS First Boston and for a large public accounting firm. He spent more than a decade as head of the crisis practice at the consulting firm Clark & Weinstock. Fred founded Logos Consulting Group, dedicated solely to crisis management and communication, in 2002. Fred also heads the Logos Institute for Crisis Management and Executive Leadership, which provides executive education and coaching to help leaders protect or restore their organizations' reputations. He has advised hundreds of companies and thousands of executives. Fred has been on the NYU faculty since 1988, where he was recently involved in helping build the new MS degree in public relations and corporate communication; he teaches courses in communication strategy and communication ethics, law, and regulation in that program. He also teaches crisis management in NYU's Stern School of Business Executive MBA Program, and has taught many courses in crisis communication, spokesmanship, communication ethics, public policy, and related fields in NYU's Center for Marketing. He also is a frequent guest speaker at the Wharton School at the University of Pennsylvania and other academic institutions. Fred received a BA with honors in politics and philosophy from NYU, two graduate certificates in classical Greek languages and literature from the Latin/Greek Institute of the City University of New York Graduate Center, an MA in philosophy from Columbia University, and an honorary doctorate in humane letters from Mount Saint Mary College.

About the Contributors

Chapter Contributor Biographies

Unless otherwise specified, the chapters were authored by John Doorley and Helio Fred Garcia. The other authors' biographies follow, in chapter order:

Chapter 4, New Media, by Andrea Coville, CEO of, and Ray Thomas, consultant to, Brodeur

Andrea Coville   A founding partner of Brodeur, Andrea Coville leads its global executive team, plays an active role as a senior client consultant, and is involved in the company's branding, marketing, and strategic positioning. Formerly president of Brodeur Worldwide (and before that, general manager and managing partner), Andy has worked with IBM, Philips, IKON Office Solutions, Baan, Fidelity Investments, Pitney Bowes, and 3M, among other clients. Before joining Brodeur, Andy was with the West Coast-based PR firm Franson & Associates and at Infocom, an entertainment software company. She began her career as a journalist writing for New England-area newspapers and magazines. Andy earned a bachelor's degree in English literature and journalism at the University of New Hampshire.

Founded in 1985, Brodeur is a leading strategic communications group with branded offices and partners operating from eighty offices in over fifty countries worldwide. Brodeur specializes in public relations, marketing, and corporate communications in sectors such as technology, finance, healthcare, and consumer marketing.

Ray Thomas   Ray Thomas is a consultant to and former chief operating officer of Brodeur. He also led the agency's advanced technology practice and provided corporate communication, investor relations, and strategic marketing counselling for selected clients. Ray's twenty-seven years of corporate and business communication experience with Burroughs, Data

General, and EMC spans all areas, including integrated marketing communication programs, sales communication, and mergers and acquisitions (M&A) activity. He joined Brodeur in 2000 as senior vice president of business technology and became executive vice president in 2001. He was named COO in December 2005. Ray holds a bachelor's degree in mathematics with a minor in English from the University of Detroit.

Chapter 5, Employee Communication, by the authors with significant input from Jeff Grimshaw, partner, CRA, Inc.

Jeff Grimshaw   Jeff Grimshaw is a partner with CRA, a communication consulting firm focused on increasing organizational effectiveness. Jeff and his colleagues have worked with dozens of Fortune 500 companies. Their work includes:

⇒ Coaching hundreds of leaders to enhance their credibility, influence, and relationships in order to promote change and deliver business results.
⇒ Elevating internal communication as a truly strategic business function that aligns employees with the leadership agenda.
⇒ Conducting qualitative and quantitative research to show what's working, what's not, and what to do about it.

Before joining CRA in 1993, Jeff worked for a member of Congress for several years.

Chapter 6, Government Relations, by Ed Ingle, managing director of government affairs, Microsoft Corporation

Ed Ingle   Ed Ingle oversees Microsoft Corporation's lobbying activities in Washington, D.C., and has over twenty years of public policy and political experience. He was named managing director of government affairs for Microsoft in August 2006. He previously served in the White House as a senior aide to President George W. Bush. Ingle was a consultant for twelve years with the Wexler & Walker government relations firm, where he lobbied Congress and the Executive Branch on behalf of corporate clients. He served in the Reagan White House Office of Management and Budget from 1985 to 1989. Ingle has a bachelor's degree in journalism/public relations from the University of Tennessee, and a master's in public administration and policy from Indiana University.

Chapter 9 Global Corporate Communication, by Lynn Appelbaum, APR, associate professor, The City College of New York, and Gail S. Belmuth, vice president of global corporate communications, International Flavors & Fragrances Inc.

Lynn Appelbaum   Lynn Appelbaum, APR, is an associate professor at The City College of New York (CCNY), where she is program director of the advertising and public relations specialization in the Department of Media & Communication Arts. She has taught at CCNY since 1993.

Prior to her academic career, Appelbaum managed media relations for NBC News' "Today." She served as public affairs director for Cooper Union, and marketing director of Merkin Concert Hall in Manhattan. She continues to consult for agencies and nonprofit organizations. Appelbaum has conducted a major research study of diversity in public relations. She serves on the executive committee of the board of directors of The Public Relations Society of America-New York (PRSA-NY) and was awarded the chapter's Dorf Mentoring Award. She has written about mentoring in PRSA's *Strategist* and about crisis communications in PRSA's *Tactics*.

Gail S. Belmuth   Gail S. Belmuth, former vice president of global corporate communications, International Flavors & Fragrances Inc. has twenty years of global corporate communication and international political consulting experience. Currently on hiatus to raise her toddler daughter, Ms. Belmuth has held senior positions in corporations and communication agencies including Burson-Marsteller and Banner McBride, and has run her own consulting practice. Former clients include Unilever, Textron, Cemex, the National Cable Television Association, the governments of Russia, Kazakhstan, Bolivia, El Salvador, and Panama, and a presidential candidate in Colombia. Ms. Belmuth graduated Phi Beta Kappa, magna cum laude from Brown University with a degree in Russian Studies. She completed post-graduate work at Leningrad State University.

Chapter 10, Integrated Communication, by Tim McMahon

Tim McMahon   Tim McMahon heads McMahon Marketing, specialists in corporate branding and integrated communication. Additionally, he is counsel to The Dilenschneider Group Inc. a global communications consulting firm based in Manhattan. From 1997 to 2002, McMahon headed corporate marketing and communications for ConAgra Foods. Early on he was in charge of national advertising for Pizza Hut and headed marketing at the fastest-growing restaurant chain in the country. He graduated from the University of Nebraska–Omaha and holds a master of arts degree in strategic communication and leadership from Seton Hall University and is currently pursuing a PhD at Gonzaga University. He has owned and operated successful restaurants, radio stations, and an advertising agency.

Chapter 13, Corporate Responsibility, by Anthony P. Ewing

Anthony P. Ewing   Anthony P. Ewing is a lawyer, management consultant, and expert on corporate responsibility. As a partner at Logos Consulting Group, Anthony has advised clients in a range of industries, including healthcare, technology, financial services, and manufacturing. Anthony's corporate responsibility practice has helped companies and trade associations to engage stakeholders, define corporate human rights standards, and implement compliance programs and partnerships. He also advises nonprofits on strategic planning, board relations, and strategic communications. Anthony teaches a graduate seminar on business and human rights offered jointly by the Columbia University business and law schools. His writing and research examines corporate human rights programs and corporate responsibility best practices. Anthony holds a BA in political science from Yale University and a law degree from Columbia University.

Sidebar Contributor Biographies

Susie Adams   Susie Adams is vice president of public and community affairs of Duke Power. She is responsible for electric company communications to customers, employees, regulators, government officials, and the financial community. Adams graduated from Clemson University with a bachelor of science degree in administrative management, and earned a master of arts degree in speech communication from the University of Georgia.

Sharyn Bearse   Sharyn Bearse began her career as a secretary and worked her way up to director of corporate and employee communications at Merck when it was one of the world's most respected companies. During her tenure, Sharyn's group won numerous awards for communication initiatives with employees and shareholders.

Rosalind Bennett   Rosalind Bennett is a communications specialist at Duke Power. She is responsible for a variety of communication activities, including content management for the company's external and internal Web sites. Bennett graduated from the University of North Carolina at Chapel Hill with a bachelor of science degree in industrial relations.

Kenneth P. Berkowitz   Kenneth P. Berkowitz, a graduate of Brooklyn Law School with a master's degree in trade regulation law from NYU Graduate School of Law, had a unique position at Hoffmann-La Roche Inc. U.S.A., a major healthcare products company, based in Basel, Switzerland. As vice president of public and regulatory affairs and drug safety, his responsibilities included virtually the entire corporate communications and public affairs spectrum as well as drug regulatory and safety issues. He is now a healthcare industry consultant and served as president of the Healthcare Marketing and Communications Council.

Roberta Bowman   Roberta Bowman is vice president of external relations and chief communications officer of Duke Energy, responsible for the company's brand and reputation, corporate communications, and philanthropy. She is also president of the Duke Energy Foundation. Bowman graduated from Tufts University in Medford, Massachusetts. She has spent nearly thirty years in the energy industry and public relations profession.

Sandra Boyette   Sandra Boyette is senior advisor to the president of Wake Forest University. Prior to that appointment, she was Wake Forest's vice president for public affairs, and then vice president for university advancement. She is a graduate of the University of North Carolina–Charlotte; holds a master's degree in education from Converse College; and earned her MBA at Wake Forest.

Barbara M. Burns   Barbara M. Burns, APR, Fellow of the International Public Relations Association (IPRA), heads up BBA Communications, Inc, a New York City consultancy specialized in international practice. Barbara is the 2001 recipient of the PRSA Atlas Award for Lifetime Achievement in International Public Relations. She is president-elect of the PRSA New York chapter, and serves as the UN representative in New York for IPRA.

Lou Capozzi   Lou Capozzi is chairman of the Publicis Public Relations and Corporate Communications Group. He leads all of the PR firms and related agencies in the world's fourth-largest communications holding company. Formerly CEO of Manning, Selvage & Lee, Lou was also vice president of corporate communications for Aetna Life & Casualty and earlier held communications positions in both public relations firms and corporations. A journalism graduate of NYU, he holds an MBA in finance from Bernard Baruch Graduate School of Business.

Steve Doyal   Steve Doyal is senior vice president of public affairs and communications for Hallmark Cards, Inc. A 30-year communicator at Hallmark, Steve leads the company's corporate communications, public relations, and government affairs functions. He also is responsible for reputation management and crisis preparedness, and serves on the company's ethics committee. He is a graduate of the University of Missouri School of Journalism and is a trustee of the University of Missouri-Kansas City and Baker University.

Mel Ehrlich   Mel Ehrlich is a New York-based communications consultant and writer/editor specializing in pharmaceuticals and healthcare. He is also a PR skills trainer. He teaches public relations at the Marketing and Management Institute at New York University's School of Continuing and Professional Studies.

Bill Heyman   Bill Heyman is president of Heyman Associates, the largest executive recruitment firm specializing in public relations and corporate communications. He and his colleagues are involved in several initiatives to improve the quality of public relations practice.

James E. Lukaszewski   James E. Lukaszewski, ABC, APR, Fellow PRSA, is chairman of The Lukaszewski Group. Jim is a corporate advisor with special experience and knowledge in crisis communication and community relations. For more information visit his firm's Web site at http://www.e911.com.

Raleigh Mayer   Raleigh Mayer is principal of MK Coaching, a communications counsel and training firm. Formerly vice president of public affairs for the New York City Marathon, Mayer is also an assistant professor of marketing at NYU and CCNY.

Alan Nelson   Alan Nelson, a CRA partner, is an authority on leadership communication and communication strategy. His clients include senior leaders at Carlson, EDS, Korn/Ferry International, McDonald's, Merrill Lynch, Morgan Stanley, and PepsiCo. He has led dozens of studies examining the relationships between corporate communication, culture, and performance.

Julie M. Osborn   Julie M. Osborn, illustrator, was born and raised in Danville, California. She traveled south for college to the University of California, Dan Diego, where she majored in studio art and minored in Japanese. In the fall of 2005, she moved to New York for a change of pace at NYU's School of Continuing and Professional Studies, where she is currently working toward her MS in Digital Imaging and Design at the Center for Advanced Digital Applications.

Jay Rubin   Jay Rubin, a public relations writer and consultant to some of America's best-known companies, is president of Jay Rubin & Associates. He also writes speeches for various senior executives in the communications and consumer products industries, conducts business writing seminars on-site at companies, and serves as an adjunct faculty member at NYU's MS Degree Program in Public Relations and Corporate Communication.

Judy Voss   Judy Voss, APR, is director of professional development for the PRSA, the world's largest organization for public relations professionals. The PRSA Web site can be found at http://www.prsa.org.

CHAPTER 1

Reputation Management

> *If you don't know where you're going, any road will take you there.*
> *(This may not be an ancient proverb, but it should be.)*

In 1998 Abercrombie & Fitch published a back-to-school catalog with a section advocating that college students drink creatively, rather than just participate in the standard beer binge. The section, headed "Drinking 101," contained recipes for the Woo-Woo, the Beach Hemorrhage, and other potent mixtures. The organization Mothers Against Drunk Driving was irate. Within days, NBC's Today Show was set to interview MADD's president, but the clothing company refused to send a spokesperson (issuing just a brief statement). The question is: Should the company have sent a spokesperson?[1]

When that question is asked of communication or PR majors (this book's coauthor John Doorley has done this with many classes) most students say yes; often the teacher is the only dissenter. The reason for dissent: The company had not formulated any policy expressing embarrassment, let alone shame, and there was no commitment to mitigate the damage— for example, recall the catalog and help wage responsibility-in-drinking campaigns. Most college students are not of drinking age, and the company appeared to care little about the health of the people who wear their clothing. What could the spokesperson have said, in lieu of repudiation and correction, that would not have made the matter worse? For as Will Rogers was fond of saying: "When you find yourself in a hole, the first thing to do is stop digging."

Eventually, of course, the company had to issue statements and provide stickers for existing catalogs that advocated responsibility in drinking. MADD and most PR observers agreed it was too little too late.

It turns out that A & F has published catalogs for their young audiences with nude models, and been criticized for not featuring people of color. It seems that A & F is not concerned about their reputation with older audiences, believing perhaps that the younger audiences will not care about the social issues and may even want their clothing all the more. One has to hand it to the company: It is a bold marketing strategy, and a very risky reputation strategy, especially over the long term. Creating demand is one thing, but alienating the people who pay the bills, as well as groups that devote their lives to a cause, is another. (By the way, what is the name of that organization of mothers that almost single handedly forced the United States government into the nationwide drinking-age limit of 21?)

****

This Chapter Covers

⇒ Reputational capital

⇒ Identity

⇒ Can reputation be measured?

⇒ Can reputation be managed?

⇒ "Intangible asset"—the wrong perspective

⇒ Comprehensive reputation management

⇒ Confusing communication with performance and behavior

⇒ Sidebar: It's all about the relationship

⇒ The ten precepts of reputation management

⇒ Reputation management: The best corporate communication strategy

⇒ Sidebar: Systems theory

⇒ Best practices

⇒ Resources for further study

⇒ Questions for further discussion

Shakespeare called it "the purest treasure mortal times afford." Men have fought duels and killed for it. Companies and other institutions have succeeded or failed because of it. Warren Buffett said: "If you lose dollars for the firm by bad decisions, I will be very understanding. If you lose reputation for the firm, I will be ruthless." It seems that Mr. Buffett was paraphrasing Othello: "He who steals my purse steals trash … but he that filches from me my good name … makes me poor indeed."[2]

The business scandals of the first years of the twenty-first century demonstrated how important it is to build, maintain, and defend reputation. The scandals spread to nonprofits, government, universities, and sports, and the public seemed to tire of the press reports. But fatigue did not convey immunity, so people demanded change: tougher laws, more governance, and greater accountability. At the same time, academic researchers and public relations professionals intensified efforts to quantify and manage reputation, heretofore thought of as an intangible asset.

Reputation scholar Charles Fombrun, professor emeritus, Stern School of Business, New York University, an editor-in-chief of the journal *Corporate Reputation Review*, defines reputation as the sum of the images the various constituencies have of an organization.[3]

John Doorley and Fred Garcia (this book's coauthors) accept that definition but also like their own—which leads us to:

> Reputation = Sum of Images =
> (Performance and Behavior) + Communication
>
> This definition helps make it clear that performance and behavior, as well as communication, are critical components of reputation.

Reputational Capital

Just as people develop social capital that helps them build relationships and careers, corporations and other organizations develop reputational capital that helps them build relationships and grow their organizations.

A good reputation has both intangible and tangible benefits. It is important for audiences, from customers to employees to consumer advocates, to feel good about an organization, and it is important to build a good reputation to sustain an organization through the tough times. But a reputation is worth much more than that. Companies with the better reputations attract more and better candidates for employment, pay less for supplies, gain essentially free press coverage that is worth as much if not more than advertising, and accrue other benefits that actually contribute to profits. Reputation adds value to the actual worth of a company—that is, market capitalization (the number of shares outstanding times the price per share) includes more than just the book value or liquidation value of assets. The reputation component of market capitalization, reputational capital, is a concept closely related to "goodwill," and it is worth many billions of dollars in many large corporations. It has a value in not-for-profits, government, and universities as well. For instance, a good reputation helps a university attract students and donors.

Although CEOs agree that reputation has a value—is an asset—few firms actually treat it as such. Few companies or nonprofits take a rigorous, quantifiable approach to reputation management—measuring, monitoring and managing reputation assets and liabilities—yet such an approach is intrinsic to the concept of asset management. Most organizations have no idea what their reputations are worth, yet reasonable measurements (absolute or relative) can be agreed upon and taken. Most companies do not have a system in place for regular, periodic accountability on variations in reputation, yet without such a system opportunities will be missed and problems will become magnified. Measurement, acknowledgment, and planning make possible proactive behaviors and communications to take advantage of reputational opportunities and minimize problems—thereby building reputational capital.

Although CEOs agree that reputation has a value—is an asset—few firms actually treat it as such.

Identity

To reputation scholars like Fombrun, "identity" is the raison d'etre of an organization. It is, simply, what the organization stands for above all else. To distinguish this concept from other uses of the term (such as corporate identity programs that try to position the company in a particular way through all its communications and graphic vehicles), Paul Verbinnen of Citigate Sard Verbinnen coined the term "intrinsic identity." (We use that term in this book.)

Of course organizations, like individuals, have multiple identities. Research by George Cheney of the University of Colorado, in *Rhetoric in an Organizational Society: Managing Multiple Identities*, is consistent with the proposition that multiple identities need not pose any conflicts, as long as there is a clear, dominant identity.[4] Johnson & Johnson, for example, seeks not just to develop, make, and market quality healthcare products for patients, it also seeks profits large enough to attract shareholders, reward employees, and stoke research. But the commitment to serving patients and the healthcare community, as expressed in the company's credo and demonstrated in the response to the Tylenol® tampering crises in 1982 and 1986, has clearly been the dominant identity over the years.

Other companies, such as the venerable General Electric and the relative upstart Starbucks, have each stayed true to a dominant identity: respectively developing and marketing consumer and technology products of the highest quality, and employing the best people to obtain, market, and sell quality coffee and collateral products in a warm and welcoming venue. Starbucks is not at all embarrassed to proclaim the ideals of mutually beneficial and profitable relationships with employees and communities. A Starbucks ad running in national media in 2005 stated: "It's about idealism, and community, and sustainability. It's about remembering how things should be, and striving to get there."[5]

Other organizations, sadly and notably, have recently failed to stay true to the dominant identities that made them successful:

The Catholic Church. The scandals over the sexual abuse of young children by some priests, which came to light starting in the Boston Diocese in 2002, were shocking and horrible enough. Catholics and non-Catholics recognized that evil could exist anywhere. But what drove many Catholics away from the church was the coverup by the church hierarchy, from bishops to cardinals. In numerous instances, they knowingly sent offending priests to other parishes without telling the legal authorities or the people in the new parish, leaving the priests free to commit the same crimes over and over. The average priest believes he exists to give spiritual and emotional guidance to the people in his parish, but many of the bishops and cardinals forgot that raison d'etre; instead, they believed they had to protect the church's image at all cost.

In his first public statement as Boston's new archbishop, Sean P. O'Malley made explicit reference to the need to return to the Church's intrinsic identity:

> *"We can only hope that the bitter medicine we have had to take to remedy our mismanagement of the problem of sexual abuse will prove beneficial, making all of us more aware of the dreadful consequences of this crime and more vigilant and effective in eradicating this evil from our midst. How we ultimately deal with the present crisis in our Church will do much to define us as Catholics of the future. If we do not flee from the cross of pain and humiliation, if we stand firm in who we are and what we stand for, if we work together, hierarchy, priests, religious and laity, to live our faith and fulfill our mission, then we will be a stronger and a holier Church."* [6]

The New York Times. To its credit, *The New York Times* broke the story itself in a front-page exposé on May 11, 2003. Reporter Jayson Blair had plagiarized content from other newspapers, had fabricated whole stories, and had invented scenes for stories that appeared in the paper, including major front-page ones over a period of years. There were warning signs bold and numerous enough to have stopped him early on, but the top editors ignored them. Why did the people charged with seeing that the country's "newspaper of record," the one that exists to report "all the news that's fit to print," publish the unfit? An explanation that makes sense is that one of the paper's other identities—including its commitment to affirmative action (Blair is African American) and a desire not to rock the boat about a reporter thought to be a favorite of the executive editor—superseded, in this case, its commitment to quality. So while the paper can be proud of its various identities, it cannot be anything but humbled by its failure to live up to its commitment to quality journalism, above all else.

In the wake of the Blair scandal, *The Times* has reaffirmed its commitment to its intrinsic identity, and has established numerous structures, including a new public editor and a new standards editor, to try to assure that it is not distracted from its mission again.

It is important for employees to understand and be committed to the organization's dominant intrinsic identity. For example, if the CEO truly believes the organization is committed above all else to quality products, but the average sales person believes the dominant identity is the sales quota, there exists a prescription for disaster. For in difficult times, what the employees believe the organization stands for will determine what they will do, just as surely as it did with Blair and the church.

> For in difficult times, what the employees believe the organization stands for will determine what they will do.

Another benefit of a clear identity is that it can drive behavior, performance, and communication, as it should. Then, internal and external constituencies will all understand what the organization is about.

Can Reputation Be Measured?

Fombrun maintains that reputational capital is the difference, averaged over time, between market capitalization and the liquidation value of assets. Many chief financial officers disagree with that formula, believing that the difference overstates the value of reputational capital. But even those CFOs agree that much of that difference is reputational capital. The more common approach to measuring reputation is to take comparative measures against similar organizations. The annual Fortune magazine survey of America's Most Admired Companies is among the most widely known and respected by both industry leaders and academics. But it surveys only three constituencies: senior executives, (outside) board members, and securities analysts. A more comprehensive approach would include surveying all the major constituencies, including employees, customers, and the press.

Another is the Harris-Fombrun Reputation Quotient (by Harris Interactive in association with Charles Fombrun). It evaluates reputation among "multiple audiences," according to twenty attributes that are grouped into what are referred to as "dimensions of reputation": products and services; financial performance; workplace environment; social responsibility; vision and leadership; and emotional appeal. The results of that survey are widely covered by the press, including each year, Ronald Alsop of *The Wall Street Journal*, author of *The 18 Immutable Laws of Corporate Reputation*.

Can Reputation Be Managed?

There are many organizations with "reputation management" in their names and their number has increased markedly since the Sarbanes-Oxley Act became law in the wake of U.S. corporate scandals. Yet most of them are actually reputation measurement organizations that offer little in the way of reputation management. There are many conferences on reputation management, yet they too focus on measurement or only on specific parts of reputation management, such as crisis communication. They do not produce a plan or a document that aims to manage reputation as other assets are managed—including the plusses and the negatives associated with any asset.

Some academics believe that reputation can be managed, while others believe it cannot be. While more research in the field of reputation management is needed, the pro-management body of academic literature is certainly as strong as the contrary studies, if not stronger. And one thing is certain, as recent business scandals have demonstrated in the sharpest relief: reputations can surely be mismanaged, and in many cases, not managed at all. There is a clear need for a new approach that will help companies and other organizations measure, monitor, and manage their reputations, and the factors that contribute to reputation, organization-wide, over the long term.

"Intangible Asset" – The Wrong Perspective

The reason most organizations do not have formal programs to manage reputation is that they view it as something "soft"—intangible. Yet as nebulous as reputation can seem, it has real, tangible value (dollars, for example) that can be measured. So the historical view of reputation as an intangible asset is the wrong approach. Moreover, such a view is analogous to that of some parents who say they need not be that concerned about their young children's character, because "they will be influenced by their peers anyway when they become teenagers." Such laissez-faireism—whether in parenting children or organizations—is a prescription for disaster, as recent history has clearly demonstrated.

So the historical view of reputation as an intangible asset is the wrong approach.

Like all other assets—a building or a product, for example—reputation has its liability side. So any reputation management plan has to measure, monitor, and establish a plan for managing both the reputation assets and vulnerabilities/liabilities. The important thing is to have a plan. If the following is not an ancient proverb, it should be: "If you don't know where you're going, any road will take you there."

So a major question for leaders of organizations is: Can reputation be managed? It follows that those who believe it can be managed—perhaps not totally, but which asset can be?—must establish a plan to do so, as they would for any other asset.

Comprehensive Reputation Management

"Comprehensive Reputation Management" (*Copyright 2003, John Doorley*) provides a formal framework for managing reputation. It is one way for an organization to get its arms around this asset, and a way to manage reputation problems, vulnerabilities, and opportunities. It has been vetted before the leadership of The Conference Board, many industry leaders and CEOs, numerous academic researchers, and heads of corporate communications at thirty major companies. Paul Verbinnen and Rich Coyle of Citigate Sard Verbinnen made significant contributions.

Comprehensive Reputation Management =
A long-term strategy for measuring, monitoring, and managing an organization's reputation as an asset. Comprehensive Reputation Management is to reputation what risk management is to other assets

This strategy results in the management of an organization's intrinsic identity (what it stands for) and external images, giving an organization a methodology for working to converge the two. The Comprehensive Reputation Management methodology is applied to the major areas of an organization—for example, finance, human resources, investor relations, manufacturing, marketing, and public affairs. Each area gets involved in a process that is a way of approaching total reputation management—(performance and behavior) + communication—and is distinct from brand management (the marketing value of a name) or corporate identity programs (which usually boil down to institutional advertising).

These are the six major components of Comprehensive Reputation Management:

1. *Customized Reputation Template.* The measurement tool begins with a basic template that is then customized for each organization. In some cases, the organization may simply want to improve its ranking in an established poll, such as *Fortune* magazine's, which is based on eight criteria or attributes: innovativeness, quality of management, employee talent, financial soundness, use of corporate assets, long-term investment value, social responsibility, and quality of products/services. Certain of the financial measures may be more important to some companies than to others, as might be environmental performance and community relations (under "social responsibility") and so on.

    Reputation Criteria: Basic Template for Comprehensive Reputation Management program includes:

    ⇒   Innovation
    ⇒   Quality of Management
    ⇒   Employee Talent
    ⇒   Financial Performance
    ⇒   Social Responsibility
    ⇒   Product Quality
    ⇒   Communicativeness (Transparency)
    ⇒   Governance
    ⇒   Integrity (Responsibility, Reliability, Credibility, Trustworthiness)

    The first six are the time-tested *Fortune* criteria, with the three financial measures collapsed to one. Communicativeness is part of the template because there has now been more work done to demonstrate the link between an organization's transparency and its reputation. (See reference to *Corporate Reputation Review* paper in The Best Communication Strategy section, later in this chapter.) Governance is listed because it is now, especially post Sarbanes-Oxley, an important part of the reputation mix. Integrity is this model's way of encompassing the four character traits that research by Fombrun and others has shown to have a direct effect on reputation: responsibility, reliability, credibility, and trustworthiness.

The basic template can then be customized for the particular organization, and the resultant customized template becomes senior management's acknowledgment of which reputation factors are most important. The customized template becomes the tool for measuring changes in reputational capital. The template can also be customized by constituency, because different constituencies care more about different attributes.

2. *Reputation Audits of Internal and External Constituencies.* One audit assesses what employees believe to be the intrinsic identity (what the organization stands for) and compares that with what senior leadership believes the intrinsic identity to be. The gap between the two views is analyzed and a plan (part of the Reputation Management Plan) to converge them is created. A second audit measures how external constituencies view the organization, and the sum of those constituency images constitutes reputation. The gap between identity and reputation is analyzed, and a plan (part of the Reputation Management Plan) to converge the two is created.

3. *Reputational Capital Goals.* Goals are established for performance within an industry group, for example, or versus competitors. For example, a company might establish a goal of moving up into the top quartile of its industry sector. Progress toward that goal can then be measured, monitored, and managed.

4. *An Accountability Formula.* This is based on changes in reputation measured against the customized template. If the organization is slipping according to one reputation attribute (for example, communicativeness) particular departments, such as public relations, can be given the responsibility of correcting that impression through proactive communication initiatives.

5. *A Reputation Management Plan.* This is the deliverable that the Comprehensive Reputation Management process produces. It is a strategic performance (behavior) and communication plan for convergence of identity and reputation—a plan to move the images the various constituencies hold about the organization closer to the

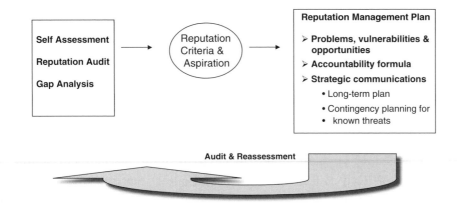

Figure 1.1

intrinsic identity. The very act of having to list their reputational assets and liabilities helps the various units focus on reputation management. The Reputation Management Plan includes: a summary of the internal and external audits; measures of reputational capital; a statement of reputation challenges and potential problem areas by company or organizational unit; the respective goals and opportunities; and corporate or organizational message strategies. With objectives, strategies, timelines, and so forth, the Reputation Management Plan becomes a strategic guide for units of the organization to follow, short—and—long term.

6. *Annual Follow-Up Audit and Assessment According to the Standards in the Reputation Management Plan.*

Confusing Communication with Performance and Behavior

Pushmi-Pullyu. In Kurt Eichenwald's *Conspiracy of Fools*, Enron CEO Kenneth Lay proclaims to his public relations officer Mark Palmer, not long before the collapse of the company: "The reason we can't right the ship is we're not doing a good job in dealing with the press."[7] In other words, Lay saw a communication problem, not a performance or behavior problem. On the other hand, a major article about professional basketball in *The New York Times Magazine* of February 13, 2005, maintained that the National Basketball Association does not have a "drug problem or a thug problem (or a PR problem)." Instead, the players, despite their unprecedented athleticism, do not play with teamwork, the way the sport used to be played. "It has a basketball problem."

In the contest between the steak and the sizzle the steak will, inevitably, prove more important. Or, as in Enron's case, the sizzle will always evaporate. Wendy's television commercial from the 1980s, "Where's the beef?" said it best.

In *The Story of Doctor Doolittle*, by renowned children's author Hugh Lofting, the good doctor comes across a mythical, rare animal in Africa. It is a llamalike creature with one head at the front, where it would normally be, and one at the base of its spine, and it is called Pushmi-Pullyu. "Lord save us," cries the duck. "How does it make up its mind?"[8]

The Pushmi-Pullyu metaphor (devised by John Baruch, LittD, former CEO of Reed & Carnrick) is a fitting one to represent the problem that public relations and corporate communication practitioners face: the confusion of behavior or performance with communication—of the substantive issue with the communication about it. While the communication objectives and strategies should always be in synch with the business objectives and strategies, they are distinct. Communication cannot make a bad product good, at least over the long run. Of course it can make a good or fair product seem worse, as it did with the Exxon Valdez crisis in 1989. (Many observers agreed that Exxon did a pretty good job operationally in cleaning up the oil spill, but the communications were a disaster.) In 2006, the mishandling of communication regarding the hunting accident involving Vice President Dick Cheney clearly made the matter worse, and played right into the hands of the press and its insatiable appetite for sensationalism.

Pushmi-Pullyu is a syndrome that explains the generations-old lament of corporate and organizational communicators about their lack of a "seat at the table." The reason this has been a problem, of course, is that, too often, an organization develops an ill-advised product or position, or takes such an action, and then asks the communications group to justify it. The performance/behavior head is turning in one direction and saying one thing, and then it expects the communications head to turn and speak in a different direction.

The Pushmi-Pullyu Syndrome: "A pattern of behavior whereby an organization performs or behaves in one way but expects the communications professionals to explain that performance away. Assembled in that fashion, two heads are not better than one—and they should be merged so that performance/ behavior and communication can turn and talk in a confluent direction."

Merck. When John Doorley was hired in 1987 to form Merck's first corporate communications department the company was not widely known outside of business and healthcare circles. But it was on fire with success—with important new medicines and excellent profits—under the leadership of P. Roy Vagelos, MD, whose own reputation as a scientist and businessman was impeccable. The ensuing public relations campaign, led by an aggressive media outreach initiative, produced quick results. For instance, an October 19, 1987, cover story in *Business Week was* headlined, simply, "The Miracle Company." The campaign continued through the nineties, fueled by an outstanding science and business story, and Merck landed on everyone's most admired list (including a record seven years as America's Most Admired Company in *Fortune*'s annual cover-story survey). It was all PR, essentially free, with virtually no corporate advertising.

Since 2000 the company has been hit by the perfect storm of dreadful events. Several late-stage investigational medicines failed in the clinic, and the company's pharmaceutical research, which had always been cyclical, hit a nadir. The profit picture began to look bleak and the company missed some of its own earnings projections. Then, in the fall of 2004, the company decided to recall the painkiller Vioxx, because of cardiovascular side effects in certain patients. Amidst what at this writing may turn out to be the largest wave of product liability suits ever, the company fights for its reputation against charges of side effect coverup.

In October 2004, presumably because of the ongoing litigation, the company chose not to aggressively discuss the matter with *The Wall Street Journal* reporters whose seminal front-page article exploring the allegation appeared on November 1, 2004. The company had provided an outside attorney as spokesperson and did not address questions about individual documents. Yet the *Journal* is one of the publications that could be most disposed to letting the company make its case, and Merck's failure to do so in the article predictably produced pack journalism reports on the major TV expose magazine shows. On May 30, 2005, after enormous reputation damage, the company launched a multimillion-dollar advertising campaign, which, the company said, had been in the works for a few years. If the campaign is to be successful, it will need to be matched by significantly improved research, financial performance, and an aggressive public relations program. The strategy of using controlled (paid) media makes sense, but only in conjunction with the more credible, albeit less controlled, communication initiatives that tell the story of performance.

Reframing the Problem. In 2002 this book's coauthor Fred Garcia was called into a company to consult on what the communications people called a "*Fortune* magazine problem." They said *Fortune* was working on a story about the company's chairman, a flamboyant, politically connected executive who had borrowed millions of dollars from the company to support a lavish lifestyle. The chairman's business and political enemies were pointing to the lifestyle, and to other personal foibles and business failures, and the company's stock was suffering. Investors and analysts were asking questions but getting no satisfactory answers. It seemed like the worst mix of Enron, Tyco, and WorldCom. Company leadership was also concerned that the weakening stock price could lead to a hostile takeover.

Fred asked the company leadership what would happen if *Fortune* magazine should be persuaded not to run a story: would the problem be solved? They acknowledged that they would still be as vulnerable to take-over and to critics' capitalizing on the company's weakness in other ways. "You don't have a *Fortune* magazine problem," Fred told them, "you have a governance problem." He met with the general counsel and several board members. They discussed various scenarios under which they could rem-edy the company's weaknesses. Regardless of the scenario, one thing was consistent: success required the chairman to resign and to repay his loans to the company. The only meaningful question was timing: could he leave before the company suffered more harm, or would he resist, leading to calls by shareholders and others for his resignation, declines in the stock price, and eventually his ouster? Given the alternatives, the Board persuaded the chairman to leave quickly. He resigned within two weeks, and repaid his loan. The company's stock price rebounded. There was no takeover. And no *Fortune* article.

The solution to the struggle represented by the Pushmi-Pullyu meta-phor—the solution to the push and pull of substance and communica-tion—is to have the entire organization behave and communicate as one.

It's All About Building The Relationship

By Kenneth P. Berkowitz, Esq.

A critical first step in reputation management, it seems to me, is the building and cultivation of relationships with key constituencies. Show me a successful PR practitioner or lobbyist, and I will show you some-one who has developed strong individual relationships and cultivates them in a planned, concerted way on an ongoing basis. Building and maintaining relationships, as is true of reputation, should be viewed as a full-time effort.

The best way to establish a relationship is to understand that it must benefit both parties—in this case, the organization as well as other con-stituencies, the government including regulatory agencies, news media, customers, suppliers, employees, and other important constituencies. It should come as no surprise, therefore, that a critical first step is to identify the critical constituencies of the organization. Practitioners should then identify or, as necessary, conduct research to determine the constituency's needs and then use that information for the benefit of both parties, what the academics call the "two-way symmetrical" model (Media Relations Chapter 3). What often happens is that PR departments do the research and then try to exploit it for the organization's benefit alone ("two-way unsymmetrical"); this seldom proves a productive strategy over the long run. And once an established relationship "sours," it may prove to be unsalvageable.

Along those lines, relationships have to have a degree of unselfishness in order for the parties to be respectful of each other. It's a dot-connected world—Word gets around. And a PR practitioner or company lobbyist cannot afford to just disconnect from a relationship when it becomes unproductive: for example, when the reporter retires or a legislator loses an election, or when the constituency acts against the interest of the organization. Disagreement must be anticipated, as one can never expect both parties to be in agreement on all issues.

So that this aspect of relationship management is not viewed as "soft" and static or unmanageable, formal strategies and objectives should be established and monitored. The strategies and objectives should also force practitioners to go out and meet face-to-face on an ongoing basis with their constituencies, which is a hard thing even for some public relations people and lobbyists to initiate. You almost need to treat your constituencies as sales people would treat their customers. Here are five such strategies that I have encouraged my colleagues to implement over the years:

(1) Target key areas that really matter to your organization. Public relations practitioners and lobbyists have to focus first on areas where the organization has business or other interests, particularly areas where they can make a difference. It does little good to try to meet with reporters at each of the one hundred top dailies, or to establish relationships with every congressional or state legislative staffer (and remember that staff can be as important as the elected official). While you need to target the capitals (Brussels, Washington, and the state capitals, for example) absolutely do not forget the communities where the organization has a large business, factory, distribution facility, or employee base.

(2) Target the leaders but do not stop there. This can be a very difficult challenge unless you have sufficient resources at your disposal. Research can identify who the thought leaders are within particular constituencies and who or what influences their views on issues. Seek to cultivate relationships with as many of them and/or their staffs as possible. But do not stop here; instead, identify others (individuals or organizations) who may have important roles to play.

(3) Identify the emerging players. Who are the up-and-coming staffers and journalists, for example? A particularly good time to establish relationships is when a new official is elected or a staff member or reporter comes on board. PR practitioners who cultivate those people before they become major players can hope to establish strong relationships before anyone else even tries to. Once the staffer or journalist reaches the top, stand in line.

(4) Use the organizational resources. Work with key groups in your organization so that you have all the necessary data and facts at your disposal depending on the particular issues. Do not be fearful of bringing your experts to meet with constituencies. While preparation is critical, it is often the expert that reporters or governmental representatives would appreciate meeting with on an issue. It does not undermine your relationship, but should strengthen the other party's view of you and your organization. At the same time, make sure that you are always kept in the "loop."

(5) Always be the first to tell the "news" to your constituency—particularly if it is bad news. This is very important in maintaining strong relationships and credibility. Once a person has heard from others, it becomes extremely difficult to change views or opinions and could undermine existing relationships.

The U.S. healthcare industry, which I have always been proud to be a member of, is embroiled in controversy over pricing, access, and other significant issues. Never before has the industry faced such grave challenges. Yet few industries produce the societal benefits the healthcare industry does. If the U.S. industry is to continue to lead the world in the discovery, development, and marketing of medicines and other healthcare products, we must rebuild our reputation. And if we are going to succeed we have to build stronger and more productive relationships with all our constituencies. One relationship at a time.

The Ten Precepts of Reputation Management

These precepts are meant to help professionals who spend their workdays communicating on behalf of organizations. Because the precepts are intended to help with reputation management, they have as much to do with performance and behavior as with communication.

1. *Know and honor your organization's intrinsic identity.*

   Jim Burke, the CEO of Johnson & Johnson during the Tylenol®
tampering cases of 1982 and 1986, said he deserved little credit for
the extensive product recalls, which were undertaken at much risk
to the franchise and the finances of the company. He explained
that the company credo—its intrinsic identity—puts the health
of the patient first. That credo begins: "We believe that our first
responsibility is to the doctors, nurses, and patients, to mothers
and fathers, and all others who use our products and services."[9]
When a company acts always in ways that reflect its first responsibility to the people who use its product, and people are dying after
using its product, the decision to pull its product is an easy one.

   The Johnson & Johnson case stands in stark contrast to the sexual abuse scandal in the Catholic Church, where bishops put what
they perceived to be the interest of the organization above the emotional and spiritual well-being of the people they exist to help. Of
course organizations have multiple identities (for example, quality
products and competitive profitability), but as George Cheney and
other researchers have demonstrated, the identities must be com-
patible, and one must be dominant. That dominant, or intrinsic,
identity must be clear to the members of the organization. It is
what the organization stands for, and it will often determine what
the employees will do as a first resort, in good times and bad.

2. *Know and honor your constituents.*

   The American Red Cross, among the most successful and highly
regarded charities in U.S. history, had good intentions when it
decided to withhold from the families of the victims of 9/11 some
of the monies donated for them. The fund had generated an over-
whelmingly generous response, and the leadership of the Red Cross
reasoned that not all the monies were needed by the families, and
that it would be prudent to save some to help when future disasters,
man- and God-made, strike. Donors were outraged, and a major
crisis ensued.

   The moral: do not presume to know the will of your constituents, and do not presume that good intentions alone are sufficient
to protect against criticism that the organization is acting against
the interests of its key constituents.

3. *Build the safeguards strong and durable, for they are the infrastructure
   of a strong reputation.*

   Former U.S. Federal Reserve Chairman Alan Greenspan maintains that greed was the root cause of most of the recent business

scandals, but he acknowledges that weakened safeguards let the greed flourish. The misuse of company funds by the Rigas family at Adelphia Communications illustrates the point. According to the U.S. Securities and Exchange Commission, the scandal represents "one of the most extensive financial frauds ever to take place at a public company." Not only did the internal controls—from company lawyers to accountants to the board of directors—fail to function, the external ones—from auditors to bankers to regulators—did as well. The moral: strong, efficient safeguards, internal and external, are in an organization's best interests.

4. *Beware the conflict of interest, for it can mortally wound your organization.*

   Few firms in history had better reputations than Arthur Andersen, and a statue of the company namesake and founder stood tall at the company's training facility as a reminder of what he stood for: the meticulous and rigorous auditing and reporting of a client's finances. Andersen's primary duty was to the shareholders of companies whose books it audited. But by 2001 Andersen's imperative to boost revenues and profits had eroded structures intended to assure the independence of auditors. Andersen allowed itself to act in its own short-term interest and against the interests of its clients' shareholders. The compromising of audit standards and auditor independence was discussed publicly within and outside the firm for years before the damage became apparent and severe.

   After the Enron/Andersen scandal broke in late 2001 and early 2002, a committee of some of society's most respected leaders, including former U.S. Federal Reserve Chairman Paul Volker and former Merck CEO P. Roy Vagelos, was convened to save it. But by then the firm's intrinsic identity—meticulous, honest auditing—had already been so compromised that the core had been ruined; Andersen was convicted of a crime and soon closed its doors.

   Paul Volker once said that it is only the people or organizations that have not accomplished very much who could be free of all potential conflicts. Nevertheless, when it comes to major conflicts or conflicts that threaten the viability of an organization, it's like U.S. Supreme Court Justice Potter Stewart said of pornography: it may be hard to define, but you know it when you see it.

5. *Beware of the " CEO Disease," because there is no treatment for it.*

   It is the same malady the Greek gods said destroyed so many tragic figures, and it is called hubris. Chief executives command tremendous incomes, power, and prestige. Thousands of employees almost genuflect when they walk by, and powerful people from all sectors of society treat them with deference. It must be difficult not to fall into certain traps, such as wanting to be surrounded by employees who always agree with them. Ask anyone who has worked in corporate communications for a long time: There is a "CEO Disease" (and heads of governments, nonprofits, and universities are not immune).

One of the manifestations of hubris is an inability to see that a looming problem requires immediate attention. Many CEOs mishandle initial phases of a crisis out of either arrogance or willful blindness, caused by a misplaced sense of invincibility. The outcome is otherwise manageable crises that result, ultimately and after much hardship, in the CEO's ouster. The year 2004 saw more forced CEO turnover than any year since such statistics have been compiled. According to the consulting firm Booz Allen Hamilton's annual CEO succession survey, the "giant sucking sound heard in the business world during 2004 was the extraction of chief executives from seats of power ... The first quarter of 2005 brought headline-generating forced successions at Disney, Hewlett-Packard, Boeing, and AIG, linked to shareholder dissatisfaction, scandal, or both."[10]

6. *Beware of organizational myopia, for it will obscure the long-term view.*

Especially during times of crisis, organizations tend to focus on the short term. It's part of the corporate and organization condition, and not falling into that trap is one of the lessons of crisis management (Chapter 12). Sometimes organizations are given plenty of advance notice of issues looming large, but few heed the warning signs.

7. *Be slow to forgive an action or inaction that hurts reputation.*

Warren Buffett said it best to a group of Salomon Brothers managers after a 1991 trading scandal hit the bank in which he had an interest. The quote, at the beginning of this chapter, bears repeating: "If you lose dollars for the firm by bad decisions, I will be very understanding. If you lose reputation for the firm, I will be ruthless."

8. *Do not lie.*

People tell lies, most of which are small and harmless, and some of which may even be good things ("Honey, do I look heavy in this dress?"). Similarly, organizations are not always completely forthcoming with information and, indeed, that is sometimes a very good thing (Media Relations, Chapter 3). But lying is of course a slippery slope, eventually dragging the organization into a deep hole from which there is no extrication. Organizations can often get away with lying for a while, but that's all. Sometimes, efforts to mislead have significant adverse consequences, a lesson learned by President Nixon with Watergate, President Clinton in the Monica Lewinsky scandal, and by Martha Stewart, who was prosecuted, convicted, and imprisoned for lying to law enforcement officers.

9. *Dance with the one that "brung" you.*

This aphorism, popular within sports teams, applies to organizations as well as individuals. By the fall of 2000, it was becoming clear that Firestone tires were leading to traffic accidents, and many of them were on the Ford Explorer. Bridgestone-Firestone blamed Ford and vice versa. A business and public relations crisis ensued, and in May 2001 the two companies severed their business relationship that had endured for almost one hundred years. Most analysts agreed that the crisis was compounded by the lack of cooperation, and although the relationship was later revived, the damage had been done. Likewise, it is not uncommon today for a firm that is downsizing to give pink slips to employees, and then have a security guard publicly usher them to the gate—even those employees with excellent, long-term records. Thankfully, however, many other companies take monumental initiatives to be loyal to their employees, customers, and other constituencies. Aaron Feurstein, owner of Malden Mills in Lawrence, Massachusetts, was able to retain all his employees after a fire destroyed his factory in 1995. He said he would simply not abandon his employees, and quoted from the Torah, or Jewish Law: "He is poor and needy, whether he be thy brethren or a stranger."[11]

10. *Reputation is an asset and must be managed like other assets.*

Reputation is intangible, but it has great, tangible value (worth many billions of dollars in large corporations, for instance). It is therefore an asset. Failure to acknowledge reputation as an asset can be self-fulfilling. By ignoring reputation and factors that harm or help it, companies often behave and communicate in ways that cause harm to the reputation. Successful stewardship of reputation not only protects against the downside, but can affirmatively enhance the enterprise value of an organization. Because the component parts of reputation (performance/behavior and communi-

---

Reputation = Sum of Images =
(Performance and Behavior) + Communication

cation) can be managed, one should devise a strategy and plan to measure, monitor, and manage it on an ongoing basis.

Reputation Management
The Best Corporate Communication Strategy

The remaining chapters of this book flow from a discussion of ethics (Chapter 2), to a discussion of approaches to working with the various corporate communication constituencies (Chapters 3–10), to ways of handling certain major responsibilities (Chapters 11–13), to the challenges facing those who seek to build a career in corporate and organizational communication (Chapter 14).

The premise of Chapter 1—that reputation can be measured, monitored, and managed—begs for the adoption by corporate communications departments of a long-term strategy of reputation management, customized for the particular constituencies, and in synch with an intrinsic identity that the entire organization understands and believes in.

A growing body of scholarship shows links between reputation and business performance, and the ability of public relations, particularly corporate communications, to impact reputation. Such studies include:

Journal of Public Relations Research, "Measuring the economic value of public relations," Yungwook Kim, 2001. "This study established a two-step model to measure the economic value of public relations by testing two relationships: the impact on reputation as a goal of public relations, and the economic impact of reputation on companies' bottom lines." The study showed a positive causal relationship between public relations and reputation, and a positive causal relationship between reputation and revenue.

Southern Economic Journal, "A latent structure approach to measuring reputation," Quagrainie et al., 2003. "The study provides estimates of reputation as a dynamic latent variable that is determined by price premiums and market data." It showed a positive effect between reputation and the prices a company can charge.

Corporate Communications, "Measuring corporate reputation," Bradford, Stewart Lewis, 2001. "This paper considers how corporate reputation is most influenced by the actions of an organization rather than a successful (or otherwise) PR campaign, and how a communication strategy can best influence reputation." The paper established that it is important to measure and manage reputation by constituency.

Corporate Reputation Review, "The concept and measurement of corporate reputation …," de la Fuente Sabate et al., Winter 2003. "This paper … leads us to a new definition of corporate reputation, one that not only introduces the perceptions of how the firm behaves towards its stakeholders, but also takes into account the degree of transparency with which the

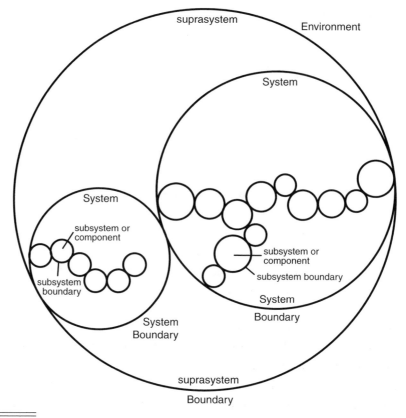

Figure 1.2

firm develops relations with them." The paper established that information transparency (communicativeness) affects reputation and the ability to do business.

Positive reputations have a positive effect on a company's ability to do business.

Since reputation is the sum of performance/behavior and communication, an effective corporate communication strategy must be that inclusive. As with individuals, the relationships an organization has will succeed or fail based on performance/behavior and communication. In other words, relationships must be sound and aggressively fostered. Such a strategy can ensure that the organization moves forward, avoiding the Pushmi-Pullyu Syndrome and the reputation pitfalls.

Systems Theory

Communication is the means by which an organization functions, and it is axiomatic that the better the communication the more productive the organization. That proposition is supported by communication theories, most notably in the case of corporate communication by General Systems Theory. It provides a communication framework which conceives of organizations as living things composed of interrelated components or parts. It provides a way of thinking of an organization not as an amalgam of distinct, seemingly unrelated disciplines, such as finance, customer service, or research, but rather as a whole that comprises components bound together by certain commonalities. As a system, the organization is part of a community that is part of other communities and they all interact, wittingly or unwittingly, in a planned or unplanned way. Systems theory can help communicators and leaders of organizations adopt a working philosophy that communication is the only way to unity and synergy within the organization, and to openness and harmony with systems (for instance, publics) in the environment outside the organization.

"One of the fundamental concepts of General Systems Theory can be traced to Aristotle," explains Rutgers University Communication Professor Brent Ruben, "who said in *Politics* that a state is composed of villages, which are in turn made up of households, which contain families.[12] Conceiving of entities in terms of wholes and interrelated parts is a basic concept in the general system framework of today."

The modern-day father of systems theory in organizational communication was Ludwig von Bertanffly, who conducted his research in the 1950s and 1960s. He was influenced by researchers who were working at the time to identify and express the generalities that tie the scientific disciplines together, so that biology and physics, for example, could be viewed in an interrelated way, rather than as separate, highly specialized fields. For example, cybernetics, which can produce a self-regulated machine that can perform functions greater than any part could, represents a specific application in the physical sciences; Gestalt psychology, which approaches psychotherapy from the perspective of the whole person, including the diverse systems of which he is a part, as opposed to an analytical approach, represents an application in psychotherapy.

Within the communication framework of systems theory, an organization can be pictured as a series of systems and subsystems within a supra system (see Figure 1.2). For example, a company could be pictured as a system, the departments as subsystems, and the particular industry as the supra system that functions within the environment of society. Of course, each supra system, system, and subsystem has a boundary and contains components (individuals). The boundaries are porous, opening subsystems to systems to supra systems to the environment. Subsystems and components are identified by the processes they perform. (Systems figure reproduced with the permission of Ruben, Gibson et al. of Rutgers University.)

Systems theory provides a framework for organizational communication based on the following properties and principles common to all systems. The properties and principles have implications for all communication enterprises, with employee communication, media relations, government relations, investor relations, and community relations being among the most obvious:

⇒ Just as in a biological system where information flows from one cell to another, information in an organization flows across the borders in what theorists like Professor Ruben call the "metabolism of information." It follows that the more effective the communication, the more productive the organization.

⇒ No part of a system, no person within an organization, can exist by himself or herself. This is the theoretical basis for tearing down the "silos," which became a theme throughout industry in the 1990s.

⇒ Systems are dynamic. Feedback, from one component to another and with the environment, is essential. Implications for dialogue and engagement are clear in communication enterprises ranging from classroom learning to employee communication. The old communication model of sender-receiver may work for thinking in terms of transferring information; it is not helpful for understanding more complex processes involved with attitudes and behavior.

⇒ Participation in the system is mandatory. One cannot not communicate. (That is the phrase attributed to communication scholars Watzlawick, Beavin, and Jackson). [13] Engagement is essential.

⇒ Human communication systems are "open systems." As opposed to closed, self-contained systems, which, for example, produce predictable chemical reactions in a test tube, the reactions of the things that go into an open system cannot be precisely calculated in advance; that is, the output cannot be calculated from the input. The open system has properties distinct from its parts; the total, therefore, is not equal to the sum of the parts.

⇒ There are generalities that tie the parts together but one must be careful here. To say something meaningful about the whole—for example, the employee audience—is to omit specifics about the parts. "The key is to find the optimum degree of generality," Professor Ruben states. The implications for audience segmentation (internal or external audiences) are clear.

⇒ The environments within and surrounding the supra system, systems, and subsystems shape those parts, and the reverse is true as well. Likewise, the environment shapes the individual's view of reality, and the individual actually shapes the environment. That is, the environments of a company (everything from the physical and cultural environments within and around the company to the country in which the company is based) shape the employees and vice versa. This point illustrates the great potential of communication.

Systems Theory: a framework that supports many of the principles expressed in the following chapters.

"The systems approach," Professor Ruben states, "has been a particularly useful foundation for what may be thought of as the quality approach to organizations. The dominant metaphor for the Quality School is team, which relies on communication for success." Sports metaphors about teamwork may be clichéd, but they have solid foundation in theory as well as practice.

Professor Ruben: "Communication is the lifeblood of human systems. It is the means through which leadership functions, the mechanism by which parts relate to one another, the process by which systems relate and adapt to their environments. In organizations, quality and effective multidirectional communication go hand in hand."

Best Practices: Reputation Management

1. Understand and value the components of reputation, including integrity, governance, and communicativeness (transparency).
2. Establish a formal mechanism to periodically measure reputation.
3. Establish a formal mechanism—for example, a regularly scheduled meeting of senior officers, or a "Reputation Management Plan"—to manage reputation on an ongoing basis. The very act of establishing and adhering to a formal mechanism clearly expresses leadership's commitment to protecting the reputation asset.
4. A formal mechanism (for example, a Reputation Management Plan) can help your organization converge brand reputation and the broader corporate reputation with intrinsic identity (what the organization stands for).

Resources for Further Study

Ronald J. Alsop, *The 18 Immutable Laws of Corporate Reputation, A Wall Street Journal Book*, Free Press, New York, 2004.

Paul Argenti, *Corporate Communication*, Dartmouth University, The Amos Tuck School of Business Administration, McGraw-Hill, 1998.

The Corporate Communication Institute at Fairleigh Dickinson University.

The Corporate Reputation, an electronic newsletter by Peter Firestein, president of Global Strategic Communications Inc., at http://www.firesteinco.com/reputation.

Corporate Reputation Review: An International Journal, Henry Stewart Publications.

The Expressive Organization: Linking Identity, Reputation and the Corporate Brand, Majken Schultz, Mary Jo Hatch, and Mogens Holten, Eds., Larsen Oxford University Press, New York, 2000.

Charles J. Fombrun, *Reputation: Realizing Value from the Corporate Brand*, Harvard Business School Press, Boston, 1996.

The Institute of Public Relations, http://www.ipr.org.uk/reputation.

Measurement of "intangible assets." Refer to the work of Professor Baruch Lev of New York University, the Stern School, http://www.stern.nyu.edu/~blev/main.html - 9k.

Michael Morley, *How to Manage Your Global Reputation: A Guide to the Dynamics of International Public Relations*, New York University Press, 2002.

Leslie Gaines Ross, *CEO Capital: A Guide to Building CEO Reputation and Company Success*, John Wiley & Sons, New York, 2003.

Questions for Further Discussion

1. Why do you think *The New York Times* was for so long blind to reporter Jayson Blair's plagiarism and fabrications?
2. Why is it that most by far of the organizations that claim to provide reputation management services are really selling reputation measurement? Do they really not know the difference?
3. Can you think of examples of the Pushmi-Pullyu Syndrome in your organization? Should that animal, exciting though it may be to watch, ever be permitted to exist in an organization?
4. Are companies whose products largely share the company name (Coca-Cola, Johnson & Johnson, etc.) at an advantage or disadvantage in terms of reputation management?
5. Is it easier to manage the reputation of an organization in a free or totalitarian society?

CHAPTER 2

Ethics and Communication

> *Management is doing things right; leadership is doing the right things.*
>
> – Peter F. Drucker

In August 1990, Iraq invaded Kuwait. In the days that followed, Hill & Knowlton undertook a major campaign to mobilize U.S. public opinion to defend Kuwait and go to war with Iraq. Hill & Knowlton was the largest and, by some accounts, the most powerful public relations firm in the world.

Working for an entity it described as "Citizens for a Free Kuwait" (CFK), Hill & Knowlton staged a number of public events that it said represented the interest of private Kuwaiti citizens in the United States and Canada. After the 1991 Gulf War, investigative reporter John R. MacArthur wrote a book called Second Front: Censorship and Propaganda in the Gulf War, *which called into question the legitimacy of much of Hill & Knowlton's work, including the identity of Citizens for a Free Kuwait.*

Although Hill & Knowlton insisted, both to MacArthur and to the CBS television news magazine 60 Minutes, *that its client was a group of concerned citizens and not the government of Kuwait, MacArthur concluded that Citizens for a Free Kuwait was a front group for the government. "The 'Citizens' part of the organization was a fiction, as was the pretense of being an ordinary nonprofit charity. After the war, when it grudgingly owned up to its true status, CFK reported to the Justice Department receipts of $17,861 from seventy-eight individual U.S. and Canadian contributors, and $11,852,329 from the government of Kuwait."[1]*

Jack O'Dwyer, editor of a leading public relations trade newsletter, characterized the veracity of Hill & Knowlton's claim by analogy: "If the manufacturer of a suit that was 99.85% cotton called it a wool suit because it was 0.15% wool, you'd expect the company to be arrested."[2]

Hill & Knowlton's work for a front group while denying that it was working for the government of Kuwait was just one of the many ethical issues exposed by MacArthur. His book set off a fierce debate about the ethics of communication and the role of professional communicators in mobilizing public opinion.

The controversy severely damaged the reputation of Hill & Knowlton, of the public relations industry, and of the Public Relations Society of America (PRSA), which was paradoxically silent about the scandal while its members, the media, and critics were calling for it to take a stand on the controversy. Six months after the scandal broke, the chair of the association's "PR for PR Committee" called the PRSA its "own worst enemy."[3]

Six years after the CFK scandal, the PRSA began a complete overhaul of its ethics process. The PRSA's new Member Code of Ethics, ratified by the society's membership in October 2000, specifically addresses front groups. Its provision on The Free Flow of Information says that a member shall "reveal the sponsors for causes and interests represented." Under "Examples of Improper Conduct Under This Provision" it includes a clause that specifically describes front groups purporting to represent one interest but secretly representing another interest.[4]

And today the PRSA has a mechanism for commenting on ethical issues, comprising Practice Advisories, which provide standards on ethical issues in the news, and Practice Commentaries, which provide topical comment on ethical behavior.[5]

* * * * *

> Communication ethics: normative standards of behavior that govern the practice of pubic relations with integrity.

This Chapter Covers

⇒ Why ethics matters
⇒ What is ethics?
  – Ethics and morality, legality, etiquette, and aesthetics
  – Ethics as habits
  – Codes of ethics and normative standards of behavior
⇒ Ethics and organizational communication
  – International Association of Business Communicators Code of Ethics for Professional Communicators
  – Public Relations Society of America Member Code of Ethics
  – International Public Relations Association Code of Athens
⇒ Ethics of communicating
  – Are press releases unethical?
  – Are video news releases unethical?
  – Corrupting the channels of communication
  – Front groups
⇒ Ethics of running a business
  – Confidentiality
  – Preventing conflicts of interest
  – Ethics of routine business relationships

⇒ Ethics of representation
⇒ Helping companies behave ethically
⇒ Sidebar: Case study: Citizens for a free Kuwait
⇒ Sidebar: Historical perspectives on communication ethics
⇒ Ethical communication best practices
⇒ Resources for further study
⇒ Questions for further discussion

Introduction: Why Ethics Matters

The ethical practice of corporate communication and public relations is a given for many professional communicators. And celebrated ethical scandals such as the Citizens for a Free Kuwait debacle are considered by many practitioners to be aberrations.

But to much of the outside world there is something vaguely unethical about the entire enterprise. Such phrases as "just PR" or "spin" suggest that people see a meaningful difference between truthful and candid discussion and the kinds of activities that professional communicators are thought to engage in. This has been a perennial concern for practitioners of the craft, from the roots of professional communication in the fourth-century BC through the formative years of the modern practice of public relations in the twentieth-century AD, to the present.

The irony is that most professional communicators not only practice ethically but also deliberately want to do so. And many corporations, learning the lessons of Enron, WorldCom, Andersen, and other celebrated corporate scandals of 2001–2, now recognize that inattention to ethical issues exposes them to far worse consequences than they may have previously understood.

Inattention to ethics risks significant harm to reputation and to other important intangible corporate assets—including employee morale and productivity, demand for a company's products, confidence in a company's executives, and stock price performance. Ethical lapses also lead directly to changes in senior leadership of a company. Inattention to ethics and the consequences of unethical behavior, as evidenced in the collapse of Enron, Andersen, and other well-known companies, can even affect an organization's ability to survive.

What is Ethics?

Despite a general desire to practice corporate communication ethically, many professional communicators have only a passing knowledge of ethics and the way ethical standards have evolved in business generally and in the professional practice of communication in particular.

Ethics and Morality, Legality, Etiquette, and Aesthetics

Individuals and companies often get into ethically murky situations because they confuse ethics with morality, legality, etiquette, or aesthetics—that is, they confuse actions with motives, crimes, politeness, or feelings.

Many people associate the word "ethics" with some sense of morality, and often use the words "ethics" and "morality" interchangeably. And although there is a high degree of overlap between the words, they mean different things and should not be confused.

Ethics concerns behavior—what people do—and the behavior at issue is often public. Morality concerns motivation—why people do things. And because morality involves intention and attitudes, it is generally within the realm of personal conscience, and is typically private. Sometimes morality drives ethics; that is, sometimes personal conscience leads to admirable public behavior. But sometimes the admirable public behavior takes place for other reasons.

Although some people might wish that all actions be done for the right reasons, from an ethical perspective motives are less important than the actual behaviors. Take a simple example: lying. As an ethical issue, it is a matter of indifference whether people refuse to lie because they are afraid of getting caught, because they have become habituated to not lie, or because of a strong moral commitment to honesty. From an ethical perspective, the person who does not lie—for whatever reason—is behaving ethically. Similarly, someone who lies for benevolent or moral reasons—for example, from a desire not to hurt someone's feelings or to protect a loved one—commits an ethical offense. It doesn't matter that the motive was positive, even that the motive was moral. All that matters in such a case is that the lie—the public behavior—is unethical.

The same applies in the corporate world. It is more important that a company insist on ethical behavior by its employees than that it do so for some moral reason. Some companies' leaders are genuinely driven by a moral desire to practice business ethically—to do what is right. Others are driven by a desire to avoid the distraction and costs associated with ethical lapses. And some insist on ethical behavior because they know that having and policing a strong code of ethics protects them under U.S. federal sentencing guidelines should they or their employees be convicted of a crime. But the motive for a company's behavior is less important than recognizing that its behavior is acceptable or unacceptable. And because morality is a private matter, it is often difficult to discern a company's, or an individual's, true motive. Sometimes people and companies act from a mixture of both moral and practical motives.

Ethics is also often confused with legality; unethical behavior with illegal behavior. In broad overview, morality, ethics, and the law are all part

Individuals and companies often get into ethically murky situations because they confuse ethics with morality, legality, etiquette, or aesthetics—that is, they confuse actions with motives, crimes, politeness, or feelings.

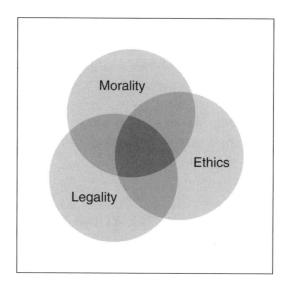

Figure 2.1

of a continuum of sometimes overlapping considerations. Take again, for example, lying—telling a deliberate untruth with the intention of deceiving. Lying can be seen to be a moral failing. Lying to someone in a business context can be seen to be an ethical lapse, the violation of a codified or implied rule stating that people in business not lie to each other. And in some circumstances, such as lying under oath or to a criminal investigator, lying may trigger legal action. So, for example, Martha Stewart's lie to federal law enforcement officials may have been a moral lapse, and it may also have been an ethical lapse. But Ms. Stewart was prosecuted, convicted, and sent to jail not for moral or ethical lapses but for violation of the criminal law.

It may be useful to think of morality, ethics, and legality as three circles of a Venn Diagram, with some overlap among the three areas, but each a distinct set of issues with its own distinct worldviews, considerations, and consequences.

Sometimes people compartmentalize the three, and fail to recognize that the violation of one of these may also be a violation of others. For example, in 2002 it became widely known that many Roman Catholic priests in the United States had sexually abused children, and that the bishops who ran the church in the United States had known about the problems for years and had done little to stop the abuse.

Abusing children was clearly immoral—in the vocabulary of the church, a sin. And it was also a clear violation of priests' own codes of ethics, particularly their vows of celibacy. But what seemed to be unaddressed was the fact that such behavior is also a crime. Before the scandals became widely known in 2002 few Roman Catholic priests had been prosecuted; afterward many were, including some of the most notorious abusers. Now some dioceses have established zero-tolerance policies, including recognition that allegations of abuse should be turned over to law enforcement authorities for investigation and prosecution.

Sometimes legal and ethical duties conflict: For example, the ethical duty to maintain confidentiality, such as a reporter's promise to keep the identity of a source secret, and the legal duty to answer questions when testifying under oath in a trial or in a grand jury investigation. In 2005 the U.S. Supreme Court refused to consider an appellate ruling that journalists could not refuse to identify their sources to a grand jury investigating the leak of classified information about a Central Intelligence Agency operative. As a result, a *The New York Times* reporter, Judith Miller, went to jail rather than violate her promise—described by her and *The New York Times* as an ethical obligation—to protect the identity of her source.

Similarly, some actions may be perfectly legal but also unethical, such as representing two companies with conflicting interests. While such client relationships may violate ethical standards, unless there is a contractual prohibition against such a relationship the law is generally silent about them.

It is also common for people to confuse ethics with etiquette: what is polite. For example, some people consider it impolite to criticize others. So they sometimes withhold criticism, or even tell a "white lie"—that is, an innocent untruth not intended to deceive, but to flatter—in order to avoid giving offense. While this kind of behavior is often seen to be admirable, the conflict between etiquette and ethics often comes into full focus when a desire to avoid offense leads to more than an innocent untruth, but to a full-blown lie; that is, a deliberate untruth intended to deceive. Often the duty to be truthful conflicts with the desire to be polite, and ethical people sometimes need to tell hard truths to others; failure to tell those hard truths may be seen as unethical. More significantly, because ethics refer to habitual behaviors, the default to etiquette over ethics can habituate someone to default to politeness over truthfulness, leading to inadvertent ethical lapses.

> Sometimes legal and ethical duties conflict.

Similarly, ethics is often confused with aesthetics: what is pleasurable. People say things that make them and others feel good, regardless of the underlying truthfulness of the statement. Or they avoid saying things that may be unpalatable to them or to their audiences. Like etiquette, the desire to feel good and help others feel good is often admirable, but can lead to habitual behaviors that conflict with ethical duties.

Ethics as Habits

The English word "ethics" comes from the ancient Greek word that translates into the English word "habits." The word began to take on its current meaning when it was used by the Greek philosopher Aristotle (c. 384 to 322 BC) in his book *The Nichomachean Ethics*, which describes habitual behaviors that lead to happiness. Over the years "ethics" has come to mean habitual behaviors that are appropriate in certain circumstances. So ethics consists of the behaviors that are habitually practiced by an individual and, collectively, by a group of individuals. As individuals form groups that serve particular purposes, they establish formal or informal codes of conduct to govern relations among themselves and between their group and other groups. Over time these codes of conduct describe socially acceptable patterns of behaviors.

It is useful to keep the word "habits" in mind when discussing ethics, because ethics describe behaviors that are repeated over time and that therefore become unconscious. As an ethical issue it is a matter of indifference whether an individual refuses to lie because of fear of getting caught or because of a strong commitment to morality. But as an individual becomes habituated over time to avoid lying, the original motive may be forgotten. Someone who initially refuses to lie because of fear of the consequences may, over time, become habituated to not lie, even when there are no likely negative consequences. In other words, the behavior becomes habitual.

Similarly, it can be risky to permit suspect behaviors, even when the reasons are defensible, because over time these suspect behaviors may become habits: so someone who lies in certain circumstances may be habituated to lie in others, and it becomes more and more likely that such a person will lie as a first resort.

> We are what
> we habitually do.
> — Aristotle

Codes of Ethics and Normative Standards of Behavior

One reason groups develop formal ethical rules is to establish normative standards for behavior that can then become habitual among members of the group. Such rules are an ordinary part of social interaction.

Over the years, and especially in the twentieth century, professional societies developed their own codes of professional behavior, establishing behaviors that are required, permitted, and forbidden among their members. So doctors in the United States are bound by the *Code of Medical Ethics* of the American Medical Association; lawyers by the *Code of Professional Responsibility* of the American Bar Association; accountants by the *Code of Professional Conduct* of the American Institute of Certified Public Accountants; and so forth.

In the 1920s, Edward L. Bernays, the first professional communicator to call himself a "public relations counselor," called for a code of ethics to govern the behavior of the emerging profession of public relations. "The profession of public relations counsel is developing for itself an ethical code which compares favorably with that governing the legal and medical professions. In part, this code is forced upon the public relations counsel by the very conditions of his work. While recognizing, just as the lawyer does, that everyone has a right to present his case in its best light, he nevertheless refuses a client whom he believes to be dishonest, a product which he believes to be fraudulent, or a cause which he believes to be antisocial."[6]

In that very description of the choices a practitioner makes, Bernays previewed some of the ethical challenges facing public relations practitioners in the twenty-first century. Today the Public Relations Society of America's *Member Code of Ethics*, the International Association of Business Communicators' *Code of Ethics for Professional Communicators*, and the International Public Relations Association's *Code of Athens* (named for the city where the code was ratified), set standards to which their member practitioners are expected to abide.

Ethics and Organizational Communication

Many practitioners of corporate and organizational communication are not members of industry associations, and many associations do not have corporate members. So technically a significant percentage of professional communicators are not bound by such industry codes of conduct. Further, membership in these associations is voluntary and is not a requirement for most jobs in corporate and organizational communication. And the maximum penalty for being found to have violated the code is removal from the association, an association that many communicators did not belong to in the first place. Some people argue that removal from a voluntary organization that does not affect employment is not a sufficient penalty to deter unethical behavior, and that therefore such codes are meaningless.

But because the codes are normative, they provide standards that both members and nonmembers can use as guides for effective action, and to which clients and others can subject any given behavior to determine whether it is appropriate. In other words, regardless of the strength of the sanctions involved, the descriptions of normative behavior provide value by setting standards against which any individual's, group's, or company's behavior can be evaluated.

Indeed, the International Association of Business Communicators (IABC) "encourages the widest possible communication about its Code," publishes the code in several languages, and grants permission to any individual or organization to copy and incorporate all or part of its code into personal or corporate codes (with attribution to IABC).

As members and nonmembers of various professional associations adapt their behaviors to these groups' normative standards, and the behaviors become habitual, they establish even stronger norms. Violations of the code, even when committed by nonmembers who are subject to no disciplinary procedures, nevertheless can be recognized as inappropriate, and as aberrations from the professional practice of communication.[7]

> The descriptions of normative behavior provide value by setting standards against which any individual's, group's, or company's behavior can be evaluated.

International Association of Business Communicators
Code of Ethics for Professional Communicators

The International Association of Business Communicators' *Code of Ethics for Professional Communicators* offers three overarching rules:

⇒ First, that members of IABC "engage only in communication that is not only legal but also ethical and sensitive to cultural values and beliefs"
⇒ Second, that they "engage in truthful, accurate, and fair communication"
⇒ And third, that they adhere to the articles of the *Code* itself.

The IABC *Code*, in turn, consists of twelve normative statements, each describing the behavior of professional communicators. These include:

Professional communicators disseminate accurate information and promptly correct any erroneous communication for which they might be responsible …

Professional communicators give credit for unique expressions borrowed from others and identify sources and purposes of all information disseminated to the public …

Professional communicators do not accept gifts or payments for professional services from anyone other than a client or employer.[8]

The complete *IABC Code of Ethics for Professional Communicators* may be found at http://www.iabc.com/members/joining/code.htm.

Public Relations Society of America Member Code of Ethics

After the Citizens for a Free Kuwait scandal broke, the Public Relations Society of America (PRSA) came under sharp criticism. The association was criticized for not taking a position in the public discussion of communication ethics, and for having a code that was difficult to follow, not particularly helpful to individual practitioners, and out of date.

The PRSA's Board of Ethics and Professional Standards, which led the revision of the code in the late 1990s, recast the code to emphasize the standards that apply to the professional practice of public relations.[9] This board focused on the fact that the most effective codes are normative, and can therefore serve as guides to the ethical practice of the craft as a whole, not just to the association's members.

The new *Member Code of Ethics* was prepared by the PRSA Board of Ethics and Professional Standards, which consisted of nine senior public relations practitioners. They were assisted by the Ethics Resource Center, a Washington-based ethics consulting organization. The Ethics Board convened a series of discussions with members in 1998 and 1999, leading to the launch of the new Code in 2000.[10] In their introduction to the new *Code*, the authors note that "the primary obligation of membership in the Public Relations Society of America is the ethical practice of public relations," and observe that the new Code "is a way for each member of our society to daily reaffirm a commitment to ethical professional activities and decisions."[11]

Unlike the prior code (and unlike several others associations' codes, including IABC's) the new *PRSA Member Code* also includes examples of behaviors that would be considered unethical, providing more concrete guidance to members and others of what would be considered inappropriate behavior. It not only lists required and forbidden behaviors in the abstract; it demonstrates by example and analogy the kinds of behaviors that are inappropriate, making it more likely that proper behaviors will be habituated, that improper behaviors will be avoided, and that practitioners will find the code useful as a guide to the real-world practice of professional communication.

The *PRSA Member Code of Ethics* consists of three parts: values, provisions, and a pledge.

Member Statement of Professional Values. These values, each of which is defined with several bullet points, include advocacy, honesty, expertise, independence, loyalty, and fairness. They provide a conceptual framework for the ethical practice of public relations.

PRSA Code Provisions. For each provision there is a plain English description of each of the code's principles, including a statement of intent, guidelines, and examples of improper conduct.

For example, the *Principle* "Disclosure of Information" is described as follows: "Open communication fosters informed decision making in a democratic society." Its *Intent* is described as "to build trust with the public by revealing all information needed for responsible decision making."

The guidelines include:

Be honest and accurate in all communications. Act promptly to correct erroneous communications for which the member is responsible. Investigate the truthfulness and accuracy of information released on behalf of those represented. Reveal the sponsors for causes and interests represented.[12] The *Examples of Improper Conduct Under this Provision* section includes the following: "A member deceives the public by employing people to pose as volunteers to speak at public hearings."[13] *The Pledge*, which each member signs, affirms his or her commitment to, among other things, "conduct myself professionally, with truth, accuracy, fairness, and responsibility to the public."[14]

The complete PRSA Member Code of Ethics can be found at http://www.prsa.org/_About/ethics/index.asp?ident=eth1.

International Public Relations Association Code of Athens

The International Public Relations Association (IPRA)'s *Code*, drafted in Athens, Greece, in 1968, begins with several *Considerations*, including the observation that "the use of the techniques enabling them to come simultaneously into contact with millions of people gives Public Relations practitioners a power that has to be restrained by the observance of a strict moral code." The *Code* then includes thirteen clauses, each framed in the imperative mood, describing things members shall do, and shall refrain from doing.

For example, one of the three *Endeavors* says that a member shall endeavor "To conduct himself/herself always and in all circumstances in such a manner as to deserve and secure the confidence of those with whom he/she comes into contact." One of three *Undertakings* says that a member shall undertake "To carry out his/her undertakings and commitments which shall always be so worded as to avoid any misunderstanding ..." And two of the four clauses describing forbidden behaviors require that members refrain from both "subordinating the truth to other requirements" and "circulating information which is not based on established and ascertainable fact."

The complete IPRA Code of Athens may be found at http://www.ipra.org/aboutipra/aboutipra.htm.

These three association codes of ethics describe, each in its own way, normative standards of behavior for professional communicators around the world. Although the specific provisions apply directly only to members of the respective organizations, they create a framework for understanding appropriate standards of conduct for all professional communicators. And although there are variations among the codes, they are generally consistent in broad overview and collectively serve as useful benchmarks against which to assess the typical ethical challenges that professional communicators face.

> Although the specific provisions apply directly only to members of the respective organizations, they create a framework for understanding appropriate standards of conduct for all professional communicators.

Ethics of Communicating

Ethics of communicating involves behaviors one engages in that are intrinsic to the process of shaping public opinion by means of communication.

Effective communication starts with a climate of belief, and credibility is the strongest asset a professional communicator can have. Most of the ethical questions relating to the practice of communication involve credibility in one way or another. The most significant issues of credibility involve truthfulness and falsity of communication, and disclosure of the client or cause on whose behalf a communication is being made.

Some critics of professional communication assert that the very idea of public relations is itself unethical, and use words such as "propaganda" and "spin" to suggest that such activities are inherently misleading. Public relations critics John Stauber and Sheldon Rampton assert that the business of public relations represents a significant social problem. They claim that

"Today's PR industry is related to democracy in the same way that prostitution is related to sex. When practiced voluntarily for love, both can exemplify human communication at its best. When they are bought and sold, however, they are transformed into something hidden and sordid."[15]

Stauber is executive director, and Rampton is research director, of the Center for Media and Democracy, which publishes *PR Watch*, dedicated to investigative reporting on the PR industry. In their 1995 book *Toxic Sludge is Good for You: Lies, Damn Lies and the Public Relations Industry*, Stauber and Rampton attribute sinister motive to the practice of public relations: "Public relations exists to manufacture the necessary illusions that bridge the gap between the dream and reality of American society ... If the PR industry were *only* based on 'lies and damn lies,' it might be easier to see through its deceptions. But PR's cunning half-truths and 'spins' appeal to us and work on us because they come from us, from the constant plumbing of the social mind by surveys, opinion polls, focus groups, and information gathered as we apply for bank loans, purchase goods with credit cards, place birth announcements in newspapers, vote, and make phone calls."[16]

Stauber and Rampton particularly object to press releases, video news releases, and other techniques common to the practice of public relations that involve providing information to journalists for their consideration and publication.

While Stauber and Rampton acknowledge that not every instance of public relations practice is by itself illegitimate, they also argue that the craft is more often used in the service of illegitimate corporate gain: "Citizens and individual PR practitioners can use ethical public relations techniques to right social wrongs, clean up the environment, promote minority rights, protect working people, and make communities better. But we consider it an illusion to imagine that PR is a 'neutral' technology that can simply be adopted uncritically to achieve socially responsible ends."[17]

But a close look at many of the arguments used by Stauber, Rampton, and other critics shows them to be oversimplifications of the corporate communication process, to project to the entire profession the unethical behavior some of its members, to confuse criticism of PR with the practices of journalism, or to use PR as a foil in the service of a political agenda—in Stauber's and Rampton's case the argument that it benefits large corporations at the expense of ordinary people. Indeed, the introduction to *Toxic Sludge is Good for You*, by journalist Mark Dowie, lays out the political agenda of the book: "A single public relations professional with access to the media, a basic understanding of mass psychology, and a fistful of dol-

> Stauber and Rampton attribute sinister motive to the practice of public relations.

lars can unleash in society forces that make permanent winners out of otherwise-evident losers—whether they be products, politicians, corporations, or ideas. This is an awesome power we give to an industry that gravitates to wealth, offers surplus power and influence to those who need it least, and operates largely beyond public view."[18]

In particular, much of the criticism also seems to blend critique of the practice of corporate communications and public relations with criticism of journalists' reliance on PR's work product.

Are Press Releases Unethical?

For example, some critics of public relations and corporate communication point to the tools used to communicate—especially press releases, video news releases, and related handouts that are provided to the news media—and suggest that these very tools are somehow sinister and misleading.

> Much of the criticism also seems to blend critique of the practice of corporate communications and public relations with criticism of journalists' reliance on PR's work product.

But most of the tools are neither. Press releases are corporate announcements written in the style of a newspaper story that a news organization may choose to use or not use. Some press releases are printed verbatim in newspapers; some are excerpted. Many press releases serve simply as a starting point from which a reporter will write his or her own story, often lifting language or quotes from the press release. Among the criticisms of press releases is the observation that quotes lifted from a release convey to the reader of the news story the impression that the reporter actually spoke to the person quoted. The suggestion is that using the quote misleads readers, giving a false impression that the reporter spoke with the newsmaker.

But a close review of such practices suggests that if there is an ethical issue, or a credibility issue, inherent in such practices, the ethical challenge is on the part of the news organization. News organizations are certainly free to ignore a press release, and many press releases are never printed in news media. News organizations are also free to supplement a release with their own reporting, including speaking with the person quoted in the release. They are also free to label the quote in such a way that lets a reader know that the quote came from a press release. Such formulations include "in a statement the company said …" or "in an announcement Mr. so-and-so said …"

From a professional communicator's perspective, the ethical duty is different: to assure that the announcement genuinely represents the point of view of the client on whose behalf it is distributed, that the source of the information is clearly and accurately identified, and that there are no deliberate falsehoods in the text of the release. So long as these ethical duties are met, the communication is generally considered ethical. All three professional association codes of ethics—IABC's, PRSA's, and IPRA's—require that all communication, including news releases and related materials, be truthful and that the source of the communication be clearly identified.

One of the counterarguments to the suggestion that press releases by their very nature are unethical is to note that often press releases are required by law and regulation. For example, under U.S. laws and regulations governing corporate disclosure in the securities markets (See Chapter 8, Investor Relations), companies whose stock is publicly traded are required to issue press releases to the media and investment community describing their financial performance and other significant news. In fact, a significant percentage of business news is the routine excerpting of such corporate press releases.

The same regulations that require press releases as a financial disclosure device also establish standards for accuracy and truthfulness of such communications. In general, these announcements may not be "materially misleading" or contain "material omissions"; that is, they must be accurate and complete. Releasing deliberately inaccurate or incomplete information may be considered securities fraud, and companies and individuals may be subject to civil or criminal penalties. Releasing information known by the communicator to be false or misleading is also a breach of ethics.

Are Video News Releases Unethical?

Video news releases (VNRs) are the broadcast equivalent of print news releases. Some video news releases are simply edited footage of a news event, such as a speech, presentation, testimony, or meeting, provided to television networks in much the same way as a press release. News organizations can choose whether to use any, part, or all of such video footage as part of their larger reporting on a story. Some VNRs are packaged to resemble local television news stories, including tightly scripted voice-overs, well-edited graphics, and compelling images. Television stations are free to use or not use such video news releases as they choose, including editing the footage to add their own reporting, interviews, or images.

Stauber and Rampton argue that video news releases are unethical because, among other things, they take advantage of news organizations' limited resources: "Canned news and industry-supplied 'experts' are effective because they appeal to budget-conscious news organizations. When a TV news show airs a video news release, the PR firm that produced the segment pays for all the costs of scripting, filming, and editing. Likewise, PR-supplied experts enable reporters to produce authentic-sounding stories with a minimum of time and effort. The public rarely notices the self-serving bias that creeps into the news along with these subtle subsidies."[19]

In 2005, ten years after Sheldon and Rampton's book appeared, VNRs were again in the news. The U.S. government and several public relations firms retained by U.S. government agencies were severely criticized for distributing video news releases that gave the impression that they were objective news reports that happened to promote government programs. Some of the criticism was that the VNRs deliberately mischaracterized the identity of the party on whose behalf the VNR was issued. But much of the criticism focused on the very idea of a VNR.

This scandal triggered renewed criticism of such news practices. *The New York Times* reported that at least twenty U.S. government agencies, including the Census Bureau and Department of Defense, had distributed hundreds of video news releases in recent years. "Many were broadcast on local stations across the country without any acknowledgement of the government's role in their production."[20]

In response to the 2005 VNR criticisms, the U.S. Federal Communication Commission warned broadcast and cable news organizations, according to *Reuters*, "to properly identify the source of video news releases that some government agencies have circulated through commercial TV outlets despite criticism. Congressional investigators earlier this year concluded that repackaged news stories created by the Office of National Drug Control Policy constituted covert propaganda."[21]

One of the FCC's Commissioners told *Reuters*, "People in this country have a right to know where their news is coming from, but it's getting almost impossible to know. Everyone understands that a story cannot be judged without knowing its source, but increasingly the source goes unreported."[22]

The scandal also prompted the Radio-Television News Directors Association (RTNDA), citing its own *Code of Ethics and Professional Conduct*, to remind its members of their duties: "News managers and producers should clearly disclose the origin of information and label all material provided by corporate or other noneditorial sources. For example, graphics could denote 'Mercy Hospital video' and the reporter or anchor script could also acknowledge it by stating, 'This operating room video was provided by Mercy Hospital.'"[23]

RTNDA also directed its members to subject VNRs to the same news standards as they do their own work: "News managers and producers should determine if interviews provided with video/audio releases follow the same standards regarding conflicts of interest as used in the newsroom. For instance, some releases might contain interviews where subjects and interviewers are employed by the same organization. Consider whether tough questions were asked and if the subject was properly questioned."[24]

PR Watch published an article by Rampton addressing the 2005 VNR scandals. Rampton made two points: first, that use of VNRs isn't limited to government, and second, that VNRs and other communication tools are illegitimate: "In fact, corporate public relations is the biggest single source of video news releases, just as corporate PR is the biggest single source of other types of PR that pollute the media ecosystem."[25]

Rampton's critique, while colorful, isn't particularly helpful to professional communicators. In fact, both the FCC's and RTNDA's discussions of the controversy focused on disclosure of the source of the news as the key ethical issue, and place the burden and the ethical criticism rightly on journalists. That is, to the degree there are ethical issues inherent in VNRs, they are primarily issues affecting journalists' use of the VNRs and their disclosure of the source of the content. From a professional communicator's perspective, the ethical standards regarding a VNR are the same as those regarding a print news release: the source of the material should be clearly identified by the communicator, and the content should be accurate and truthful. If these standards are met, the VNR generally passes ethical muster.

Corrupting the Channels of Communication

One ethical concern facing professional communicators is the integrity of the channels of communication, particularly regarding the independence of news organizations and news commentators. The integrity of the communication process is impaired by, among other things, payments to reporters, so that their interest in providing objective coverage is or appears to be compromised. This includes providing bribes, inappropriate favors, hiring relatives, and otherwise mingling the reporter's private interests with those of a professional communicator's client or employer.

The PRSA *Member Code of Ethics* specifically calls for members to "maintain the integrity of relationships with the media, government officials, and the public."

In early 2005 *USA Today* reported that the prominent conservative commentator and columnist Armstrong Williams had received $240,000 from a public relations firm, working for the U.S. Department of Education, to promote the Department's initiatives on Williams' television program.[26] A firestorm of controversy ensued. As a result of the disclosure, *Tribune Media Services*, which syndicated Williams' column, dropped the columnist, saying, "Accepting compensation in any form from an entity that serves as the subject of his weekly newspaper columns creates, at the very least, the appearance of a conflict of interest. Under these circumstances, readers may well ask themselves if the views expressed in his columns are his own, or whether they have been purchased by a third party."[27]

The U.S. Department of Education initially defended its payments to Mr. Williams as legal, but after significant criticism the outgoing Secretary of Education, Rod Paige, said, "All of this has been reviewed and is legal. However, I am sorry that there are perceptions and allegations of ethical lapses."[28]

One ethical concern facing professional communicators is the integrity of the channels of communication, particularly regarding the independence of news organizations and news commentators.

As the Williams controversy became public it was also learned that syndicated columnist Maggie Gallagher had promoted the Administration's "healthy marriage" initiative while receiving $21,500 from the U.S. Department of Health and Human Services.

At a press conference President George W. Bush was asked about the accumulation of scandals involving VNRs and payments to columnists. He replied, "All our Cabinet secretaries must realize that we will not be paying ... commentators to advance our agenda. Our agenda ought to be able to stand on its own initiative."[29]

The PRSA's *Member Code of Ethics* offers guidance on less dramatic, but sometimes challenging, ethical choices. In its *Examples of Inappropriate Conduct* under its *Free Flow of Information* provision, the *Code* offers two cases of inappropriate behavior: "A member representing a ski manufacturer gives a pair of expensive racing skis to a sports magazine columnist, to influence the columnist to write favorable articles about the product. A member entertains a government official beyond legal limits and/or in violation of government reporting requirements."[30]

Front Groups

Another challenge to the integrity of the communication process is the establishment of "front groups," or organizations that purport to have a certain, usually public purpose, but that in fact are acting on behalf of an undisclosed interest.

Citizens for a Free Kuwait is the most notorious example in recent memory, but is hardly the only such group. At the same time the Kuwait story was in the news, Greenpeace criticized a Washington PR firm for what it called a "phony citizens group," to lobby against increased fuel efficiency standards. The group, called "The Coalition for Vehicle Choice," was funded by the major automobile manufacturers.

Ironically, Edward L. Bernays, who in the 1920s called for a code of ethics for public relations, was a master of creating front groups. It all started in 1913 when Bernays, just out of college, was working at a medical magazine called *Medical Review of Reviews*. Bernays published a review of a play called *Damaged Goods*, which dealt with the effects of syphilis. The play violated social taboos against discussion of sexually transmitted diseases. Bernays persuaded Richard Bennett, a popular New York actor who wanted to produce the play, to let Bernays underwrite the production. According to his biographer, Bernays realized that in order to create interest in *Damaged Goods* Bernays needed "to transform the controversy into a cause, and recruit backers who already were public role models. The twenty-one-year-old editor formed a Medical Review of Reviews Sociological Fund Committee, then attracted members with an artful appeal that played on Bennett's reputation as an artist as well as the worthiness of battling prudishness."[31]

Committee members included John D. Rockefeller, Jr., Mr. and Mrs. Franklin D. Roosevelt, and Mrs. William K. Vanderbilt, Sr. Rockefeller offered a typical endorsement: "The evils that spring from prostitution cannot be understood until frank discussion of them has been made possible."[32]

Despite weak reviews, *Damaged Goods* was a big success, and sold out in New York. It then went to Washington, where it was performed for Supreme Court justices, members of Congress, and members of the Administration. Bernays' biographer says that using a third-party group of luminaries to lend credibility to a commercial or political cause became Bernays' preferred method of operating.

"This was the first time [Bernays] or anyone else had assembled such a distinguished front group. And its success ensured not only that he would use this technique repeatedly but also that it would continue to be employed today, when it takes a detective to unmask the interests behind such innocuous-sounding groups as the Safe Energy Communication Council (antinuclear), the Eagle Alliance (pronuclear), and the Coalition Against Regressive Taxation (trucking industry)."[33]

In the 1940s Bernays was retained by Mack Trucks to help recover market share in freight hauling from railroads. He devised an extensive campaign to improve the quality of interstate highways to make shipping cargo by truck more feasible. And he created a number of front groups, including Trucking Information Service, the Trucking Service Bureau, and Better Living Through Increased Highway Transportation, which in turn created state chapters to run local campaigns to influence members of Congress. Bernays was successful, and in 1950 Congress approved $556 million in new highway construction funds, and in 1952 increased the funding level to $652 million. The U.S. interstate highway system remains the living beneficiary of Bernays' campaign, which also set the standard for contemporary lobbying and political action committees.[34]

Today front groups that purport to represent one interest but actually serve a hidden interest are violations of most ethical standards, which require disclosure of the interests on whose behalf communication is taking place. PRSA's new *Member Code of Ethics* specifically requires identification of the ultimate beneficiary of any front group. It requires that a member "reveal the sponsors for causes and interests represented." Its *Examples of Improper Conduct Under This Provision* includes this clause: "Front Groups: A member implements grass roots campaigns or letter-writing campaigns to legislators on behalf of undisclosed interest groups."[35]

> Bernays' biographer says that using a third-party group of luminaries to lend credibility to a commercial or political cause became Bernays' preferred method of operating.

Ethics of Running a Business

Professional communicators need also to abide by ethical standards that apply to any professional situation. These are ethical situations that any organization might face, involving mostly the interpersonal relationships between the organization and its employees, customers, business partners, and other companies.

Some of the particular ethical duties include:

Confidentiality
Preventing conflicts of interest
Ethics of routine business relationships

Confidentiality

Professional communicators are often in a position to know things before the general public, and sometimes also to know information that should never be revealed because they include trade secrets, personal information about fellow employees, or proprietary information.

Under U.S. securities law and regulations there are strict prohibitions about revealing "material nonpublic information" or to disclose selectively. So professional communicators are sometimes subjected to legal and regulatory requirements to keep secrets. (See Chapter 8, Investor Relations, for more detail.)

Sometimes professional communicators are bound by contractual obligations to keep certain information confidential.

But even absent legal, regulatory, or contractual requirements, professional communicators may also be required to maintain confidences for ethical reasons. For example, the PRSA *Member Code of Conduct* has an entire provision on *Safeguarding Confidences*. The *Intent* of the principle is "to protect the privacy rights of clients, organizations, and individuals by safeguarding confidential information." The *Guidelines* require that members "safeguard the confidences and privacy rights of present, former, and prospective clients and employees. Protect privileged, confidential, or insider information gained from a client or organization." In *Examples of Improper Conduct Under This Provision* the *Code* notes "a member changes jobs, takes confidential information, and uses that information in the new position to the detriment of the former employer."[36]

Similarly, the IABC *Code of Ethics for Professional Communicators* contains two articles on the subject: "Professional communicators protect confidential information and … do not use confidential information gained as the result of professional activities for personal benefit."[37]

Preventing Conflicts of Interest

One of the persistent ethical challenges for professional communicators involves conflicts of interest. Sometimes the conflict is between the individual and his or her employer or client, such as when a professional communicator receives payment from an entity whose interest may be opposed to the communicator's employer or client.

The PRSA *Member Code of Ethics* has a provision on *Conflicts of Interests* that includes two guidelines on such personal/professional conflicts, saying that a member shall "act in the best interests of a client or employer, even subordinating the member's personal interests," and "avoid actions and circumstances that may appear to compromise good business judgment or create a conflict between personal and professional interests." The *Code* lists an *Example of Improper Conduct Under This Provision*: "The member fails to disclose that he or she has a strong financial interest in a client's chief competitor."[38]

Similarly, the IABC *Code of Ethics for Professional Communicators* contains an article that says "Professional communicators do not accept undisclosed gifts or payments for professional services from anyone other than a client or employer."[39]

Sometimes the conflict arises from a professional communicator having as clients two organizations whose interests are in conflict.

Note, however, that simply representing two competing companies does not necessarily result in a conflict of interest. For example, two competitors may have a common interest in legislation, and each could use the services of a government relations professional seeking to influence legislation that would benefit the clients' industry as a whole, and therefore both clients. Similarly, a communicator may represent two competing companies for different functions; for example, doing internal communications for client A and government relations for client B.

Many professional communicators have significant expertise in a particular industry, and represent more than two companies who compete with each other. Some companies require exclusivity from their communication advisors, and usually pay a premium for that exclusivity. But others recognize that they ultimately benefit from an advisor with significant industry expertise.

One way to manage such multiclient relationships is full disclosure to all parties of the various relationships. The assumption is that there is no conflict if each party is aware of the various relationships.

The PRSA *Member Code of Ethics* requires members to "disclose promptly any existing or potential conflict of interest to affected clients or organizations," and to "encourage clients and customers to determine if a conflict exists after notifying all affected parties."[40]

> Simply representing two competing companies does not necessarily result in a conflict of interest.

Similarly, the IABC *Code of Ethics for Professional Communicators* says that professional communicators "do not represent conflicting or competing interests without written consent of those involved."[41]

In any event representing more than one company in a given industry, or representing two competing companies, underscores the need for professional communicators to maintain strict confidentiality of proprietary client information, so as not to deliberately or inadvertently reveal to one company the business plans, strategies, staffing, sales volume, or similar sensitive data of another such company.

Ethics of Routine Business Relationships

Professional communicators are bound by the same ethical standards as other professionals, including fair treatment of customers, business partners, and employees. Routine business ethics challenges, such as accurate billing, paying employees for hours worked, providing safe workplaces, and adhering to legal and regulatory requirements apply to professional communicators as they do to employees in other industries.

Sometimes the ethical challenges of professional communicators in routine business matters cast the profession in a negative light. For example, at the same time in 2005 that the public relations industry was being criticized for VNRs and for paying columnists to support clients' policies, it was revealed that a public relations firm in Los Angeles had overbilled its client, the City of Los Angeles, and had also billed the city for work not performed. After an investigation the public relations firm, Fleishman-Hillard, agreed to a settlement with the City of Los Angeles valued at $5.7 million, and apologized to the citizens and city officials of Los Angeles,[42] and a Fleishman-Hillard executive pleaded guilty to fraud.[43]

In a similar ethics and legal crisis, two former senior executives of the advertising agency Ogilvy & Mather Worldwide were convicted in 2004 of ordering employees to alter time sheets, resulting in overbilling their client, the U.S. Office of National Drug Control Policy. In 2005 both were sentenced to more than a year in prison and were fined. U.S. Federal District Judge Richard Berman further ordered the more senior executive, Shona Seifert, as part of her sentence, to write a code of ethics that could be used by the advertising industry to prevent such billing practices in the future.[44]

Ethics of Representation

One area that provokes much discussion and disagreement is the question of representation, the suggestion that there may be something ethically suspect about working with certain clients or companies. Where should professional communicators draw the line? Are there whole categories of companies, industries, products, causes, and people that a professional communicator should refuse to help?

The PRSA *Member Code of Ethics* says that PR professionals "provide a voice in the marketplace of ideas, facts, and viewpoints to aid informed public debate," and that they "respect all opinions and support the right of free expression."[45] Some might interpret these statements of professional values as providing justification for representing all interests, however personally offensive, dishonest, distasteful, or ethically suspect those interests may be. Others suggest that just because all parties may be equally entitled to representation, there is no duty on any given practitioner to agree to work with any given client.

As Edward L. Bernays pointed out in 1928, "While recognizing, just as the lawyer does, that everyone has a right to present his case in its best light, [a professional communicator] nevertheless refuses a client whom he believes to be dishonest, a product which he believes to be fraudulent, or a cause which he believes to be antisocial."[46]

In practice many professional communicators, and the firms that hire them, understand that whether to work with a given client is often a matter of personal choice. The IABC *Code of Ethics for Professional Communicators* makes such a choice explicit: "Professional communicators refrain from taking part in any undertaking which the communicator considers to be unethical."[47] The IPRA *Code of Athens* has a similar provision, requiring that members refrain from "taking part in any venture or undertaking which is unethical or dishonest or capable of impairing human dignity and integrity."[48] And the PRSA *Member Code of Ethics* does require that members "decline representation of clients or organizations that urge or require actions contrary to this Code."[49]

> Others suggest that just because all parties may be equally entitled to representation, there is no duty on any given practitioner to agree to work with any given client.

Such activities could include not just the ethics of communication and the ethics of running a business, but also the nature of the organization for which the communicator would work.

Among the industry categories that are often cited by practitioners as causing concern are:

⇒ Tobacco companies
⇒ Individuals or companies accused or convicted of a crime
⇒ Companies that harm the environment
⇒ Companies that use animals in medical experiments
⇒ Foreign governments whose policies are thought to be repressive or contrary to a practitioner's national government's interests
⇒ The military, especially in time of war
⇒ Manufacturers of handguns or other weapons
⇒ Chemical companies
⇒ Alcohol beverage companies

⇒ Causes that advocate policies contrary to a communicator's own values, religious beliefs, or political views

⇒ Companies with abusive workplace practices, or that employ child, prison, or slave labor

⇒ Companies based in countries with poor records of human rights, financial fraud, or political oppression

The list could continue for quite a while, and some companies have affirmative policies specifying the industry sectors for which they will work. (Note that this list does not imply that any one category of product or company has any particular relationship with any other. Rather, the list is a sample of the kinds of clients that sometimes cause practitioners to raise concern about the clients or issues they are comfortable representing.)

Some communicators differentiate between the company they work for and that company's parent. For example, in the United States for some time tobacco companies also owned food processing companies, and communicators who would never promote tobacco had no difficulty working for the food processors that were owned by tobacco companies. Others saw no difference between working for a benign division of a company they found objectionable and promoting the objectionable product, and avoided such companies altogether.

Sensitivities change over time. For example, in the 1980s fur companies and nuclear energy companies were considered by some communicators to be objectionable. In the 1990s companies that tested products on animals were often seen to be controversial, as were the countries of China, Indonesia, and Turkey.

Edward L. Bernays, over the course of a long career, saw his own sensitivities change. In the 1920s and 1930s he was an ardent promoter of tobacco companies, and is credited with making it socially acceptable for women to smoke in public. Bernays' biographer, Larry Tye, notes that Bernays shifted his views as the science became clearer: "When the surgeon general and other medical authorities released incontrovertible evidence of the dangers of smoking, Bernays used his talents of persuasion to help undo the addictions he'd help build. In 1964 he unveiled a bold and detailed plan to transform smoking into 'an antisocial action which no self-respecting person carries on in the presence of others.'"[50]

Beyond categories such as industry sector or national policy, some representation choices concern the character of the individuals. Several PR firms routinely require prospective clients who are rumored to be involved in organized crime to pay for independent private investigations of their activities to validate the prospects' claims that they had been falsely accused.

One common concern about representation is helping governments rally public support for a war. In a 1992 CBS *60 Minutes* program about the Citizens for a Free Kuwait controversy, correspondent Morley Safer summed up this view: "The troubling part of the story is the belief by the public relations industry that, with enough access, enough money, and knowing which buttons to push, war can be marketed, just like soft drinks and toothpaste."[51]

A close look at the history of public relations, however, shows that mobilizing public opinion has been an integral part of the United States going to war (in every war except Vietnam). From Committees of Correspondence in the American Revolution, to war cries such as "Remember the Maine!" in the Spanish-American War, to the use of sophisticated public relations techniques in the run-up to the War with Iraq in 2003, professional communicators have been active in most U.S. military operations. Edward L. Bernays himself practiced his craft on behalf of U.S. involvement in World War I and World War II.

Professional communicators who work with the military argue that there is nothing inherently suspect about working for a military operation, including during a war, but note that they continue to be bound by the usual ethical requirements, including the duty to communicate honestly and accurately. John R. MacArthur, who revealed the Citizens for a Free Kuwait controversy and whose book, *Second Front: Censorship and Propaganda in the Gulf War*, examines ethical failings of both the news media and the public relations industry, notes that truth is often a casualty of war: "In modern wars, exaggerated or manufactured enemy atrocities have frequently played an important part in the cause of boosting war fever at home ... Slaughtered and mutilated Belgian babies were a tremendous propaganda triumph for the Allies [in World War I]. In retrospect, the success of these manufactured stories possessed ominous implications for future wars, especially the one to liberate Kuwait."[52]

Every professional communicator, as part of his or her ethical development, needs to reflect on the kinds of companies, causes, people, and circumstances that cause ethical concern, and be ready to make decisions on whether to represent such causes or not.

Helping Companies Behave Ethically

The corporate scandals of 2001–3 demonstrated that a company's ethical lapses can cause significant harm to reputation, operations, morale, customer demand, stock price, and in some cases even a company's survival. Often, ethical slippage is a leading indicator—a kind of early warning—of legal problems. From Enron to Andersen to the Roman Catholic

Church, ethical lapses that were apparent to insiders and observers were ignored by organizations' leaders, only to reemerge in criminal conviction, civil penalties, and in Enron's and Andersen's cases, dissolution.

Increasingly, corporate communication departments are seen as the conscience of a company and play an important role in helping a company behave ethically. Recognizing the relationship between ethical lapses and reputational harm, many companies now see commitment to ethics as an integral part of managing their reputation and preserving the value of the company's intangible assets.

On a more practical level, U.S. Federal Sentencing Guidelines, which set rules for punishment for corporate crimes, mandate that companies with strong ethics codes, training programs, and compliance procedures can be subjected to less severe penalties if they should be convicted of certain crimes.

Sometimes the professional communicator's ethics role is informal, helping the company navigate day-to-day communication decisions in an ethical way.

Sometimes the corporate communicator's ethics role is paired with the company's program of corporate social responsibility (see Chapter 13, Corporate Responsibility). And sometimes the corporate communicator's role is paired with the company's own code of ethics.

Some companies have robust ethics codes and training programs. For example, General Electric's code, called *Integrity: The Spirit & Letter of Our Commitment*, runs for thirty-five pages. It starts with a single-page GE Code of Conduct, which requires that GE people obey laws and regulations, be honest, fair and trustworthy, avoid conflicts of interest between work and personal affairs, foster an atmosphere of fair employment practices, strive to create a safe workplace and protect the environment, and sustain a culture in which ethical conduct is recognized.[53] The balance of the document provides extensive procedures for implementing the code.

Sometimes companies overhaul their codes following ethical lapses. For example, from 2002 to 2004 The Boeing Co. suffered reputational harm through a series of scandals involving the recruitment of Pentagon officials for senior positions in the company while these officials were still overseeing Boeing and other defense contractors for the government. Eventually Boeing's chief executive officer, Phil Condit, was forced to leave the company. He was replaced by retired vice chairman Harry Stonecipher, who promptly instituted a revised *Code of Conduct*. The new single-page *Code* includes the following sentence: "Employees will not engage in conduct or activity that may raise questions as to the company's honesty, impartiality, reputation, or otherwise cause embarrassment to the company."[54] It also requires that employees promptly report any unethical conduct.

> Increasingly, corporate communication departments are seen as the conscience of a company and play an important role in helping a company behave ethically.

Ironically, soon after implementing the *Code*, Mr. Stonecipher was discovered by a fellow employee to be in a romantic affair with a female subordinate. The employee, following the *Code's* requirements, reported his suspicions to the company's board, which promptly investigated. Mr. Stonecipher was fired for violating his own code.

Commentators noted that the Board's dismissal of their new CEO demonstrated that the *Code* worked and that the company took ethics seriously. The *Seattle Post-Intelligencer* quoted University of Washington business professor Jonathan Karpoff saying that Boeing reacted so dramatically to the CEO's affair because of its recent ethical challenges. "Everyone's on pins and needles when it comes to manipulating the numbers, but now it's spreading out to all aspects of a firm's leadership—especially in light of the lapses Boeing has been involved in over the years," Karpoff said. The newspaper also quoted Kirk Johnson, vice president at ethics consulting firm Integrity Interactive Corp., saying, "This story demonstrates that ethics programs work, and that they do have teeth."[55]

Some companies' commitment to ethics is triggered by a series of ethical scandals that impair their ability to do business effectively. For example, in 2004 Japanese banking regulators revoked Citigroup Private Bank's license to operate in Japan. Citigroup's chief executive officer, Charles Prince, formally apologized to the regulators, including participating in a seven-second ceremonial bow. A photograph of Mr. Prince bowing before regulators appeared in newspapers around the world on October 26, 2004.

Citigroup's Japan problems were just the latest ethical challenge in a series of mishaps over several years. Citigroup was involved in financing Enron, WorldCom, and Parmalat, each of which was found to have committed financial fraud. Its European traders were implicated in a controversial trading strategy named "Dr. Evil," although the company was later cleared of wrongdoing in that strategy. And it had been implicated in scandals involving the independence of its research analysts.

In March 2005, Mr. Prince announced a new ethics initiative, telling *The Wall Street Journal* that the project would consume "at least half his executive time and energy over the next several years." He told the newspaper, "This is job one. If I don't own this, I don't think it will succeed."[56] Mr. Prince specifically linked the ethics initiative to restoration of Citigroup's reputation, saying it was intended to make Citigroup the most respected financial-services company.

Mr. Prince recognized that even the best ethics code won't protect a company's reputation if the company's culture isn't responsive to ethical considerations and ethical responsibilities.

> Even the best ethics code won't protect a company's reputation if the company's culture isn't responsive to ethical considerations and ethical responsibilities.

Indeed, Enron Corp., which has become synonymous with corporate corruption, had a sixty-five-page ethics code that included all the usual requirements and prohibitions that highly respected companies' codes contain. These include four core values: respect, integrity, communication, and excellence.

An elaboration of the *respect* value is particularly ironic, given Enron's ultimate demise: "We treat others as we would like to be treated ourselves. We do not tolerate abusive or disrespectful treatment. Ruthlessness, callousness, and arrogance don't belong here."[57]

An introductory letter to the code from Kenneth L. Lay, chairman and chief executive officer of Enron, said, "We want to be proud of Enron and to know that it enjoys a reputation for fairness and honesty and that it is respected. Gaining such respect is one aim of our advertising and public relations activities, but no matter how effective they may be, Enron's reputation depends on its people, on you and me. Let's keep that reputation high."[58]

The letter was dated July 1, 2000. Less than two years later Enron was out of business, brought down by a series of ethical and legal shortfalls. And in May 2006, Mr. Lay was convicted of numerous fraud and conspiracy charges.

Another company to go out of business in the wake of the Enron scandal was Enron's auditor, Arthur Andersen. The firm went out of business just six months after it emerged as inextricably linked to the Enron scandal, following Andersen's conviction for obstruction of justice. Andersen's conviction was overturned by the United States Supreme Court in May 2005, too late to save the company.

A close look at the firm in the years before the scandal shows that Andersen's Enron entanglements were a symptom of a much larger problem, particularly an inattention to the ethical standards that had helped propel Andersen to the heights of respectability and profitability.

Barbara Ley Toffler, formerly a professor of ethics at the Harvard Business School, and presently a professor at Columbia University Business School, ran Arthur Andersen's Ethics & Responsible Business Practices consulting group. After the firm's demise in 2002, she wrote a book diagnosing the root causes of the firm's collapse. She writes that:

> *Arthur Andersen was a great and venerable American brand that had, over the course of the twentieth century, become a global symbol of strength and solidity ... In my years working at Arthur Andersen, I came to believe that the white-shoed accounting firm known for its legions of trained, loyal, honest professionals—a place that once had the respect, envy, and admiration of everyone in Corporate America—had lost its way. The accountants and the consultants forgot what it meant to be accountable. The fall of Arthur Andersen, I believe, was no murder. It*

was a suicide, set in motion long before there was ever an indictment. Yet while the guilty verdict sealed Andersen's fate, by the time it came it was merely a formality, the last nail in a coffin whose grave had been primed for burial.[59]

Toffler says that her attempts to bring ethical problems to management's attention were rebuffed. She says that it was clear to her, and to anyone who chose to see, that Andersen's culture had shifted powerfully to a short-term focus on profitability at the expense of its core values of independence and client service, to what she termed "billing our brains out," regardless of the value delivered to the client, of unethical entanglements, or of suspect behavior. She describes a culture where every employee who had or might have anything to do with a client had to figure out a way to sell more services to clients, regardless of the client's need. "Some would call this client service—but in my experience it seemed to be more about raping the client than serving it."[60]

Toffler's business was advising clients on ethical business practice, not serving as an in-house ethics officer for her own firm. But internal ethical issues came to her attention, including a partner who she says had taken his and a client's daughters to a New York Yankees game in a limousine, which waited for the entire game, and then took them home. The partner directed that the expenses for the trip be billed to the client as an audit-related expense. She recounts, "I could find no indication that ethics was ever talked about in any broad way at Arthur Andersen. When I brought up the subject of internal ethics, I was looked at as if I had teleported in from another world ... The end result was the continual reinforcement of the idea that it was okay to play with numbers ... The laxity of this approach would come back to haunt the Firm later: Billing Our Brains Out or compromising quality was what we all had to do to get ahead—or to keep up."[61]

According to Toffler, "there was simply too much similarity of thought, too much acceptance that the way things were done was the best simply *'because that's the way we do it'* to see that this culture was turning on itself."[62]

She concludes, "I believe strongly that the suicide of Arthur Andersen—and the assault on the investing public's trust—could have been avoided had people paid attention to the danger signs flashing everywhere in the late 1990s."[63]

One of the critical roles of a professional communicator is to serve as an early warning system for such danger signs. As the entity formally charged with protecting and advancing an organization's reputation, the corporate and organizational communication function needs to be fully engaged in discussions of all of an organization's reputational threats, including the implications of unethical behavior.

> The corporate and organizational communication function needs to be fully engaged in discussions of all of an organization's reputational threats, including the implications of unethical behavior.

Case Study: Hill & Knowlton and Citizens for a Free Kuwait

The most significant communication ethics scandal of the 1990s concerned Hill & Knowlton's work for its client, Citizens for a Free Kuwait (CFK). The scandal was triggered in 1992 by publication of *Second Front: Censorship and Propaganda in the Gulf War*, by *Harper's Magazine* publisher John R. MacArthur. Much of the book focused on the U.S. government's management of the media in the 1991 Gulf War, and the media's acquiescence to the government's groundrules. But the revelations about ethically suspect behavior involving the PR firm and its client set off a firestorm of criticism against the firm and PR in general.

This chapter opened with a discussion of the front group, Citizens for a Free Kuwait. The failure of Hill & Knowlton to identify its real client was just the starting point in a discussion of systematic ethical wrongdoing.

What is The Congressional Human Rights Caucus? And Who is Nayirah?

One of the more serious criticisms of H&K's work involved what MacArthur described to the CBS news program *60 Minutes* as the Kuwaiti's and Administration's need for a "defining atrocity."[64] That defining atrocity concerned allegations that the invading Iraqi army had systematically pillaged hospitals in Kuwait, removing dozens (in some reports, hundreds) of premature babies from incubators, leaving them to die on the hospital floors. The most riveting account of the incubator story came from a fifteen-year-old Kuwaiti girl identified only as Nayirah.

On October 10, 1990, Nayirah testified at a meeting of the Congressional Human Rights Caucus. Although it had the appearance of a full-fledged congressional hearing, in fact it was merely an informal gathering of like-minded members of Congress. MacArthur points out that, "The Human Rights Caucus is not a committee of Congress and therefore it is unencumbered by the legal accoutrements that would make a witness hesitate before he or she lied ... Lying under oath in front of a congressional committee is a crime; lying from under the cover of anonymity to the caucus is merely public relations."[65]

The nature of the caucus and its relationship to H&K and CFK is a critical one. According to MacArthur, the cochairs of the caucus, Congressman Tom Lantos (D-CA) and Congressman Edward Porter (R-IL), were also cochairs of the Congressional Human Rights Foundation, whose rent-free offices were in H&K's Washington offices. After the caucus meeting at which Nayirah testified, the Congressional Human Rights Foundation, which had paid for travel and lodging for

Congressmen Lantos and Porter, and for their wives, received a $50,000 contribution from CFK.[66]

At the caucus' October 10 meeting, Nayirah was introduced only as a fifteen-year-old girl with first-hand experience of the events to which she was testifying. Her full identity was withheld, it was said, in order to protect her family in Kuwait from reprisals.

Nayirah, who had been coached by H&K and whose testimony was later included in H&K's press materials about the caucus meeting, told the caucus, "While I was [at the al-Adan hospital] I saw the Iraqi soldiers come into the hospital with guns, and go into the room where fifteen babies were in incubators. They took the incubators, and left the babies on the cold floor to die."[67]

Nayirah's story, distributed by H&K via video news releases, press releases, and other tools of the trade, was widely covered, and referred to often by President Bush and by members of the U.S. Senate and House of Representatives.

As the U.S. Senate debated a resolution authorizing the United States to go to war against Iraq, the babies-pulled-from-incubators story had become the war's defining atrocity. It was mentioned often by President Bush. More significantly, the war resolution passed the U.S. Senate on January 12, 1991, by a five-vote margin; six senators who voted for the resolution referred to the baby incubator story in justifying their vote. MacArthur argues, "The significance of the baby incubator story in the larger propaganda campaign against Saddam Hussein and for the war option cannot be underestimated. Without it, the comparison of Hussein with Hitler loses its luster; to make the case effectively, one had to prove Hussein's utter depravity."[68]

After the war ended, MacArthur discovered that Nayirah was no ordinary refugee, and questioned whether her anonymity would have made any difference in protecting her family from reprisals: She was in fact a member of the Kuwaiti royal family, and the daughter of Kuwait's Ambassador to the United States (and, because CFK was a front group for the Kuwaiti government, the Ambassador was also H&K's client). He further discovered that five of the other six Kuwaitis who spoke at the United Nations used false identities. He says that H&K claimed that the fact that the witnesses used false identities had been revealed at the time, but he was unable to find any proof of this. He further notes that several of them were prominent Kuwaitis, whose identity would have been known in Kuwait, including the head of the Kuwaiti Red Crescent. MacArthur muses, "Why would a well-known public health official—even one working for the Kuwaiti government—need to hide his identity if not to mislead the media and human rights investigators and to make follow-up inquiries more difficult?"[69]

After the war, leading human rights organizations, including Amnesty International and Human Rights Watch, went to Kuwait to investigate reports of atrocities, and each concluded that the baby incubator atrocity had never taken place.

Aftermath and Backlash

MacArthur revealed his findings in a *The New York Times* op-ed article on January 6, 1992, just before the one-year anniversary of the war. The article, based on his book, was the first salvo in what would be an escalating and nearly yearlong scandal. Within weeks the criticism included an editorial in *The New York Times* called "Deception on Capitol Hill" and criticism of Hill & Knowlton—and of public relations in general—by CBS *60 Minutes*, ABC *20/20*, *Newsweek*, *The Wall Street Journal*, and *The Washington Post*. *TV Guide*, with a circulation of more than 15 million, ran a story that accused Hill & Knowlton of "systematic manipulation of the news."[70]

Hill & Knowlton defended its work for CFK, and rebutted MacArthur's and the media's criticisms. Thomas E. Eidson, H&K's president and CEO in 1992, defended both the accuracy of Nayirah's testimony and the firm's insistence that it worked for a citizens group and not for the government of Kuwait.[71]

In the aftermath of the CFK scandal, with H&K's and PR's integrity impeached, the firm became the subject of intense scrutiny about other clients it represented. Soon after the Kuwait story broke, H&K was sued for "PR fraud" by creditors of its client, the disgraced Bank of Credit and Commerce International (BCCI), and its work for the Church of Scientology was criticized as well. It was also criticized for its work for governments of countries implicated in human rights abuses, including Turkey, Indonesia, and China. It suffered severe decline in staff morale, client defections, and ultimately turnover of most of the people at the top of the company, including nearly every senior person involved with the CFK business.

Inside PR magazine, which published a yearly report card on major public relations firms, assessed the damage to Hill & Knowlton in its July/August 1992 issue: "What was the greatest PR agency in the world has come to be regarded as a pariah by many prospective employees. Internally, morale is resurgent, but a reputation for petty politics and the controversies of the past two years make H&K in the '90s look about as attractive as Dow [Chemical] in the '70s … Crisis-plagued and battered in the media, new management faces an uphill battle."[72]

Hill & Knowlton's battering in the media served as a proxy for the public relations industry as a whole. Senior PR executives opined that employees of H&K had violated the PRSA *Code of Ethics*, but the PRSA was largely silent on the scandal, creating a vacuum of opinion and leaving the impression that H&K's behavior was acceptable and common PR practice. The PR profession was in crisis, but the industry association seemed paralyzed and either unable or unwilling to take a public stand on the scandal. The board of the PRSA met in New York in late January, but refused invitations to speak with the PR trade media.

In the aftermath of the scandal PRSA saw defections from its own ranks, including coauthor Fred Garcia, who resigned both from the PRSA and from a leadership position in the association's New York chapter because of the association's mishandling of the ethics issue and its failure to defend the profession.

Over the course of the mid-to-late 1990s Hill & Knowlton recovered, and is again a strong and respected firm. But it lost significant market share, momentum, and clout. And PRSA eventually took the initiative and after a multi-year self-assessment recast its *Member Code of Ethics* and became more active in defining and defending the profession.

Historical Perspectives on Communication Ethics

The professional practice of public relations is not a twentieth-century invention. Neither are the ethical challenges facing it. Concern about the integrity of professional communication goes back much farther than 1923, when Edward L. Bernays was worried that people viewed it as some "vaguely defined evil, 'propaganda.'"[73]

In fact, professional communication emerged as a profession 2,500 years ago. And it was criticized in much the same way it is now: Those who practiced it were said to care little for the truth.

A careful review of the critique of classical public relations can be helpful in pointing the way to solving the problem of communication ethics in the twenty-first century.

The historical antecedents of professional communication may be found in fourth-century BC Greece. While Plato never used the term "public relations," he had a deep awareness of the importance of crystallizing public opinion, and of the methods and proper uses of persuasion. Unlike Aristotle, whose *Rhetoric* provides a theoretical construction of oral persuasion, Plato (c. 427 to 346 BC), did not articulate a discrete theory of persuasive communication. But his *Gorgias* provides a sharp criticism of the practice of professional communication in his day,

But his *Gorgias* provides a sharp criticism of the practice of professional communication in his day, and his *Republic* articulates the appropriate method for shaping public opinion.

and his *Republic* articulates the appropriate method for shaping public opinion.

Classical Rhetoric

Classical Greece was an oral society. While today most communication is done in print, on television, or on the Internet, in Greece most public discourse was spoken.

But like today, in classical Athens public opinion determined matters both large and small, from whether to build city walls to the appointment of generals to sentences at criminal trials. And also like today, there was a growing demand for expert help to shape public opinion. To meet that demand, a new class of professional persuaders, called *rhetoricians*, emerged. They called their craft "rhetoric," which Aristotle later defined as "the faculty of discovering the possible means of persuasion in reference to any subject whatever."[74]

Aristotle differentiated this general persuasive nature of rhetoric from the specific natures of other pursuits: "This is the function of no other of the arts, each of which is able to instruct and persuade in its own special subject; thus, medicine deals with health and sickness, geometry with the properties of magnitudes, arithmetic with number, and similarly with all the other arts or sciences. But Rhetoric, so to say, appears able to discover the means of persuasion in reference to any given subject."[75]

Rhetoric as a distinct practice emerged in the fifth century BC on the then-Greek island of Sicily. Citing a lost book of Aristotle, the Roman orator Cicero says that following a political upheaval, two enterprising Sicilians, Corax and Tisias, developed a method of instructing others how to argue persuasively, so as to recover property confiscated by the prior regime.[76] Corax, in addition to teaching clients how to argue persuasively and providing them with a set of rules for dealing with difficult questions, also wrote speeches for his clients to deliver in court, and was the author of the first handbook on rhetoric. His pupil Tisias, who also composed a handbook on rhetoric, later became tutor to the great Greek rhetoricians Gorgias, Isocrates, and Lysias.

Rhetoricians should not be confused with other distinguished Greeks who used persuasion as part of other pursuits. Statesmen such as Pericles were powerful speakers, but were primarily engaged in governing. Sophists such as Protagoras used techniques similar to those used by rhetoricians but claimed that their teaching instilled virtue in their pupils. Rhetoricians, on the other hand, were concerned neither with governing nor with instilling virtue. Rather, they provided communications services to those who paid for them. These services were remarkably similar to those offered by modern professional communicators. They included speechwriting, speaking on clients' behalf, and coaching clients how to argue their cases persuasively. This latter service included anticipating difficult questions and framing appropriate answers, similar to modern media training.

By Plato's day rhetoric as a distinct discipline was well established in Greece. The foremost rhetorician was Gorgias of Leontinium in Sicily, who is reputed to have lived 108 years (c. 483 to 375 BC). Gorgias' view of rhetoric differentiated it specifically from other persuasive pursuits such as governing and instilling virtue. Gorgias claimed that his only object was to foster persuasive skills on any subject whatever. Cicero, again citing a lost book of Aristotle, reports that Gorgias further encouraged speakers to exaggerate or extenuate, as the occasion might require.[77]

Plato's Critique

Plato wrote his *Gorgias* in about 387 BC and related events said to have taken place when Gorgias was in his eighties and at the pinnacle of his influence, around 403 BC. The work, in dialogue form, pits the Platonic protagonist Socrates in argument with Gorgias and Gorgias' disciple Polus regarding the nature of rhetoric.

Socrates and Gorgias agree that, if it is anything, rhetoric is a form of persuasion. Gorgias defines it as "the ability to persuade with speeches either the judges in the law courts or statesmen in the council-chamber of the commons in the Assembly or any audience at any other meeting that may be held on public affairs."[78]

He agrees with Socrates' further characterization, "You say that Rhetoric is a producer of persuasion, and has therein its whole business and main consummation."[79]

Socrates begins his critique of rhetoric by securing Gorgias' acknowledgement of the difference between knowledge and belief. While knowledge can only be true, belief can be either true or false. Gorgias further agrees that rhetoric, as a persuasive medium, is not concerned with instilling knowledge:

Socrates: "This rhetoric, it seems, is a producer of persuasion for belief, not for instruction in the matter of right and wrong."

Gorgias: "Yes."

Socrates: "And so the rhetorician's business is not to instruct a law court or other public meeting in matters of right and wrong, but only to make them believe."[80]

Gorgias asserts that the rhetorician will persuade the public on all matters, even when competing for public opinion against experts.

Socrates: "Now, do you mean to make him carry conviction to the crowd on all subjects, not by teaching them, but by persuading?"

Gorgias: "Certainly, I do."

Socrates: "You were saying just now, you know, that even in the matter of health the [rhetorician] will be more convincing than the doctor."

Gorgias: "Yes, indeed, I was—meaning, to the crowd."

Socrates: "And 'to the crowd' means 'to the ignorant?' For surely, to those who know, he will not be more convincing than the doctor."

Gorgias: "You are right."

Socrates: "And if he is to be more convincing than the doctor, he thus becomes more convincing than he who knows."

Gorgias: "Certainly."

Socrates: "But he who is not a doctor is surely without knowledge of that whereof the doctor has knowledge."

Gorgias: "Clearly."

Socrates: "So he who does not know will be more convincing to those who do not know than he who knows; supposing the [rhetorician] to be more convincing than the doctor. Is that, or something else, the consequence?"

Gorgias: "In this case it does follow."

Socrates: "Then the case is the same in all the other arts for the [rhetorician] and his rhetoric: there is no need to know the truth of actual matters, but one merely needs to have discovered some device of persuasion which will make one appear to those who do not know to know better than those who know."[81]

Pressed by Gorgias and his disciple Polus to provide his own definition of the art of rhetoric, Socrates responds that it is not an art at all: "It seems to me, then, Gorgias, to be a pursuit that is not a matter of art, but showing a shrewd gallant spirit which has a natural bent with dealing with mankind, and I sum up its existence in the name of flattery."[82]

Asked to elaborate further, Socrates identifies rhetoric as a semblance of a branch of the art of politics.[83] By semblance, he means an unreal image or counterfeit: It uses the same techniques, and vocabulary, and claims to be directed toward the same end.

Socrates elaborates on the nature of such a semblance by analogy. Consider, for example, the health of the body. Maintenance of health, which Socrates calls gymnastic, has a semblance, self-adornment. While gymnastic is concerned with maintaining a body's health, self-adornment is concerned with the appearance of health. Gymnastic strives for a body that is robust and functioning at its best. Self-adornment, on the other hand, strives for a body that appears healthy, without regard to whether it actually is healthy.

Similarly, medicine is concerned with the restoration of health in an ill body. The doctor prescribes the proper foods, herbs, and beverages to be ingested to restore health. The semblance of medicine is cookery, which provides foods, herbs, and beverages that are pleasing to the body without regard to whether they will help restore health. Socrates summarizes:

"Cookery is flattery disguised as medicine; and in just the same manner self-adornment personates gymnastic: with its rascally, deceitful, ignoble, and illiberal nature it deceives men by forms and colors, polish and dress, so as to make them, in the effort of assuming an extraneous beauty, neglect the native sort that comes through gymnastic."[84]

Socrates asserts that rhetoric, as practiced by Gorgias and his followers, is a semblance of something else, which in this instance he calls justice. "As cookery is to medicine, so rhetoric is to justice."[85]

Socrates' specific objection to rhetoric, it must be noted, is that it is concerned merely with persuasion, without regard to whether those persuaded have received knowledge or merely belief, which may in turn be either true or false.

So, to state his objection more briefly, rhetoric is the semblance of justice because it is concerned with persuasion without regard to whether the beliefs it generates are true or false. We can construct the following matrix for justice (where T = True, F = False, B = Beneficial, H = Harmful).

Justice
T F
B H

Rhetoric, on the other hand, is concerned with what is beneficial to the persuader without regard to whether it is true or false. We can construct the following matrix for rhetoric:

Rhetoric
T or F
B H

Notice that Plato's objection is not that rhetoric persuades by instilling beliefs that are necessarily false. In his analogy, cookery is perfectly capable of providing foods that could restore health; it is merely unconcerned with whether its foods restore health or not. Similarly, self-adornment is concerned with providing the body with the appearance of health, even when the body is already healthy. It is unconcerned with whether the body is or is not healthy.

> Socrates' specific objection to rhetoric, it must be noted, is that it is concerned merely with persuasion.

The objectionable nature of Gorgias' rhetoric is its lack of concern whether its statements are true or false; it would be objectionable even if its statements turned out to be true.

Translating this into modern vocabulary, we can create a matrix that helps us understand the ethical use of professional communication: So a modern professional communicator can ground his or her professional judgment on the degree to which he or she promotes statements that are both true and beneficial to his or her client. As a general principle, a professional communicator does not promote statements that are harmful (with the possible exception of disclosure in the investment markets, which may require such communication). But an ethical communicator is concerned with whether his or her statement is true; an unethical communicator is not necessarily one that deliberately promotes falsehoods, but someone who is unconcerned with whether a statement is true or false. We can construct a similar matrix to differentiate between ethical and unethical communication (where T = True, F = False, B = Beneficial, H = Harmful).

Ethical Communication

T F

B H

Ethical communication promotes statements that are both truthful and beneficial to a client.

Unethical Communication

T or F

B H

Unethical communication is concerned with statements that are beneficial, without regard to whether those statements are true or false.

The ethical practice of professional communication is one where the professional communicator deliberately seeks to promote only true and beneficial statements, avoids false statements, and cares about the difference.

Ethical Communication Best Practices

The ethical practice of public relations requires both a desire to behave ethically and an understanding of ethical issues in professional communication. Here are some of the best practices:

1. Understand the letter and spirit of the various industry association codes of ethics, both for communication professionals and for the industries on whose behalf you communicate.

2. Recognize that codes of ethics are valuable because they establish normative standards of behavior that become habitual through repetition.

3. Understand the difference between ethics, morality, legality, etiquette, and aesthetics.

4. Know where you draw the line. Ultimately you need to know which behaviors are acceptable to you and which are unacceptable. If you think this through in advance you'll be better able to navigate ethical challenges when they present themselves.

5. Identify likely inadvertent violations of ethics codes before they happen, and call attention to them. Do not argue just on the basis of morality, but on the basis of practical business issues, including the likelihood that the unethical behavior will be discovered, and the negative consequences to the organization if this should be the case.

6. Note that the most likely ethical violations for public relations and corporate communication professionals include:
   – Conflicts of interests
   – Kickbacks from suppliers
   – Establishing or participating in front groups
   – Failing to protect proprietary and other confidential information
   – Issues of truthfulness and credibility

7. When in doubt, seek counsel of more experienced practitioners.

Resources for Further Study

Council of Public Relations Firms

The Council of Public Relations Firms represents the business of public relations in the United States, and includes more than 100 public relations firms. The Council's members agree to abide by its Code of Ethics and Statements of Principles. Its overriding principles are that openness and transparency are not only in the public interest, but also necessary tools for meeting clients' objectives. Its Web site is http://www.prfirms.org/who/code.asp.

Ethics Resource Center

The Ethics Resource Center in Washington, D.C., is the oldest not-for-profit association in the United States devoted to organizational ethics. The ERC conducts research, including an extensive National Business Ethics Survey, and publishes a free monthly electronic newsletter, *Ethics Today Online* (http://www.ethics.org/today/et_subscribe.html).

The Center publishes a number of guides to ethical practice, including *Creating a Workable Company Code of Ethics: A Practical Guide to Identifying and Developing Organizational Standards*. The Center also sponsors character development and ethics courses for educational institutions and for corporate ethics officers. The Center advised the Public

Relations Society of America in its overhaul of the PRSA Member Code of Ethics. The Ethics Resource Center can be found at http://www.ethics.org.

Global Business Standards Codex

This survey of business ethics standards around the world was conceived by several Harvard Business Schools scholars and described in detail in the *Harvard Business Review*. See *Harvard Business Review*, "Up to Code: Does Your Company's Conduct Meet World-Class Standards," by Lynn Paine, Rohit Deshpandé, Joshua M. Margolis, and Kim Eric Bettcher, December, 2005, page 122. Reprints can be ordered at http://www.hbr.org.

International Association of Business Communicators (IABC)

The IABC, based in San Francisco, has more than 13,000 members in more than sixty countries. It publishes guides to best practices, and offers professional development programs. The IABC can be found at http://www.iabc.com; its *Code of Ethics for Professional Communicators* can be found at http://www.iabc.com/about/code.htm.

International Public Relations Association (IPRA)

IPRA, based in Surrey, UK, is a membership organization of public relations professionals from nearly one hundred countries. IPRA has more than fifty years of experience in sharing and promoting professional development. IPRA has published several Codes and Charters seeking to provide an ethical framework for its members' professional activities. IPRA can be found at http://www.ipra.org; its various Codes and Charters can be found at http://ipra.org/aboutipra/aboutipra.htm.

Public Relations Society of America (PRSA)

The PRSA, based in New York City, is the world's largest organization of public relations professionals. It was founded in 1947 and as of 2006 had 20,000 members. The PRSA can be found at http://www.prsa.org. The PRSA's *Member Code of Ethics* can be found at http://prsa.org/About/ethics/index.asp?ident=eth1.

Questions for Further Discussion

1. What are the differences among morality, ethics, legality, aesthetics, and etiquette as they relate to any particular practice of corporate communication?
2. Codes of ethics are normative standards of behavior, and as such can be used by individuals or organizations who are not members of the organization that drafts the code. What are some of the other advantages of codes of ethics as normative standards of conduct?
3. Are print and video news releases, by their very nature, unethical?
4. How can a professional communicator resolve conflicting duties? For example, if asked a factual question by a reporter about a sensitive issue, the duty to keep confidences and the duty to be truthful may conflict. What are some ways to resolve the apparent conflict?
5. Is there a meaningful difference between public relations and propaganda?

CHAPTER 3

Media Relations

*That we teach others how to treat us is as true
in press relations as anywhere else.*

In the spring of 1998, an administrative assistant in Merck's Corporate Communications Department tried to fax an eighteen-page, confidential internal memorandum on the planned restructuring of the company's relationship with Astra, the Swedish pharmaceutical firm, to an outside investment banker counseling Merck. The machine jammed and she pushed what she thought was the "redial" button, but inadvertently sent the fax to The Star Ledger, *New Jersey's largest newspaper. To her credit, she told her boss, John Doorley, immediately, and John knew he had to contact his boss, Ken Frazier, senior vice president and general counsel.*

The restructuring of the joint venture that marketed Prilosec for the prevention and treatment of gastroesophageal reflux disease (GERD) was weeks from culmination, and premature disclosure would pose countless communication and regulatory problems, as well as trust issues with Astra. Ken agreed that John would contact Iris Taylor, a reporter at The Ledger *with whom he had a long-standing, trusting relationship. Ms. Taylor retrieved the fax and returned it to John as requested, promising she would not read it. Although the eighteen pages were coded for confidentiality, a business reporter covering the pharmaceutical industry would have been able to unravel it. The deal, valued at over $3 billion when it was announced weeks later, could have collapsed.[1] It was saved because the Communication Group and other people at Merck, including two CEOs, had invested much time and effort over many years in building a good reputation with that reporter. The relationship meant more to her—and she believed to her newspaper—than an ill-gotten scoop. The company's investment in the relationship, often intangible and hard to quantify, paid off handsomely that day.*

* * * * *

What each constituency believes and feels about an organization contributes to its reputation. But there is one group that influences every other constituency that matters to a company, a group that can affect the company's reputation quickly and profoundly: the news media.

Media relations is one of the core disciplines in public relations and corporate and organizational communication, and it is often one of the most visible. But it is also one of the most difficult for senior management to understand.

> *Media relations consists of all the ways an organization interacts with the news media. These include the ability to build long-term relationships with reporters whose area of responsibility, often called a "beat," includes covering the organization every day. Media relations also includes managing ad hoc contact with reporters who may be calling the company for the first and only time in their careers. Media relations also includes the processes of seeking media coverage and of responding to reporters' requests for interviews or information. And it includes developing procedures to measure, monitor and manage the contact between an organization's employees and reporters.*

This Chapter Covers

⇒ The case for a centralized media relations function
⇒ Organizing the media relations function
⇒ Media relations as a lightning rod
⇒ Sidebar: The four models of public relations
⇒ Moderating expectations
⇒ The journalist and the spokesperson
⇒ Fear of the press
⇒ The press' right to know
⇒ The press' penchant for bad news
⇒ The good news about the press
⇒ Press relations from a position of power
⇒ Success in media relations
⇒ Best practices
⇒ Qualities of a good media relations person
⇒ Resources for further study
⇒ Questions for further discussion
⇒ Sidebar: The art of the pitch, by Raleigh Mayer
⇒ Sidebar: Choosing the right tools to convey your message, by Jay Rubin

The Case for a Centralized Media Relations Function

An organization should not communicate through the news media until it knows what the facts are, and then only when the organization is prepared to disclose those facts. And it needs to communicate with a single voice.

But to the outside world, it is neither intuitive nor self-evident that an organization must have a strict policy governing which people can communicate with the media about the organization, its activities, products, policies, and positions. Why should the researcher who conducted the breakthrough research for the organization not take the call from the reporter who is inquiring about that research? Why should the chief financial officer or senior accountant not take a phone call about the company's latest sales and earnings press release? Why should any employee not be permitted to express his or her opinion on what is happening at the company?

Outsiders, especially young journalists and young employees (sometimes, even including those in the communications department) tend to sense a conflict between forthright communication and managed communication, and they tend to believe that "open and forthright" means "tell everyone everything right away." Yet such a strategy would be irresponsible—in fact, anarchic. And in light of securities regulations, it could also present a company with legal liability and regulatory problems.

To an organization's constituencies, anyone from the organization who speaks about the organization is seen to be speaking for the organization. But often, different people speak from different perspectives, using different vocabulary, and based on different levels of knowledge about an issue. The result can be confusion, inaccurate communication, and reputational harm.

> It is neither intuitive nor self evident that an organization must have a strict policy governing which people can communicate with the news media.

When speaking with reporters, it is even more important for communication to be centralized. Reporters, especially when covering breaking news, are often less interested in understanding a complex issue than in harvesting quotes to bring a story to life. The way reporters use quotes is different from the way most constituencies use the information they receive. Speaking with a reporter without knowing how one's words are likely to be used can lead to what are often seen by the person quoted to be misquotes. But in our experience, most instances of a "misquote" are really accurate quotes based on people speaking imprecisely, with limited knowledge, or with little understanding that only one or two sentences—out of dozens or hundreds spoken—would be quoted. Good organizational practice dictates that only people who have been trained to speak effectively with reporters be authorized to do so.

One of the best examples of the consequences of uncoordinated press communication concerns the nuclear accident at Three Mile Island. The accident that occurred there on March 28, 1979, was the country's first nuclear accident, and it provoked a torrent of press inquiries.[2] Within minutes, local journalists, including wire service reporters, were on the scene. They interviewed several employees of the Metropolitan Edison utility company who were not fully informed, were not communicating with each other, and were unfamiliar with the utility's plan for corrective action. As a result, the various employees related inconsistent information about what had happened and about what was being done in response. The result was confusion, fear, and the sense that the utility did not know what it was doing. The press coverage, which would have been quite negative in any case, was made much worse by the perception that the utility was unprepared for such a situation, and that the public was at greater risk than it actually was. What had begun as a manageable situation was turned into a communication disaster by the utility itself, acting in unwitting concert with local journalists, who in many cases had little understanding of science or science writing.

Even when reporters know a company or industry well, it is still important to limit their access to information and people in a company. For example, we have been struck over the years by how individual pharmaceutical researchers viewed the promise of a particular research project differently. If ten scientists were working on a new medicine, seven might think it held little promise, two might be cautiously optimistic, and one might think it was the next penicillin. Allowing reporters random access to any or all of the researchers would present a confusing picture of the therapeutic potential of a given medicine. While robust internal debate can be a good thing, the tendency of the media to oversimplify would lead such a story to be cast as confusion, disagreement, or internal strife, rather than the natural give-and-take of a scientific enterprise.

Unrestricted communication to the news media can cause more than just confusion. It can be irresponsible, and sometimes even illegal. For example, it would be both irresponsible and potentially a violation of securities laws and regulations for an executive to prematurely reveal to a reporter that the company is in negotiations on a potential merger. The very coverage of a merger negotiation would have an adverse impact on the negotiation itself, often limiting the flexibility of one side or the other. Similarly, the securities market's reaction to the news may affect the price of the various companies' stocks as investors buy or sell stock on the news, potentially affecting the economics of the merger. And the news would give competitors, and other potential merger partners, a heads up on what the organization was planning, often triggering reactions on the part of competitors, including a possible bidding war for the company that may be acquired. So premature disclosure could result in the derailment of a merger that appeared to be headed to a successful conclusion. Just as significant, merger discussions and other material information are subject to strict disclosure rules, and premature or selective disclosure of such negotiations could subject the company or individuals to civil or criminal liability.

Enlightened organizations establish clear guidelines on who can speak to reporters on what topics, maintain press logs for tracking who has spoken to whom, on what topics, what was said, what follow-up is required, and when a story is likely to appear.

Organizing the Media Relations Function

Media relations typically resides within a corporate communications function, but it can also reside in other corporate structures, including:

⇒ Marketing
⇒ Product divisions
⇒ Regional offices
⇒ Investor relations (in the case of the financial media)

In large companies, there is often a breakdown of responsibility, with different people responsible for different kinds of media relations, including:

⇒ Corporate media relations, for articles about the corporation as a whole, including governance issues, industry trends, senior leadership, sales and earnings, and issues affecting the entire corporation.

⇒ Product media relations, sometimes residing with a single person, sometimes with a different person responsible for each product category. These individuals focus on inquiries about, or stories featuring, individual products. These can include the general interest consumer media (newspapers, magazines, television, electronic), or can include industry trade publications.

⇒ Marketing public relations, focusing on initiating coverage of the company, its products, issues, and people. This function often is responsible for creating special events, promotional campaigns, and other opportunities to affirmatively show the company in a positive light.

⇒ Financial media relations, usually coordinated carefully with the investor relations function, responsible for distributing news of interest to the investment community, and in fulfillment of a company's securities law disclosure requirements.

⇒ Regional media relations, usually a separate function in each geographic region, and often reporting to the management of the region, with only a dotted-line reporting responsibility to corporate media relations.

There are many other configurations of the media relations function. The most effective functions are those that fit the strategic and operational needs of their organizations. But to succeed, the function must be well coordinated, regardless of the structure or reporting responsibilities. Many companies manage the coordination by having well-defined policies for who is responsible for which relationships with which kinds of media; who is responsible for handling inquiries on which topics, and the like. They also have frequent, often weekly conference calls with all media relations staff to assure up-to-date understanding of pending stories and developments, and to share insights, resources, or information.

Most companies also have clear policies directing all other employees to refer any press inquiries, on any topic, to certain people in the media relations department.

Media Relations as a Lightning Rod

Reporters who cover a company or industry speak constantly with industry observers, participants, critics, and supporters. They sometimes develop insights that are even deeper than a company's management may have at any given time. They can serve as an early warning system of trouble ahead. And they are often seen within a company to have an anticompany agenda or bias.

In a major article in the March 18, 1991, issue of *Business Week* magazine, reporter Joseph Weber wrote that Merck's research pipeline was not as promising as in the 1980s and that "an inevitable cooling off has begun." He projected that earnings growth would decline over the coming years.[3] The article was viewed by some senior people within Merck as extremely negative and unfair. Of course, in 1991 Merck senior executives were beginning to realize that a downturn in financial performance was coming, but that is different from reading about it in a major publication. The *Business Week* article produced a firestorm of criticism within senior ranks at Merck, and several executives began to routinely criticize Weber's subsequent articles. This book's coauthor John Doorley had viewed Joe Weber as an astute, very intelligent, tough journalist, and thought he had always been fair. John liked him. But after months of internal pressure, John began to change his view and to look upon Weber's frequent calls to Merck as cynical or unfair. With Weber's help, John arranged a meeting in late 1991 with him and his editors at *Business Week* headquarters in Manhattan. Accompanied by John's boss and another colleague, John openly criticized Weber, whom he had alerted in advance. Weber and his colleagues listened. He never retaliated in any way, and some at Merck thought that his coverage became fairer.

Some months after the meeting at *Business Week*, John reviewed Weber's recent and older articles about Merck. It became clear, as it had been until John succumbed to internal pressure, that Weber had remained, all along, a good and fair reporter. A few years later, Weber was promoted to head of the Toronto bureau of *Business Week*. John wrote him a congratulatory letter that included John's personal view that the earlier criticism of him was wrong. John copied the senior people at Merck and the editors of *Business Week* who had attended the 1991 meeting. John acknowledged his mistake and hoped he had learned from it. (At this writing Joe Weber was Chicago bureau chief for *Business Week*.)

Journalists will often know about problems in an organization early on. It is important that communicators feel free to pass along to senior management negative comments and questions without fear that management will want to "kill the messenger." And it is important for senior leadership to see these negative comments or questions as possible precursors of trouble ahead, not with the individual reporters but with the business performance or practices in question. In other words, communicators need beware of the Pushmi-Pullyu Syndrome (Chapter 1).

For example, several years before the accounting scandals about American business broke onto the front pages, several journalists openly questioned the accounting methodologies and inherent conflicts of interests that would bring down major companies in 2002. Similarly, many journalists questioned the independence of Wall Street research for several years before New York State Attorney General Elliot Spitzer and the Securities and Exchange Commission forced major Wall Street firms into a financial settlement and structural changes to assure that analysts' opinions are in fact independent of the investment banking agendas of their employers.

At least one thing is certain from the communication post mortem of these business crises: Not enough corporate and organizational communicators listened early on, and few raised their voices internally against practices that were clearly wrong and often indefensible.

> It is important that communicators feel free to pass along to senior management negative comments and questions without fear that management will want to "kill the messenger."

Four Academic Models of Public Relations

In the seminal public relations text, "Managing Public Relations" (New York, 1984, Holt Rinehart and Winston), James Grunig and Todd Hunt identified four models that generally guide the communication philosophy of practitioners.[4] We believe it can be helpful for public relations practitioners to examine their own communication philosophies to try and determine which model they generally follow. Although it can be helpful to look at these models in terms of communicating with various constituencies, the models can be especially helpful with media relations. The following definitions of the models, which have stood the test of time, are Grunig's and Hunt's; the commentaries are by Doorley and Garcia.

1. Press Agent / Publicity Model. The guiding principle here is to get favorable publicity—not to try to ensure accuracy and truthful reporting. Commentary: This model can place the goals of accuracy and truth in second place to publicity. While this model can produce good results for the client organization, at least over the short term, it can be bad for the various constituencies (for example, the media, customers, employees, and the community). The term "spinning," which came into vogue twenty years after this model was defined, is just another label for it. This is the approach that gives public relations a bad reputation.

2. Public Information Model. The focus here is on the communication of objective information, generally without regard to the self-interests of the organization or client for whom the PR person works. Commentary: In theory, the constituency wins. The client organization, often a government agency or nonprofit, can also win. But we would argue that public relations practitioners have a responsibility to advocate for the client, not just to disseminate information. And if the advocacy is up front—that's why organizations have letterhead!— then the advocacy is transparent and ethical.

3. The Two-Way Asymmetric Model. The PR practitioner conducts research to determine the views of a particular constituency and then uses that information to help achieve the client's objectives. Commentary: The client organization can win, at least over the short term. But the constituency probably loses, and we would argue that this is a myopic and sometimes unethical approach.

4. Two-Way Symmetric Model. The PR practitioner conducts research to determine the views of a particular constituency and then uses that information to help achieve the objectives of both the client organization and the constituency. Commentary: This is the approach that will most often produce a win-win outcome. It can be useful in conflict resolution and in any public relations program. It can help address ethical questions, including that of advocacy versus objectivity, by looking at the interests of both the client organization and its constituencies.

> If the news report turns out badly for the organization, the media relations person will usually take at least a small hit.

Moderating Expectations

When a story turns out well for the organization, the people interviewed are seen to have done a good job, and they might pass along a brief compliment to the media relations person. If the editors are pleased with the news report, the journalist might thank the media relations person as well.

On the other hand, if the news report turns out badly for the organization, the media relations person will usually take at least a small hit, regardless of how the report arose or the accuracy of it. If the journalist's editors are unhappy with the report, the journalist is generally unhappy with the media relations person because of, for example, inadequate access.

To be effective, the media relations professional needs a supportive boss. If he or she does not have a superior who will absorb at least some of the criticism for the bad news reports and take only some of the credit for the good ones, the media relations person might be able to survive for a while, but he or she cannot do the job well over the long term. It is impossible. Polish the resume. It is time to leave.

The good news is that most heads of public affairs (or whatever function media relations reports into) have the honesty and courage required to support their people. Fortunately for us—John Doorley over the years at Roche and Merck, and coauthor Fred Garcia at two corporations and a number of firms—most of our bosses fell into that category.

One challenge, an occupational hazard, is the tendency of some executives to assume that the media relations professional is an advocate for the news media. Sometimes this is framed as "being on the reporter's side"; sometimes as having "gone native" and caring more about maintaining relationships with reporters than protecting an organization's reputation. Most of the time such criticism misses the mark. The best media relations people are advocates in two directions: they need to clarify and focus the organization's viewpoint for reporters. But they also need to help management better understand what a reporter is up to and whether and why it is in the company's interests to engage with the reporter.

Nevertheless, it is extremely important that the media relations person take substantial responsibility for the news that appears. We have known press relations people who would say, " I don't write the news reports, you know." Our answer to them, assuming they were actively involved in cooperating with the journalist, was: If the article had turned out well, would you be saying the same thing?

One key to effectiveness in media relations is to manage the expectations that company executives have, both inflated expectations about positive news or the ability to avoid bad news, and negative expectations about a crisis. And it is usually best to put it in writing.

The Journalist and the Spokesperson

In many ways reporters and company spokespeople are similar. They go to many of the same events and conferences, and share interviews with the same important people. They often have similar academic and professional backgrounds—in fact, many media relations professionals began their careers in journalism. Both address (talk or write about) the same subject matter. But their jobs are different. The journalist's job is to write stories that his readers or viewers want to read or watch. The media relations professional's job is to manage the company's engagement with the journalist in ways that ultimately benefit the company, or are, at minimum, fair. The two jobs are not mutually exclusive. In fact, each depends on the other for success. But the jobs are not the same.

So media relations people should try to build good working relationships with journalists, meaning that each party tries to understand and respect the perspective of the other. It means treating each other with dignity and honesty. It means that the media relations person needs to respect the time-table that reporters work under. But it does not mean that the timetable should be the sole driver of a company's response to an inquiry. It means that a spokesperson should deal forthrightly with the journalist, even when they disagree. But it does not mean acquiescing to every request or with-holding criticism when it is deserved. And it sometimes means giving the other party the benefit of the doubt, as in the story about the misdirected fax that began this chapter.

Most important, building good relationships does not mean that the spokesperson and reporter should conspire with each other as if they were partners in a common enterprise. Often media relations people confuse good working relationships with friendships. While such relationships have much in common with friendships, they are not the same. In fact, friend-ships can complicate things, mostly by letting down the guard that is often necessary to prevent one party from taking undue advantage of the other.

This is particularly difficult when the spokesperson and journalist have a preexisting friendship. For example, in the late 1980s, Fred was head of corporate communications at a major investment bank. One of his jobs was to be the primary spokesperson for the bank to the major national and international media. At the time the investment banking reporter at a leading business magazine was a college classmate of Fred's. They had been friendly for years.

> Often media rela-tions people con-fuse good working relationships with friendships.

Although they were friends, neither ever forgot what his job was. Often the reporter would publish stories that were sharply critical of Fred's bank. Fred often acted as gatekeeper, declining to grant the reporter access to executives on stories that Fred feared might be negative.

Sometimes the reporter even misled Fred in order to get access. At one point he persuaded Fred to grant an interview with the CEO for what the reporter called a "general industry trends piece." When the story appeared it was in fact a scathing criticism of the CEO's leadership style. When called on the carpet by Fred, the reporter sheepishly admitted that he would not have gotten the interview if he had been candid about his story. His defense: "You can't blame me. I was just doing my job. I needed to get the story, and that was the only way I could. It wasn't personal."

Fred had never let his guard down; he had simply been misled. From then on, he became even more careful, as the friendship grew less trusting. The reporter would often gossip about leaders of other investment banks, trying to draw Fred into the gossip. Fred never took the bait. Sometimes the reporter would gossip about the executives of Fred's own bank. Again, Fred would not take the bait. When the reporter protested that Fred was being too rigid, behaving less as a friend and more as a corporate spokesperson,

Fred would ask what he had in his jacket pocket: he always carried his reporter's notebook. Fred asked what would happen if he said something newsworthy in a moment of informality, and the reporter confirmed he would have no choice but to find some way to use it in his coverage of the bank. The reporter never forgot that despite all else, he was always a reporter, and working a competitive beat. Fred never forgot either. His reply to the reporter's complaint: "I'm just doing my job. It's nothing personal."

So journalists and media relations people work on the same projects, but often with completely different perspectives. Journalists are sometimes skeptical and they often see media relations people as impediments. Media relations people sometimes fear the journalist's penchant for bad news or oversimplification. The secret of good media relations is to find the common goal and work toward it together: a timely, fair news report or feature that accomplishes what the reporter wants—a story people are interested in—and that also accomplishes what the spokesperson wants—a story that is fair, and more favorable or less negative than it would have been without his involvement.

Fear of the Press

Isn't the spokesperson who is afraid to speak an oxymoron?

We believe that many media relations people are not very good at their jobs, and that this is so because many of them are afraid of journalists. "Now, please don't quote me on that," is the constant refrain. It's much like a salesperson ending a call with: "Now please don't buy any." Is not the spokesperson who is afraid to speak an oxymoron?

Especially in large organizations, there is a danger that media relations people become mere order-takers, responding to press inquiries and helping provide journalists with information, but not necessarily working to change a journalist's perceptions of the organization. And especially in a large organization that receives many press calls daily, there is a tendency for media relations people to see their job as fielding inquiries—catching, rather than initiating coverage, pitching. Sometimes this is for good reason: because the volume of incoming calls is so high. But sometimes it is inertia or even fear that suppresses a media relations person's appetite for initiating discussions with reporters.

One reason fear develops in media relations people is the constant scrutiny and criticism within an organization of what is stated and not stated in press reports. Senior officials in organizations often react out of all proportion to the slightest problem in a news report. A mistake by the spokesperson is out there for the world to read, see or hear—colleagues, bosses, CEOs, family, friends, and neighbors. The spokesperson begins to doubt his or her ability to synthesize and express a view on behalf of the organization.

Yet the spokesperson is paid to convey certain facts and points of view. While there are times when one should speak "for background," or even "off the record," or indeed not at all, constant pleas for the journalist not to print or broadcast certain information give the journalist another reason to want to ignore the media relations person. After all, the journalist usually wants to speak with someone else in the organization anyway, with the media relations person being a distant second choice (and, generally, the spokesperson at the PR agency third).

Often media relations people are afraid of the media because they are intimidated by the prestige of the institution. For a twenty-five-year old, or even a forty-year old, a call from a senior reporter at *The New York Times*, or from a producer at CBS's *60 Minutes* can cause panic or worse. When the stakes are so high, it is easy for media relations people, especially those who are not particularly confident in their own abilities or their stature in their organization, to worry that their own words may come back to haunt them.

Some journalists, especially young ones and those with the news organizations that specialize in sensationalist stories, play "Gotcha journalism," hovering over the interview subject like jackals. We have witnessed instances where executives said something they did not mean to say—statements the journalists knew to be inaccurate and unintended—and the journalists used the misstatements because they buttressed the story angle. And there are surely a small number of journalists, like some people in other professions, who are simply bad people who will cheat and lie, and they do that by omitting a quote, by deliberately misquoting someone, and sometimes by inventing quotes or stories outright. We suspect that journalists who have no qualms about such matters are cynics who believe that the people they might interview (the rest of the world) are duplicitous and untrustworthy, and that the journalist's dishonesty is therefore necessary to get the truth out to the public. Nevertheless, in more than a combined forty years of press relations work with thousands of journalists, we have seen only very few examples of what we perceive to be blatant unfairness.

One was on July 29, 1994, when a journalist for *The New York Times*, Gina Kolata, took remarks from an interview John had given her four months earlier on a completely different subject and put it in a page-one article about the possible conflict of interest that Medco, a pharmacy benefits management organization recently acquired by Merck, would henceforth face in handling prescriptions for patients.[5] The powerful last paragraph of the article had the reporter writing: "Mr. Doorley of Merck said critics have to consider the drug industry's point of view. Something has to be done to restore profits." The remarks were not printed as a direct quote but they appeared to have been written to produce that effect. Doorley had made

Nevertheless, in more than a combined forty years of press relations work with thousands of journalists, we have seen only very few examples of what we perceive to be blatant unfairness.

such remarks—at least remarks to that effect—in an entirely different context, but, when used in the July 29 article, they buttressed the conflict-of-interest theme and made Merck look like it put profits before patients. John and Merck appeared callous and greedy.

The New York Times refused to publish John's letter to the editor, even though he spoke with editors there and explained what had happened. He received a letter, dated August 17, from news editor William Borders: "As to the quotation from you with which the article ended, you don't seem to dispute that you said what she (Kolata) said you said, only the context. I am afraid I cannot agree. There is nothing wrong with using in July a quotation from an interview four months earlier, so long as the context is fair, and in this case I think it is. You were talking about the need for Merck to be more profitable, and certainly the Medco arrangement moves toward that goal."[6]

John subsequently realized that this newspaper would seldom publish letters critical of its journalism (unlike National Public Radio, for example, which broadcasts critical comments every week). In late 2003 *The New York Times* appointed a public editor as one of the mechanisms for assuring high-quality journalism in the wake of a scandal where a reporter (see Jayson Blair, Chapter 1) had been inventing stories. Under pressure from the public editor, the *Times* changed its letters policy, and now sometimes discusses lapses in journalistic standards in its expanded corrections column.

A second incident of journalistic unfairness involved John's colleague, Sharyn Bearse. On October 24, 1995, a reporter for *The Star Ledger*, New Jersey's largest newspaper, phoned Sharyn and asked if it was true that Merck had committed infractions against the Cuban embargo when some of the company's midlevel executives had visited Cuba about a year earlier. Sharyn answered that the Merck employees who visited Cuba did so at the request of the Pan American Health Organization and that they had not violated the embargo. The reporter's call had come out of the blue, precipitated by a surprise Clinton administration press release about Merck's embargo infractions, something the administration officials had said they would not do. But Castro was visiting the United Nations in New York City, and apparently someone in the administration could not pass up an opportunity to criticize "Big Pharma." After Sharyn spoke with the reporter, she and John contacted Merck attorneys who explained that, technically, the Merck employees had violated the embargo—a distinction John and Sharyn had not understood—by having certain chemicals tested at a Cuban laboratory under a routine agreement that nevertheless constituted a contract and was therefore a violation of the embargo.

Sharyn and John agreed she would phone the reporter—it was the Communications Department's policy to correct misstatements and to do so as soon as possible—and tell him that what she had said earlier was not technically correct, and that she would like to amend her statement. The reporter, instead of simply changing Sharyn's statement as most would do, constructed a narrative that made Sharyn look as if she had been duplicitous, rather than simply mistaken. The scenario in the next day's page-one article, headlined "Merck Pays $127,500 In Fines For Cuba Deal," implied that Merck had business plans for Cuba.[7] Lost in the story was the fact that any such business in Cuba would have amounted to a minuscule percentage of Merck's 1995 annual sales of $16.8 billion. But the reporter weaved a captivating tale.[8]

However, such journalism is not a reason to be afraid of the press, because it is the exception, not the rule. The press relations person has to begin a relationship with a journalist presuming trustworthiness, just as one should begin other relationships in life that way, both because trusting relationships are more productive as well as for the sake of one's own sanity and soul. If a particular journalist should be untrustworthy or unethical, it will become clear soon enough.

A degree of anxiety can increase performance. It is reasonable and good to be anxious when dealing with journalists because they are human and make mistakes. They sometimes misunderstand what is said or they mistranscribe quotes. And today, in the ever-faster-paced media world, there are more and more opportunities for mistakes.

Another reason for having a healthy degree of anxiety about the press is that every journalist brings a perspective to an assignment. Some are better than others at being objective, but no one can wipe clean the slate of life's experiences, opinions, predilections, and prejudices. A big part of the media relations person's job is to figure out what the journalist's perspective is. If the perspective is favorable and accurate, reinforce it. If it is unfavorable, try to understand why, and then deal with the problems and issues.

Still another reason for healthy anxiety is one's own inadequacies as a spokesperson. How many people can talk with absolute precision for, say, an entire hour? Can one swear, at the end of the interview, that he or she said "appraise" rather than "apprise" or, "Yes, I disagree" rather than, "No, I don't disagree"?

Spokespeople say things ranging from insensitive to inappropriate to dumb. We all do so in our personal discourse, out of carelessness, naiveté or ignorance, sometimes even offending the very people we care most about. Media relations people can say things that are inaccurate or reveal information that should not be revealed. One of the biggest fears of public relations professionals in technology-based companies should be that they might unwittingly reveal something proprietary. The rule most companies follow is: if the information has been presented before a scientific forum or

> Spokespeople say things ranging from insensitive to inappropriate to dumb.

published in a scientific journal, it is considered public. But of course few rules are that simple. Sometimes, for example, scientists present information at a sidebar session (a "poster" session) and not in front of the entire conference. Sometimes, a scientist overstates or understates a scientific development and that might not be easily apparent from the transcript.

Similarly, public relations people who work on Wall Street must be acutely aware that everything they say is subject to securities laws and regulations, and has the potential to move markets. Fear of civil and criminal liability has a tendency to focus one's mind, and to make one default to precision or to silence.

The Press' Right to Know

If a journalist does not ask a question in precisely the right words, yet the spokesperson knows what information the journalist is seeking, does the spokesperson have an obligation to give the desired information?

For example, a journalist phones the spokesperson for the publicly owned ABC Company and says: "I understand that Ms. X (a senior officer in the organization) has resigned." The fact is that, as the spokesperson knows, Ms. X will formally resign the next day, but has not done so yet. So the spokesperson answers: "No, that is not true." The journalist failed to phrase the question precisely or broadly enough, and the spokesperson took advantage of that. "Gotcha journalism" in reverse, one might say.

> To deny certain rumors but not others is to implicitly confirm the others.

Did this spokesperson handle the matter well? The answer is that it depends on the circumstances. If Ms. X is in line to succeed the CEO, the resignation announcement could be considered "material," meaning that a shareholder or prospective shareholder might buy or sell stock on that information. The spokesperson could not prematurely acknowledge the resignation to that one journalist, because that would constitute selective disclosure and possibly violate securities laws or regulations. Similarly, securities laws prohibit statements that are "materially misleading." Saying, "It's not true that Ms. X has resigned," while technically true when spoken, may no longer be true when the newspaper is published. Such a statement could be seen to be materially misleading. A safer approach would be to avoid commenting on the resignation at all. The story about the resignation would still appear, but without the company's comment, one way or the other.

Such considerations apply when journalists raise questions about rumored business development activities. If a journalist asks: "I understand that you have acquired XYZ company," and the spokesperson knows that the acquisition agreement, while expected soon, has not yet been reached, the spokesperson can answer "No." A better answer might be: "As a matter of policy, ABC company does not comment on rumors about our business (or organization)." This is a particularly effective response if used consistently. The spokesperson can explain to journalists (as well as securities analysts and others who inquire) the reason for the policy: To deny certain rumors but not others is to implicitly confirm the others. Of course when rumors rise to the level where they have a significant (for example, "material") effect on the organization, a denial or confirmation may have to be issued before the organization would otherwise plan to do so. But that should be a rare exception. Armed with a no-comment-on-rumors policy, the spokesperson need not even make the internal inquiries to determine the truth about the rumor. In fact, he or she should not delay in giving the response: "As a matter of policy, ABC does not comment on rumors."

While the press arguably has the right to ask any question, the press does not have the right to know everything. Reporters often assert that they are proxies for the public at large, and that "the public has a right to know." They often assume that such an argument is persuasive, and in fact sometimes inexperienced media relations people fall into the trap of assuming that the public has some such right. In fact, the public does not have a right to know everything reporters might choose to write about. While companies have disclosure obligations, those obligations are very clearly specified in securities regulations, as is the timing and manner of such disclosure. But there is a big difference between a company's duty to disclose certain kinds of information in a certain manner, and the public's or press' right to know whatever it wants to know.

The press does not have a right to know proprietary information; personal information; information that is not fully developed; or information that might threaten security.

Proprietary Information

Inventions must be patent protected before they can be discussed outside the organization. The trade secret is another valid way of keeping information confidential until the appropriate time for disclosure. If a journalist asks a question about a proprietary matter, it is perfectly acceptable to say, "The matter is proprietary, and we don't discuss proprietary information." The reporter does not have a right to know trade secrets or other appropriately confidential information.

Personal Information

Individuals have the right to protect information that is truly personal and none of the public's business. So, also, do individuals within organizations have the right to protect their personal information. Publicly traded organizations have a duty to disclose some private information about a small number of their senior-most executives (usually, their salary, bonus, and stock holdings). But for most employees their compensation, personnel files, and other work-related personal matters are not public, and should be protected.

When Fred was a spokesperson at a major investment bank in the 1980s, Wall Street compensation was a hot topic, and Fred would frequently be asked about particular executives' compensation. As a matter of policy the bank did not disclose compensation information except for the small number of executives required by law. Fred would often say something like, "As a matter of policy we don't comment on executive compensation." Often reporters would persist, asking to confirm ranges: "Does he make more than $10 million? Does he make less than $20 million?" Fred's reply would persistently be, "That's a question about compensation and we don't comment on employee compensation." With one *The Wall Street Journal Reporter,* Fred and the reporter had this type of exchange for every salary level from $1 million to $20 million, always with the same response, over a period of a half hour. The reporter later told Fred, "You can't blame me for trying to get you to crack. And besides, I had to be able to tell my editor that I had grilled you on every salary level." The interaction was a kind of dance, with each party knowing precisely what the other would do, but duty-bound to do the dance anyway.

> The interaction was a kind of dance, with each party knowing precisely what the other would do.

Information That Is Not Fully Developed

Even "sure things" fall apart. The train may be moving smoothly along the tracks, but even the conductor does not know with certainty what may be lurking in the tunnel or around the corner. In any case, spokespeople should never acknowledge anything before the organization agrees to the timing. The reasons range from illegality (for example, selective disclosure) to certain unemployment for the spokesperson. And sometimes the premature disclosure of a pending event may prevent the event from happening at all.

Preparation can prevent such problems. If something new is brewing in an organization, the communications people should be brought in early so that the best response can be prepared for the announcement day, and another for the interim period.

Some situations are so difficult that a "no-comment" response or a euphemism is called for. The phrase "no comment" has become, through movies and television programs, a caricature of evasion. And the phrase itself is awkward. Because of the baggage the phrase carries, it can cast a negative impression with both the reporter and with those who read, view, or listen to the story. But there are ample ways of avoiding comment without using that two-word phrase. Among the possibilities are:

⇒ "We don't discuss financial projections."

⇒ "As a matter of policy we don't comment on (rumors/employee matters/investigations,etc.)."

⇒ "It is proprietary."

⇒ "We cannot reveal the identities of the victims until next of kin have been notified."

Even a "no comment" is always better than a lie. The U.S. Supreme Court has ruled that "no-comment statements" are the functional equivalent of silence. But it also ruled that denying a rumor that happened to be true was the functional equivalent of a lie, and held the offending company liable for the lie.

So as a rule, some form of "no-comment" statement, however phrased, is the less bad alternative between inappropriate disclosure of private information and lying.

Some form of no-comment statement is preferable to "was not available for comment," since a big part of the spokesperson's job is to be available.

"Let me check and get back to you" can be a useful response when the spokesperson is caught off guard or unaware. The problem with this response is that the spokesperson has to get back to the journalist, who will expect some enlightenment after an hour or two of grace. It is far better to be prepared with an immediate response.

If the journalist and the spokesperson have a good relationship, the spokesperson will often have to work hard to see that confidentiality concerns do not damage their relationship. For example, if a journalist is hot on the trail of breaking news for three days, and the spokesperson cannot reveal anything until the fourth day, the spokesperson might gain the necessary internal approvals to tell that journalist first on the fourth day or to give him or her a special interview opportunity at the right time.

Security Concerns

Spokespeople have a profound obligation—especially in this day and age—to protect the security of the organization and its people. Yet anecdotal research suggests that most corporations do not train their communications people to guard against lapses that could pose a security threat.

The Press' Penchant for Bad News

"Does the press have a penchant for bad news?" is a question much like the one we used to ask as kids about the Pope being Catholic, and the bear doing something in the woods. The answer is yes, and nobody can credibly take another position. "If it bleeds, it leads," is the mantra of local television news directors.

Journalists can argue that their behavior reflects society's desires and the discussion can become arcane, but the answer is still yes—there is a penchant for negative news. Realizing that is important for two reasons:

First, if there is bad news brewing in your organization, the press will probably find out about it and report it, so why not generally address the matter up front? When patents are about to expire on a major product in a technology-based company, for example, the business press covers the matter early and thoroughly. The best way for a company to deal with this is to understand that patent expirations are important and legitimate stories, and be ready with the best answers to such questions as "what will happen to the company's profitability?" Similarly, management turmoil, weak sales, and other negative information will often find its way to reporters before the company is fully ready to discuss it.

Second, the penchant for bad news interferes with coverage of good news, if only because the newshole (that is, the total amount of space in any given print or broadcast story minus the space or time for advertisements) is only so big. The 1988 story of Merck's introduction and donation of Mectizan to prevent and treat river blindness in millions of people is literally one of the greatest stories in history. Yet it proved extremely difficult over the years to get coverage of the story (with some notable exceptions such as the cover story in *The New York Times Magazine* of January 8, 1989).[9] Journalists would often say that people in the West are not interested in stories about people afflicted with river blindness who live mainly in developing countries in Africa. Yet all one has to do is note how prominent the coverage is of the bad news out of Africa about AIDS, wars, famines, and other horrors. Would not one think that the media would rush to cover the story of a pill (taken just once a year) that prevents or treats a parasitic disease that ravages entire populations, with blindness being only one of the symptoms? As if that were not enough to ensure coverage, the company that discovered and developed the medicine has committed to continuing to donate it to the millions of people who need it for as long as necessary.

> If the story is positive and important, and journalists are not covering it, the spokesperson should challenge them.

After the 1974 resignation of President Richard M. Nixon in the wake of the Watergate scandal, there was an influx of young people into journalism. They were following the example of Carl Bernstein and Bob Woodward, whose dogged pursuit of a "third-rate burglary" resulted in the downfall of the most powerful person in the free world. Romanticized by the movie *All The President's Men*, journalism was seen as a vital mechanism for democratic accountability.

But the thrill of the chase often became the foremost concern of some journalists. In the late 1980s, Fred had lunch with the newly appointed reporter in charge of the investment banking beat at *The Wall Street Journal*. It was a time of turmoil in investment banking, punctuated by insider-trading scandals that served as the basis for the popular movie *Wall Street* with Charlie Sheen. *The Wall Street Journal* had recently won a Pulitzer Prize for its coverage of the scandals. The once-powerful firm Drexel Burnham Lambert ceased to exist, and its charismatic head of junk bonds, Mike Milken, was on his way to jail. During the lunch Fred innocently asked the reporter what his goal was in covering the industry. In all seriousness the reporter said, "My goal is to bring down a major investment bank before I'm thirty." Fred thought the reporter was joking, and asked him, "No, really, what's your goal for your beat?" The reporter, with a straight face, replied, "No, really. That's my goal." After several seconds of awkward silence, Fred asked, "Well, how old are you?" The reporter was twenty-eight, which gave him two years to accomplish his goal.

Sure enough, the reporter wrote story after story that proved to be both very damaging and untrue. Numerous attempts to change his behavior proved unsuccessful. After a while, the only course left was for the chairman of the bank to send a forceful letter to the publisher of *The Wall Street Journal*, describing in great detail the various violations of the *Journal's* own standards in the reporter's coverage. It worked. The reporter turned his attention to other firms.

While, in the aftermath of Watergate, journalism came to be seen as investigative, over the last three decades—and particularly with the advent of all-news-all-the-time cable news coverage—journalism has morphed into a kind of entertainment medium, with production values and story lines similar to the dramatic features offered on television entertainment programs. Whereas in the "early years" CBS's news division was not considered a profit center, it now has to justify its existence in terms of advertising dollars. The result can be positive: production values and fast-breaking news. But it can also be negative: ignoring important stories for the sake of interesting ones.

In the fall of 2004, just before the presidential election, Fred had the opportunity to speak with Walter Cronkite, the celebrated CBS news anchor from the 1960s and 70s. Cronkite was once considered the "most trusted man in America." Speaking about his own craft, Mr. Cronkite said that the competition from cable news, and the premium on conflict, had changed his profession in profound and disturbing ways, and deprived the audience of what it needed to make informed decisions about pressing issues.

The Good News About the Press

Journalists are usually not in the field for the money, and many of them could do better financially on the "other side," in public relations. They are journalists because they believe in what they are doing and take great pride in it. Most believe that theirs is a noble profession.

Many press relations people, as well as leaders from business, government, and other fields, become jaundiced about journalism. This book's coauthors always felt grateful for journalism, believing that the social, personal, and business freedoms we have could not endure without it. When our clients' story is not being properly reported, we tend to look, first, at the performance of the sender (ourselves) in the classic academic communication model, the message, the channel (in this case the journalist), and then at the other information or attitudes ("noise") that might be causing interference.

Noise

Sender → Message → Channel→ Receiver→ Feedback

Noise

Of course there is one other piece of potentially good news about the press: They can get very excited about good news from time to time. But new inventions can be oversold, and breakthroughs in basic biomedical research can be headlined cures for cancer. Advice to media relations practitioners: Beware of the good hype as well as the bad. You cannot have it both ways.

Press Relations from a Position of Power

Journalists often ask the questions an organization hopes would not be asked.

It is easy to think that journalists hold all the power in the relationship with companies and other organizations, but this is not necessarily the case.

Journalists often ask the questions an organization hopes would not be asked. They are pressing, even threatening: "You know, I am going to cover the story with or without your help, and I believe I already have what I need." The spokesperson feels powerless. The senior-most people in the organization brazenly prescribe responses from afar—"Just stick to the prepared response"—until they get calls from the journalist directly or are about to be interviewed. Then the brazenness collapses into what they would call anxiety but some might call fear.

"Power" often implies something underhanded or Machiavellian, so heads of communications and senior officers in organizations may want to call it "strength" or "influence." But the fact is that a person in a stressful relationship must not feel powerless. Companies and other organizations have the ability to shape the stories that appear about them, but they need to wield that influence responsibly and carefully.

We know of one case where an individual reporter who was grossly unfair to an organization was frozen out of that organization's public relations information chain. Sometimes—rarely—this is necessary, and the journalist may move on to another beat because of a lack of access. But there is a big difference between "black balling" one reporter versus the entire news medium. The most famous instance of the latter was Mobil Oil's 1984 declaration that it would henceforth not communicate in any way with *The Wall Street Journal*. [10]

Again, there is seldom a need to even consider such extreme remedies. But it is critically important for an organization and its spokespeople to realize that it is not powerless in the face of the awesome power of the press.

Day to day, the best way for spokespeople to leverage power is by managing access. Journalists have to go through the communications office to get to the senior officers, and managing access in a fair way will rebound to the credit of the entire organization.

Enduring power in media relations flows from relationships built on fairness, respect, and credibility. One of the keys to power in the relationship with journalists is to be very good at the media relations discipline, knowledgeable about your own industry, and well-versed on what journalists do and why.

Success in Media Relations

Everyone in media relations chants the same mantra: success in media relations depends upon building solid relationships with the press. Of course knowing it and doing it are two different things. How to do it? The formula is simple: success as a communicator will be in direct proportion to one's skills as a communicator, one's conviction, the quality of the product, position, or story one is selling to the press, and one's preparedness.

Communication Skills

Communication is one of those things that most people think they are good at. After all, it involves speaking, reading, and writing. Most people have been speaking from the first year or so after they were born, and learned to read and write in first grade.

But true communication skill requires more than just speaking, reading, and writing. It involves using those behaviors to influence the attitudes and behaviors of others. And like any other set of skills, it can become stale and fall into disuse. Effective communicators regularly upgrade their communication skills.

For example, this book's coauthors have both taken numerous writing courses and won writing awards, but we still work hard at improving our craft. Over the years, we would routinely invite writing instructors to hold workshops for our professional staffs, and we would participate ourselves.

Conviction

Journalists are like kids and puppy dogs: if you do not mean what you say, they can smell it. For example, we knew of a young woman in corporate communications for a healthcare company who intellectually accepted the need for animal research of investigational medicines. But she did not have a firm conviction that, while the best tools of science should be mobilized to minimize the number of animals used, some animal studies must be performed before an investigational medicine can be administered to a man,

> Journalists are like kids and puppy dogs: if you do not mean what you say, they can smell it.

woman, or child. As a result, she was often ineffective in interviews on the topic. It was not a function of knowledge or understanding, but of being able to enthusiastically represent a position.

Eventually, her superior asked her not to take any more calls about animal research, assuring her that her career would not suffer. There were many other things she could do well, and there were also other people in the group who had enough conviction in the appropriateness of responsible animal testing of medicines to withstand a badgering from any reporter or activist and still hold firm.

Quality of Product or Story

If the thing you are selling to the press is not a page-one story, do not try to get coverage there. If your product or story is not what your organization says it is, the lie or omission will eventually be uncovered. Do not lie. Sounds easy, but it is not. Be willing to stand up in your organization and object to a story line that obscures, blurs, or distorts the truth. Let your uncompromising position be known within the organization—you will not have to blurt it out, because the opportunity to let people know how you feel will come.

Similarly, if you are trying to interest a reporter in a story, you need to package it in ways that get the reporter's attention and make it more likely that the reporter will become the story's champion. This usually requires doing much of the legwork for the reporter before even pitching the story. The general rule of thumb for a major story is that the media relations person needs to do 80 percent of the work on the story, and the reporter will be able to do the other 20 percent. Trying to interest a reporter in a poorly planned, weak, or otherwise uninteresting story is a waste of the reporter's time as well as your own, and can prevent the reporter from seeing the media relations person as a valuable resource.

Preparedness

Be knowledgeable about your organization, and its products, services, and people. Otherwise, you are just an obstacle to the press. Unfortunately, too many media relations people think their job is simply to arrange interviews. There is a time to call upon the experts in your organization to grant interviews, but the communications people should be able to field a significant percentage of incoming calls and be well enough informed to approach a journalist with the basics of a story. If you know what you are talking about—that is, understand your industry, not only your company—journalists will begin to rely on you. When they start calling you for guidance on a story that does not directly involve your organization, you know you have accomplished something. If you have arranged for someone in your organization to be interviewed, make sure he or she is prepared.

The Art of the Pitch

By Raleigh Mayer,
Principal of MK Coaching

Successful pitching to reporters begins with a clear understanding of the outlet, its audience, and the utilization of appropriate tone, timing, and content.

A Pitch is Not:
- A high-pressure sales presentation
- Press release text
- Advertising copy
- A plea or solicitation
- A social conversation

A Pitch Is:
- An invitation to cover a story
- A concise, compelling, and customized invitation to interview an expert, preview an event, report on a phenomenon or trend, test a product or service
- An idea for a compelling story, and a road map for how to get the story

Successful pitching requires comprehensive knowledge of the targeted media, including:
- Prior and current coverage of your industry
- Style and bias of the outlet
- Format of specific columns, departments, segments
- Preferences and interests of individual journalists

Successful pitching requires comprehensive knowledge of your story, including:
- Answers to basic questions about the event, person, business, market
- How to bring the story to life for readers or viewers
- How to get access to others, including those who are not part of your organization

Pitching on Paper
Lead With:
- Question
- Juxtaposition
- Comparison
- Observation
- Riddle

After Lead:
- Support or expand on your claim or theme
- Who you are and why you are writing
- Present relevant facts, statistics, or documentation
- Name what you are asking or offering: interview, story, profile, attend event, and so forth
- Conclude with a promise to follow up
- Keep to one page if possible

Pitching by e-mail:

Make it Compact:
- Put the lead in the subject line
- Condense body copy to one or two paragraphs
- Include contact information in signature
- Do not send attachments unless asked

Pitching by Phone:
- Conduct it conversationally
- Identify yourself clearly
- Deliver the lead and let the reporter respond
- Have prepared message points ready
- Organize your desk so you can concentrate during call
- Give up graciously if the reporter declines or defers pitch
- Thank the reporter for considering it

Pitching By Voicemail:
- Be concise
- Be prepared to leave pitch as voicemail message
- Give compressed pitch—still powerful, but short
- Leave your name and number at both beginning and end of message
- Do not be careless in leaving message

If Pitch is Declined:
- Pitch different angle to same reporter
- Pitch same angle to different desk of the same outlet (if relevant)
- Pitch new angle to another section
- Pitch competing reporter at different outlet

After the story appears:
- Thank the reporter (a handwritten note has the most impact) but do not gush
- Keep in contact with reporter

- Update reporter of relevant developments, even if there is no immediate benefit to you
- Deliver next pitch with same level of professionalism as the last one

If there are errors:
- Let the reporter know, politely, of the errors
- Do not confuse contrasting opinions with errors of fact
- Contact editors only if you believe willful or harmful errors are not being taken seriously

What Reporters Dislike:
- Unprepared or unknowledgeable pitches
- Pitches delivered too fast or in a convoluted manner
- Pitches delivered on deadline
- PR people who cannot answer basic questions or provide access to the right people
- PR people who whine that the story was not as positive as they had hoped
- PR people who call to follow up on a release without adding anything new
- PR people who call to ask when/if story has appeared
- Unsolicited e-mail attachments
- Overly ornate or poorly designed press materials; including those with tiny typeface

Choosing The Right Tools To Convey Your Message

By Jay Rubin,
President, Jay Rubin & Associates

Marshall McLuhan's catchphrase, "the medium is the message," may be too radical for many public relations professionals to accept. But you would be hard-pressed to find anyone in the business who does not recognize at least some kernels of truth in that statement. PR veterans know from experience that the tools they choose to pitch their stories have a significant impact on the coverage they receive.

So how do you decide which tools are best to convey your message? You usually rely upon a combination of research, experience, and gut feeling. It may also be helpful to consider the same six words so often associated with news content. Here is a set of who, what, when, where, why, and how questions (and some possible answers) worth considering as you shape your pitching strategy.

Who warrants your personal attention?

It is a rare public relations department that has the time, resources, or inclination to personally contact every name on its press lists. Mostly, you will reach out to all your prospects with the same e-mail press release (typically a one-to-two-page document explaining the news value of your message). Or you can buy space for your press release on one of the paid wire services (e.g., Business Wire, PR Newswire) that link up with newsrooms in a wide variety of geographic and subject categories.

You are then able to follow up with those reporters who *really* count. Pick up the phone. Customize e-mail pitch letters. Send personalized cover notes along with your press release. Offer to set up interviews. Break the news while you break bread with a reporter. Your individual attention sometimes brings extra weight to your message. More important, it allows you to tailor your pitch points to the different needs of reporters.

Occasionally, you may consider scrapping the press list and devoting 100 percent of your energy to a single media outlet. If you give an exclusive on a story, you should be confident about significant coverage and that you will not seriously damage your relationships with other key contacts.

What will increase your odds of successful coverage?

Publicists use e-mail press releases most often because they can promote virtually any type of news—hard or soft, urgent or evergreen. Reporters favor a standard press release format because it allows significance, timeliness, and other criteria to be quickly evaluated.

If your news is big enough, enhance your coverage opportunities with an e-mail press kit (generally including a press release, one or more photos and captions, a quick-reference fact sheet, a biography, and other appropriate background information). Remember to also keep a supply of kits in hard copy. Some press contacts may request a print version, and the kits can subsequently be used as reference materials.

When pitching TV and radio programs, publicists often provide materials that can be integrated into on-air reports. These include B-roll (video and sound that can be edited into a news report), video news releases (self-standing pieces that can be aired as is or edited), or natural sound (audio recorded by a microphone). If your topic is newsworthy and your client is polished, you can also embark on radio and television tours (a series of appearances at stations in different cities).

When must your message be received?

The old days of stuffing press releases into envelopes or being at the mercy of a busy fax machine thankfully are over. Modern media now demand the immediacy of e-mail. However, one fundamental has not changed: the importance of knowing deadlines.

It is not enough to just know the main deadlines for a newscast or a newspaper. These and other outlets may also have e-mail bulletin services or frequently updated Web sites. Get to know *every* means of distribution the media have to report your story, and exactly when they are likely to do so.

Where is your message best delivered?

Be ready to take advantage of opportunities beyond e-mail on the computer screen. A press conference; a press breakfast, lunch, or dinner; or an after-hours reception can be ideal ways to reach reporters assembled at a trade show. Industry gatherings are also prime time for company executives to deliver newsy speeches or panel presentations, be interviewed, or just meet and greet reporters who are otherwise hard to reach.

Off the convention circuit, press conferences are on the wane. The same format (scripted remarks by executives, followed by questions from reporters) can now be handled through a telephone conference call with much less expense to the company and much more convenience to all involved.

Why should a reporter care?

Sometimes e-mails, pitch calls, and other routine tactics are not enough to grab attention. That is when a special event, a community service project, an endorsement, or a gimmick can help pique media interest and give you the platform to promote your news.

If you are having trouble attracting national attention, you should also consider pursuing local coverage. National outlets may give you a second look once a media bandwagon starts rolling in various cities. At the same time, do not overlook the importance of hometown news. When your news is limited to certain areas, suburban weeklies may be more accessible and more valuable to you than metropolitan dailies.

To promote important and complex issues not fully appreciated by the media, try scheduling editorial board meetings. These sessions, usually with a small group of journalists from the same publication, allow you and your associates to directly present your case. Op-ed articles can also be terrific vehicles to explain your viewpoint.

Keep an eye on influential chat rooms, blogs, Web sites, and other information purveyors in cyberspace. But be sure to exercise caution before you decide to jump into the frequently freewheeling Internet fray.

> *How much will it cost?*
> E-mail is commonplace for more than just utility; it also has a negligible impact on an overall PR budget. The same cannot always be said about disseminating press releases on a paid wire service, commissioning a video news release, or picking up the tab at a fancy trade-show luncheon. Spend wisely and *always* to promote stories with real news value. Trying to dress up a mundane message is one of the quickest ways to deplete your budget and your credibility.

Best Practices in Media Relations

1. *Be quick (but not foolhardy).* Communication groups should have their own policy—for example, "return 90 percent of press calls within one hour"—based on their resources and the demands of the press reporting on their organizations. But we do not subscribe to the often-stated PR principle to call every reporter back right away. First, it is not always possible. Second, some journalists—those who have not been fair or responsive to your organization—do not deserve a quick response. That we teach others how to treat us is as true in press relations as in anything else. But as a general rule, the earlier you can get back to a reporter the more influence you can have on the story. That is because the reporter, especially one on a breaking story, cannot wait for your call to write the story. He or she will write it whether you return the call or not. Returning a call at the end of the day may permit the insertion of a small quote or no-comment statement into a nearly completed story. But returning a call before the reporter has invested time and energy, and before the reporter has committed to deliver a story of a certain length to his or her editor, often makes it possible to shape the story or even to prevent a false story from appearing.

2. *Know the media.* Understand the missions of the various print, broadcast, and electronic media. *The Wall Street Journal* is not *The New York Times* and *The New York Times* is not the *Los Angeles Times*. Research! Know the consumer, professional, and trade media covering your industry. Understand those umbrella terms and use them correctly.

   Both coauthors read the *Columbia Journalism Review*, *The American Journalism Review*, and many first-person, behind-the-scenes accounts of life as a reporter. We require the same of our media relations students. Understanding what is important for reporters, the experience of being a reporter, and the pressures reporters face in doing their jobs every day is a critical part of being an effective media relations professional.

3. *Know the reporters.* Of course you can only know a small number of journalists well. But media directories have brief biographical sketches of journalists, and full bios are available through services such as Bulldog Reporter or directly from the journalist. We cannot imagine arranging an interview for a senior executive

or official without obtaining a bio of the journalist and without reviewing that journalist's past news reports, features, or editorials. Research! Visit the journalists at the bureau or for lunch. Most spokespeople are not good at this, but doing so is tremendously important. A good time to ask to meet informally with a journalist is a few days after you have been helpful to him or her. It is also effective to call a journalist when he or she first begins covering your organization, and to go to lunch or grab a cup of coffee to get to know each other. Most journalists new to a beat are eager to make such contacts, and generally welcome such approaches. Once they are established it can be much harder to schedule such time with a reporter without having a story to discuss.

4. *Have a plethora of standby statements.* Most companies know what is likely to become public prematurely. The most enlightened companies have standby statements ready to distribute on such topics well before a reporter calls. The statement should generally be ready for faxing or e-mailing to a reporter. One way to avoid questions on a sensitive subject is to say "we have a standby statement on that; should I e-mail it to you?" Invariably—literally—the answer will be yes, thank you, and goodbye. This avoids the possibility of misspeaking or of being misquoted, and the journalist has the precise words the organization wants to express.

5. *Have a plethora of Qs and As.* If the spokesperson has days to prepare for a tough interview on a narrow subject and the journalist only has an hour or so, the spokesperson can anticipate every single, reasonable question. If the subject is broad—for example, growth prospects for a particular industry—the challenge becomes greater. But even then, the proposition is irrefutable: The more Qs and As the spokesperson has prepared, the greater the chances for success.

6. *Media training.* Speaking with reporters is different from speaking with other people, because they use your words differently than most people do. In particular, most conversations are private, unstructured, and informal, while interviews are always public, and should be formal and structured. Executives often behave with reporters the same way they behave with everyone else, and often with adverse consequences.

One way to prevent such negative outcomes is to prepare the executive not just on the subject matter to be discussed, but also on the skills necessary to communicate that content most effectively through the news media. The skills for effectiveness in print interviews are in some ways different from those necessary for television, radio, or the Internet.

One advantage of media training is that it is often videotaped—even training for print interviews. One reason for the taping is for the executive to see how he or she really comes across. It can be eye-opening, and much more effective than telling the executive how he or she did.

Another advantage of media training is that it provides a safe setting to ask the executive difficult questions that would not be as acceptable in a rehearsal at the executive's desk.

Finally, the training provides a safe environment for an executive to fail—far better to fail in rehearsal than on CNN. The training can reveal how weak a particular response to a difficult question may be, and provide an opportunity to improve. It can reveal the gaps in information before the actual interview. Finally, the training can reveal character issues that would be catastrophic in a real interview. We have seen senior executives lie when pressed by a tough media trainer. Like a kid caught with his hand in the candy jar, a person armed with weak information tends to lie. It is far better to expose the lie and the weakness that triggered it in an exercise than with a reporter.

7. *Have B-roll.* Have plenty of television footage of production, products, and so on. When the deadline or a crisis occurs is not the time to be developing B-roll.

8. *Prepare before and after interview memos.* When possible, sketch in a preinterview memo the objectives for the interview and other relevant information. The postinterview memo can be a way of preparing colleagues and bosses for the news report and of learning for the future.

9. *Do everything you can to build your organization's reputation.* The media relations person represents the organization as much as anyone and is in a position of great leverage in this regard.

10. *Do not do anything that puts your organization's reputation at risk.*

11. *Make it interesting.* Given a choice between "interesting" and "informative," the journalist will choose "interesting" almost every time.

12. *Never speak on background—unless you know what you are doing.* To most PR people and journalists, the phrase "on background" means that the information can be used, but cannot be attributed to or associated with the spokesperson or organization he or she represents. It is an indispensable part of an ongoing media relations program, and can be helpful in many cases—for example, when you are not sure of something but think the journalist should investigate, or when what you say might seem inappropriate in a news report quoting your organization. Make sure the journalist and you are working from precisely the same definition of terms, and that you explicitly note when you are "on background" and "off."

13. *Never work with a reporter under "embargo"—unless you know what you are doing.* The rule should be: Do not issue a press release to a world of journalists and mark it "embargoed"—unless you actually want and expect someone to break the embargo. The embargo can be a useful tool, especially when the story is complicated and a journalist would need time to understand it, and when you have a mutually trusting relationship with the journalist. How can a publicly owned company issue a press release on a complicated matter after the New York Stock Exchange closes and expect it to be covered accurately on the evening news or in the morning papers? Make sure that the journalist and you have precisely the

same understanding of what the agreement is. Make sure both parties understand exactly when the news can be released.

14. *Never speak "off the record"—never.* The term means that the information will never be reported. Fuhgeddaboudit!

15. *Call every reporter back right away—Fuhgeddaboudit!* The golden rule taught in public relations courses is that a PR person must return a reporter's call as soon as possible, and in general that is a good rule to follow. The reason, of course, is that the journalist is usually under deadline. But there are exceptions, dictated by common sense.

    Again, if a reporter has been unfair to the client or organization you represent, or if the reporter's news media often does a poor job, it does not make any sense to treat that person with the same degree of responsiveness you would the better reporters. Journalists talk, and it often becomes clear to one who feels mistreated by an organization he or she is covering that colleagues in the press do not feel that way. The light can go on. In any case, the PR person has power, as does the organization or client he or she represents, and it can and should be used.

16. *Keep a press log.* There are two reasons. First, it can be circulated within your organization so that others know what you are doing with the press and so that PR people in the organization are not tripping over each other. Second, it will provide a record so that, in the future, you can reach out to all journalists who, for example, have inquired about a particular product or issue.

17. *Have a "return-call policy."* It is a good idea to have a policy that says, for example, "we return 90 percent of all press calls within one hour." (Arrange lunch breaks and so forth accordingly.) Setting business objectives is as important in press relations as anywhere else.

18. *Be available nights and weekends.* It is the deadline, stupid. There is no other way to run press relations. If there is more than one person in the press relations shop, spread the overtime work around. If you are the only one, make sure your superiors know what overtime work is required.

19. *Correct every mistake in the press about your organization.* There are essentially three remedies: a letter to the editor; a correction notice for publication or broadcast; and a letter or call to the journalist to clarify the matter with him or her but not necessarily for publication or broadcast.

20. *Broadcast, cable and the Internet can get the story out faster and more broadly—sometimes.* Broadcast can be faster indeed. But the print media usually break the major stories that prove of long-term interest. Getting your story right in just one of the leading newspapers (for example, *The New York Times, The Wall Street Journal, Washington Post,* or one of the major foreign papers) can be worth much more than a press conference, media tour, and an appearance on Oprah combined.

21. *If a journalist can cover a fire he can cover anything—not true.* PR has its myths and journalism has its. Therefore, it becomes important to know the background of the journalist the PR person is working with. In addition to the reporter's bio,

sources such as *The Bull Dog Reporter* summarize the kinds of subjects the reporter usually covers.

22. *Get the journalist's agreement, when time permits, for review of quotations, before publication.* Especially if the matter discussed in the interview is complex, the journalist should agree to give the interviewee the opportunity to review quotes before publication. More journalism schools are adopting this position, and John cannot see the fairness or journalistic good of any other. On complicated stories, John's position is: No review of quotes, no interview.

23. *Journalism support programs.* A great way of building relationships with the press is to fund programs that support good journalism. Of course this has to be a mutually productive but hands-off relationship. The benefits of a media relationship initiative will sometimes be hard to see, day to day, and some people in the organization might even think the initiative is counterproductive: "If you had not been reaching out to that reporter so often, he wouldn't now be all over us at a time when we don't need the attention."

But over time, the relationship is beneficial in a number of ways. It provides a bridge for two-way interaction independent of any one story. It provides opportunities for executives and others to get to know reporters well, and vice versa. And, above all, it reflects the organization's honest desire for fair journalism.

24. A media relations person should always be working toward measurable results that support organizational objectives.

Qualities of a Good Media Relations Person

The list is brief:

⇒ Good communication instincts (some people are simply not communicative by nature and should not be in media relations).
⇒ Good communication skills. The job interview can reveal much about speaking abilities. To assess writing ability, always give a writing test.
⇒ Toughness and an ability to withstand criticism.
⇒ Honesty.
⇒ Good research skills.
⇒ An ability to shine when under intense deadline pressure.
⇒ Teamwork skills.
⇒ (See Sidebar by Bill Heyman in Chapter 14.)

Resources for Further Study

Scott M. Cutlip, Allen H. Center, and Glen M. Broom, *Effective Public Relations*, 9th ed., Pearson, Prentice Hall, Upper Saddle River, NJ, 2006.

James E. Grunig and Todd Hunt, *Managing Public Relations*, Harcourt Brace Jovanovich, 1984.

David W. Guth and Charles Marsh, *Public Relations, a Values-Driven Approach,* 3rd ed., Allyn & Bacon, Inc., Needham Heights, MA.

Ray E. Hiebert, Ed., *Public Relations Review: A Journal of Research and Comment,* Elsevier, Amsterdam.

Carole M. Howard and Wilma K. Mathews, *On Deadline, Managing Media Relations,* 3rd ed., Waveland PR Inc., Prospect Heights, IL.

Irv Schenkler and Tony Herrling, *Guide To Media Relations,* Pearson, Prentice Hall, Upper Saddle River, NJ, 2004.

Herb Schmertz with William Novak, *Good-bye to the Low Profile,* Little, Brown, Boston, 1986.

Questions for Further Discussion

1. Should media relations people proactively mention to journalists the reason the organization adheres to a centralized communication policy?
2. Do you think the Grunig-Hunt models of public relations apply today? Which one do you practice? Are you ethically committed to that model?
3. Does the press really have a right to ask anything at all?
4. Is there any reason PR people should not be as zealous about accuracy as the best journalists?
5. When the subject of the interview is technical, is it appropriate to ask the journalist before the interview to agree to clear the quotes before using them? What if the journalist will not agree?

CHAPTER 4

New Media

By Andrea Coville,
Chief Executive Officer, Brodeur

and Ray Thomas,
Consultant, Brodeur

> *And then came the Internet and everything changed.*

"Music in Color"

Brodeur was in its third year of working with Toshiba America Consumer Products when Tina Tuccillo, vice president of Marketing Communications, told us about plans for a new device to compete with the iPod. Everyone knows the iPod story. Apple invented a marvelous MP3 device and did an even more remarkable job of bringing it to market. It took the world by storm. So how do you compete with that?

Enter gigabeat®, the first in the Toshiba gigastyle™ family of hard-drive-based products—portable audio players, camcorders, DVD recorders, and more. Combining innovative storage with simplicity and seamlessness for the consumer, gigastyle would deliver more music, more video, more control, and more options, along with sleek, innovative designs.

Prior to announcing the gigastyle family at the 2005 Consumer Electronics Show in Las Vegas, Toshiba enjoyed a reputation as a world leader in high technology products and a pioneer in DVD and DVD recorder technology. The company was known primarily for televisions—flat panel TVs, rear- and front-projection TVs, direct view TVs, and home theater projectors. How could Toshiba extend its leadership to the MP3 market, which was clearly dominated by Apple and quickly becoming crowded with new players?

We believed it would take a concerted and integrated marketing effort that would leverage all types of communication, including new media. In the end, the launch plan would encompass a launch party, a microsite, TV spots, a direct mailer, e-mails, magazine ads, online ads, Times Square signage, and radio promotion.

While some of these components would have had a natural place in a product launch circa 1985, Toshiba applied them with a new-media twist. For example, ads were placed in Rolling Stone, a traditional print publication, announcing a promotion—a chance to win a gigabeat. But to participate, readers first had to register at a Web site, http://www.gigabeat.com. Dedicated to gigabeat and the nascent gigabeat community, gigabeat.com offered innovative product guides, music links, accessory information, and product updates. In other words, Toshiba used a traditional medium to direct consumers to a new medium.

One of the key differentiating features of the gigabeat is its 2.2-inch color screen, which owners can use to display family photos, cover art, or other images of performers. Hence the theme of the gigabeat advertising *campaign: "Because Music is Just Better in Color™." The campaign featured performers with colorful names—Blues Traveler, Joan Jett and the Blackhearts, and the emerging band Vendetta Red. TV spots were placed on MTV properties such as VH-1™, MTV™, Comedy Central™, and TV Land™. Joan Jett and the Blackhearts hosted the gigabeat launch party at the Times Square Studios in New York, where Blues Traveler was the featured act.*

The gigabeat campaign drew on extensive research into consumer decision making. And from the start, the entire marketing strategy was carefully tracked and the impact of each element measured.

The gigabeat launch brought Toshiba extensive market visibility. The launch party was attended by nearly one hundred journalists. Gigabeat appeared in more than one hundred publications and on dozens of Web sites and portals. The Web activities—carefully integrated with the traditional media—clearly played a central part in this success.

Digital media enable companies to introduce and market products in more targeted and personalized ways.

* * * * *

This Chapter Covers

⇒ A different world

⇒ An abridged history of new media

⇒ New media and the consumer electronics revolution

⇒ A sampling of today's new media tools

⇒ Are the new media truly different?

⇒ Examples of digital marketing

⇒ The impact of new media on TV

⇒ New media terms

⇒ A new media timeline (Sidebar)

⇒ Best practices marketing in the new media world

⇒ Resources for further study

⇒ Questions for further discussion

A Different World

Two decades ago, the channels available for the launch of a comparable product were simpler. Back before the Web, a new product introduction was generally started with a well-written press release and supporting statements from partners and customers. The rules were straightforward:

⇒ Issue the release over one of the newswire services

⇒ Mail (print/fold/stuff in envelope/add postage) copies of the release to the prescribed media list

⇒ Call the media to make sure they got the release and try to arrange interviews

⇒ Scan the media in the following days and weeks to find the coverage

Those were just the basics. There have always been creative approaches used for "major" announcements, such as full press kits (the fancier the better) including product pictures and appropriate backgrounders; interesting Associated Press wire photos; extravagant "shrimp events," often in New York, where media, industry analysts, financial analysts, and customers could gather to eat free food and learn all about the new product; and many other more creative strategies and tactics. A "global" announcement would mean repeating some or all of the above in each country. But the channels available to reach people were much more limited. There were two or three wire services and a handful of major TV networks. Publications had predictable print schedules.

> The Internet ushered in the new media era. It completely changed the dynamics of communication and rewrote the book on public relations. But the change did not happen overnight.

An Abridged History of New Media

On the technology side, we can credit thousands of inventions over nearly four decades that resulted in the digital communication capabilities available today:

⇒ The computer evolution—from mainframes and minicomputers to personal computers, laptops, notebooks, and handhelds

⇒ Telecommunications—from the formation of ARPANET, the first computer network—precursor to the Internet, to the development of Ethernet, local area networks, wide area networks, broadband, and wireless networking, with all the related enablers from fiber optics to satellites

⇒ The development and evolution of browsers—from Mosaic, which started at the University of Illinois, to Netscape, Internet Explorer (which in January 2006 controlled 83 percent of the market), Mozilla, FireFox, and Safari

⇒ Software—from operating systems to database management systems, customer relationship management, many layers of middleware,

3-D user interfaces, and to thousands of applications, including voice over Internet protocol (VoIP)

⇒ Search engines—from Alta Vista in 1995 to the latest from Google, Yahoo, Microsoft, and others—that enable users to find information on the Web

⇒ Text messaging—which evolved from the British Broadcasting Corporation's 1969 work on "videotext," a new interactive format for transmitting text and graphics

⇒ The evolution of e-mail from its initial technical uses to business systems and ultimately to today's IM (instant messaging)

⇒ The wireless content phenomenon, enabled by the convergence of technologies for cell phones, personal digital assistants (PDAs), mobile television, and other wireless devices, and especially by the more recent development of Really Simple Syndication (RSS) and other consumer content-management tools

⇒ The quick rise and pervasiveness of blogging (from Web logging), podcasting (which takes its name from the iPod), and VODcasting (derived from Video-on-Demand)

New Media and the Consumer Electronics Revolution

The pace of technology change is not abating. In the first few months after the 2005 Consumer Electronic Show in Las Vegas, the marketplace was bombarded with numerous new devices, joining the already bewildering array of gadgets for accessing music, e-mail, video, storage, photos, games, the Web, phone calls, and cell phone ring tones.

In addition to Toshiba's gigabeat, other examples included:

⇒ Blackberry, which had 2.5 million subscribers at the end of 2004 and growth of 135 percent that year, introduced the 7100 series—small, sleek, friendly devices that allow on-the-go access to e-mail, phone, and Internet. Blackberry will be adding applications like IM and GPS (Global Positioning System).

⇒ VCinema, a start-up company, launched its Digital Theater service that integrates the best qualities of TV with the flexibility of the Internet, allowing customers to legally download and create their own video libraries from a vast array of IP-based content. Users can watch what they want when they want.

⇒ Sony announced its new PSP, or personal play station, which can be used to play games, music, or movies just about anywhere.

⇒ Motorola launched its Ojo Personal Video Phone, which has a 5.6-inch screen and promises to eliminate the breakup and distortion of most video phones.

The pace of technology change is not abating.

⇒ Sling Media introduced a device that digitizes whatever is playing on TV at home and puts it on the Internet using streaming technology.

We will focus here on the elements that make up new media today and how these media can be used creatively in marketing and corporate and organizational communication.

A Sampling of Today's New Media Tools

Web site/Microsite Design

Over the first decade since the development of the browser, standards have evolved for Web site design. These range from technical standards to informal but generally accepted ways of presenting content. Globalization of sites, which ranges from multiple language implementations to country-by-country home pages within a corporate entity, has become standard for multinational companies and those who want to be accessible everywhere.

There are also microsites tailored to specific purposes, where consumers can be directed or linked through other forms of advertising. A microsite is a separate page of a Web site that has a separate URL than its home page. Microsites are especially helpful during new product launches and other campaigns because they make it possible to track responses to advertising. In addition, organizations are creating their personal online identity.

> Consumers want to know they can find information in specific places on a site.

Making Your Corporate Online Identity:

Top Things to Include
　　Logo
　　Imagery
　　Symbols (Icons)
　　Typography
　　Color Palette
To have a successful online identity, these elements must be consistent across all digital mediums.

Consumers want to know they can find information in specific places on a site, so the current trend is toward fixed but flexible designs, with at least an annual review to update the look and feel. Content, of course, is updated on an ongoing basis. And finally, organizations need an information architecture that works for them.

Intranets/Extranets

While the external focus is critical to branding, the internal site or intranet is equally important. It is the central repository for shared information, so it must be managed as an information library as well as an internal marketing resource. Content needs to be kept current.

Extranets are special sites set up to manage and exchange information during a project or for continuing work with a particular client or vendor. In setting up an extranet, a firm always needs to stop and consider the needs of its audience. It is important to engage the audience in the design and development of the site and to monitor activity to ensure users are getting the intended benefits.

Blogs

Blogs, short for Web logs, are running commentaries on whatever their authors are interested in. The contents often focus on politics or media criticism and usually include feedback from readers. Blogs frequently contain comments on products or services. According to one blog expert, Bob Cox, president of the Media Bloggers Association, 8 million people write online journals as of late 2005. And, according to another source, some 32 million people read blogs. One could interpret these numbers to mean that each blogger averages four readers, but that would be highly misleading. Some well-known journalists, business executives, and entertainment personalities have created blogs that are followed extensively, while many bloggers are amateur journalists with few readers.

All bloggers have one thing in common: the ability to express ideas and opinions and offer others the chance to respond. Bloggers come from all parts of society. Examples include *San Jose Mercury News* columnist Dan Gillmor, Sun Microsystems President and Chief Operating Officer Jonathan Schwartz, and Graham Hill of Treehugger, who publishes a blog focused on "green design." Robert Scoble is a "technical evangelist" for Microsoft. He started the blog *Scobleizer*. Everything in it is his personal opinion and is not read or approved by Microsoft before it is posted. Scoble's blog has become so popular that his name is becoming as synonymous with Microsoft as Bill Gates!

Anyone can create a blog using easy-to-use software from Google and Microsoft. *Fortune* magazine's David Kirkpatrick even created "the idiot's guide to blogging."[1]

⇒ Step One: Go to Google's Blogger.com or Spaces.MSN.com and create an account. (If you're willing to pay for a more professional look, go to TypePad.com.)

⇒ Step Two: Come up with a name for your blog, peruse the templates, and click on one you like.

⇒ Step Three: Write something interesting.

⇒ Step Four: Want to find out if anyone's reading your blog? Register at a service like Feedburner to see how many readers you have and what posts they like best.

Because blogs can contain commentary and consumer opinion on a company's brand, many companies make use of search engines focused specifically on blogs. These include BuzzMetrics, Intelliseek, and Cymfony (for search and measure), and GoogleBlogSearch, Technorati, Feedster, and PubSub (for general blog search purposes).

Really Simple Syndication (RSS)

RSS allows Web sites to automatically push regularly updated information to consumers as needed. It is a means of delivering syndicated online content. RSS has become widely used by online publishers as well as by shopping portals. RSS helped the proliferation of blogs and brought them into the mainstream. Anyone publishing online can set up a feed to syndicate content, and users can take advantage of such sites to monitor news or activity on a company or product. Feeds can be built into personalized pages. Someone interested in buying a specific item on eBay, for example, can use RSS to monitor activity on it to determine the optimum bid price.

Podcasting is the process of broadcasting an audio program to MP3 players through RSS. A listener subscribes to free podcasts made available via RSS feeds; intermediary software downloads and stores the audio on the MP3 player for use at the listener's convenience. Radio shows have begun making their content available as podcasts. In addition to audio, the file-sharing technology behind podcasting will allow other types of data to be attached, such as photos or video.

Anyone can make a blog.

VODcasting is very similar to podcasting. The difference is that the content is video instead of audio.

Search Engines

No discussion of new media would be complete without including search engines. "Google it" has become a common expression, a tribute to the dominance that the Google search engine achieved in helping Internet users find information. Yahoo and Microsoft also offer powerful search engines, and a number of other companies have developed similar technology. Convera Corporation, for example, offers Excalibur Web Search, "a private label search service for online publishers and other organizations seeking more authoritative and relevant results from the World Wide Web." The Excalibur Web Search platform uses advanced semantic analysis, combined with broad and deep knowledge resources, to understand the meaning of Web content and how it relates to a user's query.

Search engines rely on simple keywords and page-rank analysis. Web pages are ranked based on how many pages are linked to them. This means that if a company wants its brand to stand out, it needs to increase its possibilities. Some companies set up "link farms" to improve their rankings. Some also retain search engine optimization firms that promise to increase

Web site traffic through search engine placement, keyword-related advertising, keyword phrase research, search engine optimization consulting, optimized code creation, link popularity and page rank assessment and analysis, and paid inclusion.

Companies are also recognizing the need to monitor their brand through search engine technology. As Alan Earls of *Computerworld* noted, "Reputation management is increasingly the focus of new technologies and techniques, ranging from human-aided Web searches to advanced analytical software running on enormous server farms dedicated to teasing trends and shades of meaning from millions of Web pages."[2]

Rich Media

Rich media are defined as new media that offer an enhanced experience relative to older, mainstream formats. Some popular formats commonly considered rich media include Macromedia Flash and Shockwave, along with various audio and video formats. The Interactive Advertising Bureau (IAB) has announced a set of guidelines for rich media advertising focused on in-page and over-the-page ad units. These guidelines give advertisers and their agencies the ability to develop advertising content consistent with the specifications accepted by many of the leading interactive publishers. The purpose of the guidelines is to lend efficiency to the online ad-creation and media-buying communities. The goal is to enable advertisers and agencies to create compelling rich media advertising that will be usable across the majority of publishers.

> As in any direct marketing campaign, there are three key elements to effective e-mail marketing: the offer, the creative, and the content.

Rich media enable much more interactive sites. VFM Interactive, for example, provides such services for hotels and resorts. Using sites where their videos, virtual tours, and other interactive content are posted, a viewer can see a property's interactive content simply by clicking on a link or icon. The interactive content is then displayed through one of VFM's proprietary interactive content viewers. (See "Rich Media" in Chapter 5.)

As user-friendly technologies, rich media are used on CDs and DVDs, in specially designed kiosks, in presentations, and in virtually every form of marketing today. Rich media are becoming increasingly popular in advertising.

Using e-mail: Is it mailing-list abuse or creative marketing?

E-mail

As a marketing technique, e-mail faces numerous challenges because of consumer reactions to its abuse. However, e-mail marketing can be extremely effective when used with permission-based mail lists (assuming creativity in the marketing program itself!). One of the benefits of e-mail marketing is the opportunity for personalization. As in any direct marketing campaign, there are three key elements to effective e-mail marketing: the offer, the creative, and the content.

Laws must be observed. The CAN-SPAM (Controlling the Assault of Non-Solicited Pornography and Marketing) Act of 2003 establishes requirements for those who send commercial e-mail, spells out penalties for spammers and advertisers that violate the law, and gives consumers the right to ask e-mailers to stop spamming them.

The law, which became effective January 1, 2004, covers e-mail whose primary purpose is advertising or promoting a commercial product or service, including content on a Web site. A "transactional or relationship message"—e-mail that facilitates an agreed-upon transaction or updates a customer in an existing business relationship—may not contain false or misleading routing information but otherwise is exempt from most provisions of the law.

More information on the CAN-SPAM Act can be found at the Federal Trade Commission Web site, http://www.ftc.gov.

Database Management

Organizations typically have large databases filled with customer and product information. Integrating the data with Web marketing programs offers excellent opportunities for businesses to reach customers and improve sales. Companies can also acquire databases for use in new media marketing programs.

The new media era has been supported by extensive customer relationship management (CRM) solutions from Siebel, SAP, and Salesforce.com. The Salesforce.com solutions, for example, provide integration by linking easily to everything from desktop tools to enterprise resource planning (ERP), accounting, and other third-party applications.

A note of caution: database security is critical. Several major security breaches have opened access to credit card records and other supposedly secure data. Citadel Security Software Inc., a leader in enterprise vulnerability management and policy enforcement solutions, began issuing a daily security news service that provides up-to-the-minute threat alerts, recommends actions to thwart attacks, and presents headline news in a radio-style broadcast. This free subscription service enables network security professionals to stay abreast of new vulnerabilities and quickly develop plans to mitigate risks and maintain security compliance.

Webinars

Webinars are Web-based seminars.[3] By connecting to the Web and simultaneously to a telephone conference number, a broad audience of attendees can participate in a seminar without having to leave their desks. Webinars can be as effective as on-site presentations without the travel expense.

Webinars consist of slide presentations delivered via the Web in combination with a phone-bridge (traditional tele-conference) that allows the audience to listen and interact with the teacher/speaker. Participants can ask questions by submitting them online; if desired, the phone lines can be opened up for questions and discussion. During the presentation, the audience can be polled with predetermined or impromptu questions in order to assure that the message is being understood. A presenter can also take the audience to another predetermined Web site or add a slide with new information. The moderator advances the slides of the Webinar. Finally, at the end of the presentation, the audience can be surveyed for feedback.

Other than the method of delivery, Webinars are very similar to any other presentation. The content is critical, and the presenter needs to be knowledgeable and articulate. Since the speaker does not physically see the audience, it is important to recognize what it is like to be on the receiving end. It's best to keep sentences short and keep slides simple and to the minimum. It's also wise to send detailed information to the participants in a follow-up mailing.

Cell Phones

Another target for advertisers in the new media age is the cell phone, which some are calling the "third screen," following the TV screen and PC screen. By tapping into the extensive use of text messaging among the 18- to 34-year-old crowd, advertisers have found a new market.

Worldwide revenue from mobile information and entertainment is expected to reach $39 billion in 2007, according to Ovum Consulting. Peter Fuller, executive director of the Mobile Marketing Association, gave an interesting perspective in an *Advertising Age* article in November 2004[4]: "I'd liken it to 1997, just before the dot-com boom," says Mr. Fuller. "It's the next consumer touch point, and everybody wants to be part of it."

Marketers have begun using the third screen for a variety of purposes, from wireless carriers offering mobile content like ring tones, screensavers, games, and e-books, to McDonald's, Unilever, and Kellogg Co. placing text messaging codes on cereal boxes and in TV ads to entice people to participate in campaigns. Mattel even introduced a "Barbie Cell Phone" targeted at the junior set. Organizations including Major League Baseball and the National Football League essentially set up their own networks, delivering live scores and game information on cell phones.

Text Messaging: Customized ringtones, real-time sports scores, and a "Barbie cell phone" for a target market.

With the variety of Blackberries, personal digital assistants (PDAs), and other mobile devices available today, the opportunities for personalized marketing abound.

The following table summarizes the new media tools discussed above.

Tool	Pro	Con	Audience
Web sites	Visibility	Expense	All
Extranets	Efficiency	Expense	IR Employees
Blogs	Uncensored	Credibility	Customers, Media
Search Engines	Traffic	Expense	Customers, Media
Rich Media	UserFriendly	Bandwidth, SP	Customers, Media
E-mail	ROI	Privacy	All
Databases	Personalization	IT Challenges	Customers
Webinars	Interaction	Expense	All
Cell Phones	Ubiquitous	Screen Size	All

Are the New Media Truly Different?

From the point of view of professional communication and reputation management, the new media do differ in at least three key dimensions: interactivity, measurement, and variety.

Former General Electric CEO Jack Welch once noted about the so-called new economy, "There is no such thing." Similarly, one could argue that the traditional principles of good corporate and organizational communication apply to the "new" media just as clearly as they do to the old. That is, public relations people still have to segment audiences and construct messages uniquely designed for each market segment. Above all, a successful campaign must be built around an objective and a well-defined strategy. From a tactical perspective, however, working with the new media differs in several important respects.

Twenty years ago, the media available to advertising and public relations professionals were largely limited to TV, radio, print, and live events. Today, as we have seen, many new channels have been added to the list. All, of course, new as well as old, communicate by the same familiar means: still or moving images, sounds, and spoken or written words. For all the glittery new gizmos, do the new media truly differ from the old?

From the point of view of professional communication and reputation management, the new media do differ in at least three key dimensions: interactivity, measurement, and variety.

Interactivity

When a news story appears on television, viewers really have just one choice: to watch it or not to watch it. But consumers visiting a Web site can gather information in as much depth as they like—from a general impression of a company, product, or service to specific details about product features and specs. By entering their own e-mail address, they can receive future updates on products or services of interest.

Feedback mechanisms are fundamental to communication on the Web. Virtually all company Web sites provide a message board or simple e-mail link for customer questions, comments, or problems. Blogs can be another source of feedback. In fact, some senior executives establish their own blogs primarily as a way to get direct feedback from customers.

E-mail, message boards, and blogs enable a company to discern patterns in consumer responses. These patterns can then be used to guide the development of next-generation products that will better meet customer needs. Using blogs for reputation management allows executives to see the feedback early and act on it before it does damage to the company's brand.

Of course, customer feedback is not, in itself, a new phenomenon. Companies have long used surveys and focus groups to gain insight into consumer perceptions, and customers have long communicated with manufacturers, retailers, and others via the phone and conventional mail. But the Web enables companies to get feedback in real time and makes it easier to measure and analyze the feedback received.

Measurement

Technology allows measurement at several levels:

⇒ Participation in online marketing programs can be directly measured. When the consumer goes to a Web site, keystrokes can be captured and participation can be closely monitored.

⇒ Public relations programs can be tracked, from the number of sites that pick up a press release to every story that results.

⇒ Competition can be monitored. At Brodeur, we offer a "brand dashboard"—a competitive intelligence tool that allows our clients and our account teams to keep a watchful eye in real time on industry trends, the competition, and media coverage. The dashboard uses news feeds powered by the Factiva/Dow Jones publication database or by any other XML news feed such as eWatch, Lexis-Nexus, or Northern Light.

Variety

Professional communicators now have many more communication channels from which to choose. This diversity presents both opportunities and challenges. Today's consumers are inundated by news and information in many different forms. A company with a finite budget must select those media that will best reach the target audience. Often, this will mean using many of the media available to assure that no parts of the audience will be left out.

The larger palette of colors afforded by new media gives marketers the chance to exercise greater creativity in designing campaigns. It is as if companies can now express their brand identity with a larger palette of colors. By selecting a mix of new and old media, as well as by shaping message content and design, companies can amplify their power to influence public perceptions.

Examples of Digital Marketing

Following are some examples of companies that have implemented integrated digital marketing programs:

Xerox

⇒ • Xerox.com
⇒ • Newsroom
⇒ • Press Release
⇒ • Events Calendar

GE

⇒ • GE.com
⇒ • CD
⇒ • Viral Campaign
⇒ • Microsite

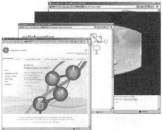

DuPont

⇒ • Microsite
⇒ • CD
⇒ • Online Magazine
⇒ • Contest

Pepsi

⇒ • Billboard
⇒ • Banner Ads
⇒ • Point of Sale
⇒ • iTunes Application

The Impact of New Media on TV

Nowhere have new media had a greater impact than on television advertising. Contrast 1960, when in the United States there were 5.7 TV channels per home, 4400 radio stations, and 8400 magazine titles, with 2004, when there were 82.4 TV channels per home, 13,500 radio stations, and 17,300 magazine titles—plus 25,000 Internet broadcast stations and 4.4 billion Web pages indexed by Google.[5] The three major TV networks no longer carry the majority of programming. An advertiser's ability to reach consumers has drastically changed.

It should come as no surprise that the explosion of new media has been accompanied by a precipitous decline in television ad recall, from just under 40 percent in 1965 to around 10 percent by the year 2000. The three primary turning points were cable TV going mainstream in the early 1970s, the introduction of the remote control in the late 1970s, and the advent of the World Wide Web in 1993.[6]

GartnerG2, in a November 2004 report, talks about "digital media titans driving the slow death of prime time." Clearly, what had been a prime time bonanza for advertisers and a $60 billion market has been dramatically altered by new media.

Further complicating an already fragmented and scrambled marketing mix, more consumers than ever have the ability to skip TV ads completely, thanks to the advent of the DVR (digital video recorder). In addition, cable and satellite providers are offering video on demand (VOD). The Forrester research firm predicts that by the end of 2006, 97 percent of the country's 34 million-plus digital cable subscribers will have VOD, and 17 million will own DVRs. Today's DVR users already reduce their exposure to ads by 54 percent.[7] Forrester notes, "Technology is disrupting TV content production, distribution, and consumption. As a result, the industry is unable to deliver advertisers a solution on a plate, because it confronts a radical change in the viewing paradigm."[8]

Consumers are blocking ads in other media, too. From national "do not call" lists to the elimination of pop-up ads, consumers are making it clear that they want more control over anything that disrupts their way of working, playing, or relaxing.

As a result of these trends, dollars formerly spent on mass marketing are now devoted to targeted marketing. *Business Week* cites the example of McDonald's:

> *McDonald's now devotes a third of its U.S. marketing budget to television, compared with two-thirds five years ago. Money that used to go for 30-second network spots now pays for closed-circuit sports programming piped into Hispanic bars and for ads in* Upscale, *a custom-published*

> Don't touch that dial! Mass marketing becomes target marketing.

magazine distributed to black barber shops. To sharpen its appeal to young men, another of its prime target audiences, McDonald's advertises on Foot Locker Inc.'s in-store video network. The company zeroes in on mothers through ads in women's magazines such as O: The Oprah Magazine *and* Marie Claire, *and on Web sites like Yahoo! and iVillage Inc. "We are a big marketer," says M. Lawrence Light, McDonald's chief marketing officer. "We are not a mass marketer." [9]*

For marketers, the evolution from mass to micromarketing is a fundamental change, driven as much by necessity as by opportunity. Today, American society is far more diverse than it was in the heyday of the mass market. The country has fragmented into countless market segments defined not only by demography, but also by increasingly nuanced and insistent product preferences. "All the research we're doing tells us that the driver of demand going forward is all about products that are 'right for me,'" says David Martin, president of Interbrand Corp. "And that's ultimately about offering a degree of customization for all."[10]

New Media Terms

With brand advertising moving, increasingly, to the Web, a new ad lingo has emerged. Following are some new media terms as *Fast Company* magazine defines them:

Adverblog A mock blog that's actually an ad. Pioneered by Wieden+Kennedy's campaign to promote Sega's ESPN NFL Football game.

Mouseover A user interacts with the ad (sometimes inadvertently) by rolling the cursor over it—without even having to click.

Roadblock or takeover An advertiser pays up to $1 million for all the ad space for a full day on the home page of Yahoo, MSN, or AOL (sometimes all three).

Skyscraper ad Vertical column running along the side of a Web page.

Viral film A short film downloaded from the Web. Pioneered by BMW, which hired acclaimed Hollywood directors to make 10-minute films starring its cars.

Webisodes A twist on viral films: advertiser-produced series that draw consumers to the brand's Web site. Pioneered by American Express.[11]

A New Media Timeline

1969: ARPANET. It began as an experimental network of four computers, a project commissioned by the U.S. government. ARPANET (the name comes from DARPA, the U.S. Department of Defense's

Advanced Research Project Agency) evolved during the 1970s into a network of computer networks that became known as the Internet.

1969: Text messaging. The British Broadcasting Corporation began testing a new format called videotext, a computerized, interactive system that would transmit text and graphics. The British system requires the use of a telephone, a modified television set, and keyboard. The generic term videotex includes computer communications services such as teletext and viewdata.

1970: Alohanet. This was the first wireless computer networking system, developed by Norm Abramson at the University of Hawaii.

1971: E-mail. An electronic mail (e-mail) program is invented by Ray Tomlinson of Bolt, Beranek and Newman and becomes the most popular application for ARPANET. There are now over 650 million e-mailers in the world. Analysts estimate that 35 million e-mails were sent daily in 2005.

1972: Ethernet. Bob Metcalfe, a researcher at the Xerox Palo Alto Research Center, wrote a memo about the potential of a local network technology called Ethernet. In 1976 Metcalfe and David Boggs publish a paper called, "Ethernet: Distributed Packet-Switching For Local Computer Networks."

1973: The Wire Services go digital. United Press International (UPI) announces that it will begin installing computer terminals in all of its one hundred United States bureaus. The Associated Press (AP) announces that it plans to develop electronic darkrooms. By 1973 AP is using computer terminals throughout its domestic system.

1974: Newsrooms get VDTs and CRTs. A large number of newspaper newsrooms replace their typewriters with computer front-end systems that include video display terminals (VDTs) and cathode ray tubes (CRTs).

1975: The First PC. In the January 1975 issue of *Popular Electronics,* the cover story describes the Altair 8800, the first successful personal computer. For $395 you can order a kit to build the Altair yourself or you can buy it assembled for $495. The Altair 8800 comes with 256 bytes of computer memory and uses Intel's 8080 processor.

1975: Microsoft begins. Ed Roberts, the creator of the Altair personal computer, works with Bill Gates and Paul Allen to develop Altair's first programming language, a version of the BASIC computer language. The partnership between Gates and Allen is the beginning of the Microsoft company.

1976: Apple. The Apple I personal computer is introduced by Steve Jobs and Steve Wozniak. Also in 1976, Jobs and Wozniak leave their jobs at Atari and Hewlett-Packard to form the Apple computer company.

1976: Word processor and floppy disks. Wang Laboratories introduces a cathode ray tube-based word processor system. During 1976 Wang also develops 5-1/4" floppy disks.

1977: PCs proliferate. The TRS-80 Model 1 microcomputer is released by Tandy and Radio Shack. The Commodore PET personal computer is introduced, which comes with two built-in cassette drives and 4 to 8K of memory. The Apple II personal computer is introduced. It has 4K of memory and is one of the first PCs to use color graphics and floppy disks.

1977: Electronic mail. An electronic mail system is developed at the University of Wisconsin that provides e-mail to over a hundred computer science researchers.

1981: The IBM PC and Microsoft disk operating system (DOS). This was not the first PC or operating system, but this was the IBM-Microsoft combination that truly launched the "IBM-compatible PC" revolution.

1983: NEXIS. The Nexis database service begins offering exclusive access to *The New York Times*. Nexis is a full-text information service with material from newspapers, magazines, and many other sources. Nexis's parent company, Mead Data Central, also purchases the *Times'* Infobank service.

1984: The Macintosh. The Macintosh personal computer is introduced by Apple. It is one of the first personal computers to use a 3-1/2" disk drive, a mouse, and a graphical user interface.

1985: Microsoft Windows graphical user interface. In the evolution of the DOS operating system, Windows changed the world as much as the arrival of the PC. It has helped make PC software easier to use.

1985: Desktop Publishing. Affordable desktop publishing begins with the introduction of the Apple LaserWriter, the HP LaserJet, and software programs such as Aldus PageMaker.

1987: NSFNET. Funded by the National Science Foundation to connect five supercomputer research centers, NSFNET is called the backbone of the Internet and will eventually take the place of ARPANET. NSFNET will help guide and manage the Internet's incredible growth until it is decommissioned in April 1995.

1988: Prodigy. The Prodigy dial-up service is launched. Prodigy evolved from an unsuccessful videotex program called Trintex, which started in 1984. Prodigy offers news updates as part of its service. From a historical standpoint, Prodigy serves as a bridge from videotex to the new media projects of the 1990s.

1990: WWW. The World Wide Web (WWW) prototype is created at the European Laboratory for Particle Physics, also known as CERN.

1991: Gopher. The Gopher Internet navigation system is released by researchers at the University of Minnesota. Gopher inventor Mark MaCahill is reported to have called it "the first Internet application my mom can use."

1993: Mosaic. Mosaic, the first graphical Web browser, is released by the National Center for Supercomputing Applications at the University of Illinois at Urbana–Champaign. Marc Andreessen leads the group of computer programmers who developed this browser.

1994: Netscape. The Netscape Communications Corporation is founded by Marc Andreessen and Jim Clark, and the company releases the beta version of its Navigator Web browser.

1994: Yahoo. The Yahoo Internet index is started as a personal list of sites by David Filo and Jerry Yang, Ph.D. candidates in electrical engineering at Stanford. Yahoo stands for "Yet Another Hierarchical Officious Oracle."

1995: The Alta Vista search engine: The Internet is the world's biggest library, but finding anything without a search engine would be practically impossible. Alta Vista is the first.

1995: Windows 95 operating system. Released by Microsoft, Windows 95 includes software for MSN and the Internet Explorer Web browser.

1996: PDAs. The first personal digital assistant (PDA) to achieve popular success is introduced. Earlier PDAs, such as the British Psion Organiser and the Apple Newton, were too complicated or expensive for consumers. However, in 1996 the Palm Pilot 1000 sparks interest in the handheld computer market.

1998: Search engines abound. A study in the journal *Science* reports that even the best search engines index no more than 34 percent of the 320 million available Web pages.

1998: Blogs. The Charlotte Observer uses a Web log to report the story of Hurricane Bonnie.

1999: Google. Beta testing of the Google search engine is finished.

2001: iPod. The iPod, Apple's hard-drive-based MP3 digital audio player, is introduced.

2004: Podcasting. The term podcasting describes the downloading of Internet radio and similar programming to portable digital audio devices.

In deference to experts who have tracked new media, like David Shedden, director of the Poynter Institute's Eugene Patterson Library, this sidebar includes only the major developments in new media history. For more detailed timelines, we refer you to:

http://www.poynter.org—The Poynter Institute is a school for journalists, future journalists, and teachers of journalists.

http://www.personalcomputerworld.com "Disruptive innovations: 27 life-shaping technologies," Martin Lynch, April 1, 2005, Personal Computer World, VNU Business Publications Ltd.

http://www.babel.massart.edu —"A Timeline of New Media," created by Eleanor Ramsay for *Teaching in New Media*, Massart, 2003.

Best Practices Marketing in the New Media World

What does it mean to do marketing in a new media world? How does one reach a "targeted" audience? How do advertisers cope? What is the right mix of media?

At this point in the new media revolution, there are no definitive answers. What is clear, though, is that marketers need to recognize the complex mix of media available and to take great pains to match the marketing spend to the target audience.

While much is in flux, certain fundamental principles continue to apply. Here are seven best practices for marketing in the new media world.

1. Start with the Customer, Not the Medium

Remember that every message is ultimately aimed at the consumer of your product or service. That can be a retail consumer or a buyer inside a business. You aren't talking to the press; you are talking through the press to your customer. You aren't talking to the investment community; you are talking through it to your customer. You aren't talking to analysts, industry associations, or other external brand influencers; you are really talking to your customer.

The same holds true for internal audiences such as your line managers, sales force, or employees. While there are times when you may have specific internal messages for them, when it comes to describing your business, products, and services, they too should be treated as customers. They can be your best ambassadors and are often an organization's largest single audience.

When you consider the customer your audience, you are much more likely to achieve brand impact and business impact. The brand impact will come from consistent message delivery, increased value perception, and improved relationships with customers and channel partners. As your product or service becomes the solution of choice, the business impact will be manifested in increased market share, revenues, profits, and market value.

2. Develop Solid Positioning

The best media-reaching techniques cannot compensate for undifferentiated positioning.

Positioning is fundamental to communication. Every organization needs to review its positioning regularly. Positioning is about getting to the essence of your business, and it is the first step in building a brand.

Positioning is where you would like your brand to reside in the customer's mind relative to other available alternatives. The positioning process identifies your most unique, meaningful and memorable values. The branding process positions these values in your customer's mind in order to form or change the customer's attitude toward your brand and, ultimately, to impact the customer's behavior.

Several popular global brands are examples of effective positioning. Volvo is accepted for its safety. Federal Express is known for its guaranteed delivery. VISA is everywhere. Dell means direct. BMW stands for driving excellence. Few would argue with these qualities. But how did they come to be? It was not by accident, but by each of these companies taking the time to define its position in the market, then systematically perpetuating this positioning in all forms of communication. Ultimately, each brand owns its "identity" and customers clearly understand what each stand for.

Positioning is a clear articulation of:

⇒ the problem your brand solves for its primary audience;
⇒ the compelling benefits of your products and services;
⇒ the differentiation of your products/services/solutions from those of your competitors;
⇒ believable, supportable messages based on core competencies.

3. Target, Tailor and Personalize Your Messages

Clear messages are more important than ever. Digital technology has leveled the playing field in marketing. Your voice online can be just as loud as anyone else's. Approximately 80 percent of the American public has access to the Internet, so anyone who wants to can find you as easily as they can find your competitor. You combat this effect and differentiate your messages by segmenting your audience, tailoring messages within each segment, and taking advantage of the technology to address messages to individuals. Remember that messages drive beliefs, opinions, preferences, and, ultimately, behavior.

4. Integrate (or strategically align) all communication elements and campaigns.

Integrated marketing is defined as the coordination and blending of a variety of promotional vehicles in mutually reinforcing ways, implemented at specific times during a marketing campaign to ensure the message is consistently received by its target audience. (See Chapter 10.)

The Toshiba gigabeat launch plan was an integrated combination of traditional and new media elements, with the traditional applied with new media twists. Each element—the launch party, microsite, direct mailer, e-mails, magazine ads, online ads, Times Square signage, and radio promotion—had a purpose and a targeted audience, and everything carried the Toshiba branding and messaging. The net result was an initiative where the whole was greater than the sum of the parts.

Aligning all communication efforts is even more critical in the new media age. When we first met Tina Tuccillo at Toshiba, she told me that Toshiba believes in arming its unified product sales, training, advertising, public relations, trade show, and online teams with consistent, integrated messages and themes. She was looking for a single agency that could manage Toshiba's entire communication efforts.

By maximizing its reach in the most cost-effective way and leveraging new media approaches, Toshiba has been able to keep a consistent, positive position in the consumer electronics marketplace. The proof is found in Toshiba's leadership in many of the television and digital audio video product categories in which it competes. This is a tribute not only to Toshiba's outstanding product quality, but also to its ability to promote a strong brand image. Toshiba executes an integrated marketing campaign built on the foundation of "Image is Everything™."

5. Personalize and Measure

In the digital world, personalization and measurement are two sides of the same coin.

The capture of digital logins, keystrokes, and other information opens the way to new methods of personalized marketing. It also makes it possible to know what prompted a particular consumer to act, thereby permitting deeper and more useful forms of measurement to emerge.

6. Recognize and Accept the Fact that Every Published Communication Is Potentially Accessible Anywhere

The obvious benefit is that you can reach millions instantly; the drawback is that wrong information spread through the Internet and the blogosphere can become a communicable digital disease.

Yes, a press release is a published communication. But so is the anonymous comment about your product in a chat room. In other words, thanks to various forms of technology, your information is accessible through multiple channels, no matter how it was first disseminated. For example, an executive is interviewed on CNBC. Within minutes, the transcript of the interview is placed online and can then be copied, pasted, or quoted in blogs, print, or elsewhere. The proliferation of blogs and RSS feeds have brought a new transparency to communication. Corporate speak and jargon are not acceptable. It is critical that you acknowledge the blogosphere, learn from it, and respond honestly to your audience community.

If you're interested in using a viral marketing technique to enhance your corporate reputation, this dynamic makes your work easier. But during a time of potential crisis, such as a lawsuit, product malfunction, or ethical scandal, the viral spread of information becomes an issues-management challenge. You must be prepared for the bad as well as the good. If you view all communication management through this lens, you will have a better chance to manage your organization's reputation.

7. Use Technology As a Means, Not an End

Technology is an enabler. It makes communication easier, faster, and more dynamic. But it does not take the place of creativity, strong messaging, well-thought-out strategy, or good writing.

Resources for Further Study

Database and Other Computer Security

http://www.citadel.com/, Citadel Security Software Inc. provides daily security news on free subscription basis.

http://www.us-cert.gov/cas/techalerts/TA06-038A.html, US-CERT United States Computer Emergency Readiness Team: National Cyber Alert System.

New Media History

http://www.babel.massart.edu, "A Timeline of New Media." Eleanor Ramsay, Teaching in New Media, Massart 2003.

http://www.personalcomputerworld.com, "Disruptive innovations: 27 life-shaping technolgies," Martin Lynch, April 1, 2005, *Personal Computer World* (VNU Business Publications).

http://www.poynter.org, Eugene Patterson Library, David Shedden, director.

SPAM—More Information on the U.S. CAN-SPAM Act

http://www.ftc.gov, U.S. Federal Trade Commission Web site.

To Find Feeds

http://www.syndic8.com, A master list of syndication feeds.

http://www.feedster.com, Search engine which finds sites with syndication feeds.

To Search Blogs

BuzzMetrics, Intelliseek and Cymfony (for search, measure and word-of-mouth research and planning) http://www.buzzmetrics.com, http://www.intelliseek.com, http://www.cymfony.com.

GoogleBlogSearch, Technorati, Feedster, and PubSub (for general blog search purposes) http://www.google.com/search?hl=en&lr=&q=Googleblogsearch&btnG=Search, http://www.technorati.com, http://www.feedster.com, http://www.pubsub.com.

To Search and Aggregate Feeds Displayed in Your Browser

http://www.bloglines.com, BlogLines (subscription).

http://www.pubsub.com, PubSub (subscription).

To Set up Custom Real-Time Feeds on Targeted Topics

http://www.factiva.com, Factiva/Dow Jones publication database.

http://ewatch.prnewswire.com/, eWatch XML news feed flat-fee-service from PR Newswire.

http://www.lexisnexus.com, Lexisnexus: subscription-only legal, government, business, and high-tech information service.

http://www.northernlight.com/, Northern Light flat-fee enterprise-wide business news feed.

What's an Ad? Analysis and Opinion about New Media in Advertising

http://www.fastcompany,   http://www.fastcompany.com/magazine/95/open_design-collins.html

American Association of Advertising Agencies, http://www.aaaa.org/eweb/startpage.aspx

Interactive Advertising Bureau, http://www.iab.net/

adverblog advertising & online marketing, http://www.adverblog.com/

Forrester Research, Inc., "Left Brain Marketing," April 6, 2004.

Questions for Further Discussion

1. How has the Internet changed the way public relations and corporate communication are done?
2. What are the relative advantages and disadvantages of using e-mail as a marketing/PR technique?
3. Are the new media different from the old media?
4. Does using new media require changing the content of communication?
5. How has new media changed the velocity of public opinion formation?

CHAPTER 5

Employee Communication

By the authors, with significant contributions by
Jeff Grimshaw,

Partner, CRA, Inc.

> *The challenge: To align the hearts, minds, and hands of the employee
> constituency through dialogue and engagement.*

In its presentations to corporate leadership teams, CRA, Inc., a consultancy that specializes in internal communication strategy, likes to show an employee video they describe as "probably the best employee communication product ever."

"What you are going to see," CRA partner Jeff Grimshaw tells his executive audience, "is the CEO and CFO of a company you've probably heard of talking about the values that should govern everything that happens in the company: Respect, integrity, communication, excellence. Those are great values—but it's the production values that make this the best employee communication video we've ever seen. The music, videography, scripting—all of it is first rate."

As the video begins to play, members of the leadership team nod their heads in approval. It truly is a compelling employee communication product. A full minute passes before someone in the group gets a quizzical look on his face that transforms into a broad grin: "Wait a minute, that's Ken Lay and Jeff Skilling!" the leader says, as they all realize they are watching the Enron "Vision and Values" video.[1]

After giving the group a few minutes to savor the delicious irony of Enron leadership casting themselves as the standard bearers of respect, integrity, communication, and excellence, Grimshaw makes sure his audience gets the point: "For many years," he says, "the employee communication function justified its existence by producing appealing products to convey information: videos, newsletters, town hall meetings, etc. But today, employee communication is all about managing meaning inside the organization in a way that supports leadership's business objectives. That happens only when employees see consistency between the messages sent through formal channels and the symbolic messages sent through leaders' decisions and action. When there is a gap between formal communications and symbolic communications (Enron being a poignant example), employee communication becomes, in the best case, a meaningless waste of money—and in the worst case, a manifestation of hypocrisy and a target of employees' derision."

* * * * *

Historically, organizations have charged the employee communication function with communicating to employees information about the organization's products, services, organizational structure, policies, and procedures—and changes to the above. And while leadership expressed support for the function ("Employees are our most important audience"), they attributed little strategic importance to the function and the people—often tucked into the corner of public affairs or human resources—who staffed it.

Today, employee communication has made measurable gains in everything from respect within the organization to salaries for staff. A variety of factors has propelled the evolution of the employee communication function, many of them involving greater clarity in the organization about the link between employee communication and business results.

This Chapter Covers

⇒ Employee communication: The stepchild of public affairs and human resources
⇒ Making progress: Employee communication today
⇒ Employee communication drives organizational performance
⇒ The new role of employee communication
⇒ The five traits that distinguish the best employee communications shops
⇒ Best practices in employee communication
⇒ Resources for further study
⇒ Questions for further discussion
⇒ Sidebar: Message hierarchy
⇒ Sidebar: The evolution of strategic employee communication at Hallmark
⇒ Sidebar: Maximize your message through media selection

> Employee Communication: The function charged with aligning the "hearts, minds, and hands" of the employee constituency through dialogue and engagement.

Employee Communication: The Stepchild of Public Relations and Human Resources

Before elaborating why and how employee communication is taking on a more important role in organizations, we should pause to reflect on why the function was for many years relatively weak.

"They're only tacticians."

In many organizations, employee communication (the functional group) provided good writers with modestly paying entry-level jobs in public affairs or human resources. Leaders in these organizations considered the company publication—deprecatively dubbed the "house organ"—as employee communication's most important responsibility. This was good news for people with journalism degrees. The bad news: Leaders saw these people strictly as tacticians—and summoned them to craft a coherent and grammatically correct internal memo or newsletter article, with an appropriately positive spin, only after a decision had been made (never during the decision-making process itself).

We know of a recent case where a head of public relations for a large corporation told the employee communication group: "Our number one audience is senior management. Make sure they are happy with everything you do." In other words, the employee communications shop exists not to strategically engage the employee constituency but rather to ingratiate senior management. Underlying this assertion is the assumption that employee communicators are essentially "internal vendors" who exist only to deliver what they are told to and are easily replaced.

We suspect that sexism, combined with the demographics of the employee communication function, also contributed to its nonstrategic status. Over the years, a majority of employee communicators were women, who, some assumed, were less interested in or capable of pursuing northward-bound career paths. Meanwhile, men were more likely to work in the communications functions thought to have more strategic value—media relations and crisis communication, for example.

Challenges to Change

The employee communication function has struggled for more than a decade to assert a stronger role for itself—and those efforts continue. According to a recent assessment by The Minnesuing Group, a forty-member peer group of top internal communicators, three enduring obstacles to internal communicators "earning the proverbial seat at the leadership table" are: (1) leaders who do not understand the relationship between internal communication and the business outcomes they are trying to produce—and the failure of the employee communication function to clearly and credibly articulate the link; (2) a demand for tactical communications support that saps all existing capacity and makes it difficult for the internal communications function to shift from a tactical to a strategic focus; and (3) the lack of a well-defined competency model for the strategic internal communications function.

To this list of challenges, past and current, we would add:

⇒ The dynamic between public affairs and human resources, which has also made it difficult for the employee communication function to assert a stronger role for itself. Nowhere in corporate America, and perhaps in other sectors as well, were turf wars more disruptive and destructive than with public relations and human resources.

> The bad news: Leaders saw these people strictly as tacticians—and summoned them to craft a coherent and grammatically correct internal memo or newsletter article, with an appropriately positive spin, only after a decision had been made (never during the decision-making process itself).

The two functions have been, and too often still are, like Disney and Miramax, Shaq and Kobe, the Pentagon and the State Department. With HR believing that it too had stewardship for employee communication, the employee communications shop found it difficult to control its own destiny.

⇒ In many cases, the legal group has also been quick to enter the fray—and like HR, eager to tell employee communicators what they cannot say. The unintended consequence: The rumor mill became a more reliable source of information—further jeopardizing the credibility and utility of the role played by the employee communications function.

⇒ IABC vs. PRSA. The professional communicator organizations themselves tended early on to isolate employee communication from the other public relations disciplines. The International Association of Business Communicators (IABC) began as an organization for employee communicators, and the Public Relations Society of America (PRSA) tended for years to underemphasize employee communication. The unintended consequence of this isolation: As organizations began to confer more strategic status on their other communications functions, employee communications got left out.

Making Progress: Employee Communication Today

Anyone who has spent even a few years in public affairs knows the answer to the following riddle: The president of an organization meets three professional employees in the cafeteria line: (A) the media relations manager, (B) the investor relations manager, and (C) the employee communications manager. Who does the president stop to talk with? The answer is clearly (A) and (B), because the employee communicator walked away, knowing it was time to get a table and wait for his friends. But if the internal communication field continues to evolve at its current rate, that joke will not retain its currency for long. In a growing number of organizations, employee communicators are taking on broader and more strategic responsibilities, enjoying greater access to leadership, and making more money. And, according to Heyman Associates, employee communication remains poised for vibrant growth.[2]

Barry Mike, a former vice president and director of employee communications at a very well-known consumer and financial services company and now a consultant, cites eight business trends that have helped to set the stage for the "new and improved" employee communication function:[3]

1. *Growing cynicism.* As this chapter's earlier reference to Enron's "Vision and Values" video suggests, business scandals and greedy

> In a growing number of organizations, employee communicators are taking on broader and more strategic responsibilities, enjoying greater access to leadership, and making more money.

CEOs have helped ironically to produce an enlightened attitude toward employee communication. Research by The Conference Board shows that employees in American industry are less content, more suspicious, and less trusting than in the past. In this environment, organizations need employee communicators who can manage meaning and bolster trust—not just produce slick videos and other products.

2. *Organizations have dramatically flattened.* Starting with the downsizing movement of the late 1980s, organizations have increasingly debureaucratized themselves, flattening their structures and, most importantly, pushing decision making closer to the front lines. They have recognized that important customer and process information is embedded at lower levels and, therefore, decision making needs to be close to the source of information. Today, with more employees making important business decisions, and with less management oversight of those decisions, business performance has never been more dependent on employee understanding of organizational objectives, directions, and goals.

> For the most sophisticated organizations, the need for speed has turned employee communicators from newsletter writers into information processors and knowledge management experts.

3. *The rate of change is increasing.* The traditional "by the book" mentality epitomized by slow-moving monopolies like public utilities and phone companies is now obsolete. Everything is changing too fast to work according to long-standing, codified procedures. The emphasis is now on flexibility and elasticity. Employees, more than ever, need to know the context within which the organization operates to ensure that they are moving in the same direction.

4. *Speed has become a differentiator.* It used to be that only price and quality differentiated products. But information technology has allowed speed to become a competitive differentiator—raising expectations of convenience, customization, and quality that were not possible before. Speed means that traditional bureaucracies, and anything else that slows the flow of information to those who need it, wherever they are in the organization, are impediments to success. For the most sophisticated organizations, this has turned employee communicators from newsletter writers into information processors and knowledge management experts.

5. *Lifetime employment is dead.* The old, implicit employment contract that offered a job for life in return for loyalty has been dead for at least ten years. In the context of flattened, faster organizations where there are simply fewer levels within which to ascend, organizations can only offer employees the ability to grow their capabilities, expand in new challenging roles, and learn on a continuous basis. All of these demand a more sophisticated employee commu-

nication infrastructure than ever before, one in which information and knowledge are proactively managed.

6. *"It's all about the people, stupid."* Human capital is increasingly a key competitive differentiator. The ability of companies to copy even the most proprietary products and produce them at lower costs (common in China, for example) has led some business thinkers to suggest that over time the only differentiator will be the knowledge and skills of an organization's people. Employee communication can play a vital role in building people capability.

7. *The desire for purpose.* Freud said that the two most important things in life are love and work. This has become even more true in the post-9/11 era, at least in the United States, which has compelled people to search for greater meaning and purpose in their lives. Effective employee communication can go a long way toward helping employees feel like they are part of, and contributing to, something "bigger than themselves."

8. *A rising service sector has increased the importance of internal branding.* In the increasingly powerful service sector, the brand promise is more and more often realized in the interactions between the service provider and the customer. Business success becomes more dependent, then, on service personnel understanding a brand promise and their role in delivering it. Employee communications then becomes a vital extension of marketing and strategic planning in ensuring the delivery of the brand promise.

Employee Communication Drives Organizational Performance

More and more evidence is emerging to support the relationship between internal communication effectiveness and business performance, which may be the strongest motive for organizations to change the way they manage employee communication. What are the links between communication and performance?

Link #1 – Employee communication drives overall business performance. Internal communicators welcomed a Watson Wyatt study that found:[4]

⇒ A significant improvement in internal communication effectiveness is associated with a 29.5 percent increase in market value.

⇒ Companies with the highest levels of effective internal communication experienced a 26 percent total return to shareholders from 1998 to 2002, compared to a 15 percent return experienced by firms that communicate least effectively.

⇒ Firms that communicate most effectively are more likely to report turnover rates below or significantly below those of their industry peers that communicate less effectively (33.3 percent versus 51.6 percent).

Link #2 – Employee communication influences retention. It is a truism to say that employees are a company's most important audience. Employees discover, develop, and make the products, deliver the services, and hold the organization's intellectual capital in their heads. Leadership communication and credibility heavily influence whether top performers stay. For example, employees at Emmis Communications, one of *Fortune* magazine's "100 Best Companies To Work For," cited "great communication by the CEO" as one of the reasons they chose to stay, even after the company cut employee pay in 2001.[5]

> Companies with the highest levels of effective internal communication experienced a 26 percent total return to shareholders from 1998 to 2002, compared to a 15 percent return experienced by firms that communicate least effectively.

Link #3 – Employee communication promotes identification and mobilizes employees. While younger employees today are more transient, having several more employers during a career, there are still many employees who believe deeply in (or want to believe deeply in) the organizations for which they work. It is all about identity, which reputation scholar Charles Fombrun defines as the core thing the organization stands for; it is, Fombrun says, the company's "character."[6] This being the case, employees are an organization's most potentially powerful constituency, one that can recruit other employees, lobby government, even vastly affect the reputation of the organization with all the other constituencies. That is why, when public relations people are asked to name the most important audience, they often cite employees. It is probably not a coincidence the top two hundred companies in *Fortune* magazine's "Most Admired Companies" list spend a much larger share of their communication budgets on employee communication than other firms do.

Link #4 – Employee communication facilitates change and buy-in. When organizations assess the root causes of technology initiatives and other major projects that have failed to deliver the benefits promised, in most cases, "poor communication" inevitably emerges as a key contributor to project failure. This is why in a variety of organizations, the IT (information technology) function, which is all too familiar with the consequences of poor communication, has surprised many by moving ahead of the rest of the organization in elevating internal communication (with both IT employees and their internal clients) as a truly strategic business function. In fact, we know of several CIOs who have significantly increased the size of their internal communication functions while significantly decreasing their overall headcounts.

Link #5 – Employee communication influences leadership credibility. Leaders cannot not communicate. Intentionally or unintentionally, everything they do—including the decisions they make, the actions they take, and the way they reward and recognize people—sends messages to the organization. Effective employee communication cannot compensate for poor decisions or disingenuous rhetoric—at least not indefinitely (the Enron "Vision and Values" video being a case in point). But effective employee communication can help leaders articulate their strategy and interpret key activities and decisions in a way that makes sense to employees. Effective employee communication can also help leaders ensure that their symbolic communication matches their rhetoric—or more simply stated, that their words are consistent with their actions.

The Evolution of Strategic Employee Communication at Hallmark: Employee Engagement Scores Are Rising

By Steve Doyal,
Senior vice president, Public Affairs and Communications, Hallmark

Over the course of our nearly one-hundred-year history, employee communication at Hallmark has evolved into an integrated, highly influential function that links directly with all aspects of the business. Today, the communications group reports directly to the CEO—a position that yields influence, gains insight, and carries responsibility not given to Hallmark communicators in the past.

Communication stages

During my thirty-plus-year tenure with Hallmark, the company's communication function has evolved significantly. The stages of evolution could be characterized as reporting, followed by prioritizing, and growing into influence and interpretation:

⇒ Reporting—In this stage, those charged with communication responsibilities collected information, wrote it appropriately, and distributed the information as effectively as possible. This was a reactive approach, absent any strategic communication framework.

⇒ Prioritizing—In this stage, reporting evolved to include some prioritization of key messages and a degree of context relevant to the audience or business. This, too, was a relatively reactive approach, but signaled a move toward using employee communication as a business enabler.

⇒ Influencing and interpreting—In this most recent and current stage, the professional communicators at Hallmark became strategic business partners helping shape business decisions, counseling executives on strategic communication, elevating business literacy, and building employee engagement.

When I started in communications at Hallmark, our group was pretty good at the craft. A premium was placed on employee communication, but it was used to help people in the organization feel like one happy family, rather than address relevant business issues.

As an example, Hallmark has published a daily newsletter every workday for more than fifty years. At its inception *Noon News* shared headlines from news outlets outside the company and information about employees that helped them feel connected to and valued by the organization, such as birthdays and anniversaries.

<u>Evidence of business impact added to communication accountability</u>

Noon News was held relatively captive to the original content design until the communication function began proving the value of better-informed employees who understood the business.

Evolution of the employee communication function occurred as Hallmark leaders witnessed the ability of well-crafted, prioritized communication to not only inform, but also to motivate employees and move the business forward. It was the professional communicators' abilities to sort through a glut of business messages and place them into meaningful order and context that helped clarify the company's direction during the last two decades of the twentieth century. Our better-informed employees more clearly understood the actions they needed to take to support Hallmark's success.

An example of message prioritization occurred in 1999 when Hallmark was on the verge of announcing a comprehensive change initiative that included completely new alignments within the company and of our more than 20,000 employees. There were new leaders, a new vision, new organization structures—all part of the changes that needed to be communicated. With a model line of 40,000 greeting cards and related products distributed through more than 43,000 retail locations in the United States alone, our company needed to become more consumer focused and take cost and complexity out of the organization. Hallmarkers needed to understand the case for change and what the changes meant to them if we were to be successful.

Fortunately, we had a long-established philosophy about handling communication within Hallmark, so we were able to build centralized solutions that supported Hallmark's beliefs and values. That philosophy, generally known at Hallmark as the five Cs of communication, states that communication solutions encompass:

⇒ A conscience that weighs proposed actions against the principles that guide the company.

⇒ Cultural integrity that helps the company protect and benefit from our heritage and define our future.

⇒ Communication that (1) is calibrated to the particular needs of our institution and audiences, both internal and external, and (2) articulates key messages in ways that reflect the company's culture and mission.

⇒ Counsel that is consistent, sound and sensitive to the needs of both management and ownership.

⇒ Cost effectiveness achieved either through internal efficiencies and expertise or the wise use of external resources.

The strategy of our 1999 campaign was a multiphased, multidisciplined approach to sharing information about what the new organization would look like, how it would better position Hallmark for the future, and what benefits employees should expect from these changes. Large-format, face-to-face meetings were the foundation of the communication. A special print publication provided details about the changes and served as a reference for employees during these preintranet days. Smaller, follow-up meetings were conducted between managers and their work groups, and supported by communication packets of overheads, question-and-answer guides, and other sources of information.

Ongoing measurement of the effectiveness of the changes demonstrated the value of the communication approach from first, a centralized corporate perspective, and second, an employee appreciation of the need for the new structure, the changes, and the various business initiatives essential to a successful change process.

Business partners, not just support organization

Today, Hallmark's greatest impact from communication comes in the form of influence and interpretation. Communication is seen as an enabler to business success. We have moved from a centralized function creating one-size-must-fit-all solutions to a hybrid organization that continues to serve Hallmark from a centralized function, but also deploys senior-level communication strategists to sit on every major business area's leadership team. Our communication strategists work as consultants with leadership teams in business areas to facilitate change initiatives.

The centralized corporate communication function continues to serve as the funnel for daily news via *Noon News*, the corporate intranet, and CCTV, the company's internal TV system. The result of our current communications structure is exponentially greater influence within the company on the success of the business. With no additional resources, our communications function is having a greater impact than any time in the past.

To accomplish this requires professionals who have broad skills across multiple disciplines, who can think strategically about the business, and can identify the communication implications of business strategy.

In many cases, communication strategists also play a role as managers of people and/or a function. For example, the communication strategist for our greeting card business unit also is our business communications manager, supervising our employee communication and media productions staffs. The communication strategist for our marketing division also has responsibility for national public relations programs and supervises PR program managers. The expectations on individuals in these roles is high, but the professional satisfaction is unequaled.

The success of Hallmark's hybrid approach to employee communications has relied on flexibility, collaboration with internal business partners, and highly skilled and dedicated employees. The model has provided professional development for many people, has elevated the value of communications for Hallmark, and has been a key contributor to rising employee engagement scores as measured by the Gallup organization. Those scores lead us to believe that, regardless of the difficult business situations, Hallmarkers are prepared to do what is needed to succeed.

> Leaders cannot *not* communicate. Intentionally or unintentionally, everything they do—including the decisions they make, the actions they take, and the way they reward and recognize people—sends messages to the organization.

The New Role of Employee Communication

As employee communication evolves as a strategic business function, practitioners have adopted a variety of different metaphors to explain their expanded roles and operations.

1. Employee communication is the guardian of leadership credibility. The annual *Fortune* magazine survey citing "The 100 Best Companies To Work For" measures the quality of employee communication by measuring credibility. One can argue that employee communication has to be many things (for example, quick and efficient) just as other functions must. An organization can survive certain breaches in speed and efficiency, but without credibility, employee communication will lose its audience; employees might listen and heed commands but they will not be engaged.

"According to research," states Fraser Seitel in *The Practice of Public Relations*, now in its ninth edition, "communications must be continuous, respectful and candid to reinforce a consistent management message."[7] Credibility, defined as trustworthiness, is the thread that ties together continuity, respect, and candor, and it is strong enough to maintain consistency of communications. It follows that the focus of employee communication should always be on maintaining credibility, for to damage that is to destroy trust—to destroy relationships.

"There should be in the corporate and PR leadership mindset," says Steve Doyal, senior vice president of public affairs and communications for Hallmark, "a policy of absolute intolerance of actions or inactions that damage credibility."

2. Employee communication is the facilitator of employee engagement.
Studies show that internal communication can align employees' passions and energies (including discretionary effort) with the goals and strategies of the organization. Once that happens, studies suggest, employees can influence, as much as any group can, the success of a corporate branding or corporate reputation initiative.

Two U.K. researchers who draw that conclusion, Simon Hardaker of QinetiQ, and Chris Fill of the University of Portsmouth Business School, assert that there are two types of engagement, intellectual and emotional, and that the employee communications function must nurture both.[8]

They illustrate this in the case history of QinetiQ, a defense supply organization that was until 2003 a part of the Ministry of Defence in the United Kingdom; in that year, after a hundred years as a government unit, it was sold to a for-profit company, the Carlyle Group. QinetiQ leadership faced two communication challenges: (1) explain the privatization transaction and what it would mean to employees (intellectual engagement); and (2) support the radical change from government-owned and safe to entrepreneurial (emotional).

The intellectual engagement initiatives were informational and could be considered one-way communication, whereas the emotional engagement initiatives were intended to produce dialogue and ambassadorial enthusiasm on the part of employees. Engagement was necessary in order to have the employees feel and be perceived as part of the corporate brand: innovative solutions for government agencies and private defense organizations.

In order to engage employees, the communications group had to understand the employee audience thoroughly. "Effective marketing communication," Hardaker and Fill state, "is often based upon a solid understanding of the target audience in terms of behavior, information processing and media consumption." A large number of the QinetiQ employee population are scientists and engineers, who have a cognitive, rational approach to information. This kind of audience segmentation data was key to the choice of media and messaging.

The communications group actually adopted a 30/70 strategy, with approximately 30 percent of employee communication and materials aimed at explaining the change and 70 percent at motivating and imbuing the entrepreneurial spirit. Some of the main communication initiatives were:

⇒ An employee brochure that was a précis version of the new corporate business plan.

⇒ Roadshows at the company's three major sites featured the CEO, who encouraged a discussion of company strengths and weaknesses. Cascade briefings complemented the roadshows so that all employees could be involved in dialogue and building employee involvement in the corporate brand.

⇒ Online Web chats with the CEO, an intranet, and a variety of face-to-face meetings cultivated an environment of communication.

⇒ An internal, closed-circuit radio system, accessed initially through telephones and later through desktop PCs, allowed the CEO to communicate key developments. One broadcast attracted 2,000 employees, three hundred of whom gave immediate feedback.

⇒ A new system for broadly disseminating the published work of QinetiQ scientists so that their work will be better known by internal and external audiences and so that they will receive greater recognition for their work. Whereas a scientist's work is often unknown to those who do not read the peer-reviewed journals, the QinetiQ communications group now publicizes over 1,000 research papers in lay terms on subjects including ocean monitoring and satellite systems that have defense implications.

To measure the effectiveness of the engagement campaign, the communications group measures staff engagement, not staff satisfaction. "Both intellectual and emotional engagement appear to have been established," Hardaker and Fill state, "to the extent that employees at QinetiQ represent a significant brand value."

3. Employee communication is the steward of senior leaders' *strategic agenda*.

CRA helps organizations elevate internal communication as a truly strategic business function by implementing tools, processes, and practices that position the function as the steward of the leadership agenda. As illustrated here, there are three basic components to the operating model.

Step One: Establish the strategic agenda. This involves exploring with leadership the answers to three questions:

⇒ What change have you as a leadership team committed to deliver? What business results have you committed to produce?

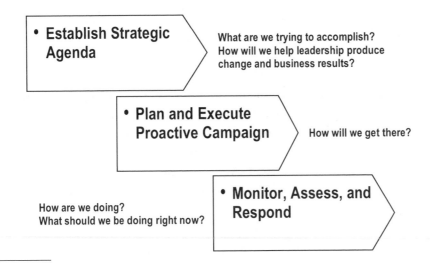

Figure 5.1

⇒ In order to produce those results, what internal constituencies do you need to effectively inform and influence?

⇒ To meet your goals, what exactly do you need each of those audiences to know and understand? What do you need them to recognize, believe, or feel? And what do you need them to do?

Step Two: Plan and execute a proactive campaign. This step involves a disciplined, rigorous campaign plan that supports the strategic agenda. If someone suggests an idea for a new communication activity or vehicle, but cannot explain how it maps to the strategic agenda and how it will do more to support the strategic agenda than devoting the resources elsewhere, it does not get done. That is true no matter how clever it is and regardless of the fact that another organization won a Gold Quill award from IABC the previous year for doing this exact same thing.

> To meet your goals, what exactly do you need each audience to know and understand? What do you need them to recognize, believe, or feel? And what do you need them to do?

Step Three: Monitor, assess and respond. The third component of the operating model involves assessing the extent to which the efforts to support the strategic agenda are working—and why. It means inventorying and strategically responding to emergent communication needs and opportunities (including leadership decisions and actions; rumors, concerns, and challenges; and progress and successes). It is about the employee communications functions gathering and synthesizing new information and "reserving the right to get smarter," all focused on delivering on leadership's "know, believe, and do" goals.

According to CRA's Jeff Grimshaw, the mantra underlying the strategic agenda-based approach is this: "In this organization, there are no longer 'communication projects,' only business initiatives that require significant and purposeful communication activity. We don't declare victory based on whether a particular communication activity is successful, for the activity is only a means to an end. We declare victory based strictly on the outcomes that we work with senior leadership to produce."

Employee Communication vs. Internal Communication

The discussion of the "new role of employee communication" may be the best place to weigh in on the distinction between "employee communication" and "internal communication." At various points in this chapter, we have invoked both terms and treated them as interchangeable, which is how these terms are used in many organizations.

Increasingly, however, organizations are coming to view employee communication as merely a subdiscipline (albeit the major subdiscipline) of internal communication. Employee communication implies that we are referring to audiences over whom there is positional authority, either directly or indirectly. But internal communication also includes two other emerging disciplines:

⇒ Cross-departmental communication. For many of the departments within large organizations, effectively informing and influencing their own employees is, at most, only half the battle. This is especially true for shared services organizations, IT in particular. According to the Gartner Group, successful CIOs spend 10 percent of their time on functional issues and 90 percent on relational issues. To do this, CIOs require a robust communication strategy and infrastructure, including support for effectively building and managing relationships with "key audiences of one."

⇒ Organizational effectiveness. The popularity of Lean, Six Sigma, and methods for improving quality and efficiency has exposed poor internal communication (up, down, and across) as a root cause of suboptimal organizational performance. In the years ahead, we anticipate that employee communicators will have opportunities, if they seize them, to play an essential role in driving improvements in organizational effectiveness—by working with other support functions and consulting directly with work teams and individuals on how to improve the effectiveness and efficiency of their communication activities.

> If someone suggests an idea for a new communication activity or vehicle, but can't explain how it maps to the strategic agenda and how it will do more to support the srategic agenda than devoting the resources elsewhere, it doesn't get done. That's true no matter how clever it is and regardless of the fact that another organization won a Gold Quill award from IABC the previous year for doing this exact same thing.

Message Hierarchy

By Alan Nelson,
Partner, CRA, Inc.

Nod knowingly if this sounds familiar: A wave of consultants comes into your organization, puts the leadership team into a room for six hours, and has them hash out—word by word—some declaration of mission, vision, and/or values that is meant to reflect the "big picture" and promote strategic alignment. The consultants then leave, the marketing department puts the messages on posters and mouse pads, and almost immediately thereafter the energy and intent of the exercise starts to dissipate.

The reason is simple: The messages often strike those who did not help create them as esoteric, irrelevant—or worse, completely divorced from the reality of what is really happening in the organization. Unable to vertically "connect the dots" between these messages, employees find it difficult to determine how the work they do, and how various initiatives underway in their business, fit into the big picture defined so carefully by the leadership team. This, in turn, promotes confusion and breeds conspiracy theories to explain what is going on, which saps energy, damages productivity, and tarnishes the credibility of leadership.

The alternative: Undercommunicate the aspirational messages (mission, vision, and values)—and then craft and overcommunicate a strategy message: a message that simply and clearly connects the aspirations of the business (where we want to be) with the initiatives underway in the business (what we are doing today). The strategy message, in essence, says "here's how we'll get there."

The right strategy message will also preserve leadership credibility even in the midst of change (because employees can make sense of what is happening), and will promote a strategically aligned and engaged workforce (since employees will know "what really counts"). But strategy messages work only when they reflect the following criteria.

⇒ Simple and universal—anyone can understand it, and everyone needs to know it. Make certain it passes the "Grandma May" test: If my Grandma May, who is a very bright woman but also a

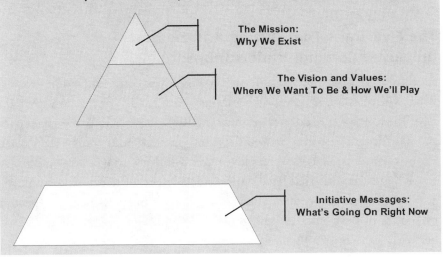

The Mission:
Why We Exist

The Vision and Values:
Where We Want To Be & How We'll Play

Initiative Messages:
What's Going On Right Now

butcher with a limited education, cannot understand the message, it is too complex.

⇒ Conversational—if it contains words like "strive" or "leverage" or other words you learned from a consultant, take them out—or risk communicating a message that no one will want to repeat (and at which Grandma May would roll her eyes).

⇒ Explains what we are doing and why—but not how. You will want to position the "hows," including all substantive actions, decisions, and initiatives, within the context of the strategy.

⇒ Actionable—employees at all levels, with help from their immediate leaders (who themselves must consider the strategy credible) can translate the strategy into specific behaviors. Bad example: "scale the business"—hard for the guy in HR to make actionable to his people. Better example: "help our business grow as fast as it can"—much easier for the guy in HR to make actionable to his people. ("Heck, folks: we're going to have to recruit and hire a bunch of people here!")

⇒ Valid—without resorting to spin or lexical slight of hand, leaders can explain all of their decisions and actions—even the ones with unpleasant consequences, within the context of the strategy. ("Here's why we hired Mary from the outside: She's an expert in recruiting, and will help us grow the business as fast as we can.")

The bottom line: If you are not sure how your various messages fit together what chance do your employees have? Clarify your message hierarchy, make it simple without simplifying—and make sure you have an appropriate strategy message you can continually invoke to help employees link what is going on right now with the organization's higher-level aspirations.

The Five Traits That Distinguish the Best Employee Communication Shops

As thinking about the strategic role of employee communication evolves, what will distinguish the organizations that "get it" from those that do not? The following list draws heavily on CRA's and others' experiences over the past decade, examining what specific practices and traits are in place in organizations that view employee communication as a strategic function—organizations that have built a track record of harnessing employee communication to produce change and deliver business results. The five categories of best practices and traits are People, Processes, Media, Feedback/Metrics, and Content.

1. People

The Employee Communication Lead. In the new employee communication function, the lead (whether VP, director, or manager) plays the role of strategist. This requires having relatively unfettered access to the senior team and their decision-making processes. And it involves coaching senior leaders to achieve strategic communication objectives.

To operate effectively—in fact, to operate at all—at this level, the communicator must position herself or himself with the senior team as a "trusted advisor." Professional services gurus Maister, Green and Galford in the book *The Trusted Advisor*, say that those who achieve this status do so on the basis of their[9]:

⇒ Credibility (professional competency, quality of advice),
⇒ Reliability (action, follow-through),
⇒ Personal connections with leaders (there is comfort in the relationship; they are easy to work with),
⇒ Motives (it is clear to leadership that the communication lead's only agenda is to support the leadership agenda).

To be seen by leaders as an "operator," and to play that role effectively, the employee communication lead must also understand the organization's political landscape and be highly conversant regarding the organization's field of business. In the ideal situation, one could sit in on a senior leadership team meeting and not be able to determine which person at the table is the employee communication lead, because of the nature and quality of his or her participation.

Employee Communication Staff. What is true of the communication lead should, for the most part, also be true of his or her staff. There is the same need to understand the political landscape, cultivate the informal networks inside the organization, develop business acumen, and become conversant in the organization's operational and competitive issues.

Ideally, the function should be able to trade on its enhanced status to make the case for adding to the size of the function—permitting the function sufficient capacity to operate at a strategic level while continuing to offer significant tactical support.

Senior Leaders. In best-practice organizations, senior leaders understand the link between employee communication and business results. Toward that end, they have articulated strategic communication objectives—what they need their internal audiences to know, believe, and do—and issued to employee communication the charge to help achieve those objectives. Further, they actively seek counsel and provide ready access to communication professionals as needs warrant.

> In the ideal situation, one could sit in on a senior leadership team meeting and not be able to determine which person at the table is the employee communication lead, because of the nature and quality of his or her participation.

As communicators, senior leaders in best-practice organizations understand the symbolic nature of their roles and are conscious of the fact that they are always communicating, regardless of whether they intend it. They recognize that leadership decisions and actions, and the way they reward and recognize employees, sends "louder" messages than any content delivered through formal channels. Accordingly, they are dogmatic about ensuring consistency between words and actions.

Managers and Supervisors (Anyone with Direct Reports). Recognizing that most employees in most organizations describe their immediate boss as a preferred information source, best-practice organizations equip managers and supervisors with privileged information. According to TJ and Sandar Larkin (1994, in *Communicating for Change*), the goal of providing "privileged" information is not to keep it out of the hands of front-line employees; in fact, just the opposite is true.[10] The purpose of providing privileged information to managers and supervisors is to ensure that the information is credibly and meaningfully delivered to front-line employees. After all, managers and supervisors should know better than anyone else their employees' questions, concerns, and information needs. And they should know better than anyone else how to interpret the implications of the strategic messages coming "from on high."

Informal Networks. In the *Tipping Point*, Malcolm Gladwell suggests that to effectively diffuse a message or idea, one must observe "The Law of the Few, " getting it into the hands of the organization's information mavens (the people who seem to know everything), the connectors (the people who tend to "bridge" the various clusters in the organization's informal networks), and salespeople (who are passionate about ideas and getting other people to share their views).[11] Best-practice organizations identify these individuals, and harness the "Law of the Few" by pulsing them as information sources (for example, as an early warning system for rumors or resistance to organizational changes), and by equipping them as information carriers. As Marshall McLuhan famously observed, "the medium is the message," which in this case means that the same message will often travel faster and more credibly through an organization's informal networks than it will through formal channels.

2. Processes

Audience / Constituency Analysis. "Don't try to visualize the great mass audience," said writing guru William Zinsser in his classic book *On Writing Well*. "There is no such audience—every reader is a different person."

Zinsser's point is well taken: There is no such thing as the general public, or, more on point, the employee audience.[12] But internal communicators, like marketers and advertisers, cannot generally create a different communication for each and every person in an audience. It makes sense to map out the most complete audience profile. What are the demographics and psychographics of middle management, the research staff, production workers, union leaders, and so on?

Best-practice organizations inventory, profile, and prioritize their employee audiences. And they do this at both the macro level (that is, in the course of developing the annual campaign plan) and at the micro level (that is, in the course of developing the strategic communication response to a specific need or opportunity). The analysis also includes the articulation of *strategic communication objectives*. As referenced earlier, this means asking: "Given the business results to which leadership has committed, what do we need this particular audience, as a result of our communication efforts, to know? Believe? And do?"

Proactive Communication Planning. Communicators are familiar with the custom of investing significant resources in November, December, and January toward the goal of producing a detailed employee communication plan for the coming year—and then, in February and March, beginning to watch the carefully prepared plan gather dust on the shelf. This happens for a variety of reasons, but often because emerging, unanticipated events make the plan irrelevant.

In contrast, many organizations are now moving toward a leaner, more adaptive approach to annual communication planning. First, they ensure that leadership has articulated a strategy message that will serve as the focal point and common denominator for all substantive messaging throughout the year. The assumption is that, moving forward, all substantive communications to employees will either be about that strategy, or about initiatives, activities, and decisions that they can and must make sense of within the context of that strategy.

Then, for the purposes of communication plan viability and message continuity, they plan in advance how they will stagger major communication activities—especially those that will require significant leadership involvement (for example, town hall meetings, formal cascades, etc.)—throughout the course of the coming year. They will also create a timeline for how to appropriately stagger the use of their other vehicles in the support of message continuity. What they will not do is create a lot of specific messaging and detailed planning for the second through fourth quarters of the year—since they expect that needs and nuances will change in ways they cannot anticipate. What they do know is that (1) they planned in advance to have available an appropriate mix of vehicles into which they can plug messages as needs warrant; (2) they will make sense of whatever it is the organization is talking about within the context of a core strategy message.

It is much easier to develop an annual communication plan if senior leadership has played an active role in articulating their strategic communication objectives. This allows employee communicators to pursue their proactive planning with much more discipline and rigor. They might ask themselves, for example, "We're planning on two all-hands forums, one in March and one in September. Are we putting them in next year's plan because we always do all-hands forums in March and September, and it's simply a tradition? Or are we planning those meetings because the investment of time, money, and energy that goes into them will have an impressive return on investment as it relates to accomplishing our senior leaders' 'know, believe, and do' goals?"

> Given the speed with which employees can communicate with one another, organizations that do not rapidly and credibly respond to emergent communication needs and opportunities cede control of the message to the rumor mill.

Responsive Communication Processes. Many organizations have found that fast and effective responsive communication processes are at least as important as their proactive communication planning activities. Given the speed with which employees can communicate with one another, organizations that do not rapidly and credibly respond to emergent communication needs and opportunities cede control of the message to the rumor mill.

In organizations with highly effective responsive communication processes, one will expect to find:

⇒ Active feedback and radar monitoring—with emphasis on preemption where possible

⇒ Responsive communication activities driven by explicit identification of know / believe / do goals

⇒ Relevant subject matter expertise quickly identified and "brought to the table"

⇒ Clear, credible, timely approval processes

⇒ A catalog of past responses so there are repeatable, efficient, streamlined processes for future activities

⇒ A checkpoint in planning process to formally or informally pretest message/strategy

⇒ A checkpoint in planning process to consider unintended message effects

⇒ A clear process for integrating with internal/external communication strategy

⇒ Clear leadership accountability for and sponsorship of responsive communication efforts/events

⇒ Thoroughly prepared and vetted Q&As that anticipate every reasonable question.

3. Media

Many organizations operate with vehicles that have emerged from tradition ("we've always had a four-color publication, so let's keep it going") or technology ("every department can now have its own Web site ... so we should"). By contrast, best-practice organizations rationalize their portfolio of vehicles against actual needs. With a rationalized portfolio of vehicles, the employee communication function can explain the unique and necessary role that each vehicle plays in accomplishing leadership's strategic communication objectives.

In organizations with highly effective employee communication, the vehicle portfolio typically includes:

⇒ A diversity of media and channels capable of communicating the full range of strategic and tactical information to all key audiences
⇒ Clear ownership of, and widely understood guidelines for using each vehicle
⇒ A centralized, readily accessible repository of vehicle templates/tools and guidelines.

Lean Media (For Example, Memos, Fact Sheets). Best-practice organizations have clear decision rules for when to use their lean media—and when to push information (via e-mail, for example) or merely make it available via a pull vehicle (the intranet). They also have streamlined production and approval processes.

According to CRA's Jeff Grimshaw, one challenge that many employee communication shops face is that their writers actually want to write. "Unlike most of the people with whom they went to college, the folks on the communication staff can actually string four grammatically correct sentences together into a coherent paragraph. But most employees today aren't inclined or don't have the time to read a lot of prose, no matter how elegantly it's constructed. So it's sometimes disheartening to good writers when they learn that they can deliver communication products faster—and produce a higher rate of assimilation among their targeted audience—when they stick with simple bullet points and lots of white space."

E-mail overload is another challenge. Employees in many organizations find it increasingly difficult to sort through their e-mail and extract what is of relevance. Accordingly, many employee communication shops and the leaders they are supporting often think they have delivered a particular message to an audience (because they sent an e-mail memo) when, effectively, they have not. To combat this issue, an increasing number of organizations are developing new information standards or "noise control" ordinances. Unfortunately, many organizations are findings that while implementing

> Unlike most of the people with whom they went to college, the folks on the communication staff can actually string four grammatically correct sentences together into a coherent paragraph. But most employees today aren't inclined or don't have the time to read a lot of prose, no matter how elegantly it's constructed.

information-sharing standards is easy, holding people accountable to them is not.

Rich Media (Face-to-Face). While lean media (especially e-mail) is the most convenient medium for delivering information to employees, it is not the most effective for conveying and interpreting strategic information. For strategic content, there is no substitute for "rich" (face-to-face) media.

In best-practice organizations, one finds an emphasis on leadership visibility—with a healthy balance between the visibility of senior and local-level leadership. These organizations also emphasize two-way communication and ensure that their rich media channels afford ample opportunity for upward communication.

4. Feedback and Metrics

Highly effective organizations use a variety of methods to inventory emergent communication needs and opportunities that warrant attention; determine which current communication efforts are working, which are not, and why; and inform decision making about how to improve internal communication moving forward. The "best-practice toolbox" for feedback and metrics includes the following components:

> For strategic content, there is no substitute for "rich" (face-to-face) media.

Anticipatory Scan. Employee communication leads should have a tool, and a deliberate process, for tracking and surfacing with leadership the issues and opportunities that may warrant a strategic communication response. CRA has found that implementing this type of radar tool and process is an effective way for would-be strategists to create immediate value for leaders and secure the "seat at the table."

CRA's "Flight Panel" is a tool that communication leads use to capture emergent issues and opportunities across several "radars" or categories. (Like an aviation flight panel, it highlights key data about an organization's present position as well as what is ahead.) These categories include key decisions/leadership activities, employee rumors and concerns, progress/milestones/success stories, and external issues that warrant internal coverage.

The Flight Panel facilitates a structured approach to communication leads' discussions with leadership. When reviewing the Flight Panel with leadership (in a staff meeting, a one-on-one, or some other setting), the communication lead does two things:

⇒ Says to leadership: "Here's what I'm tracking. What am I missing?"
⇒ Highlights key items on the Flight Panel, and offers his or her analysis and recommendations for a strategic communication response. ("Key" items are usually those where the recommended response requires leadership's approval and/or direct participation.)

Pretesting. It is common for organizations to send unintended messages, even when communications are carefully prepared. For example, employees are always "reading between the lines" when the organization announces key personnel changes or restructuring. Best-practice employee communication shops put in place the capacity to quickly test a communication product with the intended audience (employees who have not participated in crafting the communication piece) to assess how employees will interpret it, the unintended messages they will read into it, and what to do about it.

Measures of Communication Effectiveness. Like everyone else, employee communicators have to fight for the ear of senior management and for budget dollars. Delivering robust, credible, and relevant measures of communication effectiveness is perhaps the surest way to gain respect for employee communication—and demonstrate the predictive link between communication activities and business performance. These measures can include:

⇒ Survey measurements of progress against senior leadership's strategic communication objectives. To what extent do employees understand, believe, and do what we want them to understand, believe, and do? And why?
⇒ Leadership communication and credibility. Perhaps the most compelling approach to measuring leadership communication and credibility comes from Larkin and Larkin. In *Communicating Change*, they offered their counter-conventional argument for a one-item survey that asks only: "How would you rate the quality of communication between you and your immediate leader?" While we are not fans of lengthy surveys, we recommend doubling the length of the survey by adding a second question that asks "Why?"
⇒ Informal quick pulse (following communication activity, event, etc.). Every employee communication function should have a simple process for providing feedback to leadership after certain "command performances" (e.g., "town halls" or important presentations). Given the investment of time, money, and energy that goes into preparing for these efforts, we want to make sure we're continually assessing their success and extracting "lessons learned."

CRA recommends a "next-day feedback process" that involves conducting an informal pulse check following a "command performance" activity, and then synthesizing and sharing the information with leadership within twenty-four hours. According to one practitioner who has adopted this approach, "We've found that leaders are more likely to assimilate our feedback if we provide it to them within twenty-four hours. It also helps to position us as a rigorous and disciplined business function in their eyes."

Measures of Vehicle Effectiveness. Many organizations continue to use some iteration of the traditional communication audit to provide a periodic evaluation of their vehicle portfolio, including audience use and preferences. Historically, however, the communication audit report often becomes the research deliverable most likely to gather dust on a bookshelf (sometimes because those involved lack the appetite to take out the vehicles that the audit results say are no longer providing sufficient value). Accordingly, organizations are increasingly looking for ways to marry their vehicle effectiveness research with their overall communication effectiveness research.

Client-Focused Metrics. More and more communication shops are measuring the perceptions and satisfaction of the leaders they serve. The questions asked in these surveys can help to create dialogue with leaders about the strategic role that employee communicators want to play—and the impediments to securing a "permanent seat at the leadership table."

5. Content

There is no sense in putting in place the right people, processes, media, and metrics related to employee communication without the right content, and so a discussion of best practices must include the following topics:

The Strategy Message. Employee communication becomes much easier and significantly more effective when there is a clear, simple, and single strategic message or set of core themes that drives all content development. Unfortunately, in many organizations, there are as many as a dozen "North Star" messages—and many of them are couched in aspirational language that employees perceive, at best, as esoteric and irrelevant. By contrast, an effective strategy message is simple enough that anyone can understand it, universal enough that it applies to everyone, actionable at all levels of the organization, and describes what the organization is doing and why. In addition, it should fit clearly within the larger message hierarchy (see the message hierarchy sidebar).

Convincing Decisions. Highly effective employee communications shops (and the leaders they support) recognize that "actions speak louder than words." Accordingly, they anticipate and manage the implicit messages and symbolism conveyed by leaders' decisions and actions. And they explicitly position all leadership decisions and actions as "convincing decisions" or "proof points" that reflect the strategy message in action. Explicitly linking actions with the strategy demonstrates that the strategy is real, thereby encouraging employees to align their own efforts with it. It also helps employees to make sense of what is going on around them, even when leadership makes decisions and takes actions (consistent with the strategy) that have unpleasant consequences. (For example, communicating a layoff

> Communicating a layoff is never fun, but positioning it within the context of an existing and widely understood strategy will always make the effort easier and more effective.

is never fun, but positioning it within the context of an existing and widely understood strategy will always make the effort easier and more effective.)

Additionally, the employee communications function must ensure that reward and recognition systems send messages consistent with the strategy. This is sometimes difficult, since HR or some other entity outside of employee communication typically administers those programs. The key is to help leadership become more sensitive to the implicit and explicit messages conveyed by the organization's reward and recognition activities.

Local-Level Interpretation and Probabilities. Perhaps what made Larkin and Larkin's work seminal was the clarity and strength of their case for recognizing local-level leaders as their direct reports' preferred information sources, and equipping them with privileged information that allows them to operate effectively in this role.

Larkin and Larkin pointed out that local-level leaders tend not to want to share information provided to them in the form of poetically constructed prose. Instead, they want straightforward bullet points that provide non-spin answers to the "So what?" and "What does this mean to me?" questions that employees are bound to ask (provided they think their immediate leader may actually possess some insights).

Larkin and Larkin also pointed out that uncertainty is often more damaging than bad news—and that while leaders often pretend they have the luxury of deciding whether there should be communication about particular topics of a sensitive nature, leaders only get to decide whether they are going to actively participate in the communication that is already occurring. Toward that end, they recommended communicating probabilities in the midst of uncertainty, assigning the outcomes about which employees are speculating into one of five categories: "What will definitely happen," "probably happen," "we do not know," "probably will not happen," and "definitely will not happen."

* * * * *

Quality Assurance. Throughout this chapter, we have focused on the ways the employee communication function has changed. What has not changed is the continuing need for quality assurance standards; specifically:

⇒ Clearly articulated and understood guiding values/principles (for example, objectivity, honesty, accuracy, consistency, etc.)

⇒ Clearly articulated and adopted writing/usage/editing standards and checklists (e.g., single unifying point, active voice, brevity, etc.)

⇒ A heavy emphasis on simple, unadorned facts—especially in written communication and when conveying "bad news"

Maximize Your Message through Media Selection

By Sharyn Bearse,
Bearse Communications

Today's communicators have an unprecedented number of tools with which to work. This means that savvy communicators must be skilled at selecting exactly the right media to assure maximum message penetration across their target audience. Below is a list of the pros and cons of using the most prevalent communications media available today. The key to success, however, is to fully understand your audience's communications preferences so that the mix is not hit and miss, but based on solid communications research and principles. One tip: make sure you have one "anchor" communications media—the place where employees instinctively look to find out what is going on in the organization.

Print: An old workhorse and useful today. Pros: Print has staying power; what is printed today is there tomorrow. It is portable; people can read at their convenience without carrying devices and worrying about connectivity. In addition, reading often helps people better retain certain information, especially that which has been previously communicated verbally. Cons: Takes time to produce, can be expensive, and requires a distribution system. In addition, because of print's "lasting" power, management may be cautious about putting certain information "in concrete." Types of print communications include:

Magazines/Employee Annual Reports: Useful to communicate longer information, such as in-depth overviews, interviews, or opinions. Can almost be works of art in terms of design, use of images, and layout. People tend to keep magazines and also share them with others, such as family, friends, and neighbors. Do not use if timely communications are the goal. Magazines are expensive to produce and take long lead times.

Newspapers and Newsletters: Newspapers and newsletters usually carry a variety of information, designed for readers to skim for articles that interest them. Both can be produced faster and more inexpensively than magazines. For example, a two-page newsletter can be written, edited, duplicated on economical copier paper, and distributed to audiences in just a few hours.

Magapapers: This hybrid of a newsletter and magazine offers many of the advantages of a magazine in terms of layout, images, and design as well as ability to offer in-depth features combined with shorter articles for skimmers. While not as easy and inexpensive to produce as a newsletter, it often offers cost savings compared to magazines. That is why most of the corporate world has deep-sixed magazines in favor of magapapers.

Posters, Flyers, Brochures: Use as reminders about events or to drive people to main communications vehicle for more information about an issue.

Books: Use when permanence is required and you want to distribute to a large audience (at least 50,000) to mark a significant event, product, or anniversary. Because so few organizations publish books today, this will grab the attention of your audience and convey the importance of the event. Be prepared: this is a long, laborious, expensive undertaking. Hire a pro to guide you through.

Face-to-Face: This ranks as the most effective communications medium on the planet. Want proof? Business spends huge sums fielding sales forces, politicians endure grueling public speaking schedules to win votes, and educational institutions employ legions of teachers. Would so many devote so much if there were little return? Pros: Helps build employee trust in the organization's leaders. Wise communicators find ways to encourage employees to speak out at such sessions so that leaders get a good feel for the pulse of the organization. Cons: The speaker/leader must be good on his/her feet for full success.

Press-Conference Style: This versatile approach provides an excellent venue for top management to share information, visions, strategies, or report on the state of the business. Sessions can be carefully staged theater, taking months to organize, or quickly produced in a cafeteria or conference room to meet a pressing communications need. Prudent communicators often build entire communications programs around such events, producing associated media to drive the leader's presence and message into the organization.

Small Groups/Cascades: Use the small group approach for learning or problem solving. The structure can range from formal with an agenda to an informal chat at a meal. A cascade is best used to communicate major shifts in strategy, visions, or goals. The information flows from the top, as each leader presents the information to the level of leaders under him or her, until everyone, at every level, has had a chance to participate in a session.

Walk Abouts: These should be scheduled on a routine basis, not just during a crisis. Seeing the chief walk, talk, and listen helps boost employee morale and underscores the importance of day-to-day operations. It also gives management an opportunity to sense any burgeoning problems or rumors.

Digital: It is hard to keep up with the various media in the digital world because they change so fast, and will continue to do so as communications vehicles get smaller, more connected, and more powerful. Pros: Allows for maximum creativity in use of multiple media so that employees can choose the media that works best for them. For example, no time to watch the video, simply print off a text version to read at leisure. Good audiovisuals work almost as well as face-to-face to deliver messages and information. <u>Cons</u>: No permanence. In addition, some groups in an organization, for example, floor manufacturing employees, might not have access to the communications technology other groups have.

<u>Internet/Intranet</u>: This is the backbone of today's communications structure. Audiences should feel confident that the first place to turn for breaking news and important corporate information is your Web site. Both your Web sites—internal and external—must be current, attractive, and easy to use. Engineer a "template" method by which messages can be posted instantly, without waiting for the "techies" to show up.

<u>E-mail</u>: Allows for immediate and broad dissemination of news or information. E-mail is economical and versatile. The message can be a short few sentences about a promotion, or a longer, more complex announcement with an accompanying link to a Web page. Most e-mail systems have the ability to target employee groups—that is, level, payclass, geography, division—so that you can send custom-tailored messages to appropriate groups.

<u>Sight and Sound</u>: Whether it is through the Web or on DVD, video is the next best thing to being there. Using sight, sound, and motion can give immediate impact and leave long-lasting impressions. Because DVDs are small and easy to mail, consider using this format when you want employees' families to access the information as well as employees.

<u>Telephone Messages</u>: Do not neglect this older technology because a voice adds a personal touch that e-mail cannot deliver. Your telephone message system can route targeted group messages just like your e-mail system. Many top executives chose to send regular personal telephone messages to their organizations, rather than impersonal e-mails.

<u>Chat Rooms/Blogs</u>: This is information by, for, and of the people. Discard the notion that an organization can control the flow of information to its members. Those days are long gone. At minimum, monitor what your employees are saying to gain a sense of what they are thinking, feeling, or believing. At maximum, harness the human need for communication and sharing by establishing official chat rooms. For example, connect the problem-solving capabilities of your entire engineering staff by allowing them to post technical problems and seek help from engineers across your organization. Be really bold and have your CEO or other top executive start a blog that employees can read regularly.

Best Practices in Employee Communication

1. The best shops stick to the classic public relations process: research, planning, communication, and evaluation.
2. The lead employee communicator (VP, director, or manager) has access to the organization's senior leadership team.
3. The employee communicators are seen by senior leadership as trusted advisers.
4. The communicators articulate and promulgate a communication strategy and objectives that directly support the business or organizational objectives.
5. The communicators inventory, profile, and prioritize their employee audiences.
6. They rationalize their portfolio of vehicles against actual needs and can explain how each vehicle contributes to the strategic communication objectives.
7. They pretest messages.
8. They have a deliberate process for tracking, with the organization's senior leadership, the issues and opportunities that may warrant a strategic communication initiative.

Resources for Further Study

Blogs

CommLog: A weblog devoted to the strategy and practice of communication inside organizations. http://www.crainc.com/commlog.

IABC Cafe (blog): International Association of Business Communicators gathering place for professional communicators. http://blogs.iabc.com/chair/.

Presentation Zen blog: Garr Reynolds blog on issues related to professional presentation design. http://presentationzen.blogs.com/presentationzen/.

Books

Gergen, D. *Eyewitness to power: The essence of leadership Nixon to Clinton*. New York: Simon & Schuster, 2000.

Gladwell, M. *Tipping point: How little things can make a big difference*. New York: Little, Brown, 2000.

Larkin, T.J., and S. Larkin. *Communicating change*. New York: McGraw-Hill, 1994.

Levine, R., C. Locke, and D. Searls. *Cluetrain manifesto: The end of business as usual*. New York: Perseus, 2000.

Maister, D.H., C.H. Green, and R.M. Galford. *Trusted advisor*. New York: Touchstone, 2000.

Stack, J., and B. Burlingham. *The great game of business*. New York: Doubleday, 1992.

Questions for Further Discussion

1. The discordant relationship between human resources and public relations that exists in many companies has been tolerated for so long that it may seem unimportant to the companies. Is it?

2. The results are in: Organizations that are more communicative have larger amounts of reputational capital. Has this made the day-to-day fight for transparent, meaningful employee communication any easier?

3. Do most corporate communication departments segment their employee audiences by job demographics and psychographics? Does yours?

4. Do most employee communicators follow the classic PR process—research, planning, communication, and evaluation—or do they get lost in the frenetic rush of daily communications? What does your organization do?

5. Hallmark has published a newsletter each workday for over fifty years. Could this have happened in a company with little commitment to building the employee constituency?

CHAPTER 6

Government Relations

By Ed Ingle,

Managing Director of Government Affairs, Microsoft Corporation

> *Man is by nature a political animal.*
>
> – Aristotle

You Snooze, You Lose

In March 1990, the Energy and Commerce Committee of the U. S. House of Representatives was holding a late night, closed-door session on proposed clean air legislation. Chairman John Dingell of Michigan—one of the longest-serving members of Congress—presided over the powerful committee.

It was near midnight and the negotiations had bogged down over a key issue—how to cost-effectively reduce emissions from power plants to address acid rain pollution in the Northeast. In particular, the discussion focused on how to divvy up the new emission allowances or "credits" among the nation's largest coal-burning utilities, primarily located in the Midwest. The proposed legislation capped emissions by allocating a fixed number of credits to the largest emitting plants. Each credit represented one ton of emissions. The more credits a utility received, the more it could legally pollute. As a result, the credits became a very valuable commodity.

On this particular evening, scores of utility lobbyists and their "hired guns" (i.e., lobbying consultants and lawyers) were huddled outside the closed-door session in the foyer of the Rayburn building. Every hour or so, members and committee staff would emerge from the hearing room only to be swarmed by the lobbyists hoping to make a last-minute case for more "credits" and to hear the latest results of the negotiations.

Bob Schule, former White House legislative aide to President Jimmy Carter and then partner in the Washington lobbying firm, Wexler, Reynolds, Fuller, Harrison and Schule,[1] was on hand with his colleague, Ed Ingle, then a twenty-nine-year-old associate and former program analyst at the Office of Management and Budget in the Reagan White House. Ingle had been with the Wexler firm for less than a year and was getting valuable on-the-job training on the lobbying trade. Schule and Ingle were representing Ohio Edison, a large Midwestern utility.[2] They were joined by Bob McWhorter, senior vice president of Ohio Edison, and Bob Giese, another lobbying consultant to Ohio Edison.

Sometime after midnight, a corporate lobbyist from another large Midwestern utility, who had been sitting on the gray marble floor in the corner of the foyer, slumped over in exhaustion from the long day. His deep sleep caught the attention of many of those nearby—when suddenly Giese shouted out, "Quick, grab that guy's credits!" The foyer erupted with laughter and the startled corporate lobbyist was jarred from his sleep.

The life-long lesson for Ingle that night on Capitol Hill was this: only those companies who are present and engaged in the policy-making process in Washington will reap the benefits of their efforts. Those not present—or not paying attention—will pay the price of not having a sound corporate government relations function. In other words, "you snooze, you lose."

* * * * *

This Chapter Covers

⇒ What is government relations?
⇒ Case for a centralized government relations function
⇒ Organizing the government relations function
⇒ Understanding the key audiences
⇒ Sidebar: A profile of reputation and integrity
⇒ Setting the company's government relations agenda
⇒ Success and expectations management
⇒ Role of third-party advocacy
⇒ Role of the lobbying consultant
⇒ Role of political contributions
⇒ State and international government relations
⇒ Ethics in lobbying
⇒ Eleven best practices

What Is Government Relations?

Few professions can point to the U.S. Constitution as the basis for their existence. Many are surprised to find that the lobbying profession is one of the few. In fact, you need only look as far as the First Amendment to see the eight words that serve as the basis for this vocation:

"Congress shall make no law respecting an establishment of religion, or prohibiting the free exercise thereof; or abridging the freedom of speech, or of the press, or the right of the people peaceably to assemble, and to <u>petition the Government for a redress of grievances</u>."[3]

> *Lobbying* is the practice of advocating one's policy position to government officials with the hopes of influencing legislation, regulation, or other government action.

Lobbying can take a variety of forms. Meeting with a member of Congress, a congressional staffer, or an executive branch official to influence public policy is a direct form of lobbying. Phone or written communications

> Few professions can point to the U.S. Constitution as the basis for their existence.

(e.g., via letter, e-mail, or fax) to these same decision makers are also regarded as direct lobbying.

However, lobbying can also be deployed indirectly. A "grassroots" campaign that encourages constituents of a given congressional district or state to write a letter, send an e-mail, or make a phone call to a member of Congress or Senator can be an effective form of indirect lobbying.

> *Government relations* is a broader term that includes all forms of lobbying and nonlobbying activities that have the ultimate goal of influencing public policy.

For example, providing strategic counsel on political and policy matters to corporate executives is not lobbying, nor is managing the company's political action committee, but both can be important parts of an overall government relations function. Government relations is sometimes referred to as government affairs, and more broadly, public affairs. Regardless of the label, government relations is an important function within a corporation, and lobbying is at the heart of this function.

The lobby of the historic Willard Hotel on Pennsylvania Avenue in Washington, D.C., is thought to be where the term "lobbyist" was first coined in the 1870s during President Ulysses Grant's administration. After a long day in the Oval Office, President Grant would frequently escape the pressures of the presidency with a brandy and a cigar in the Willard lobby, where he was approached by people seeking his ear on a given issue. Grant called these people "lobbyists."[4] The term subsequently became associated with individuals who seek out legislators in the lobby or hallway outside of a legislative chamber or meeting place.

Lobbyists can work for a corporation, trade association, law firm, lobbying consulting firm, interest group, or other organization. A lobbyist—particularly a corporate lobbyist—is sometimes referred to as a Washington representative or "Washington Rep" in lobbying parlance. Almost every business or political interest is represented by one or more lobbyists in our nation's capital—interests as varied as agriculture, transportation, energy, education, technology, healthcare, women's rights, abortion rights, gun owners, labor, snack food, florists, and pest management.

The first lobbying law was enacted by Congress in 1946, and required the registration of lobbyists, their employers, and their expenses. In 1995, Congress passed the Lobbying Disclosure Act (LDA), which expanded the definition of a lobbyist and greatly tightened reporting requirements. Under the LDA, lobbyists and/or an organization must file semiannual reports disclosing the specific issues they work on, any interests by foreign

Table 6.1 Top Fifteen Corporate Lobbying Spenders (1998–2004)

1.	Altria Group Inc.	$101,220,000
2.	General Electric Co.	$94,130,000
3.	Northrop Gruman Corp.	$83,405,691
4.	Verizon Communications Inc.	$81,870,000
5.	ExxonMobil Corp.	$59,672,742
6.	SBC Communications Inc.	$58,035,037
7.	Freddie Mac	$57,740,000
8.	Boeing Co.	$57,138,310
9.	Lockheed Martin	$55,373,840
10.	AT&T	$53,349,499
11.	Fannie Mae	$50,777,000
12.	General Motors Corp.	$48,260,000
13.	Sprint Corp.	$47,276,585
14.	Microsoft Corp.	$46,020,000
15.	Pfizer Inc.	$43,522,720

Source: The Center for Public Integrity

Author's Note: At the time this chapter was written, Congress was considering further amendments to the Lobbying Disclosure Act as a result of the Jack Abramoff lobbying scandal of 2005–06. Any subsequent changes to the LDA can be found on the Web sites of the American League of Lobbyists (http://www.alldc.org) and the Center for Public Integrity (http://www.publicintegrity.org).

> It is critical for an organization to speak with one voice on all government relations matters.

agencies or businesses in their lobbying activities, and estimates of their lobbying expenses.[5] Company and organization expenses on federal lobbying from 1998 to 2004 approached $13 billion (the top corporate spenders are shown in Table 6.1). In 2004 alone, expenses were about $3 billion.[6]

Case for a Centralized Government Relations Function

Similar to the case for a centralized media relations function covered in Chapter 3, it is critical for an organization to speak with one voice on all government relations matters.

It is not uncommon for corporate executives to know a number of state and federal policymakers. In fact, these relationships can be quite beneficial to the company and generally should be encouraged. The company's government relations operation should inventory the relationships of its executives and midlevel managers, and seek to nurture them where possible. However, there is the potential for tremendous risk to the company's policy objectives if the communications with these political contacts are not closely monitored and coordinated by a central function.

At any given time, an organization or company may have numerous policy issues before Congress and the executive branch. Some of these issues may fall under the jurisdiction of the same congressional committees or executive branch officials. For instance, a large U.S. company with interests in trade policy may find itself working closely with the House Ways and Means Committee on a trade agreement before Congress. Meanwhile, the company's tax department may have an important tax issue before the same committee. If two parts of a company are talking to the same committee without coordinating through its government relations office, both policy objectives could suffer. Worse, the company risks being perceived by the committee as unorganized and unreliable, which may jeopardize the company's objectives on future policy matters.

Even very savvy and capable corporate executives and managers should not assume that they can navigate the rocky shoals of politics and policy formulation. What may seem a simple phone call, letter, e-mail, or conversation at a social gathering with a government official should not be taken lightly. Government officials may be looking for an endorsement of their idea, legislative proposal, or policy initiative that could contradict other policy objectives of the company or alienate other industry allies.

> But companies like Microsoft have learned that a "Washington presence" is critical to its overall business.

It is worth noting that some organizations may question the need for a government relations function altogether. But companies like Microsoft have learned that a "Washington presence" is critical to its overall business, and that it pays to engage in the policy and political debate and to have experienced government relations professionals looking out for the company's welfare. Bottom line: a company or organization should integrate government relations into its business plan and ensure that its efforts are coordinated and strategic.

Organizing the Government Relations Function

Government relations can reside within a number of broader functions within a corporation, including:

⇒ Legal
⇒ Communication or Public Relations
⇒ Corporate Affairs
⇒ A business unit

The location of a government relations function is driven by a number of factors, such as how a company is regulated or potentially regulated by the federal government and the enforcement exposure of a company by regulatory agencies (e.g., Federal Trade Commission, Environmental Protection Agency, Federal Communications Commission, or Food and Drug Administration). Oftentimes, a company that has heavy regulatory or enforcement exposure will locate government relations within the corporate legal department. However, in response to this same regulatory and enforcement exposure—and the likelihood of resulting communication challenges—it also is not uncommon for the government relations function to be located within the communication department.

In some companies, the government relations function falls under the corporate affairs (or public affairs) department. Corporate affairs can serve as a general catch-all for a number of functions, including government relations, communication, and community affairs. Government relations can also reside under a particular business unit of a corporation, especially in companies where that business unit may have its own unique exposure to regulatory and/or enforcement activity.

Regardless where the government relations office resides, it is imperative that there be close coordination with the communication function, both proactively on the company's policy objectives, and reactively to unexpected circumstances as they arise.

The configuration of government relations offices within an organization also varies, and is often dictated by the types of issues a company faces, the size of the operation, and the management style of the head of government relations and the needs of his or her superiors. A corporate government relations function typically covers federal, state, and local affairs. Increasingly, larger companies with overseas operations and/or customers are adding international affairs coverage to their government relations functions. Most medium to large companies will have a government affairs office in Washington, D.C., which will house the federal affairs operations, but may also include the state and international affairs functions. (State and international government affairs are covered later in this chapter.) Smaller companies will maintain a government affairs function at their corporate headquarters, which could include as few as one or two people.

A Washington government affairs office for a Fortune 100 company, for example, may include five to ten employees (although a few offices may have as many as twenty to forty employees if the company is heavily regulated or has diverse subsidiaries). The office will usually be led by a vice president, senior vice president, or managing director, who will report to the general counsel or top senior government affairs, communication, or corporate affairs executive back at headquarters. A VP or director of legislative affairs may oversee the office's lobbying activities on the Hill, and a VP or director of regulatory affairs may oversee executive branch lobbying.

Within these offices, you likely will find a combination of political and issue-specific lobbyists. For example, each lobbyist may manage a certain portfolio of issues that he or she will lobby on Capitol Hill and/or in the executive branch. Some offices may divide its lobbying portfolio by the two sides of the Hill and the executive branch; for example, a House lobbyist, Senate lobbyist, and executive branch lobbyist. Some may have a lobbyist for each political quadrant on the Hill, for example, a House Republican, House Democrat, Senate Republican, and House Democrat.

Understanding the Key Audiences

For any government relations office in Washington, there are two distinct audiences: Congress and the executive branch. Although they both consist of critical policymakers, these audiences could not be more different in many respects. Congress comprises Senators and House members elected every six or two years, respectively, whose number one goal generally is to get reelected.

The president, the White House, and the political appointees within the cabinet agencies also care about broad public sentiment, reelections (albeit limited to two four-year terms), and the congressional elections which dictate whether a president's party might control the House or Senate. However, they are less moved by the individual voter. As such, the dynamic of how they are lobbied is quite different. For example, one hundred individual voters writing letters to the Department of Health and Human Services about a Medicare provision will not demonstrably change how the HHS secretary will think about that issue. On the other hand, one hundred voters from the district back home writing to a congressman—particularly one who serves on the Ways and Means Health Subcommittee—may indeed have an impact on how that member views the issue and advocates for it in the Congress and with the administration.

> But a career employee cares less about politics and more about implementing the laws Congress passes.

Further, political appointees within the executive branch are a mere fraction of the overall federal workforce. While political appointees admittedly occupy the most senior positions within the administration, there are only about 3,000 of them across the federal government among the millions of federal employees. A senior federal career employee is naturally interested in helping the president accomplish his agenda. But a career employee cares less about politics and more about implementing the laws Congress passes via regulation and administering the federal programs under his or her jurisdiction. Lastly, each agency is different, and how you approach a given agency or various officials within an agency should be tailored accordingly.

Capitol Hill is also made up of a wide variety of important audiences. There are one hundred Senators, four hundred thirty-five House Members, and over 15,000 congressional staff—all of whom are associated with various committees, leadership offices, caucuses, and working groups. A successful government relations function will advance its public policy interests by building and nurturing relationships with these key audiences:

⇒ *House and Senate Leadership.* It is important to know the members and their staffs who serve in leadership positions in both bodies and on both sides of the aisle. The leadership sets the agenda for each legislative body, and determines which issues get considered and how they ultimately get resolved.

⇒ *House and Senate Committees.* Most policy priorities of a company will likely fall under the jurisdiction of a handful of committees. These committees are responsible for holding hearings, drafting legislation, making modifications, reporting legislation out of committee to the full House or Senate, and reconciling the differences in House–Senate conference committees. It is imperative that a company cultivate relationships and build allies with members and staff on these committees—both in the majority and minority.

⇒ *Congressional Caucuses.* There is a congressional caucus or working group on a myriad of policy issues, such as: intellectual property, agriculture, property rights, the Internet, Vietnam vets, wine, human rights, oil and gas, biotechnology, adoption, and China. These ad hoc groups are made up of members of Congress who have a personal, professional, or district-related interest with these issues. Members of these groups make great targets for building relationships around issues that are important to your company.

⇒ *Home State Senators and Representatives.* At the end of the day, the elected officials most inclined to come to a company's aid when it needs help are the members of its home state delegation. A company with a big presence in a given state or district has one thing going for it: jobs. If a company does nothing else in Washington, it must make sure it keeps its own home district Congressman and its two Senators up to date on issues of importance, and cultivate them as champions for the company.

⇒ *Congressional Staff.* The congressional staff who support the five hundred thirty-five House and Senate members are a very important part of the legislative process and should be central to any government relations strategy. This includes the personal staff in each legislator's office, as well as the committee staff. The committee staff (e.g., counsel) and personal issue-specific staff (e.g., legislative assistant) help draft the bills and brief and advise the members. Time and care should be spent in working closely with congressional staff, understanding their value to the process, respecting their relationship and influence with the members, and by all means, not end-running them or blind-siding them along the way.

At the end of the day, the elected officials most inclined to come to a company's aid when it needs help are the members of its home state delegation.

Reputation and Integrity—A Bryce Harlow Profile

One of Washington's most highly regarded corporate lobbyists was Bryce Harlow. During his forty-year career, Bryce Harlow served as a legislative aide to the House Armed Services Committee, senior legislative advisor to presidents Eisenhower and Nixon, and head of the first Washington government affairs office for Procter & Gamble from 1961 to 1978. In the foreword of the biography entitled *Bryce Harlow, Mr. Integrity*, Dr. Henry Kissinger wrote that Harlow "single-handedly created the entire modern advocacy industry."[7]

In June of 1981, about two hundred fifty of Bryce Harlow's friends and business colleagues gathered for a dinner in his honor. It was an event to mark not only his exceptional public and private service, but also his special contributions to the profession of corporate representation in Washington. The funds raised from the dinner became seed money for the Bryce Harlow Foundation, which was incorporated in 1982 as a nonprofit organization. The foundation seeks to recognize and inspire gifted leaders, in both public and private sectors, who foster high ethical standards with regard to advocacy, and to "enhance the quality of professional advocacy and increase the understanding of its essential role in the development of sound public policy."

The Bryce Harlow Foundation has continued its annual awards dinners, and the proceeds help fund educational seminars on advocacy and ethics, as well as scholarships for graduate level students interested in pursuing careers in government relations.

Vice President Dick Cheney, himself a former Bryce Harlow award recipient in 1992, was the keynote speaker at the March 2005 foundation awards dinner in Washington. In his remarks, the vice president commented on the man for whom the dinner was named: "Bryce passed away in 1987, but the foundation has carried on his legacy of service, integrity and patriotism in a way that would no doubt please him." The vice president continued, "Every day in the West Wing, I work in the office that was once Bryce Harlow's office, and he is someone I think of often. For those of you who didn't get to meet Bryce, you should know that he wasn't a famous or a physically imposing man. He used to say that it's easy to keep a low profile when you're only 5 foot 4; but when it came to knowledge about this city and the understanding of the legislative process and personal integrity and wisdom, Bryce Harlow was a man of incredible stature."[8]

Harlow's own words, published by the foundation in 1984 regarding corporate representation in Washington, ring just as true today:

> *Corporate representation is sometimes dangerous, often frustrating, and always time-consuming and difficult. It calls for an unceasing effort to educate and motivate current and potential allies—and to discourage and befuddle foes. It requires the coordination of personal visits, telephone calls, and letters from top management; the flexing of political muscle in the home districts of particularly recalcitrant members of Congress; the fine-tuning of press relations and advertising; and, throughout, a dogged determination to prevail. That may sound tedious and vexing and grim. But for the right person, corporate representation can also be fascinating, challenging, immensely satisfying, and—on balance, most of the time—fun.[9]*

Setting the Company's Government Relations Agenda

How a company sets its government relations agenda differs from company to company depending on the issues, the corporate structure, and the various personalities involved. Nevertheless, there are common elements for successful agenda setting that should be taken into consideration.

Government affairs agenda setting should not be totally top-down nor should it be only bottom-up. For example, an agenda set solely by the government relations office, without input from senior management and the business units, may be out of step with the company's most important business objectives. Conversely, an agenda set solely by senior management and/or the business units, without input from the government relations office, may not take in to consideration the realities of the current public policy and political climate in Washington. As such, a company's government affairs agenda should be the result of a healthy collaboration between the government relations function, senior management, and affected business units.

As such, a company's government affairs agenda should be the result of a healthy collaboration between the government relations function, senior management, and affected business units.

The government relations office should drive and coordinate the agenda-setting exercise given its understanding of the public policy process. The agenda should be consistent with the overall business and communication objectives of the company and should be updated annually or as changing conditions may dictate. It should take into consideration the business cycle, key lines of business, and related policy and political issues.

The government affairs agenda must also be realistic. Moving an important legislative agenda item from a draft proposal to a bill and on to final enactment can take several years in most cases. It is better to focus attention and limited resources on a realistic number of policy objectives, rather than a long list of items that will never be realized. Once set, it is the charge of the government relations office to implement the agenda. This necessarily involves developing strategy, drafting briefing materials, talking points, and conducting and/or managing the lobbying activities.

Success and Expectations Management

One of the most difficult tasks of a corporate government relations function is managing expectations within the company. Many times, success in policy and political terms to a senior executive is very different from success to a government relations office.

Politics by its very nature is the practice of the art of compromise. And in compromise, the final result almost always ends up somewhere in the middle. No one side gets everything it wants. So where politics is involved, success is not achieving the perfect, but obtaining a legislative, regulatory, or public policy result that is as close to the company's objectives as possible.

Success from issue to issue may also vary considerably. Success many times is minimizing the damage of harmful legislation that is destined to pass. After the Enron and WorldCom scandals of 2001 and 2002, Congress sought to pass tough corporate governance legislation and nothing short of an act of God was going to stop it. Therefore, success for a company during that debate was minimizing the damage of a regulatory overreach against a political backdrop that was clearly on the side of the public and not corporate interests.

On the other hand, obtaining a provision that expands the federal R&D tax credit to reduce the corporate tax burden for companies that invest heavily in research is undeniable success. But is it still success if the expanded tax credit is only approved for one year, despite the company's support for at least a three-year approval? If you are appropriately managing expectations, you bet it is. The benefits of a tax credit for one year are better than no credit at all, and the company can fight the good fight again next year to seek the tax credit's continuation.

Role of Third-Party Advocacy

Third-party advocacy has become an increasingly important tool for a company's overall government relations strategy. Medium and large companies should not only have a robust government relations operation, but they should also supplement their direct lobbying efforts through the effective use of third-party advocates. Third parties can include trade associations, coalitions, think tanks, and other interest groups which share the company's policy goals.

⇒ *Trade Associations.* Trade associations are formal organizations that generally represent companies from the same industry or "trade." Most companies are members of one or more trade associations that have a presence in Washington, D.C. Trade associations can play a vital role in a lobbying campaign by speaking with one voice on a given issue—representing numerous companies and a large, combined employee base. A company could belong to an association as large and diverse as the National Association of Manufacturers (NAM), while also belonging to more trade-specific associations such as the Business Software Alliance (an association of software companies).

Trade associations can supplement lobbying activities on an issue that is already being lobbied by individual companies, and they can also effectively serve as the sole lobbying voice in situations where companies may not wish to publicly lobby an issue. Nevertheless, a trade association cannot substitute for a company's own government relations function. On any given policy issue, a company may have unique positions on certain provisions that warrant the need for the company to lobby Congress and the executive branch in its own voice. This is a critical point that bears amplifying. Trade associations are vitally important and play a key role in a company's overall government relations function. However, companies should not rely totally on trade associations in Washington to meet their policy objectives.

⇒ *Coalitions.* Unlike trade associations, coalitions are typically more ad hoc, are established around a certain policy issue, and usually cut across multiple industries. Whereas some coalitions are created under a more formal, long-term arrangement, most coalitions are set up as temporary, informal organizations that exist only for the purpose of achieving specific policy objectives; for example, passage of class action reform legislation, corporate tax reform, immigration reform, energy security legislation, and so forth.

Member companies, and in some cases trade associations, finance coalition efforts. Those companies who pay more typically have more say over the day-to-day direction and priorities of the coalition. The funding may pay for full-time staff and/or outside government affairs consultants to manage the coalition. The coalition allows disparate companies and organizations to come together around a single cause to combine their voices for greater impact with Congress and the executive branch.

⇒ *Think Tanks.* Companies seeking to find other voices to support their views on a given policy issue may consider think tanks. A think tank is a collection of academic and government scholars, which may bring a particular political or philosophical bent to its writings and publications; for example, conservative, liberal, libertarian, or somewhere in between. They add credibility and a degree of objectivity to a debate. There are scores of think tanks in Washington. Smaller think tanks may focus on a narrow set of issues, such as defense policy, international affairs, or economic policy. Larger thinks tanks—such as the American Enterprise Institute,

Brookings, and the Heritage Foundation—support scholars who cover a wide range of issues. For example, if a particular scholar has written on the issue of energy security, a group of oil companies or its trade association may seek to cosponsor an energy-related symposium with the scholar/think tank to coincide with consideration of energy legislation before Congress.

⇒ *Grassroots Advocacy.* One of the most effective tools in a company's government relations tool box can be the use of third-party "grassroots" advocacy. Grassroots advocacy is an indirect form of lobbying in which constituents of a given congressional district or state are encouraged to write a letter, send an e-mail, or make a phone call to a member of Congress or Senator. "Grasstops" advocacy occurs when influential community leaders (e.g., local or state officials, business owners, and heads of local organizations) are targeted to communicate their feelings on an issue to their respective members of Congress, Senators, or executive branch officials.

> One of the most effective tools in a company's government relations tool box can be the use of third-party "grassroots" advocacy.

Note that corporate America was not the first to use grassroots advocacy. In fact, it was the extensive use of grassroots activities by various interest groups, such as environmental organizations, senior citizens, small business, and human rights that led companies to recognize grassroots advocacy as not only an effective tool but a necessary one. The sheer numbers of lobbying contacts made possible by a successful grassroots campaign demonstrate to lawmakers that an issue is important to their constituents and worthy of consideration.

Role of the Lobbying Consultant

A company's communication department routinely hires outside public relations consultants to supplement its work. Likewise, many companies will enlist external lobbying consultants to enhance its government relations activities and to expand its reach in Washington. Companies are hiring outside lobbyists at a record clip, according to Jeffrey Birnbaum of the *Washington Post*, who covers the lobbying industry. In a June 2005 article, Birnbaum points to a doubling in lobbying registrations from 2000 to 2005—for a total of 34,750 registered lobbyists in Washington.[10]

Debra Mayberry of Columbia Books Inc., which publishes the *Washington Representatives* directory, contends that the number of professionals who are *actively* lobbying in our nation's capital as of 2005 is actually closer to 11,500. Mayberry says that the much larger registration numbers that are reported routinely in the press are based on figures used by the U.S. Senate Office of Public Records (SOPR), which reflect a historical record of registered lobbyists, not a current record of active lobbyists. For example,

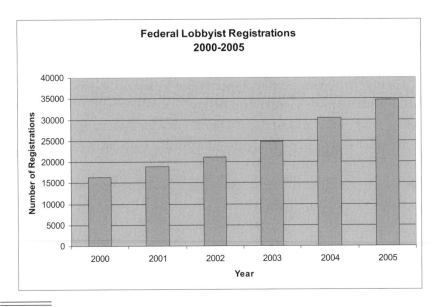

**Federal Lobbyist Registrations
2000-2005**

Figure 6.1

she notes that the SOPR does not remove registrations from its database for those lobbyists who "change careers, retire or die."[11]

Regardless of whose numbers you cite, there is no debate over the fact that the number of lobbyists in Washington has increased in recent years. One contributing factor to the increase in lobbying consultants is the declining cost of entry into the profession as a result of new communications technologies. As recent as 1995, a successful lobbyist needed a downtown office, expensive office equipment and an assistant to type memos, answer the phone, and fax materials. Today, that same lobbyist can thrive with a virtual office via a handheld communications device or "smart phone" to screen calls, receive/send e-mails, view attachments, and access the Internet—whether he or she is in the office, in a restaurant, in the car, or on the steps of the Capitol.

Meanwhile, during the same period, U.S. corporations have been under pressure to tighten their own payrolls given pressures on the economy. It is no wonder that our nation's corporations have turned to a greater use of outside lobbying consultants to help them engage in Washington and take advantage of the opportunities. According to the Center for Public Integrity, more than 22,000 companies and organizations employed 3,500 lobbying firms between 1998 and 2004.[12]

Who are these outside lobbying consultants? Some are former Senators, House members, and executive branch officials. Others are former congressional staff, White House staff, and agency staff. They may have their own one- or two-person consulting shops, or they may be part of a larger lobbying firm or law firm. Some law firms have a separate lobbying arm, composed of lawyers and nonlawyers, who handle the government relations work on behalf of clients. Other law firms have partners and associates, who may register as lobbyists and spend part of their time on government relations activities.

Lobbying firms focus exclusively on government relations services, such as: direct lobbying, strategic counseling, coalition building, grassroots activities, and government-related communication. These firms comprise lawyers, nonlawyers, and policy experts, most of whom have worked for Congress or the executive branch, or both.

Lobbying consultants help a company's overall government relations function in several important ways:

> ⇒ *Intelligence Gathering.* In Washington, as in Brussels and other capitals, information is power. The quicker you have a piece of information, the sooner you can act upon it, and your likelihood of success increases. Good consultants can greatly extend a company's "eyes and ears" capability to either help thwart bad policy or ferret out opportunities that would have otherwise gone unnoticed.
>
> ⇒ *Strategic Counsel.* There is frankly no substitute for hands-on experience when it comes to government relations. Outside consultants can clearly add depth and breadth to the company's thinking on addressing policy and political challenges and should be utilized early in a company's strategic process.
>
> ⇒ *Direct Lobbying.* Outside lobbying consultants can increase a company's "boots on the ground" capability where the tactical lobbying of members and/or staff is needed. Most important, outside consultants will invariably bring with them additional relationships with members of Congress, staff, and executive branch officials which can be leveraged on behalf of the company.
>
> ⇒ *Communication.* Some government relations consultants can also effectively supplement a company's communication function in an effort to influence government officials on a given policy issue—both in Washington and in home district media outlets. Consultants can help with message development, drafting press releases, advertorials, op-eds, and arranging for media interviews.

A company's government affairs agenda, its priority issues, and the size of its consultant budget will obviously dictate how many outside consultants it may need. It is essential that the company's internal government relations function keep the consultants current on priority issues and engaged regularly—both strategically and tactically. The company should also conduct thorough, annual reviews of its consultants to determine whether the current consultants still map well to the priority issues and are still adding value.

Outside consultants can clearly add depth and breadth to the company's thinking on addressing policy and political challenges and should be utilized early in a company's strategic process.

Finally, a company should not only ensure that it follows the letter of the law and the rules that govern lobbying activities, but it should also insist that its outside consultants do the same.

Role of Political Contributions

Like it or not, it costs a lot of money to run a House or Senate campaign. Costs are driven by television and radio advertising buys, telemarketing, direct mail, staffing expenses, and political and media consultants. Campaign costs for a U.S. House seat in a contested race can easily exceed $1 million. Costs for running a U.S. Senate campaign can exceed $20 million. Short of major reform in the current political campaign system, these costs will continue to escalate.

Consequently, companies must decide how and whether to participate in the political contribution process. Since federal law prohibits corporate donations to candidates, the only legal option for a company is to establish a political action committee (PAC). Some companies question the need for a PAC, which is money raised through personal, voluntary donations from employees of a company or organization. However, many companies with a Washington presence today either have a PAC or are seriously considering it—particularly in light of the campaign finance law, the Bipartisan Campaign Reform Act (BCRA) of 2002.

BCRA's most notable achievement was ending the prior practice of corporate (and labor organization) contributions or "soft money" going to national party committees, such as the Republican National Committee, the Democratic National Committee, and the party campaign committees for the House and the Senate. Prior to BCRA, organizations and individuals could give large, unlimited soft money donations (e.g., $100,000 or $250,000) to these national party committees as long as the funds were not used to influence federal elections. However, concerns grew as the lines began to blur between the funding of "issue ads" from soft money and the ads' impact on federal political races. Under BCRA, no corporate or labor dollars can be given to these national committees (and individuals must comply with dollar limits). BCRA did preserve "hard money" contributions—personal and PAC donations going to federal candidates—which are subject to strict contribution limits.

A common misperception is that companies with PACs are able to "buy votes" of members of Congress through their donations. When you consider that donations from the largest corporate PACs are limited to $5,000 per election (e.g., primary election or general election), it is hard to believe that a Congressman, whose campaign will likely cost more than $1 million, will change his vote based on a $5,000 donation. And when you consider a Senate campaign that may cost $5 million, $10 million, or even $20 million, a $5,000 donation is clearly not a consequential amount. It is frankly this very reason why Congress and the Federal Election Commission continue to hold PACs out as a meaningful and effective way for individuals, companies, and interest groups to participate in the political process without fear of undue influence.

So if a company cannot expect its PAC to change a member of Congress' vote, then why have one at all? In today's political environment, where the costs of campaigns are so significant, a PAC demonstrates to a Senator or Congressman that the company respects the political process and realizes that it costs money to get reelected. A contribution will not change his or her vote, but it typically will give a company the opportunity to be heard on a priority issue. Most important, a PAC allows a company to support candidates who support its issues and interests.

With that said, a PAC should not substitute for personal political contributions of corporate executives. In addition to supporting the PAC, executives should be willing to show support for key federal and state elected officials, particularly those who represent the district or state where the company is located and/or has significant facilities.

State and International Government Relations

This chapter has focused primarily on how a corporation might approach the federal government relations function. Large companies are increasingly deploying state and international government affairs operations as part of their overall government relations activities. Many of the components covered in this chapter are also applicable to state and international government relations. However, it is important to note some unique aspects and the need for coordination across all activities.

State Government Relations

A presence in the state capital of a company's headquarters is an essential part of the overall government affairs function. State governments oversee a number of areas critical to most companies, such as education, transportation, communications, electricity, and tax issues. Local governments also play an important role on many of these issues. As such, corporate state and local government affairs representation is needed to oversee this function. Other professionals also may be situated around the country in state capitals, where the company may have a large employee base and/or a customer base. These representatives are there to monitor legislative activity that may impact the company and lobby state legislators, the governor's office, and agencies.

Relationships developed with state officials can also pay dividends when an official decides to run for federal office. For example, it is common for a city mayor, state legislator, state attorney general, or governor to later run for Congress. As such, coordination between the state and federal teams is important—in terms of relationship building, political giving, and legislative activity that may give rise to federal legislation.

International Government Relations

Many large companies are only now discovering the need for a presence in foreign capitals such as Brussels (EU), Tokyo, and Beijing. The rise in recent years in global competition has brought with it increasing opportunities for U.S. companies and increasing regulatory action by foreign governments. As a result, companies are beginning to hire in-country government affairs professionals, who, like their U.S. counterparts, seek to engage in the policy and political process and build relationships with key officials. Each country and government is unique, requiring a tailored approach. Once again, close coordination between the United States and the international government affairs teams is critical. Policies that start in the United States may spread to foreign capitals or vice versa and must be closely monitored. And, in cases where foreign governments are taking U.S. companies to task through regulation and enforcement, U.S. government officials—and the pressures they can potentially bring via communications with their foreign counterparts—may serve to positively impact the outcome of these issues.

Ethics in Lobbying

It takes twenty years to build a reputation and five minutes to ruin it.—Warren Buffett

Adherence to sound ethical principles is vital to the lobbying profession, despite public perception to the contrary. The vast majority of registered lobbyists are decent and principled, and they realize that the fastest way to sink one's career is to cross the ethical line and, in doing so, implicate a government official. Just as the fate of Enron's executives serves as a reminder for all corporate executives as to the importance of strong ethical behavior, Jack Abramoff does the same for lobbyists.

The following is an excerpt from the "Code of Ethics" of the American League of Lobbyists (ALL). Established in 1979 as a nonprofit organization, ALL is the national professional association dedicated exclusively to lobbying. ALL's mission is to enhance the development of professionalism, competence, and high ethical standards for advocates in the public policy arena.

Code of Ethics of the American League of Lobbyists:

Article I – Honesty and Integrity

A lobbyist should conduct lobbying activities with honesty and integrity.

Article II – Compliance with Applicable Laws, Regulations, and Rules

A lobbyist should seek to comply fully with all laws, regulations, and rules applicable to the lobbyist.

Article III – Professionalism

A lobbyist should conduct lobbying activities in a fair and professional manner.

Article IV – Conflicts of Interest

A lobbyist should not continue or undertake representations that may create conflicts of interest without the informed consent of the client or potential client involved.

Article V – Due Diligence and Best Efforts

A lobbyist should vigorously and diligently advance and advocate the client's or employer's interests.

Article VI – Compensation and Engagement Terms

An independent lobbyist who is retained by a client should have a written agreement with the client regarding the terms and conditions for the lobbyist's services, including the amount of and basis for compensation.

Article VII – Confidentiality

A lobbyist should maintain appropriate confidentiality of client or employer information.

Article VIII – Public Education

A lobbyist should seek to ensure better public understanding and appreciation of the nature, legitimacy, and necessity of lobbying in our democratic governmental process. This includes the First Amendment right to "petition the government for a redress of grievances."

Article IX – Duty to Government Institutions

In addition to fulfilling duties and responsibilities to the client or employer, a lobbyist should exhibit proper respect for the governmental institutions before which the lobbyist represents and advocates clients' interests.[13]

Government Relations Best Practices

The following are eleven best practices that a corporate government relations professional should seek to employ:

1. *Shoot Straight.* First and foremost, always tell the truth in all of your lobbying communication, oral and written. Nothing sinks your credibility faster than appearing to play fast and loose with the facts.

2. *Be Consistent.* Do not tell one congressional office one thing and another office something else. By all means, you should customize your message to take into account your different audiences (e.g., a member of the Finance Committee versus a member of the Foreign Relations Committee). However, make sure the underlying facts of your advocacy stay consistent. Members and staff—on both sides of the aisle—routinely talk to one another and compare notes.

3. *Know Your Issues.* Do your homework before you meet with a government official. Have a clear outline of the key points you want to make, and be prepared to give your thirty-minute pitch in ten minutes if the member or staff starts the meeting late or has to leave the meeting early, which is quite common. Anticipate questions ahead of time, but never shoot from the hip on an answer if you are not sure of the facts. You should not hesitate to say, "I don't know, but I'll get back to you with the answer." Also familiarize yourself with the opposition's arguments and be prepared to address them.

4. *Know Your Audience.* As part of doing your homework, you want to know before you lobby a Congressman on an education issue that he was a former teacher (or his spouse is a teacher). Likewise, you want to know before you meet with a Senator on a tax issue that she pushed through a state tax measure (e.g., Internet tax), while in a previous capacity, that conflicts with your company's position.

5. *Know Your "Ask."* A government official will want to know why you are meeting with her and what you are "asking" her to do. For example, to a House staff person you might say, "We would like the Congresswoman to consider voting for H.R. 4545 when it comes up for a vote next week in the House." Keep your "asks" to a minimum, and make sure they are realistic. If you have several "asks" of a member or executive branch official, be prepared to prioritize them.

6. *Know Your Environment.* Beyond knowing your issue and your audience, you need to be aware of the broader political and policy environment at the time of your meeting. For example, your government relations strategy may call for the introduction of a bill by a friendly member of Congress the last week before the recess. You

need to know that the Congressman during that same week might be preoccupied with fighting a base closure commission to keep a military base open in his home district, and your strategy should be modified accordingly.

7. *Offer Solutions.* There is nothing that irritates a government official more than a lobbyist who complains about an issue, but proposes no solution to the problem. Be prepared to offer up an alternative that ideally helps the member accomplish her policy objective, while minimizing or eliminating any detrimental consequences to your company.

8. *Listen.* Effectively making your pitch is only half of the equation for a successful meeting. The other half is listening effectively. Listen carefully to what the lawmaker or official is saying. For instance, "We will take a look at your issue" is very different than, "I think we can work with you on this issue." Also, listen carefully to their questions and comments and make sure you are being responsive to their exact questions or concerns.

9. *Be Adaptive.* The policy and political environment in Washington is fluid. Conditions can change without notice as a result of unfolding events that might have a direct or indirect effect on your issues. A new presidential initiative on healthcare announced in a State of the Union speech could undercut your own proposal that you had been lobbying on the Hill. In response, you will need to be able to regroup quickly and modify your strategy to reflect these changing conditions.

10. *Believe Your Own Rhetoric.* Your lobbying strategy must be based on a sound policy argument. The world's greatest political maneuvers and strategies will not carry the day for a policy argument that does not hold water. Government officials will see through a hollow argument, particularly if you do not sound convinced yourself and are not enthusiastic about your message.

11. *Play by the Rules (And Then Some).* Make it a priority to know the laws, regulations, and rules that affect you as a lobbyist—and live by them. Routinely consult an outside ethics, election law, or political legal counsel. And even if you are meeting the letter of the law, and if something does not feel right, do not do it. Always ask yourself—"would I feel comfortable with my actions being reported on the front page of the *Washington Post*, *The New York Times* or my hometown newspaper?"

Resources for Further Study

Publications

Baran, Jan Witold. *The election law primer for corporations*. American Bar Association, 2005.

Luneburg, William V. *The Lobbying manual: A compliance guide for lawyers and lobbyist*. American Bar Association, 1998.

Wolpe, Bruce C. Lobbying Congress: How the system works. *Congressional Quarterly* (1996).

Web sites

The Center for Responsive Politics, http://www.opensecrets.org.

Library of Congress, Thomas, http://thomas.loc.gov.

The White House, http://www.white house.gov.

Wikipedia, http://www.wikipedia.org.

Questions for Further Discussion

1. How significant is it to the practice of lobbying that the First Amendment expressly includes the right "to petition the government for a redress of grievances"?
2. What is the optimal relationship, if any, between the government relations and public relations functions?
3. Given the role of money in political campaigns, how important is it for a company to have a Political Action Committee (PAC) to make contributions to candidates?
4. With lobbying ethics coming under closer and closer scrutiny, how can a company lobby effectively while preserving a reputation for integrity?
5. How important is coalition building in influencing government decision makers?

CHAPTER 7

Community Relations

> *Good fences do not good neighbors make.*
>
> —Paraphrase of Robert Frost quote

Uniontown, PA, is being transformed, almost overnight, from a place where many who drove down Main Street would roll up their windows to what will soon be a showplace, a catalyst for the renewal of Fayette County, among the poorest of Pennsylvania's sixty-seven. At this writing, the town that almost died in the 1950s and 1960s with the coal mines and the birth of the strip malls is receiving a makeover of dramatic proportion: the State Theatre has been renovated and there are cultural events held frequently; more than twenty store fronts have been repaired and reopened; three churches have been whitewashed, and the bar on Main Street where the derelicts assembled has been turned into a gourmet restaurant, called 30 E. Main. It is already being frequented by local residents, as well as lawyers, doctors, and other professionals from Pittsburgh, about a ninety-minute drive away. Several high-end stores located downtown late in 2005 and more are on their way. Jobs are being created. Local professionals who have lived for years in the suburbs of Uniontown, seldom venturing downtown, now gather with town residents, as they would have in the 1950s.[1]

One man, with the All-American name of Joe Hardy, is behind it all. He is the founder of 84 Lumber, the large, national building-supplies company named after the town of Eighty Four, some twenty miles from Uniontown. The company is adding about fifty stores each year, each about ten acres large, from Maryland to Nevada. He is starring in something that many long-term residents see as surreal, more like a movie than reality. And if it were a movie, the producers would somehow have to bring back Jimmy Stewart for the lead.

Mr. Hardy talked extensively about community involvement with John Doorley, coauthor of this book, who grew up in Uniontown, watching it thrive, almost die, and now being reborn. By the time Joe Hardy is finished remodeling Uniontown, he said, he will have spent at least $20 million of his own money. Signs are popping up all over town, with greetings like "God Bless You, Joe," and one resident even proposed that Hardy's visage replace that of General George Marshall of World War II fame, who was born in Uniontown, and who was called by President Harry Truman "the great one of the age." "It's a little embarrassing," Mr. Hardy says.

The story of why Joe Hardy is rebuilding Uniontown (population 12,422), which is the county seat, is clearly an exceptional one in scope and dramatic effect. But it illustrates how and why organizations and their leaders should get involved in the community, for the benefit of both. His six principles of relationship building have made 84 Lumber the country's largest privately held building materials supplier to professional contractors; directed the way he built and runs Nemacolin Woodlands, one of America's best resorts, in the mountains overlooking Uniontown; and made him a very wealthy man. Mr. Hardy said that his principles guide his "philanthropy and community relations, just as they guide my personal and business relationships."[2]

It seems that few people know how to practice effective community relations as well as Joe Hardy: It is how he built his businesses, and helped a lot of people in the process. And while it can be said that he has a lot of money and can afford to do good things, it can also be said that he knows how to do them well. That is why the authors adopted the Hardy-centric architecture for this chapter.

$$* \quad * \quad * \quad * \quad *$$

> *Community Relations: The strategic development of mutually beneficial relationships with targeted communities toward the long-term objective of building reputation and trust.*

This Chapter Covers

⇒ Hardy's Relationship-Building Principles.
⇒ Principle #1: Be involved. Be committed.
⇒ Principle #2: Building reputation, one relationship at a time, is good business.
⇒ Principle #3: Choose the right projects. Be strategic.
⇒ Sidebar: Duke Power's centennial of service.
⇒ Principle # 4: Keep moving ahead.
⇒ Principle # 5: Embrace diversity.
⇒ Sidebar: The path to becoming a national university.
⇒ Principle # 6: When things go wrong, make them right as fast as you can.
⇒ Sidebar: Community relationships are based on trust.
⇒ Best practices.
⇒ Resources for Further Study.
⇒ Questions for Further Discussion.

> Reputation = Sum of Constituency Images = Performance and Behavior + Communication = Sum of Relationships

Hardy's Relationship-Building Principle # 1:
Be Involved. Be Committed.

Joe Hardy: "I was born on the other side of the tracks but my mother always told me I was special, like every parent should, really. And she taught me to get involved, to show up. So, over the years, no matter what I was doing in business, I always got involved, in politics and in the community. When it became clear to me a few years ago that the three county commissioners could be of tremendous help in getting things done in Uniontown and Fayette County, I campaigned for and became a commissioner in 2004—the first time I ran for public office, and I was eighty-one. I recently participated in a policy conference at Carnegie Mellon University and was asked how one makes community programs work. I tried to tell them that it is not so complicated. It is just a matter of making up your mind to do something the community needs, something you have the ability to do, and then doing it as well as possible by working with people you trust."

The transition to a more privately funded community support system caused tremendous changes in corporate community relations philosophies, staffing, and funding.

In 1954, President Dwight Eisenhower encouraged business leaders to become more involved in politics and government, and that led to the formation of the Public Affairs Council, a Washington, D.C.-based association of corporate government relations and public affairs executives who lobby for various legislative and regulatory initiatives. Beginning in 1980, when he was elected to his first term, President Ronald Reagan made sharp cuts in federal funding for social programs. The initial cuts amounted to over $11 billion and they affected, in the first year, about 57 percent of voluntary agencies. President Reagan urged the business community to make up for the cuts by getting involved, not only with philanthropic contributions but with social service programs. Specifically, he urged businesses to double their contributions and to provide social services previously provided by federal funds.[3]

"Corporate contributions soared," writes Edmund M. Burke in *Corporate Community Relations, The Principle of the Neighbor of Choice*.[4] Burke, the founding director, in 1985, of The Boston College Center for Corporate Community Relations, explains that although corporate gifts to charity rose to $4.4 billion in 1985, they could not compensate for President Reagan's $33 billion cuts. Some argue that the corporate community relations programs that ensued were more productive than the federal give-away programs. In any case, the transition to a more privately funded community support system caused tremendous changes in corporate community relations philosophies, staffing, and funding. At the same time, the pressures on companies to increase their community support initiatives were compounded by rapid increases in the number of applications community service programs made to corporations.

Companies hired community relations specialists or redeployed staff. According to Burke, similar pressures in other countries in the 1980s resulted in major community relations initiatives by corporations in the United Kingdom, Japan, the Philippines, Australia, and elsewhere.[5]

Neighbor of Choice

The new community relations model—planned involvement that meets the needs of the community and company or organization—was a response to the realization that companies and other organizations situated in a community must obtain what Burke calls a "license to operate." [6] That metaphorical license is more difficult to obtain and retain than the licenses companies actually obtain from government or other regulatory agencies. It is issued based on the written and unwritten set of expectations between the organization and the community. For example, the community will provide certain services, such as roads and other infrastructure, and the organization will work within certain rules, abiding by standards that protect the overall community and its people.

Burke writes that the best way for an organization to obtain and retain a license to operate is to become a "neighbor of choice." Much like companies that try to become an employer of choice or a supplier of choice, companies that want to achieve favored status in the community can establish programs and practices that will tend to make them, over time, neighbors of choice. In other words, the organization will adopt community relations strategies geared toward establishing not just acceptance but real trust.

"The involvement of companies in communities has changed significantly since the 1970s," Burke writes. "It has shifted in response to changing community expectations from checkbook philanthropy to a principle about the way a company should behave in a community. Companies now need to act in ways that build community trust—to become neighbors of choice."[7] (See 'Trust' sidebar by James Lukaszewski at end of this chapter.)

Hardy's Relationship-Building Principle # 2: Building Reputation, One Relationship at a Time, Is Good Business

Joe Hardy: "I realize that reputation is a popular buzzword today in business, because of the scandals, I guess. But it's strange that companies and other organizations had to be shocked into realizing that everything in life is about relationships. And isn't it true that a person's or an organization's reputation is simply the sum of the relationships that person or organization has built? I am glad that the people of Fayette County are beginning to believe in themselves again, but the main reason for a company to be involved in the community is that it is good business. Don't get me wrong: I am not going to make money off our renovation of Uniontown; I could not sell that to our accountants, because we could not prove there will be adequate financial returns. But helping the people of Fayette County get back on their feet will help everybody (individuals and businesses) over the long term. And besides, heck, if this was Montgomery County (one of Pennsylvania's wealthiest) it wouldn't be any fun."

In his seminal text, *Reputation*, Charles Fombrun of the Stern School of Business at New York University states that: "The purpose of the typical community relations department is to convey a company's benevolence, corporate citizenship and social responsiveness. Key strategies range from pro bono activities and charitable contributions to relationship building with artistic, educational, and cultural institutions. In this way, companies integrate themselves into their local communities and surround their activities with a positive halo of goodwill."[8]

Three Reputation-Building Strategies

More specifically, Edmund Burke writes that there are three strategies organizations employ to build their reputations in the community into that of a neighbor of choice:

⇒ Build sustainable and ongoing relationships with key individuals, groups, and organizations.

⇒ Institute practices and procedures that anticipate and respond to community expectations, concerns, and issues.

⇒ Focus the community support programs to build relationships, respond to community concerns, and strengthen the community's quality of life.[9]

Those three strategies are responsive to the needs of both the community and the organization. They help build the organization's reputation so that the organization can get along in the community day to day (as neighbors must); also, the strategies build reputational capital that can be drawn upon during the inevitable tough times, such as those accompanying plant accidents or layoffs.

Moreover, a good reputation benefits the company brand in immeasurable ways, including the ability to attract and retain business clients. One of the most popular (and respected) surveys of corporate reputation is *Fortune* magazine's annual Most Admired Companies survey and cover story. Inaugurated in 1984, one of the eight criteria is "social responsibility."

And besides, heck, if this was Montgomery County (one of Pennsylvania's wealthiest) it wouldn't be any fun.

Hardy's Relationship-Building Principle # 3:
Choose the Right Projects. Be Strategic.

Joe Hardy: "Nemacolin, which I purchased in 1987 and began renovating in 1988, is now a world-class resort. Guests from all over the world would often want to go down into the valley and visit what they pictured as typical small-town America. Then they would be surprised at how rundown Uniontown was. I realized that much of the problem was physical, with dilapidated buildings and so on, and it became clear to me that I could make a difference in Uniontown by doing what had made me successful: building. I had built a successful business in building materials, and, over the years, I have cultivated many relationships with builders and contractors. I know who the good ones are, the ones I can trust to do a good job. So we renovated one building after another and tore down the ones that couldn't be fixed. I think that companies, like individuals, should contribute to their communities in ways that they are good at. People who have been fortunate usually want to give something back to the community, so they can take those skills that have made their companies successful and, well, use some imagination. Great things can happen."

> So we renovated one building after another and tore down the ones that couldn't be fixed.

To guide companies and other organizations in planning and implementing their community relations programs, Burke suggests an audit of the community's needs, strengths, and weaknesses, and an assessment of the organization with respect to its community relations plans and programs. Taking those two steps can make the difference between a community relations program that, however well intentioned, fails to meet the needs of the organization and the community, and a program that helps both.[10]

Community Audit

The community audit should be geared toward producing, first, factual information including a quantification, where possible, of the community's needs, along with an examination of the community's own resources. Other companies' community resources should also be identified in order to avoid duplication. Second, the audit should include qualitative information on such things as community attitudes toward the organization as well as the kinds of relationships people in the organization have already established in the community. Third, strategic information should be included in the audit concerning opportunities and threats to the organization in the community. For instance, is there a zoning restriction that could interfere with growth plans, or a pending environmental regulation that sets unrealistic goals? What can the organization do about the threats and opportunities?

Company Assessment

The company assessment is meant to give information that can guide its philanthropic, employee volunteerism, and community partnership programs. This information is just as important as the community audit in determining an organization's ad hoc and long-term community relations strategies and programs.

Identify the Communities

Another important aspect of strategic community relations is identifying the communities important to the organization. They include the fence line and site communities, as well as the employee community, the common-interest community, and the cybercommunity. Of course organizations can only do so much, and must prioritize their community relations efforts, just as they do their business initiatives. But the point of a communities identification effort is to be sure that important communities are not being overlooked, which is to say that the communities that are the most proximal, the largest, or the loudest are not necessarily the most important.

The relationship between an organization and a community will be only as good as the two-way communication. A communication theory called General Systems Theory (see Chapter 1 sidebar) provides a framework for understanding that no constituency is an island, that communication flows between constituencies, whether it is orchestrated or accidental, and that there is no such thing as not communicating.

The Strategic Use of Corporate Philanthropy

Books have proliferated over recent years advocating the strategic use of corporate philanthropy: the targeted use of corporate philanthropy that takes advantage of the company's strengths and business interests for the benefit of certain social causes and charities. Two philanthropic marketing strategies have been employed with special effectiveness.

The American Express Company coined the term "cause-related marketing" to describe its 1983 program which encouraged use of the American Express credit card by having the company make contributions (one penny for each use of the card and one dollar for each new card issued) to the Statue of Liberty–Ellis Island Foundation.[11]

A second term, "social marketing," describes the adoption by a company of a program that clearly benefits society, while, over the long term, possibly benefiting the company. When First Alert was about to introduce its carbon monoxide detector for the home in 1992, the company learned that only 2 percent of potential customers knew that carbon monoxide leaks in the home could be a problem. The company held up on the introduction of the product and the paid advertising, while the PR people introduced a national (unpaid) carbon monoxide awareness program, consisting of briefings to health and science reporters in print and broadcast. Society benefited, with consumer awareness of the carbon monoxide threat soaring within months to 75 percent, as did the company from a timely, successful introduction of its product.[12] (See sidebar on Duke Power's program of sharing profits with the community.)

Duke Power's Centennial of Service: Reconnecting with Our Communities

By Roberta Bowman,
Vice president of External Relations and chief communications officer,
Duke Energy;

Susie Adams,
Vice president of Public and Community Affairs, Duke Power;

and Rosalind Bennett,
Communications specialist, Duke Power

On April 30, 1904, the three founders of Duke Power, the electric utility serving the central portions of North and South Carolina, ignited a sweeping change that would drive the region's economy for generations to come. They harnessed the Catawba River to generate electricity, powering the area's emerging textile industry.

The vision of Duke Power's founders went beyond the development of an integrated electric power system and the economic transformation it spawned. They wanted to "give back" to the region that nurtured their business and make the Carolinas a vital and growing area. And so they did.

Duke Power's early years exemplified financial strength, brilliant engineering, and bold dreams. Those themes continued as the company prepared for a new world of retail competition in electric markets. In 1997, Duke Power extended its reach beyond the Carolinas through its merger with PanEnergy, a leading natural gas transmission company, and the creation of parent company, Duke Energy.

Duke Energy expanded with staggering speed into a global energy giant, engaged in both regulated businesses (including Duke Power) and unregulated businesses on five continents. The once conservative, regional company transformed itself into #14 on the *Fortune 500* list in 2002. Then, just as rapidly, the competitive energy industry changed, creating challenges for Duke Energy and the industry as a whole. The fall of Enron, California's energy crisis, and the Northeast power blackouts made headlines and tested customer relationships. Trust in the industry plummeted and electric deregulation stalled. More locally, in

2002, Duke Power experienced the worst ice storm in its history, leaving virtually all of its 22,000-square mile service area without power for days. Customer satisfaction and community relationships faltered. At the same time, the economy in the Carolinas was suffering from the decline of the textile industry, as thousands of jobs moved offshore.

Against this backdrop, Duke Power was approaching its one hundredth year of business and service (2004). The company chose to celebrate in a manner consistent with its heritage and values: by giving back to others. Rather than the customary birthday party, cake and candles, Duke Power's year-long centennial became a catalyst for reconnecting with our communities and making a real and lasting impact for years to come.

The centerpiece of Duke Power's centennial was the Carolinas Competitiveness Forum (CCF), which brought together the region's political, business, educational, and social leaders to address the economic challenges of the Carolinas and spur cooperation on a multistate level. The two-day forum was a first step towards building a solid foundation for economic growth and improving the quality of life in the Carolinas. The *Charlotte Observer* wrote, "It's fitting that Duke Power is sponsoring this forum as part of its 100th anniversary celebration. Since the company opened its first dam along the Catawba River in York County in April 1904, Duke Power has helped create the region's industrial economy."

Complementing the CCF, Duke Power announced a Community and Technical College Grant Fund to support worker training and retraining efforts in the Carolinas. The grant's intent is to make college training programs more attractive to industries considering relocating or expanding in the service area.

Later in the year, Duke Power introduced a plan to share 50 percent of its North Carolina profits from its wholesale bulk power marketing division to promote economic development in the service area. The sharing proposal reduced industrial customers' power bills and provided $5 million annually over the next few years to support company programs benefiting low-income customers who need help paying their power bills, as well as the new Community and Technical College Grant Fund. A similar plan was introduced in South Carolina to support economic growth and public assistance agencies in the company's service area.

The company also worked with chambers of commerce across the service area to establish the Duke Power Citizenship and Service Awards. These local awards pay tribute to individuals or groups that make a difference in their community by contributing their time and talent.

At the grassroots level, Duke Power also shared its history through an interactive one hundredth anniversary exhibit. The exhibit traveled to history museums and science centers throughout the Carolinas during the anniversary year. The company collaborated with host facilities for local special events during the exhibit's stay in the community. The exhibit was donated to a local museum at the end of the centennial.

Duke Power saw the centennial as another opportunity to engage our employees and retirees in the celebration as well. Each year, we recognize the value of volunteerism through a worldwide Global Service Event during the month of June. The 2004 event featured "100 days of service" in recognition of the company's one-hundred-year anniversary. Employees, retirees, and their families participated in over three hundred volunteer projects in their communities—from building wildlife habitat at area schools, to entertaining senior citizens, to knitting caps for cancer patients. Additionally, a recognition program was developed to acknowledge employees and retirees who give back to their communities.

Anniversary activities took on many other forms throughout the service area, including customer appreciation days and drop-ins at local Duke Power facilities, joint celebrations with local communities, anniversary presentations to civic and professional organizations, feature stories by local media, and acknowledgments from customers and associates.

Did the centennial succeed in raising Duke Power's reputation in its communities? A year-end survey of community leaders in both Carolinas reflected a significant increase in their overall impression of the company. Duke Power's strongest scores continued to be in "involved in the community as a good citizen" and "provides reliable service to its customers." Written comments included, "I continue to be impressed with Duke's sense of community and its willingness to take leading roles in supporting education and economic development initiatives... We're fortunate to have a power provider as dependable as Duke Power in our community." Another comment put it more succinctly: "Duke Power is back."

Centennial celebrations are what you make of them. Just as Duke Power's founders brought electricity in 1904 to revitalize a struggling reconstruction-era economy, we used the occasion of our one hundredth anniversary in 2004 to reconnect with our communities and contribute to the region's economic vitality and civic leadership.

Hardy's Relationship-Building Principle #4: Keep Moving Ahead

Joe Hardy: "Once I decided to lead a Uniontown renovation effort, I did all I could to do it right. People have commented on how workers are doing their work in downtown Uniontown in the rain, painting and sandblasting and so forth, as if there is some impossible deadline. Well, in the community, I think, just as in business, once you decide to do something you have to move ahead in a committed, planned fashion. You also have to realize that just about everything you want to do has been done, so why not take advantage of that? So I visited small towns that had been successfully rebuilt. It is good to know if something has been tried before you do it again. If it failed, why did it? If it worked, maybe you can put a twist on it, and do it a little better. I also worked with local politicians and with county and state leaders including Governor Rendell. Eddie and I have a good relationship, and I know he has a tough job. But he knows I am serious about Uniontown and Fayette County, and he knows I can be impatient. Uniontown is the county seat and it is important to help bring it back. But there are other towns in the county that need such help and I want the governor to know we are serious. We need his help and I think he trusts in our personal relationship. That can mean a lot moving forward."

Organizations have to do a better job of requiring loyalty to the organization, the brand, and to the things the organization does well.

Anyone who has worked in a community relations department has seen numerous good and effective projects abandoned, sometimes for good reasons such as budgetary, but other times because a new boss wants to institute his or her own programs. Organizations have to do a better job of requiring loyalty to the organization, the brand, and to the things the organization does well. An illustration of a company that has made and adhered to a long-term commitment to a particular, albeit distant, community is the story of Merck and the drug known as Mectizan.

A Developing-World Community

Almost alone in the history of corporate philanthropy in terms of human health benefits bestowed was Merck's decision, announced in 1987, that it would donate its new medicine Mectizan to as many people who needed it for as long as necessary, until river blindness (onchocerciasis) is eliminated as a public health problem. River blindness is endemic primarily to sub-Saharan Africa but also occurs in parts of Mexico, Central and South America, and the Middle East. The active ingredient in Mectizan, called ivermectin, was originally developed as a medicine for veterinary use. After studies indicated its effectiveness against onchocerciasas, a human formulation of the drug—now known as Mectizan—was developed. Seven years of clinical trials then resulted in the approval of Mectizan to treat onchocerciasis.

The disease has ravaged populations in tropical countries for centuries, causing, among other things, blindness. The parasite that causes the disease is spread by blackflies that bite people as often as thousands of times daily. In many African villages, more than half of the adult population would be blind as a result of the disease.

In most cases, treatment with just one oral dose of Mectizan annually will prevent the symptoms and halt the progression of the disease, including blindness, with few, if any, side effects. After much discussion within the company, then-chief executive P. Roy Vagelos, M.D., made an unprecedented decision: the company would give the drug to all who needed it, for as long as needed, for the treatment of onchocerciasis. *The New York Times'* Erik Eckholm wrote in a cover story in the paper's Sunday magazine on January 8, 1989, that: "In this case—the centuries-old torment of river blindness—developments have world health authorities cheering. In what will surely rank as one of the century's great medical triumphs, a dreadful scourge is coming under control."[13] Since then, on top of the costs needed to develop, manufacture, and donate Mectizan, the company has spent millions of dollars to help develop and support the distribution and administration infrastructure. President Jimmy Carter, whose Carter Center in Atlanta, GA, has worked with Merck on the distribution, praised the company lavishly:

"I think Merck has set a standard of the highest possible quality. [The Mectizan Donation Program has] been one of the most remarkable and exciting and inspiring partnerships that I have ever witnessed."[14]

Dr. Vagelos knew that Merck, a global company, could not ignore the needs of millions of people in communities oceans away from the company's business center. A physician and renowned researcher, as well as one of America's most successful business leaders, he knew well that the parasite which infects a person's body produces intense itching that is believed to have caused many suicides, terrible skin disfigurement, and, after migrating to the eye, blindness. "The Merck community," he said in 1987, "does not end in New Jersey where we have our headquarters, in Washington or Brussels where we get our new drug approvals, or even in the Western World where we sell most of our medicines. We discover, develop and market important new medicines and, wherever we can make a difference, we must do all that we can."[15]

Together with other initiatives such as spraying to kill the blackflies, Mectizan has made a tremendous contribution. In 2005, the company contributed Mectizan for more than 70 million people: 45 million people with river blindness and another 25 million patients with lymphatic filariasis (elephantiasis), another disease prevented by the medicine. But Merck and its partners still have a long way to go, since as many as 120 million people in more than thirty countries are at risk for river blindness.[16]

Hardy's Relationship-Building Principle # 5: Embrace Diversity

Joe Hardy: "I know that diversity is also a buzzword today and it can be used in a forced kind of way, as if government regulations and so forth are involved. But I mean it in a very positive way. On the global front, it is good business to embrace diversity. If something can be made in India for a fraction of the cost, businesses are going to do that. But the market that evolves in India can then be good for businesses and people in this country. In any case, globalization is here to stay. In the local community, just as is the case internationally, diversity means to me that we can respect people who may look, speak, or think in a different way. People in Western Pennsylvania have certain expressions, such as "youns" (plural of you), but don't let that fool you. They are as smart as anyone. And even though people here have had reason in the past to be discouraged, they can be motivated by opportunity. For example, a large number of our employees at Nemacolin are compensated not just with a salary but with performance-based incentives as well. Many of our employees at Nemacolin Resort are Fayette County residents, and most of them had never worked in a hotel. But we give them great training and they respond by helping us build what is already one of the country's best resorts, right here in Fayette County. And that means our Nemacolin workers can go on to any other hotel if they wish—the famous Greenbrier in West Virginia, for instance—because the management there wants our people. That's all good of course for everyone; even when we lose good people, it all works out is the way I look at it. So building a hotel or a new 84 Lumber Store is doing something great for a community, and if we can then go ahead and help people in Uniontown get back on their feet, that is something extra. It all depends on people, on relationships. My daughter, Maggie Hardy-Magerko, understands that; she is a very good judge of people, and that is why she is president of 84 Lumber. I myself phone many friends and acquaintances each day (sometimes seventy-five, no kidding!) just to wish them a happy birthday, and these are people from all walks of life. It's all about judging character and building relationships over the years. That's how to get things done. That's a pretty good way to live one's life, too, I think."

And even though people here have had reason in the past to be discouraged, they can be motivated by opportunity.

A CEO can be incredibly important to the planning and implementation of a community relations program. Similarly, the head of any organization, for example the president of a university, can get involved directly in the community, with impressive, long-term benefits for the organization and the community. (See sidebar on Wake Forest University's program of building relationships with various communities, local and beyond.)

Ambassadors to the Community

The success of any community relations program will in the long run depend on buy-in and support from people throughout the organization. "People in communities do not make relationships with companies," Edmund Burke writes, "but with people in companies and organizations." He identifies CEOs, facilities managers, and employees as all being important in an organization's community relations program. It is they who know the culture, the unique needs and capabilities of the community in which they live and work. "Employees are the bulk users of community services and programs," he continues. "Consequently, employee evaluations of needs and services in a community constitute valuable information for planning. They are also excellent sources of information on community attitudes toward the company."[17]

A survey of human resource executives by The Conference Board showed that a company's reputation was the third most important factor influencing people to become employees of particular organizations. (Only career development opportunities and compensation outranked reputation.) A study by the University of Missouri showed that a company's corporate social performance is positively related to its reputation and attractiveness as an employer."[18]

Wake Forest University: The Path to Becoming a National University

By Sandra Boyette,
Senior advisor to the president,
Wake Forest University

In 1956, Wake Forest College did what few institutions have done in recent history: the school moved from its home of one hundred and twenty-two years, near Raleigh, NC, to a brand-new custom-designed campus in Winston-Salem. The move was initiated by the Z. Smith Reynolds and Mary Reynolds Babcock Foundations, as well as civic leaders in the industrial Piedmont city, located one hundred and twenty miles west of the picturesque town of Wake Forest.

The "new" campus was, in many ways, a reflection of the "old": Old Virginia brick Georgian buildings; fledgling magnolia trees; and a faculty/staff residential community contiguous to the grounds. A few miles from downtown, the campus was somewhat of a town unto itself in its beautiful new environment. Although college employees interacted with the city—joining Rotary clubs, participating in Winston-Salem's rich arts life—financial and industrial executives remained the key civic leaders.

In 1967, the college became a university with a growing reputation for academic excellence; but town and gown had not yet formed any serious bonds.

By 1983 when Wake Forest's trustees selected Dr. Thomas K. Hearn Jr. as the twelfth president, Winston-Salem was headquarters to several *Fortune 500* companies and a number of other corporate giants—RJR Industries, Hanes textiles, Piedmont Airlines, Wachovia Corporation, and AT&T's North Carolina Works among them. The city's economy was thriving. As the former senior vice president for nonmedical affairs at the University of Alabama–Birmingham, Hearn had been active in Birmingham's civic and economic life, and he had great national ambitions for Wake Forest.

With the encouragement of trustees and administrators, Hearn began almost immediately to take Wake Forest into the local community. Early in his tenure, he led the United Way Campaign and established its first Leadership Circle. He founded Leadership Winston-Salem, to train and network local leaders, a step that proved invaluable less than a decade into his tenure. He encouraged Wake Forest faculty and administrators to serve nonprofit organizations in the city. He championed the growth of volunteer programs for Wake Forest students, citing the university's motto—Pro Humanitate—as the imperative.

At the same time, Hearn was taking steps that further elevated Wake Forest's national visibility as a leading academic institution, including a change in the relationship with the Baptist Convention of North Carolina, giving the university's trustees full autonomy. The college and university rankings began to proliferate at that time, too. Wake Forest held its number one spot among regional colleges and universities for several years, until it moved into the national research university category, where it remains in the top 10 percent.

A successful capital campaign—the school's largest ever—more than doubled building space, and applications increased rapidly. The Plan for the Class of 2000, initiated in 1995, created first-year seminars and added forty professors to the college faculty to preserve the advantages of small class size. Wake Forest led the nation in the introduction of technology as a tool of the liberal arts experience when students began receiving IBM ThinkPads, included as a benefit of tuition. From the mid-80s until the conclusion of Hearn's tenure in 2005, nine undergraduates were selected as Rhodes Scholars. Further, the university added a residential program in Vienna, complementing its two longstanding programs in London and Venice, and today, half of Wake Forest's undergraduates study abroad prior to graduation. The university's progress resonated positively in its "new" hometown.

By the time Wake Forest hosted its first presidential debate in 1988 (and another in 2000), city leaders were supportive partners in the effort, recognizing the boost it would be for Winston-Salem as well as the university.

But also in the late 1980s, the city's economic fortunes began to turn. Mergers and acquisitions moved corporate headquarters to distant cities. The now-famous leveraged buyout of RJR Industries rattled the confidence of even the most optimistic of the city's movers and shakers. Suddenly, Wake Forest, with its growing medical center and the associated healthcare enterprises, was the city's largest employer. Dr. Hearn became instrumental in leading the fight to reshape Winston-Salem's economy and rebuild its self-image.

Ultimately, he chaired Winston-Salem Business, an organization established to recruit new companies to the area. Later, Hearn became chair of another new organization, Idealliance. Working with this group of corporate and education executives and focusing on biotechnology as the key to economic health, he and others—including Wake Forest's senior vice president for health affairs, Dr. Richard Dean and Winston-Salem State University Chancellor Dr. Harold Martin—committed to the establishment of the Piedmont Triad Research Park. A twenty-five year plan is transforming two hundred acres of the city's industrial topography to a downtown biotech park housing several departments of the Wake Forest School of Medicine and a number of biotech companies, some of which had their beginning in the university's research laboratories.

Concurrently, city leaders—many of whom were alumni of Leadership Winston-Salem, the program founded by Hearn—began an effort to revitalize the downtown area. A blighted area of warehouses and on-again-off-again retail shops has become a burgeoning, attractive arts district. Lofts and condominiums in former office and warehouse space are beginning to attract more residents downtown, with the expectation that eventually, biotech park employees and graduate students living there will keep the area vibrant.

One could argue that Wake Forest's rise in academe gave the university the credibility it needed to become an integral component of the city and region. One could also argue that the move to Winston-Salem opened new opportunity for a larger constituency to support the university's national ambitions. Both arguments have merit. It is certain that good things happened to the university and the city because of a president willing to take on daunting community issues while moving his institution to national academic prominence.

Hardy's Relationship-Building Principle # 6: When Things Go Wrong, Make Them Right as Fast as You Can

Joe Hardy: "Things will sometimes go wrong. It is a fact of life, business, and community relations. Successful people make lots of mistakes. They just know how to admit and fix them fast."

Wal-Mart has been trying for years to build a store in one of New York City's five boroughs. Each time, small but PR-savvy citizen groups were able to block the behemoth, raising concerns about everything from traffic to alleged exploitive and unsafe workplace practices.

At this writing the company had recently lost a battle to build a store in Queens, and was beginning a new initiative in Staten Island. Immediately, some resident groups mobilized against having a store in that borough, even though many of them admit frequenting Wal-Marts in New Jersey. At this writing, the company was beginning a corporate advertising program to build support among Staten Island residents for a new store.

In founder Sam Walton's day, Wal-Mart was admired as a company that knew how to do everything right, including employee and community relations. How much of the problem now is with the substance of Wal-Mart's policies and actions, versus its communications, is unclear. But what is clear is that the Pushmi-Pullyu Syndrome of a two-headed organization (Chapter 1) applies here. In order for the company to overcome its community relations problems, it will have to behave and communicate in one way—a way that represents a marked improvement over recent times.

Community Relationships Are Based on Trust

By James E. Lukaszewski,
The Lukaszewski Group

There are many ongoing challenges to building community trust and ensuring positive relationships with customers, allies, colleagues, government, and employees. It is by far easier to recognize the pattern of those behaviors and attitudes that damage trust, or at least bring credibility into question than to catalog all the activities organizations and companies use or attempt in order to build community relationships. Put in a more interesting way, trust is a fragile but powerful substance like the lignin in trees—it is the glue that holds the fiber of relationships together. Yet, trust is the most fragile and vulnerable agent in any relationship.

The twelve most commonly seen trust-busting behaviors are listed and described below. Avoiding these behaviors or remediating them promptly will help maintain community trust and credibility.

1. Arrogance: Taking action without consulting those directly or indirectly affected. Making decisions unilaterally, without important input from key partners. Action without empathy.

2. Broken Promises: One of the crucial bases of trust is that each party can rely on the commitments of the other, both implied and explicit. When those commitments are broken without prior notification, understanding, explanation, and warning, the first element of the relationship to suffer is trust. Losing the safety of commitment can call into question most other elements of the relationship as well.

3. Creating Fear: This usually occurs when something you do damages or threatens to damage someone else without their permission, knowledge, or participation. It could be the appearance of decision; it could be the feeling of unreliability in the relationship.

4. Deception: Misleading intentionally through omission, commission, negligence, or incompetence in a relationship creates a feeling of separation and distance. It also creates a sense of disappointment because the individual, product, company, or organization failed to recognize that, at the very least, there should be a sense of candor between the parties no matter what the circumstance.

5. Disparaging Opposition: Any time you hear the phrase, "He's uninformed," or "They're just looking to raise money by their actions," or "It's politically motivated," or "They just don't understand," you immediately suspect that the exact opposite is true, and you're likely to be right. All opponents have friends elsewhere. Some of those friends are your friends as well. Victory is never achieved through disparagement. Disparagement causes suspicion, damages relationships, and creates permanent critics.

6. Disrespect: Even adversaries can trust each other to some extent, provided there is a sense of respect. When the reputation of an individual, product, or organization is minimized, trivialized, or humiliated, there is a sense of uneasiness and discomfort that often leads to frustration, anger, and outwardly negative behavior.

7. Ignoring/Avoiding the Killer Questions: Too often when preparing for adverse situations the very serious questions—those that can

kill reputation and, therefore, destroy trust—are either ignored or sanitized so as to be nearly unrecognizable. The honorable, trustworthy organization or individual prepares for the killer questions first and then determines other information that might be useful and helpful to explain or illustrate.

8. Lies: Often starting with simple misunderstandings, the truth to one individual or organization can seem untruthful to a competitor or competing interest, simply based on the critic's or competitor's point of reference in relation to a given set of facts and information.

9. Minimizing Danger: The moment you hear the phrase, "It's just an isolated incident," instinctively you know it's probably just the reverse. The moment you hear the phrase, "It's old news," you instinctively understand that something new and adverse is about to happen, even if it is based on old circumstances. We trust people who appropriately characterize situations.

10. Negative Surprise: Taking action out of character, out of sequence, out of selfish opportunity, or simply without advance notice to those directly or indirectly affected can seriously damage the relationship of trust and will cause a loss of confidence in the relationship.

11. Stall, Delay: A great source of frustration is when it is obvious that a situation could be resolved easily and quickly, but is not. Procrastination and denial go hand-in-hand. Keep in mind one of the great axioms of military strategy: timidity, hesitation, and indecision are the basic ingredients of defeat.

12. Overrate Your Preparation: One of the most serious mistakes in a relationship is the assumption that one is prepared to manage most adverse situations and that everyone else will understand what you are doing. Trust in relationships is often broken because when adverse situations occur, few step forward, most back away from the organizations most directly affected. No matter how well the situation is dealt with, trust repair and maintenance must be key parts of any preparation and remediation process.

Maintaining a relationship of trust requires constant analysis of the relationship to identify and eliminate negative behaviors, confusion, negative attitudes, and unexpected outcomes.

Best Practices of Community Relations

Here are some of the things forward-thinking companies and other organizations do to build enduring community relationships.

1. Hardy's six relationship-building principles.
2. Conduct a company assessment and community audit of the most important communities.
3. Learn from others: Celebrating major milestones, whether it is a centennial of service, a decade, or a year, is something that cuts across all industries and organizations. Research what has worked well for others before developing your plan.
4. Do a few things well: There are lots of ideas for special events and programs and the challenge is always deciding what not to do. Focus on a few things rather than many.
5. It is about the customers—not us. Find ways to involve and honor customers. The focus on economic development (see Duke Power sidebar) addressed a pressing community and customer need, while playing to the company's strengths.
6. Strengthen local partnership. Use a centennial, for example (Duke Power sidebar), as a reason to educate customers and communities about longstanding company priorities (for example, philanthropy, volunteerism, service, operational successes). Explore the potential for new community opportunities, particularly where the needs of the customers, the community, and the organization intersect.
7. Recognize and involve employees and retirees. Employees and retirees personify the organization's values through their accomplishments at work, at home, and in their communities. Find ways to say "thank you" for their support and community involvement.
8. Regional and national visibility for a college or university reflect well on its home city. (See Wake Forest sidebar.) Timely editorials in the local news, commenting on the school's achievements, can only serve to build the town and the relationship, and position the president as a community leader.
9. Local government officials need to be cultivated by universities and not-for-profits, just as prospective donors are. Regular meetings with them to discuss an organization's plans—capital improvements, neighborhood initiatives, large public events—foster trust and can help avoid conflicts.
10. Ensuring that the company's or school's president (Wake Forest sidebar) leads some purely community activities—a United Way campaign, an arts festival, a leadership training initiative—can exemplify the institution's willingness to "give back" to the community. Despite all the other demands on a president's or CEO's time, early in his or her tenure is a good time for such an activity to set the right tone.
11. Evaluate the number of events at the company, school, or other organization to consider ways that they can be expanded. Publish a regular calendar in the local newspaper as a reminder of the cultural opportunities that the company or school

offers to the community. Be certain that the president or CEO when possible welcomes audiences at a number of these events.

12. A company or other organization that is going to spend money on a community relations program or on a particular philanthropic program should set aside a percentage of the funds for communication. It is not just for publicity's sake but rather to ensure that the program will work and endure.

13. Have fun! Let's face it: Most public relations people get to plan and participate in large celebrations such as centennials (Duke Power sidebar) only once in a career. It is a great time to use skills as public and community relations professionals to honor the organization's history and set the direction for the future. Enjoy the experience!

Resources for Further Study

Books

Burke, Edmund M. *Corporate community relations: The principle of the neighbor of choice.* Westport, CT: Praeger, 1999.

Burke, Edmund M. *Managing a company in an activist world: The leadership challenge of corporate citizenship.* Westport, CT: Praeger, 2005.

The Center for Corporate Citizenship at Boston College, http://www.bcccc.net.

Grayson, David, and Adrian Hodges. *Everybody's business: Managing risks and opportunities in today's global society.* New York: DK Publishing, 2002.

The Merck MECTIZAN® Donation Program, http://www.mectizan.com.

Sagawa, Shirley, and Eli Segal. *Common interest, common good.* Boston: Harvard Business School Press, 2000.

Weeden, Curt. 1998. *Corporate social investing: the breakthrough strategy for giving and getting corporate contributions.* San Francisco: Berrett-Koehler, 1998.

Questions for Further Discussion

1. Joe Hardy has almost single-handedly been able to rebuild Uniontown, PA. If one man can accomplish that, why can large companies or multicompany organizations not rebuild some of our large, decaying cities?

2. How many companies base their community relations programs on community audits or company assessments? Does yours?

3. Could Wake Forest University have achieved its national reputation for academic excellence without an outreach into communities beyond the traditionally academic ones?

4. Duke Power went far beyond the traditional centennial celebration, bringing new meaning to the phrase "giving back to the community." Was this philanthropy, good business, or both?

5. Jim Lukaszewski says that, "Maintaining a relationship of trust requires constant analysis ..." Elaborate, based on one of your business relationships.

CHAPTER 8

Investor Relations

On Wall Street, bulls make money and bears make money.
But pigs get slaughtered.

In September 2002 a large Japanese company spun off a small molecular diagnostic company, Gen-Probe, based in San Diego, a hotbed of biotechnology. At the time Gen-Probe's stock traded at about $7.00 per share.[1]

It would have been easy for newly independent Gen-Probe to focus primarily on its core business, and to wait for Wall Street to discover it. But instead Gen-Probe actively engaged the investment community.

The company spends about thirty days annually—about 12 percent of senior management's time—telling its story to Wall Street. But engagement with Wall Street is not just promotional. Management works very deliberately to keep the Street's expectations in check. The company's philosophy is to "under-promise and over-deliver" on a range of milestones including corporate financial performance and product development timelines.

The way the company engages Wall Street is not particularly esoteric or difficult. But it is intentional. The company's investor relations program employs many traditional tools of the trade, including investor targeting, presentations at brokerage conferences, nondeal roadshows, analyst meetings, facility tours, and day-to-day phone contact with the Street.

This work has paid off. A 2004 survey of forty investment analysts by Rivel Research Group gave Gen-Probe an overall corporate reputation score of 5.1 on a six-point scale. This compares to a mid-cap norm of 4.3 in other studies conducted by Rivel. Furthermore, the respondents identified "credible management" as the most important factor in determining whether to buy or sell Gen-Probe stock, and 80 percent agreed that the management team meets this criterion.

The tangible result of Gen-Probe's investor relations focus and positive reputation is telling: this small San Diego firm has become a member of the Standard & Poor's 400 Mid-Cap Index in less than three years. Its stock price has increased more than six-fold, significantly outperforming the broad market and the biotech sector. The firm is covered by a dozen sell-side analysts, and more than 90 percent of the company's shares are held by institutional investors. In all the company has generated more than $2 billion in shareholder value.

* * * * *

A company's financial strength and market value are dependent, among many other things, on the company's reputation.

And like other elements of reputation, a company's reputation among investors should not be left to chance. Affirmative management of a company's reputation in the investment community can contribute significantly to a company's overall success.

This Chapter Covers

⇒ What is investor relations?
⇒ The goals and roles of investor relations
⇒ What does "public company" mean?
⇒ A brief introduction to the financial markets and investment
 Debt securities
 Rating agencies
 Equity securities
 Shareholders
 Board of directors
 IR levels the playing field
 Equal access to information
 Income stream
⇒ Tools of the trade: Methods of investor relations
⇒ Securities analysts: The crucial intermediaries
⇒ Sell-side analysts
 Buy, sell, hold
 Analyst reports
 Brokerage firms and investment banking role
 Regulatory separation of investment banking and research
⇒ Buy-side analysts
⇒ IR's interaction with analysts
 Consensus estimates
 The road show
⇒ IR's interaction with investors
⇒ The financial media
 Wire services
 Local papers near headquarters
 Business magazines, trade press, and newsletters
 Broadcast media
⇒ IR and corporate disclosure
 Regulatory bodies
 National sovereignty and oversight
 IR's global responsibility
⇒ Materiality
 Fraud-on-the-market theory
 Efficient market hypothesis

Defining securities fraud
Establishing personal ground rules
⇒ Disclosure
Recent disclosure regulation
Reg. FD "carve out" for working journalists
The SEC: Formal and informal disclosure in the United States
Annual report to shareholders
Informal disclosure
Timing disclosure
Disclosing more than required by law
⇒ Best practices
⇒ Resources for further study
⇒ Questions for further discussion

What Is Investor Relations?

> Investor relations (IR) is the subset of public relations and corporate communication that deals with a company's relationship with the investment community. Both current investors (who own a corporation's stocks and bonds) and potential investors (who might be persuaded to own these stocks and bonds) make up the primary audiences for investor relations.

IR is most often employed by companies whose shares are held and traded by the public. Privately owned companies may also use IR in circumstances such as trading bonds on the public markets or when such companies are owned by a dispersed group of private shareholders.

IR is unique among communications disciplines in that real people make or lose real money every day, based on information, utterances, or omissions from a corporate IR department. Since IR mistakes can cost real people real money, IR is the most heavily regulated of communications disciplines. Laws, government regulations, and stock exchange regulations dictate how IR is conducted and when. As a result, IR has exacting procedures and deadlines.

The demands of investors and regulators make investor relations among the most stimulating and academically rigorous of all communication disciplines. IR requires knowledge of corporate finance, law, accounting, and human resources. In general, IR practitioners are well compensated compared to other corporate communication professionals with similar experience and responsibility. IR practitioners may become trusted advisors within corporations and participate at the highest levels of corporate strategy.

Corporate leadership has only recently come to acknowledge the strategic importance of IR. From its establishment as a distinct discipline in the 1960s until the mid-1990s, IR was long seen as a tactical function peripheral to strategic corporate decision making. Leadership typically believed that IR took care of communications details after basic decisions were made elsewhere. During this era IR often reported to the head of corporate communications, with dotted line responsibilities to the chief financial officer (CFO).

Since the mid-1990s, IR has matured into a strategic element of business operation. The reasons are myriad. The capital markets now play a more central role in personal financial decisions because more individuals own stocks, mutual funds, and retirement funds. This increases the demand for reliable data about corporations. Furthermore, chief executive officers (CEOs) are now typically judged by how well their companies' stock performs. So CEOs are now much more keen on what IR can do. Technology and the Internet have erased barriers to information flow, giving Main Street investors access to financial data and disclosure reserved previously for Wall Street. And key to the evolution of IR as a strategic discipline are the several corporate scandals that have militated more complete, integrated, timely, and thoughtful corporate financial disclosure. Without robust financial disclosure and transparency, a corporation now risks severe damage to its reputation and ability to do business. IR provides the robust financial communications management tools corporations now require.

Today, especially in the United States and Canada, IR is viewed as a financial function with an essential, critical overlay of communications practice and theory. IR typically now reports to a CFO, sometimes to a general counsel, and in some cases directly to a chief executive officer. Because IR concerns a company's stocks and bonds, at a minimum it is now common for the head of IR to interact closely with the CEO and senior executives and make presentations to the board of directors. IR generally takes part in the corporation's strategic processes to a greater degree than corporate communication professionals without IR responsibilities. Regardless of where in a corporate hierarchy IR reports, IR practitioners must possess the core skills of stellar communications and marketing professionals. The IR professional then orchestrates the public relations, finance, accounting, legal, management, and related corporate functions in clear, timely, and complete communications with relevant audiences.

The Goals and Roles of Investor Relations

The first goal of investor relations is to ensure that a company's securities are fairly and fully valued in the marketplace. "Fairly and fully valued" means

Today, especially in the United States and Canada, IR is viewed as a financial function with an essential, critical overlay of communications practice and theory.

that the price of a company's securities, that is, its stocks and bonds, closely reflects both the present and the potential value of the company. Given that a stock's price is set by the market based on demand for that stock, investor relations involves maintaining demand. IR does this by ensuring investors have access to accurate, timely information about the company so they can appraise the attractiveness of the company's stock relative to other investment opportunities.

IR's second goal is to help fulfill the affirmative disclosure obligations of securities law and regulatory authorities. These are described in detail later in this chapter. Some securities exchanges also have their own disclosure requirements, and IR is responsible for helping companies fulfill the disclosure requirements of the stock exchanges or electronic trading systems on which their securities are traded, listed, or quoted.

A third goal of IR is to create competitive advantage. In this way IR is consistent with other corporate communication and public relations efforts. As a company tries to create competitive advantage for the products and services it sells to customers, IR works to create competitive advantage in the investment marketplace. IR uses many of the same tools as other corporate communication functions and often coordinates closely with those functions. Such tools include media relations, internal communications (especially when employees, either directly, or through unions or pension plans, own stock), and sometimes advertising.

Further, because IR is a hybrid of finance, corporate communication, law, and marketing, the IR function requires sensitivity to and coordination with each of these disciplines.

What Does "Public Company" Mean?

Some words used in IR have specialized, specific meanings that are nonintuitive and even contrary to usage in everyday English. For example, in the securities markets "public" and "private" carry meanings which derive from the description of whether a company's securities are generally available to any buyer, or whether ownership is restricted to a few. A public company is a business whose securities are available for sale or trading in the public markets, and thus to any buyer. It is a publicly traded company because its stocks or bonds can be bought or sold by any buyer or seller with access to an exchange or an electronic trading system. A private company is also a business, but its ownership is restricted to present owners and those who may buy additional securities only by invitation directly from the company or one of the current owners. There is no public market. Private company securities are legal documents, but they are not registered with regulators. They are therefore forbidden by law to be sold to and by the public at large.

Publicly traded companies are sometimes called listed companies because their securities are traded (listed) on an exchange. Listed stocks and listed companies are also referred to as quoted stocks and quoted companies because their shares are quoted on trading systems or exchanges, where buyers or sellers quote a price at which they are willing to buy or sell a given company's shares. In addition, some companies—whose private shares are not publicly available and traded to all comers—do have publicly traded bonds or similar debt securities.

What differences do such distinctions make? By definition, privately held companies have no stocks or bonds publicly available for sale and thus are not subject to disclosure obligations required of public companies by law. Privately held companies are not required to disclose their finances, profits, strategies, successes or failures, and generally they do not. Public companies are required to make full, timely, and accurate disclosures of all information a reasonable observer might believe reflects on the value of that company's securities. Investor relations is the communications skill set companies use to meet these disclosure requirements and to relay material corporate information to all reasonable public observers so they can make reasonable investment decisions.

A Brief Introduction to the Securities Markets and Investment

In any market, those who have something are put together with those who need or want it and are willing to pay for it.

IR is primarily concerned with communication to the securities markets, which are a subset of capital markets. Capital markets are places where those who have capital and those who need capital come together to buy or to sell capital. Capital is surplus cash. In capital markets, those who have surplus cash are investors, suppliers of capital. Those who need cash are users of capital. They sell something to investors in exchange for cash. They are called issuers because they issue a security in exchange for that cash. Capital raised by corporations is the concern of investor relations. But note that one of the largest users of capital and the markets is government, which issues bonds.

In theory, capital markets operate so that capital flows to its most beneficial, efficient, and lucrative use defined as where surplus cash earns the greatest return. In practice, inefficiencies of human actions and communications almost guarantee that capital may not reach its best use. IR supports the market goal of capital reaching its best use by working to eliminate inefficiencies in information and data among market participants and observers.

> IR is primarily concerned with communication to the securities markets, which are a subset of capital markets.

When a business needs capital, it can turn to several sources in addition to the securities markets. For instance, it can generate capital from internal operations by increasing productivity (and thus earnings) or by closing inefficient operations. A business also may borrow capital from a bank, or find private investors.

Sometimes a business prefers to ask the general public to provide the necessary capital. It does this through the securities markets by issuing bonds ("debt securities"), which in essence are tiny, discrete simultaneous loans from large numbers of investors, or by issuing stocks ("equity"), which in essence are very small, discrete portions of ownership in the company itself, sold to many investors simultaneously. The word securities means the supplier of capital (the investor) has secured legal standing and a claim on the corporation's assets in certain circumstances. In exchange for issuing debt or equity securities, the company receives cash, gives a security, and then puts the cash to work on the terms agreed to in the offering documents.

Owners of debt security have a right to recover their investment (for example, in a bankruptcy proceeding) before an equity holder. The greater risk equity holders undertake is therefore offset by the potential for greater return that equity holders can earn if the company does well. Debt holders are limited to a fixed rate of return no matter how well the company does.

Debt Securities

Many corporations issue bonds (which mature in five years or more) or debt securities such as notes, which generally mature in one to five years, or bills, which mature in under one year. Governments also issue debt securities. Financial news on television often implies stocks are where the action is, but the bond markets are significantly larger, both in dollar terms and in number of issuers. That is in part because governments cannot issue stock. Stock equals ownership, and governments by definition cannot sell ownership of themselves. Governments can, however, take loans and issue debt securities.

A debt security is a promise by an issuer to an investor. In exchange for borrowing the investors' money—the principal amount—issuers promise to pay a previously determined return on the investment, at a stated frequency, for a certain duration (time period). When investors acquire a debt security, they gain an income stream for a certain period of time. When the time period is over and the debt security matures, issuers also give back all the principal.

The investor's income stream is determined by the coupon, or interest rate.

For example, if an investor buys a $10,000 bond paying an 8 percent coupon over thirty years, the investor will receive $800 each year for thirty consecutive years (a total of $24,000) and also get the original $10,000 investment back. From the issuer's perspective, the issuer is "renting" $10,000 for thirty years.

Rating Agencies

Investors risk the issuer not being able to pay the income stream when due or the principal amount at maturity. Some issuers are more risky than others, and this risk is assessed by independent credit rating agencies. For a fee charged to issuers, such agencies assess risks, provide detailed reports, and assign letter grades to the risk. Investors can therefore gauge the degree of risk they may take on and whether it is worth the income stream they expect to receive. The letter grade provides a shorthand way for investors to compare risks quickly. The three agencies better known globally are Standard & Poor's, Moody's Investors Services, and Fitch Ratings.

Equity Securities

Whereas debt securities are essentially loans, equity securities represent ownership in a corporation. The word equity, which in nonfinancial contexts means fairness, in the financial markets means ownership.

Equity securities are commonly referred to as shares or stocks. Those shares typically trade on securities exchanges, such as the New York Stock Exchange (NYSE) or the London Stock Exchange (LSE). New York, London, and Tokyo are the world's largest securities markets. Paris, Frankfurt, Chicago, Hong Kong, Singapore, Seoul, Sydney, Mumbai, Shanghai, and Shenzhen also host very active markets. Additionally, many important marketplaces exist only electronically and have no physical location or trading floor. The National Association of Securities Dealers Automated Quotation (NASDAQ) exchange in New York, the Toronto Stock Exchange, the Paris-based Alternext (owned by Euronext), and London's Alternative Investment Market (AIM), owned by the LSE, are notable examples.

Shareholders

In theory, stock ownership exists in perpetuity and is thus very much unlike bonds, which carry defined maturities. As owners, stockholders (shareholders) are responsible for corporate governance; that is, shareholders are entitled to participate in certain important corporate decisions. Under the concept of shareholder democracy current in the United States and most other markets, shareholders are entitled to vote their shares on a one share, one vote basis. Shareholders vote at meetings which generally take place once per year (annual meetings), but special-purpose meetings can be called any time under procedures set out in the corporation's bylaws.

Board of Directors

At annual meetings shareholders decide issues including appointment of the company's independent auditors, election of the board of directors and other issues properly brought before the meeting under the terms of the corporation's bylaws.

Elected by shareholders, directors have a fiduciary duty, or duty of good faith, to serve shareholder interests. As owners, shareholders have the right to access certain information about the company. Some information is available from the company's proxy statement and formal filings with regulators, described below.

IR Levels the Playing Field

A key job for IR is providing the rest of the information current or prospective investors need to make informed governance and investment decisions. The concept of the level playing field means that all investors must have access to all pertinent information at the same time. Ensuring that this happens is one of the cornerstones of IR practice.

> The concept of the level playing field means that all investors must have access to all pertinent information at the same time. Ensuring that this happens is one of the cornerstones of IR practice.

In addition to a share in corporate governance, an investor also buys a share of any profits distributed. Often a company retains profits to reinvest, but the board of directors may also choose to distribute profits to shareholders in the form of dividends. Dividends are distributed on a pro rata basis; that is, each share is entitled to an equal portion of the profits. In the United States, dividends are customarily paid quarterly; in the United Kingdom, semiannually.

Equal Access to Information

Note that "one share/one vote" and "equal portions of dividends per share" do not mean one shareholder's entire voting rights or dividends are the same as any other shareholder's. The shares are equal; the shareholders may not be. Regardless of how many shares a holder owns, all shareholders and the entire investment market are entitled to equal and simultaneous access to information about the company.

Income Stream

Unlike bonds, stocks have no duration but exist as long as the company is publicly traded. Stocks also have no specified dividend amount. A board of directors at its own discretion may choose to decrease or withhold a dividend at any time, a decision often indicative of the state of the company's financial health. By tradition in the United States and Canada, dividend payout typically remains steady from period to period. In the United Kingdom dividend payouts may vary from period to period.

Investors in debt securities generally know what their income stream will be, so debt securities are known as fixed income securities. Stock investors do not know what their dividend stream will be. Therefore, and because stock prices tend to fluctuate more than bond prices, stocks are considered more speculative investments.

Tools of the Trade: Methods of Investor Relations

The first role of IR is to assure that a company's securities are fairly and fully valued in the marketplace. IR's second role is to help a company fulfill the affirmative disclosure obligations of securities law and regulatory authorities, which involves disseminating adequate corporate information. To implement these functions, IR uses many of the same tools and disciplines as other forms of corporate communication.

Press Releases

The press release—an announcement of company news—is a tool used by many other communication disciplines. The goal for most press releases is generating media coverage, and they are written so that journalists can easily incorporate their themes and language into news coverage.

IR press releases share this purpose, but the primary reason for an IR release is to notify markets of important corporate news, good or bad. The primary audiences for an IR release are investors, securities analysts and the investment market. In addition, but secondarily, the IR press release is intended for journalists working in the financial media to draw upon in news coverage.

Unlike most other forms of press releases, IR releases are intended for direct public consumption. IR press releases are almost always posted in full on the company's Web site, and they can be read directly by the public, company employees, market researchers, competitors, academics, and other audiences world wide.

Although an IR press release is meant for direct consumption, it is rarely written crisply in simple, understandable prose. More typically it is laden with numbers, legal and financial jargon, boilerplate language, tables, and appendices. Readers slog through its specialized, sometimes ritualistic language for a simple reason—money is at stake. The most common form of IRcommunication—save for government filings—IR press releases can and do move securities markets and a company's stock price. As a result, IR press releases are subject to the strict laws and regulations governing direct communications with the investment markets.

Internet and Text Messaging

IR also uses the Internet extensively. Companies can sign up investors and other parties for e-mail alerts when company news is released. Following the announcement of important news, IR can arrange for investors and others to listen to management-led conference calls via Web casts. Audio or transcripts from these calls can remain on company Web sites as long as their content is relevant. Some companies also post materials from executive addresses to industry conferences.

In addition to press releases and executive biographies, IR may also post a company's ethics and corporate responsibility guidelines, environmental policies, analysts' coverage, and news coverage and industry awards. Financial data tagged in computer eXtensible Business Reporting Language (XBRL) and hyperlinks to external sites such as the Securities and Exchange Commission are becoming increasingly common.

Mass Release for Material News

To comply with regulatory requirements for fair disclosure, companies typically follow precise procedures in releasing material news. In order to ensure that all market participants have simultaneous access to news, companies typically use third-party vendors for the timely distribution of press releases. In the United States, these vendors are the competitors PR Newswire and BusinessWire, Canada Wire in Canada, and allied national distribution networks around the globe. Using vendor facilities, a company is assured its news is distributed simultaneously and appears verbatim on the Internet. Companies can supplement vendor distribution by e-mails to proprietary lists of investors, media, and market participants.

In general, press releases are distributed before the market opens or after it closes, but breaking news releases can be distributed when markets are trading. Most financial results releases are followed by conference calls affording management an opportunity to discuss them, and investors and analysts to question management directly.

Corporate Communication Materials

IR uses many standard corporate marketing materials. These include glossy publications, fact books, background documents, executive biographies, photographs, information on products and facilities, and other materials.

Investment Conferences

Typically, IR also arranges for management speaking opportunities at investment conferences sponsored by brokerage firms for their investment clients. Such conferences are usually industry specific and last several days. Senior executives from many compa-nies each speak for about an hour including a questions and answer period. Such presentations are an opportunity for management and IR professionals to market their companies directly to the invest-ment marketplace, meet directly with current and prospective inves-tors and analysts, and build relationships.

Some companies also host day- or multiday-long meetings for investors and analysts at their corporate facilities. Such "investor days" are by invitation only. They enable investors and analysts to experience a company first-hand, tour facilities, see products, and meet a broader range of managers than those attending brokerage firm investment conferences.

Companies also make private visits to current and prospec-tive investors and analysts who influence them. These "desk-side" outreach visits can be one-on-one or small-group format and are designed to build relationships and help investors better understand a company, its management team, and its strategies.

Who Manages Financial Media Relations?

In addition to direct approaches, investors often get company information indirectly from reports in the financial news media. Some companies assign interactions with financial media to their media relations staffs, with input from IR. Other companies give IR primary responsibility for these relationships; IR will field media inquiries and initiate story ideas on the company, its management, and its successes.

The Role of Advertising

Except during mergers, proxy fights, and similar nonroutine events, IR rarely utilizes advertising. Some companies, however, do buy airtime on business news cable channels, and so forth, to adver-tise directly to the investment community. Such advertising cam-paigns are managed jointly by IR and the corporate advertising staff, or outside advertising agencies.

Blowback from the Internet

A recent IR challenge has arisen via Internet chat rooms, Web logs, and dissident-investors Web sites. Current best practices sug-gest monitoring such sites, but not engaging. They often deal in unsubstantiated gossip, and IR practitioners are at a disadvantage challenging opponents who can make up things along the way. While some IR departments are exploring company management creating proactive Web posts daily, such programs are relatively new and unevaluated.

Surveillance and Intelligence

Finally, IR is also tasked with the important function of stock-holder surveillance and market intelligence. Surveillance is a process that enables a company to know who is buying and selling its stock.

Surveillance is done by reviewing available public data at exchanges, clearinghouses, and depositories and by other means. Intelligence means monitoring industry competitors' ownership records and financial and stock performance, also via public filings and records, to identify and correct potential internal exposure. Both tasks are technologically driven and IR departments often contract with outside vendors to gather and analyze such data.

Securities Analysts: The Crucial Intermediaries

When making investment decisions, investors frequently depend on the advice of specialized investment professionals known as analysts. Analysts are experts in specific industries, market sectors, or trends. They are trained in specific academic disciplines, have had intensive financial training, and many are certified as Chartered Financial Analyst or its equivalent.

Securities analysts typically advise investors on issues ranging from asset allocation to promising industry sector opportunities, to recommendations on specific companies. Analysts can cover entire markets, specific geographic regions, entire sectors of the economy, or particular industries or companies. Some cover stocks; some bonds. But analysts all help investors to make informed investment decisions.

Sell-Side Analysts

Sell-side analysts are employed by brokerage firms and make recommendations to the firms' customers. They are called "sell-side" analysts because their advice is intended to result in a sale of shares by the brokerage firm to its customers. The research is provided to customers free of charge; the firm is compensated by the commissions it generates from the sale (or from profits from the sale of shares the firm may own and sell directly to customers).

Sell-side analysts are usually knowledgeable about companies in a particular market sector. They cover a number of companies and produce reports for customers assessing the relative attractiveness of the companies in that sector.

The primary work of sell-side analysts is predicting a company's financial performance and therefore the likely profits it will generate. Because most companies' stock price is seen as a multiple of its corporate earnings (known as a price-earnings ratio, or multiple), knowing the magnitude of a company's earnings allows an analyst to make an educated guess about the stock price the company will have in the future. For example, assume a company traditionally has a price-earnings ratio of ten-to-one. That means that for every dollar of earnings its stock is valued at $10. If an analyst thinks the company's earnings for a given year will be $2.45 per share, the analyst might project the company's shares would be fairly valued at $24.50 per share ($2.45 per share multiplied by ten). Depending on the stock price when the prediction is made, the analyst can advise whether buying the stock is a good opportunity.

Buy, Sell, Hold

Based on this educated guess, analysts advise investors to buy, hold, or sell their shares. A "buy" recommendation means the analyst recommends investors add the stock to their portfolios. A "hold" recommendation means investors who already own shares should not buy more but should not sell either; rather, they should maintain their position in anticipation of the stock increasing in value. A "sell" recommendation means that investors who own the stock should sell it, either due to company problems or because it has achieved the analyst's target price and is unlikely to increase as quickly as other stocks.

Much quantitative work goes into an analyst's projection of earnings, stock price, and buy/hold/sell recommendations. Analysts work to find any opportunity to better understand companies they cover. They meet with management, call the company IR professionals, interview customers or suppliers, and review publicly available company information, including those disclosures managed by IR.

> Based on this educated guess, analysts advise investors to buy, hold, or sell their shares.

Analyst Reports

Analysts' work is published in the form of reports on individual companies and industries. It is distributed to clients of their brokerage firms and is sometimes available on the Internet or other sources. Analysts also brief brokers at their firms about their recommendations so brokers can share those recommendations with their customers (thereby generating transactions—and commissions—for the brokerage firms).

Sell-side investors are supposed to give impartial advice and serve as independent experts serving investors. But throughout the 1990s and early 2000s sell-side analysts were criticized for being influenced by other parts of their brokerage firms—large, complex organizations with different functions often seen to be in conflict with each other.

Brokerage Firms and Investment Banking Role

Investment bankers within a brokerage firm, for example, advise large corporations and generate significant revenues by helping companies raise money in capital markets. In the 1990s and early 2000s critics complained that investment banking departments had pressured sell-side analysts to withhold criticism of companies to preserve the investment banking relationship. Analyst compensation was said to be linked not so much to accurate work as to assistance rendered when the investment banking division acquired a client. It was also alleged some analysts publicly promoted some companies' stock as attractive investments while privately believing they were not.

Regulatory Separation of Investment Banking and Research

In 2001 the Securities and Exchange Commission (SEC) and the attorneys general of several states, led by New York State, reached a settlement with leading brokerage firms requiring them to separate investment banking and research functions, assure analyst compensation was not driven by investment banking pressure, and take additional steps to protect investors from advice that was not truly independent. Alleging they had relied on tainted research, many investors also initiated lawsuits against the brokerages.

In the aftermath of the regulatory actions and lawsuits, brokerage firms have taken significant steps to restore confidence in the independence of their analysts, and to more fully disclose inherent conflicts of interest including the fact that a given firm might do investment banking work for a company covered by the analyst.

Buy-Side Analysts

"Buy-side analysts" also make predictions about stock performance. They are employed directly by large investors, known as institutional investors, which include mutual funds, insurance companies, trust companies, pension funds, and other organizations that manage investments. They are called "buy-side" analysts because they work for investment firms that buy securities that are sold through sell-side firms. Whereas sell-side analysts make public recommendations both to institutional and individual investors, buy-side analysts make recommendations only to their own company's portfolio managers. As "in-house analysts," they review much of the same information and also the recommendations of sell-side analysts before making their own recommendations to the portfolio managers.

IR's Interaction with Analysts

Much of the disclosure noted above is directed both to buy-side and sell-side analysts because they have significant influence over the investment process. Much of the time IR professionals and company management spend on investor relations involves working with, meeting with, and attempting to positively influence both kinds of analyst. Most conference calls held after release of material information are intended to give these analysts timely access to company management's perspective on this news and to provide them the opportunity to ask questions. IR professionals also spend considerable time on the phone with analysts answering technical questions, arranging meetings, and otherwise helping analysts understand the company.

Consensus Estimates

Sell-side analysts make projections of quarterly and annual earnings of the companies they cover, and information service companies publish what they call "consensus estimates" of those projections for each company. The word "consensus" is misleading, because what are called "consensus estimates" are actually averages calculated among many disparate projections.[2]

Companies are often asked to comment on consensus estimates. Some companies endorse such estimates; others build in more flexibility and make a statement such as "consensus estimates suggest that we will earn 55 cents per share in the quarter; we are comfortable with estimates in the 40 to 45 cents per share range." Analysts often reset their estimates based on companies' guidance. Because of the duties to update prior statements, once a company gives guidance it may have a duty to update that guidance if the company believes it is unable to meet the expectations caused by the guidance. As a result, some companies have a policy against making such guidance, or have designated times before earnings when they refuse to make or update guidance.

> Analysts often reset their estimates based on companies' guidance.

The Road Show

Companies often send their management teams on "road shows" where executives meet with buy-side and sell-side analysts and investors one-on-one, in small group meetings, or in conferences arranged for buy-side analysts by sell-side analysts. These meetings help analysts who make investment recommendations to better understand company strategy and management team strength, and to make personal assessments of executive talent and commitment.

IR's Interaction with Investors

Institutional investors, who typically own significant shares of a company's stock, are a core IR constituency. Such investors, through buy-side analysts or portfolio managers who run particular mutual funds or pension plans, often speak with management, participate in conference calls, and sometimes try to influence the corporate policy or management decisions.

Individual investors also contact companies, and some increasingly speak with IR professionals and listen to conference calls (either live or via archived audio on the company's Web site). Individual investors also seek information via Web sites, annual and quarterly reports, and financial media.

The Financial Media

Analysts, markets, and investors rely on the financial news media for additional key information about a company or industry. Compared to investors, the financial media has greater freedom of action, greater legal protections, and often more resources to pursue corporate information. Journalists are among the first to discern trends and discover change within a corporation or industry, and it is therefore important for investors making investment decisions to pay attention to the press.

Given the leading role journalism plays in investment decision making, investor relations and corporate media relations naturally focus considerable time and energy attempting to inform and generate accurate and positive media coverage for a corporation, its management, and its prospects.

Influential Global Financial Wire Services

English
⇒ Dow Jones News Service and its specialty wires
⇒ Bloomberg Business News
⇒ Reuters
⇒ Associated Press

Japanese and English
⇒ Nikkei
⇒ Jiji Press

European Languages and English
⇒ Agence France Presse (French and English)
⇒ EFE (Spanish and English)
⇒ Deutsche Press Agentur (German and English)

Other smaller financial news wires report in local European or Asian languages. Because of the breaking-news nature of their reporting, wire services play an integral part in the system of informal corporate disclosure.

Daily newspapers with global significance in financial news include *The Wall Street Journal* (publishing separate editions from Brussels, New York, and Hong Kong), *The New York Times*, the *Financial Times* (editions from London, New York, and Asia), the *International Herald Tribune* (from Paris, in English), *Les Echos* in French, *Handelsblatt* in German, and the *Nihon Keizai Shimbun* in Japanese. Influential regional newspapers with heavy financial news content include the *National Post/Financial Post* and the *Globe and Mail*, both of Toronto, Canada; the *Australian Financial Review* from Sydney, *Il Sole 24 Horas* from Milan, Germany's *Frankfurter Allgemeine Zeitung*, the *Asahi Shimbun* from Tokyo, the *South China Morning Post* in Hong Kong and the *Straits Times* from Singapore (these latter two publish in English). Recently several Chinese language newspapers dedicated to financial news have been formed in Shanghai and Hong Kong, but none has yet captured "must read" status.

Local Papers Near Headquarters

Local newspapers, especially those writing from a company's headquarters city, can be exceptionally influential in financial news. The *Detroit Free Press* acts as the industry "bible" for the United States automotive industry, as do the Seattle newspapers for Microsoft.

Business Magazines, Trade Press and Newsletters

Three more classes of publications hold considerable sway over financial markets and investment. First, there are business and investment magazines such as *Business Week, Fortune, Forbes, Barron's Money,* and *Smart Money*. These magazines pick up business trends and ideas first surfacing elsewhere and popularize them among wider audiences. Secondly, trade publications—for example, *Automotive Age* for the auto industry, *American Metal Market* for the metals industry, the *Hollywood Reporter* for entertainment, and *Women's Wear Daily*, in apparel—specialize in single-industry coverage that can surpass investment insight and expertise in the general media.

Finally, newsletters are a powerful but often under-recognized force in investment markets. These highly specialized publications—today often sent via e-mail rather than printed paper—can tout seemingly esoteric investment theories, obscure happenings, or shadowy market prognostications. Some newsletters have a very devoted readership and can move markets and specific stocks with alacrity.

> Some newsletters have a very devoted readership and can move markets and specific stocks with alacrity.

Broadcast Media

Broadcast media are very significant for the financial markets. Bloomberg and Reuters each run radio and television news divisions separate from their wire services. CNBC holds a premier place in United States business news and also fields separate noteworthy bureaus in Singapore and London.

IR and Corporate Disclosure

Securities markets are regulated by an overlapping set of state, provincial, federal, and trans-national governmental agencies. In addition, with several exceptions, each stock exchange worldwide has an additional layer of private regulation pertaining to any security trading on the particular exchange. Such private regulators are termed self-regulatory organizations

(SROs) and carry considerable clout in determining standards and methods listing and trading a stock.

Regulatory Bodies

The Securities and Exchange Commission (SEC) in Washington, D.C., is the chief governmental regulator in the United States. In Canada, responsibility is held at provincial level; generally the Ontario Securities Commission takes the lead because Canada's most important markets are domiciled there. In December 2001 the United Kingdom completed an extensive reorganization of securities regulation, paring seven government agencies of jurisdiction to the single Financial Services Authority (FSA), which now is the U.K. regulator. In 2003 France reworked securities regulation into the new L'Autorité de Marchès Financiers (AMF). The Australian Securities and Investment Commission (ASIC), Japan's Ministry of Finance, and the Bundesanstalt für Finanzienstleistungsaufsicht (BaFin) in Germany are other major governmental-level securities regulators. China is in the earlier stages of erecting financial regulatory framework; in part, it operates through the China Securities Regulatory Commission.

Over the last two decades technology has enabled capital to move virtually anywhere on the globe instantaneously. Such capabilities led to calls from investors, listed companies, and various national governments for greater regulatory harmonization and creation of a common, precise, legal framework for securities regulation. As it currently stands, a company listing its stock in London, New York, and Tokyo needs to follow three sets of regulations that are at times contradictory. The current situation adds expense for public companies and is said to cause unnecessary rigidity in global capital flows.

National Sovereignty and Oversight

Regulatory harmonization depends on reconciling basic issues of national sovereignty and beneficial, efficacious oversight. In 1999, the European Union adopted the Financial Services Action Plan (FSAP), which set forth as a policy goal the integration of EU member states into one financial marketplace. In 2001 it created the Committee of European Securities Regulators (CESR), an advisory body, to help guide the complex process. By mid 2004, thirty-eight discrete first-step harmonization measures had been adopted by Brussels under the FSAP framework. Yet in early 2005, the EU announced a twelve-month suspension of new directives, in large part because member states were suffering "regulatory fatigue," according to an EU cabinet aide. Basic decisions remaining to be made included naming leadership for the process going forward, membership of the Commission itself, and regulators from each country jointly and/or the financial services industry, or all three.

IR's Global Responsibility

In the United States, IR practitioners must first and foremost understand and follow the regulations of the SEC and the accounting standards of Financial Accounting Standards Board (FASB). But IR is responsible for helping companies fulfill all disclosure and accounting requirements from whatever jurisdiction they emanate.

Investors get information about a company from many sources, and any given investor may at the same time be a customer, employee, supplier, or otherwise related to a company whose stock he or she owns. The proliferation of instantaneous communication, be it via Internet or twenty-four-hour television news, means investors can access many sources of information simultaneously. Enlightened companies work to ensure that every message communicated to all constituencies is consistent and mutually reinforcing.

One key IR responsibility is ensuring informational parity among all constituencies influencing an investor's decision to buy or sell its securities. IR is a highly regulated discipline, and in the United States, IR practitioners are subject to significant civil and criminal liability if they violate certain principles.

Two essential regulatory and legal principles govern the practice of IR: materiality of information and simultaneous availability of that information to all investors. In IR these principles comprise fair disclosure. (The following legal and regularly descriptions and summaries are representative but not necessarily complete; IR professionals must follow the specific advice of their legal counsel.)

> Investors get information about a company from many sources, and any given investor may at the same time be a customer, employee, supplier, or otherwise related to a company whose stock he or she owns.

Materiality

Materiality pertains to whether particular information would have value to an investor. The U.S. Supreme Court has defined materiality as follows:

> "A fact will be considered 'material' if there is a substantial likelihood that a reasonable investor would consider it important in reaching his investment decision—that is, the investor would attach actual significance to the information in making his deliberations."[3]

But who is the "reasonable investor?" Congress, the SEC, and the courts have deliberately left the definition vague. While there are guidelines on what constitutes materiality, ultimately investors can sue if they believe a company failed to disclose material information it was required to disclose—a material omission—or, if it disclosed material information that was false, materially misleading information.

Fraud-on-the-Market Theory

The concept of materiality is central to the SEC's mandate to maintain an open and honest marketplace. It is the result of the interplay between a legal and an economic theory. The U.S. Supreme Court has affirmed what is known as the *fraud-on-the-market-theory*, which says that misleading statements affect the price of securities in the market as a whole and defraud purchasers or sellers, even if they did not rely directly on the misstatements.

Efficient Market Hypothesis

In affirming the fraud-on-the-market theory, the U.S. Supreme Court further affirmed the *efficient market hypothesis*. This economic theory asserts the price of a company's stock in an open and widely traded market reflects all available material information about the company. Material omissions or materially misleading statements distort the price of a company's stock. If performed deliberately, such material omission or misstatement could be considered fraud.

The significance of the adoption of the fraud-on-the-market theory and the efficient market hypothesis is that a company's disclosure obligations apply to a much larger universe than its investors. It has a duty to the market as a whole and can be sued for improper disclosure even by people who never heard or saw the disclosure, because improper disclosure would have had an impact on the market as a whole.

Defining Securities Fraud

What constitutes securities fraud?

In the United States a company and its officers, directors, and IR professionals are governed by the anti-fraud provisions of the SEC. In its entirety, SEC Rule 10b-5 reads:

> It shall be unlawful for any person, directly or indirectly, by the use of any means or instrumentality of interstate commerce, or of the mails, or of any facility of any national exchange,
>
> a) to employ any device, scheme, or artifice to defraud,
>
> b) to make any untrue statement of a material fact or to omit to state a material fact necessary in order to make the statements made, in light of the circumstances under which they were made, not misleading,

c) to engage in any act, practice, or course of business which operates
or would operate as a fraud or deceit upon any person, in connection
with the purchase or sale of a security.[4]

The rule does not specify particular content of communication which
constitutes fraud, simply that a person or company committed a material
omission or disclosed something materially misleading that operates as a
deceit in the securities market.

IR and Legal Liability

Many companies get legal advice and establish their own materiality guidelines; they include their lawyers in decisions about whether a particular
piece of information is material. IR people often defer, appropriately, to the
advice of counsel.

In the United States IR people are also subject to legal liability, including criminal liability, for failure to disclose material information. In most
other disciplines, if a corporate communication or public relations professional in good faith helps disseminate information about the company that
later proves to be false, the communication professional is generally exempt
from legal sanction. But in the United States the SEC has ruled that IR
professionals can be subject to civil or criminal liability if they knew or
should have known that the information transmitted was materially misleading or a material omission:

> "Although the [SEC] does not regard public relations firms to be the guar-
> antors of the information they gather for distribution, such firms should not
> view themselves as mere publicists or communicators of information with
> no attendant responsibility whatsoever for the content of such information.
>
> Indeed, these firms must be aware of their obligation not to disseminate
> information concerning their clients which they know or have reason to
> know is materially false or misleading.
>
> The obligation is particularly crucial with respect to corporate financial
> statements, which are one of the primary sources of information available
> to guide the decisions of investors.
>
> In distributing financial information, public relations firms must take
> special care to ensure that the information which they have received is pre-
> sented fairly, accurately, and completely.
>
> Public relations firms' dissemination of information concerning their cli-
> ents which they know or should have reason to know is materially false or
> misleading, in connection with the purchase or sale of securities of such cli-
> ents, may render them liable for violations of the federal securities laws."[5]

*IR professionals
can be subject to
civil or criminal
liability if they
knew or should
have known that
the information
transmitted was
materially mislead-
ing or a material
omission.*

Establishing Personal Ground Rules

IR professionals need to understand clearly what they are willing and unwilling to do and in some ways to act as the conscience of the corporation.

For example, coauthor Fred Garcia has advised large corporations on IR for more than twenty years. In that time, four separate companies have asked him to disseminate information that he considered to be materially misleading. In most cases, the cause was panic by executives afraid to disclose bad news and who wanted to publish financial results that ignored negative information—a material omission. In each case Fred called the request to the attention of senior managers and in-house lawyers, expressed his belief that such a disclosure would be materially misleading, and declined to participate in the dissemination of the information. In each case the company reconsidered and published accurate information. Also in each case, Fred continued to advise the company and suffered no negative repercussion. In most cases, senior leadership later said they would ultimately have come to the same decision before releasing the skewed information. But Fred's calling attention to the problem redirected the company's energies to creating a materially accurate release.

Materiality concerns the content of information. Information deemed to be material is subject to requirements including restrictions on when and how it may be communicated and to whom. Business-as-usual information such as internal memos, advertisements, and marketing materials are not generally considered material and therefore not subject to restrictions on dissemination. But if routine communication contains information that a reasonable investor might consider important in making an investment decision, and if that information has not yet been disclosed to the marketplace, even otherwise routine communication may be considered material.

Disclosure

Disclosure concerns the timing, scope, and manner of communication of material information. As a general rule, information must be made available to all investors simultaneously. Selective disclosure—telling only some investors material news before other investors—is a violation of U.S. securities law and regulation. The overall goal of disclosure is to provide transparency, to provide anyone who may invest in a company's securities with more than sufficient, relevant information about the company's finances and operations so that nothing is hidden or distorted in meaning.

There are two kinds of disclosure. Formal disclosure requires that specific financial information be reviewed by and filed with securities regulators on a regularly scheduled basis, in a highly structured format, under the signature of senior corporate officers. Formal disclosure is generally handled within a corporation by its legal, corporate finance, and accounting arms, with support from IR.

Informal disclosure involves market communication that is unstructured, not mediated by regulators, and distributed through a variety of communications channels. Much, but not all, communication by an IR practitioner is considered to be informal disclosure.

Since theoretically any investor could be considered a potential shareholder, companies typically reach out to the entire securities market in formal and informal disclosures. IR practitioners certainly need to focus on current shareholders' perceptions and understandings, but practitioners must also be constantly aware that every word they say carries the potential that investors who do not hold shares may be induced to buy them based on the information disclosed.

Recent Disclosure Regulation

Over the last ten years in the United States, a variety of initiatives have gone into effect designed to enhance transparency, level the informational playing field, speed the availability of corporate data, and improve corporate governance. For IR professionals, the two key initiatives to understand are *Regulation Fair Disclosure*, which became effective in October 2000, and the Sarbanes-Oxley law, which became effective in stages between 2002 and 2006.

SEC Regulation Fair Disclosure (or Reg. FD) generally prohibits disclosure of material information selectively by a corporation to analysts, or others. Prior to Reg. FD, it was common IR practice to hold special closed-door meetings for selected investors and analysts and to limit or forbid general investors' participation in management conference calls, and so forth Even though stock prices could gyrate wildly during these sessions as the privileged few took advantage of insider status to make a few bucks, the principle was that "sophisticated" information discussed in these venues exceeded that needed by the average market participant. The potential for abuse was obvious.

Under Reg. FD, corporate officers are permitted to conduct closed meetings with certain analysts or investors, but material information may not be disclosed unless it is also made available to the entire market simultaneously through other channels. If new information is blurted out by accident—for instance, by a carelessly speaking CEO—the corporation has an affirmative duty to notify the entire market of that information "promptly." The SEC has interpreted the regulation to mean in no event more than twenty-four hours later or by the beginning of the next day's trading session, whichever comes first.

> If new information is blurted out by accident—for instance, by a carelessly speaking CEO—the corporation has an affirmative duty to notify the entire market of that information "promptly."

Reg. FD "Carve Out" for Working Journalists

A company's communication with journalists acting in the course of their profession has a special exemption, or "carve out", from Reg. FD restrictions. Corporations may disclose nonpublic material information to a journalist during a briefing or dialogue without triggering Reg. FD. The SEC adopted this exception to prevent corporations using FD to avoid talking to the press.

The SEC: Formal and Informal Disclosure in the United States

Formal procedures of disclosure require release of detailed information about a business, its financial results, its management, and its management's thoughts and analysis of company operations on a regularly scheduled basis. In the United States, the SEC provides preset disclosure forms. IR professionals need to understand three of them.

First, SEC Form 10-K: for most U.S. public companies (called "accelerated filers" in SEC lingo) and due at SEC no later than sixty days after the end of a company's fiscal year. The 10-K is the primary formal disclosure document. Financial statements in a 10-K must be audited by the company's outside independent auditor, which must attest to the 10-K's accuracy. It also must contain a comprehensive discussion and analysis of the company's operations and results for the prior fiscal year; an overview of the risks the company faces; biographical information on senior officers and directors, their compensation, their stock ownership; and other information considered important by the SEC. The 10-K becomes a public document automatically upon formal filing at the SEC, and anyone can obtain it (or any other SEC filing), either in hard copy, or through the SEC's Web site on its document system known as Electronic Data Gathering and Retrieval (EDGAR).

Second, SEC Form 10-Q: due at the SEC thirty-five days after the end of each of the first three fiscal quarters. The 10-Q is a briefer version of the annual 10-K and contains unaudited financial results and the management's discussion and analysis of performance during the most recent quarter.

Third, SEC Form 8-K: Filed any time during the fiscal year within four business days of a reportable event. In August 2004 the SEC expanded the number of events considered "reportable" to fourteen, from four. They include material agreements made not in the course of regular business, creation of material off-balance sheet financial arrangements; material acquisitions or dispositions of assets, commencement of bankruptcy or receivership proceedings, change in auditors; resignation of directors or senior officers, and others. To be safe, in addition to the fourteen events specified by the SEC, many companies file 8-K's on any major event that might be considered material.

Additional Documents for Formal Disclosure

Formal disclosure includes two other documents that are not set down on SEC forms. These are the proxy materials for the shareholders' annual meeting and the company's annual report to shareholders.

Proxy

Proxy disclosure is written material distributed to each shareholder in advance of a company's annual meeting, the required yearly gathering of a company's shareholders to review performance and take major decisions through a one share, one vote election. Large corporations may have tens of millions of shares outstanding (and thus tens of millions potential votes) held by tens of thousands of shareholders. Because it is unlikely every shareholder can attend the meeting, a proxy method was developed so all shareholders can vote regardless of whether they attend in person.

A proxy is an authorization to vote a shareholder's securities. Typically, a company's senior managers ask permission to be the substitute elector; and shareholders generally grant permission routinely. Thus management usually enters the meeting with enough votes in hand to control all decisions; the annual meeting becomes a pro forma. Increasingly often, shareholders have withheld their proxy from management or given it to dissident shareholders who challenge management on key decisions. Such a situation is known as a proxy fight, which falls into the category of shareholder activism in which shareholders force decisions contrary to those of company management. Recent proxy fights have occurred over issues including forcing a company into a merger that management had recommended against, limiting executive compensation, and directing a company's public policy initiatives in human rights and the environment.

Since the proxy is the key vehicle for shareholder democracy and control, the proxy statement must contain detailed information about all matters to be discussed and voted upon at the meeting. It must clearly state when and where the annual meeting will be held. It must outline each proposal to be decided at the meeting and note pros and cons. It must include biographical information about officers and directors. The proxy material must be in the hands of shareholders thirty days before the scheduled meeting. The SEC must review and approve all proxy material before distribution.

Annual Report to Shareholders

Formal disclosure also includes the annual report to shareholders. Unlike the Form 10-K annual report filed with the SEC, the annual report to shareholders is a "free writing" which does not need preclearance by the SEC. However, it must be submitted to the SEC after distribution to shareholders with or before solicitation of proxies for a company's annual meeting. Although the annual report does not require prior SEC clearance, there is significant legal liability for material omission or misstatement in the annual report.

The annual report to shareholders must include much of the information contained in the 10-K filed with the SEC. In fact, some companies use the 10-K, wrapped with a brief introductory text, as their annual report to shareholders.

More commonly, corporations use the annual report as a corporate marketing brochure and include the technical financial and operating information in the back; the front becomes a high-quality stylized brochure with essays, pictures, and art.

Typically the IR department or the corporate communication department is charged with writing and designing the overall annual report to shareholders, leaving room for insertion of financial statements and footnotes. Not surprisingly, sophisticated investors often ignore the front part of the annual report—the marketing sections—and turn first to the financial data in the back of the annual report. Although the annual report to shareholders is mandated by the SEC, the actual audience for the report is much wider than the investment community. For some companies, the annual report is the only publication that describes the entire company. Companies therefore devote significant time and attention in creating the front part of the annual report.

Informal Disclosure

In addition to formal disclosure, companies must adhere to standards of accuracy and completeness in the process of informal disclosure, which comprises all other communications that might reasonably be expected to reach the investing public.

Communications considered informal disclosure include those directed specifically to the investment community:

⇒ News releases
⇒ Corporate promotional materials
⇒ Direct communication with securities analysts, including written and electronic, in person or telephonic
⇒ Direct communication with shareholders, including written and electronic, in person or telephonic
⇒ The investor relations portion of the company's Web site as well as other sections containing data and information an investor might consider making an investment decision

Informal disclosure also includes communication that is not necessarily directed at the financial community but in which there is significant likelihood the information might filter into the investment community. Such communication includes:

⇒ Labor negotiations

⇒ Public regulatory filings, such as those required by electric utilities, banks, insurance companies, and other regulated industries

⇒ Product promotional materials

Informal disclosure does not need to be reviewed in advance by the SEC and in general requires no SEC filing, before or after. However, informal disclosure, like formal disclosure, is governed by the SEC antifraud provisions and by Reg. FD.

Timing Disclosure

Timing informal disclosure is less precise than timing formal disclosure. Companies do not have an obligation to disclose material information just because the information exists. The SEC and the courts give corporations some flexibility in delaying disclosure.

Timing of disclosure is generally left to companies. Very often they combine formal and informal disclosure: They coordinate filing a Form 10-Q (formal disclosure) with distribution of quarterly earnings information to the marketplace as a whole (informal disclosure). Thus in practice sometimes the timing of informal disclosure is governed by filing requirements of formal disclosure.

Where no duty to disclose exists, the timing of disclosure is governed by the business judgment rule:

"The timing of disclosure of material facts is a matter for the business judgment of the corporate management of the corporation within the affirmative disclosure requirements promulgated by the exchanges and the SEC … The defendant as a defense could show either good faith or the exercise of good business judgment in its acts or inaction."[6]

The court has held that it may be inappropriate and misleading to release information prematurely, and a corporation should wait until the information is "ripe."

"The information must be 'available and ripe for publication' before there commences a duty to disclose. To be ripe under this requirement, the contents must be verified sufficiently to permit the officers and directors to have full confidence in their accuracy. It also means … that there is no valid corporate purpose which dictates that the information not be disclosed."[7]

However, once a duty to disclose exists, material facts must be disclosed promptly. Companies may also be required to disclose when they can no longer maintain confidentiality of information.

When a company does disclose—whether by choice or because it is required to—that disclosure must be accurate, complete, and not misleading.

Disclosing More than Required by Law

> Disclosing more can be a competitive advantage.

It is important to note the system of corporate disclosure currently in place is a floor, not a ceiling. It is what is required as a necessary fact of doing business as a public company in the United States But such disclosure is generally not sufficient to establish and maintain long-term investor appetite for company securities. Corporations are permitted to engage in far more disclosure than the minimum requirements, and many do.

For example, there is no requirement that companies speak to individual securities analysts or to groups of analysts. But most companies do.

Except for the annual meeting, there is no requirement for companies to meet with or speak directly with their own shareholders. But most companies stay in constant touch with their shareholders and with the analysts who influence them.

In conclusion, companies which disclose more information more frequently than required often establish a competitive advantage for their securities and simultaneously ensure investors are sufficiently comfortable to buy or hold their shares. Generally, investors are more comfortable buying and holding the stocks of companies they understand than of those they do not.

Best Practices

Effective management of investor relations can help enhance a company's reputation among its investors and other key constituencies. Among the best practices are:

1. Ground all IR activities in the corporate and financial goals of the company: IR is an integral, not incidental, part of corporate strategy and management.
2. Coordinate closely with the CFO, Media Relations, and, if employees own significant shares, with employee relations.
3. Coordinate closely with the accountants and lawyers on all formal disclosure, especially regulatory filings.
4. Do more than what is required: Make it easy for investors to access information that has been disclosed, including via the company's Web site.

Resources for Further Study

National Association of Corporate Directors

The National Association of Corporate Directors (NACD) is a professional society for corporate directors and those who advise corporate directors. It is a resource on corporate governance and other issues of significance in IR. The Web site is at http://www.nacdonline.org.

National Investor Relations Institute

The National Investor Relations Institute (NIRI) is the professional society for investor relations professionals in the United States. It offers a number of publications, seminars, and programs to enhance IR professionals' practice.It also offers a particularly useful CD-ROM, Introduction to Investor Relations. Santa Monica: National Investor Relations Institute, 2005.The CD-ROM and other information is available at http://www.niri.org.

Publications

The following publications may be useful for those in IR or who aspire to work in IR:

DiPiazza, Samuel A., Jr., and Robert Eccles. *Building public trust: The future of corporate reporting.* New York: John Wiley & Sons., 2002.

Downes, John, and Jordan Elliot Goodman. *Dictionary of finance and investment terms.* New York: Barron's Educational Series, 2002.

Investor Relations Magazine at http://www.irmag.com.

Schwed, Fred. *Where are the customers' yachts? Or a good hard look at Wall Street.* Reprinted 1995. New York: John Wiley & Sons, 1995.

Trautman, Ted and Hamilton, James. 2004. *Informal Corporate Disclosure under Federal Securities Law.* New York/Washington D.C.: CCH Publications.

Questions for Further Discussion

1. Is it more important to be an expert in finance or to be an expert in your company's business (e.g., an engineer in a technology company) to be an effective IR practitioner?

2. What is the optimal relationship between the IR function and the media relations function?

3. Why is an IR person subject to different legal standards (e.g., subject to civil and possibly criminal action if he or she conveys false information) than other communication professionals?

4. How should an IR person balance the desire to position the company as positively as possible with the requirements regarding formal and informal disclosure of material information?

5. When employees own a significant percentage of a company's stock, how should an IR person optimally coordinate with employee communications?

CHAPTER 9

Global Corporate Communication

By Lynn Appelbaum, APR,
Associate professor, The City College of New York

and Gail S. Belmuth,
*Former vice president of Global Corporate Communications,
International Flavors & Fragrances Inc.*

> *Make sure it plays in Peoria, Paris, and Phnom Penh.*

In September 2000, International Flavors & Fragrances Inc. (IFF), one of the world's leading creators and manufacturers of flavors and fragrances for consumer products, announced that it would acquire Bush Boake Allen (BBA), another major industry player. When the acquisition was announced, the combined companies had approximately 7,000 employees in seventry-five locations in forty-two countries. IFF needed to communicate rapidly, clearly, simultaneously, and positively to its internal and external global stakeholders to ensure that the news was received in a timely way and with clear, consistent messages reinforcing the company's objectives and mission.

All acquisition communication, regardless of the target audience, stressed the same information:

The rationale for merging

Next steps in the acquisition integration

A pledge to make decisions rapidly and fairly and to communicate throughout the integration

A commitment to achieve savings through consolidation and elimination of duplication

Employees: Due to timing considerations IFF and BBA senior management handled the initial announcement centrally. The initial employee communication package included videos from the two chairmen, a Q&A, and the press release. Follow-up was handled through a monthly integration newsletter and face-to-face meetings. Locally driven communication also began during the postannouncement integration period, as local decisions regarding consolidation of facilities, production, and staff became known.

Customers: There was surprisingly little customer overlap for two companies in the same industry. Therefore, while stressing the greater reach and resources available to them over the long-term, the company used the announcement as an opportunity to "check in" with customers to discuss potential service improvements.

Investment community: IFF and BBA held a conference call with investors after the close of business on announcement day, followed by one-on-one calls with individual investors. Throughout the integration period, the company reported on its progress through investor road shows in the United States and Europe, quarterly earnings announcements, and speeches at consumer product conferences sponsored by leading investment banks.

Media relations: IFF and BBA did not seek media coverage at the time of the announcement, preferring to discuss acquisition milestones when they reached them. Local media inquiries regarding the closure of individual facilities were handled locally or centrally, as appropriate.

Government/community relations: Government and community relations were not a key focus in the merger announcement, as there were no anti-trust issues and no immediate impact in the communities where the companies operated. These functions became more important as individual facilities were closed and jobs were eliminated or transferred. Appropriate spokespeople for each location, consolidation, or situation were selected on a case-by-case basis.

* * * * *

Global corporate communication is the planned, long-term, strategically designed way of managing relationships with publics of other nations. In global corporate communication—as in most corporate communication—news impacts constituents in many locations. Announcements must be coordinated to account for different time zones, languages, and perspectives. And post-announcement follow-up is often more important than the initial announcement.

This Chapter Covers

⇒ The global imperative
⇒ Global corporate communication role
⇒ Standardize or customize?
⇒ Global communication network
⇒ Internal communication
⇒ External communication
⇒ Working with PR agencies
⇒ Measuring success
⇒ Best practices
⇒ Resources for further study
⇒ Questions for further discussion

The Global Imperative

Michael Morley, deputy chairman of Edelman Public Relations World-wide, notes, "There is not likely to be a phrase you will hear in your career in public relations as often as 'think global, act local'. It is used to encourage international marketers and communicators to adapt their products or messages to be accepted in a variety of local communities around a region or around the world."[1]

A global professional communicator needs a broad range of skills beyond the traditional ones. As Robert I. Wakefield, a consultant, author, and researcher specializing in cross-cultural effects on reputation in multinational organizations, noted in the Spring 2000 *Strategist*: "Considering that problems can arise anywhere and instantly become global, professionals are needed who can see the big picture and facilitate interaction between host units and headquarters to avoid these problems. They should be skilled in communication, but also in global economics and politics, mediation, cultural anthropology, and other fields relevant to the global arena."[2]

The Global Village Is Here

Marshall McLuhan's global village is here. Today, almost one third of all U.S. corporate profits are generated through international business.[3] Global investments are growing at record levels. In 2003, Americans owned $3.1 trillion of foreign stocks and bonds, while non-Americans owned more than $4.1 trillion of U.S. securities, according to the International Monetary Fund.[4]

Several key factors have led to the shift in the global business paradigm. In Fraser Seitel's *The Practice of Public Relations*, former PRSA President Joe Epley identifies three reasons for increased interaction among organizations and global publics:

⇒ "The expansion of communications technology has increased the dissemination of information about products, services and lifestyles around the world thus creating global demand.

⇒ "The realignment of economic power, caused by the formation of multinational trading blocs, such as the North American Free Trade Agreement (NAFTA), Asia Pacific Economic Conference (APEC), Organization of African Unity (OAU), and the European Economic Community (EEC)" (now the European Union or EU).

⇒ "People around the world are uniting in pursuit of common goals, such as reducing population growth, protecting the environment, waging the war against terrorism, and fighting disease, particularly AIDS."[5]

In order to operate effectively in the new international business environment, global communication practitioners need a comprehensive understanding of the many different cultures they will encounter. They must learn not only the local business practices of a host country or an international client, but also the relevant customs and appropriate communication styles. In addition, they will need a thorough knowledge of political, economic, social, and cultural values wherever they are doing business throughout the world. Therefore, in order to fully understand the practice of global corporate communication, one must not only understand the basic principles of public relations and corporate communications, but also draw upon a broad range of global society theories, cultural theories, management theories, and communication theories (see sidebar). This expansive foundation allows the practitioner to present the most compelling and credible message in a meaningful and relevant manner.

Global reputation management draws upon core communication values and practices honest, informed, timely communication to key audiences, or as Wilcox, Ault and Agee define it, "the planned and organized effort of a company, institute, or government to establish mutually beneficial relations with publics of other nations."[6] But applying solid research, effective strategic planning, tactical execution, and evaluation assumes a more complex and critical role on a global scale.

The cornerstone for successful communication is to build relationships inside and outside the company that are genuinely mutual and beneficial to both the company and its global constituents.

Establishing trust among global stakeholders can be challenging. The growing global agenda of poverty, human rights, the environment, labor abuses, corruption, consumer issues, and cultural and religious insensitivity place corporate communication among a company's most important assets. As discussed in Chapter 13 on corporate responsibility, human rights are now a business concern.[7] Today, alongside governments, companies often are viewed as a source or cause of human rights abuse, as well as an international actor with the capacity to promote human rights.[8] Therefore, it is essential that corporate communicators make efforts to build relationships across the broad spectrum of a company's global stakeholders through effective two-way communication.

> Global communication practitioners need a comprehensive understanding of the many different cultures they will encounter.

> Establishing trust among global stakeholders can be challenging.

A Foundation for Global Communication

In *International Public Relations, A Comparative Analysis*, Hugh M. Culbertson and Ni Chen derive a four-pronged model for global communication incorporating global, cultural, management, and communication theories, relating to PR theory.

Global society theories: Globalization causes turbulence, conflict, competition, and uncertainty. This creates a pressing need for organizations to predict and adapt to changing conditions based on information and research, and to identify, respond to, and resolve conflicts as they arise. Communication professionals can contribute strongly to this process. (Robertson, 1990, Lesly, 1991)

Cultural theories: Culture is an important determinant of how communication functions within and between societies. Companies must be open to multicultural influences and take full advantage of their employees' diverse backgrounds and abilities and blend both global and local coordination.

Management theories show a need for cultural sensitivity and for "third culture" practitioners, who transcend boundaries using global media, transnational education, cultural exchanges, and so forth. Effective organizations combine both culture-free and culture-specific values (Brinkerhoff and Ingle [1989] p. 25), providing common overall goals at the global level that are then tailored to the local needs of each culture.

Communication theories focus on the increasing influence of global media. People's views of international events are heavily media dependent (Manheim and Albritton [1984] pp. 25-6), since many people have little direct experience of other countries. Activists use the media to publicize their issues and influence policymakers around the world (Hiebert [1992] p. 26). Communication professionals need to understand and respond to the issues affecting their organization (L. Grunig [1992]) through relationship building and proactive PR.

Each of these findings relates to James Grunig's "Excellence Project," a seminal theoretical PR framework. Grunig states that PR contributes to an organization's success by (1) reducing conflicts and building relationships; (2) supporting management; (3) participating in management's "inner circle"; (4) respecting publics and practicing two-way communication; and (5) respecting diversity. (Culbertson & Chen, p. 20)

Gavin Anderson, founder and former chairman of Gavin Anderson & Company, a global corporate communication agency, has identified two competing approaches to international communication—the global versus the multinational.

Global Model.

"Global public relations superimposes an overall perspective on a program executed in two or more national markets, recognizing the similarities among audiences while necessarily adapting to regional differences. It connotes a planning attitude as much as geographic reach and flexibility."[9]

Multinational Model.

"International PR practitioners often implement distinctive programs in multiple markets, with each program tailored to meet the often acute distinctions of the individual market."

Anderson argues that the global model is more effective. "Global, as opposed to multinational, businesses demand that programs in distinctive markets be interrelated. While there will always be local differences and need for customization, the programs will probably share more than they differ."[10]

Establishing Credibility and Trust

Credibility and trust is at the core of any global communication program. Effective communication hinges on the ability of a company to communicate in respectful, clear, and credible ways to diverse local constituents based on their perceptual context, needs, and interests while supporting the company's global mission and objectives. While a consistent, unified, global branding message or identity is essential, a "one size fits all" message risks alienating audiences if the message is misunderstood. A truly effective global brand adapts to local needs while maintaining its essence.

A frequent obstacle to clear communication in large organizations is distrust of central authority, particularly when that authority is far away, in another country, and part of a different culture. It is easy to believe that distant authorities with such different backgrounds and cultures cannot possibly understand local problems and have overriding self-interests at heart. While it is difficult to completely eliminate this perception, international communication professionals must strive to minimize it through policies and initiatives encouraging two-way flows of learning, communication, and information.

> A truly effective global brand adapts to local needs while maintaining its essence.

The Global Corporate Communication Role

Most global corporate communication practitioners have responsibility for the following functions:

⇒ Employee communication
⇒ Media relations
⇒ Corporate brand and issues advertising
⇒ Public and community relations
⇒ Crisis communication
⇒ Public affairs
⇒ Investor relations
⇒ Annual report and other publications

⇒ Corporate philanthropy
⇒ Corporate identity or branding
⇒ Web site

In a global context, practitioners must deal with the added aspects of cultural and language diversity, wide geographic reach, time zone differences, local and regional regulation and legislation, and huge disparities in a company's physical plant, IT infrastructure, employment and compensation practices, and budgets from one location to another. This means that many corporate cultures are more like patchwork quilts than unified entities. It is challenging to manage global reputation, image, and brand when a culture is so varied.

Standardize or Customize? That Is the Question.

One of the greatest challenges is managing a task of such enormous scope with typically modest resources. While communication professionals see the value of their contribution to the bottom line, the function is in fact a cost center, not a profit center.

One of the best ways to promote efficiency in global corporate communication is to standardize as much as possible. This includes the Web site, printed publications, and all signage and corporate identity materials. This saves time and a significant amount of money, and adds an important strategic benefit: reinforcing and strengthening the company's image and brand.

In addressing best practices for global corporate reputation management, effective management of both internal and external audiences is essential to implement a successful strategic plan. We will begin with the internal structure of corporate communication and employee communication, since without excellent internal communication across borders and cultures, it is difficult to execute a consistent and effective global message to external stakeholders. Since every global employee is a potential ambassador for a company's corporate message or brand, excellent internal communication is essential.

Most corporate communication functions are chronically understaffed.

The Global Corporate Communication Department

Most corporate communication functions are chronically understaffed. As companies grow, they rarely expand the communication function commensurately. Most organizations promise shareholders that acquisitions will create "synergies"—that is, cost-cutting and layoffs. Few growing companies can afford to ease up on profitability.

An ideal global corporate communication organization would include directors to oversee each of the areas of responsibility listed above, and would also have directors for each of the company's key geographic regions. The reality, however, is often quite different. Many global corporate communication departments consist of a director and a support person. Outside of the largest multinationals, there are rarely dedicated resources at the regional or local level.

Most organizations largely centralize their global communication staff, for several reasons. First, a centralized structure helps ensure that the organization speaks with one voice. In addition, the head of communication needs to be a member of the senior executive team. Communication staffers cannot do their jobs well without being among the first to receive important information. Other staff functions—finance, legal, human resources—tend to be concentrated centrally, though finance and human resources are likely to have larger staffs and regional representation. With limited resources it is often most effective to centralize communication, since each staff member is likely to wear several hats.

Parlez Vous Urdu? Language in Global Companies

The choice of language or languages an organization uses for official communication is key. Even in non-U.S.—or non-U.K.—headquartered companies, English is often considered the official language of business, though a company's primary language may be that of the country where the company is headquartered. Having a single official language makes the preparation of documents easier and faster. A single language also reduces the chance of translation errors.

The disadvantage of having a single official language, however, is obvious. One cannot assume that a factory worker in Bangalore, or Buffalo, will be bilingual.[11] It is not just a job function issue. Many senior executives, particularly in the United States, are not fluent in more than one language.

Having an "official company language" rarely means all business is conducted in that language. If the official language is French, for example, but a Chinese salesperson is speaking with a Chinese customer, it would be inappropriate for them to try to communicate in French. However, communication from the corporate center—annual report, press releases, Web site and memos from the CEO—would almost certainly be in French. Many international companies will routinely translate important documents such as annual reports into two or three languages (English, French, and Spanish), depending on their key global markets.

When official documents need to be translated, it is best for the translation to be done in the countries where they will be used. If the documents are intended for the media, they should be translated by someone familiar with local media usage and language. While central translation may be easier to control and cheaper, local translation will save revisions to adapt to local dialects.

> One cannot assume that a factory worker in Bangalore, or Buffalo, will be bilingual.

Communicating to global external audiences in clear and understandable terms may also be challenging since subtleties of language and expressions can be offensive out of their cultural context. Consider the case of a global hotel and gaming company that has as one of its core values a goal to "blow away the customer." When the company planned to announce a development in the Middle East, it removed the core value from its media relations materials as to not offend anyone because the phrase may be taken literally in that part of the world.[12]

The Global Communication Network

If a company cannot afford a vast global communication staff, there are still ways to provide vital local communication information and counsel as needed. Many companies create global communication networks. These networks include individuals whose functions overlap with corporate communication, such as marketing, human resources, and investor relations.[13] Network members should be heavy users of corporate communication's services. The network can be used as a sounding board, to review drafts or to source local printers and other vendors. Since these people have "regular day jobs," it is important to limit the extent to which their input is solicited. Ideally, the global communication network will be self-selecting, meaning that the individuals in it have expressed interest in serving on such a team.

Working with an international/intercultural communication team provides added challenges to mounting a coordinated communication effort. Some of these barriers include (1) a bias to communicate locally, not globally, about key initiatives; (2) a global team dominated by headquarters perspectives; and (3) a lack of understanding between corporate and local teams. While a global network can provide local market understanding, a corporate communication professional may encounter resistance to corporate directives. Local teams may be skeptical of messages from headquarters and perceive them as out of touch. Homogeneous corporate messages may not reflect the diversity of knowledge, perspectives, and experiences in the field. And when working with daily local pressures from their own country management, there may not be time to contribute to a global collaborative process.

These disparities in culture and possible mistrust of centralized communication make face-to-face meetings among communication practitioners even more important, especially before launching a major campaign. According to Bonin Bough, Ruder Finn's senior vice president and director of strategy and architecture, "The cost of arranging a face-to-face meeting of your global team before launching a campaign is essential to get everyone's feedback in the planning stage. And if you can't meet in person, then it's essential to video or teleconference. It's a chance to avoid wasteful mistakes before they happen."[14]

Internal Communication—Worldwide

The Internet is especially important for global audiences. While global perceptions will vary, the Internet is the one communication mechanism that reaches constituents globally on a 24/7 basis. The Internet is also a significant money saver; eliminating the need to print and mail many items. Fewer companies have printed employee newsletters, and increasingly investors (at least institutional investors) say they would prefer to download annual reports than receive hard copies.

Global corporate communicators need to evaluate when to adapt their Web sites for global audiences. A Web site in only one language can alienate key international stakeholders, especially where the company has local workers. While creating a multilingual site takes time and money, it is important to consider doing so in major markets.[15]

Technology in a Global Setting

Technology is one of the most important tools of effective global communication for both internal and external audiences.

Internally, intranets, extranets, and e-mails are essential tools that facilitate multi-directional global communication. Colleagues in different countries can collaborate on documents. Shared files, department web pages, and easy-to-access document drops have removed many technical and physical impediments to knowledge and information sharing (human nature may still present obstacles, however!). Video conferencing has become a meaningful communication and collaboration channel.

Technology, especially the Internet, has radically changed global corporate communication and made it more efficient. Press releases can be distributed globally and instantly. Key documents such as the annual report, executives' bios and quarterly earnings announcements can be archived on a company's Web site for easy download. Even annual shareholder meetings are no longer limited to those near headquarters if the meeting is Web cast.

Posting information and press releases on the Web site on a timely basis is essential. Too often, materials appearing on Web sites are not up to date. Companies can offend or confuse by offering "yesterday's news" on their sites.

An extranet, an interactive Web site for members of global company's PR team, is especially useful to facilitate strategy and tactics "to bring access to a company's assets" (Bough 2005).

Senior Management's Role in Global Employee Communication

Employees worldwide are more closely connected both with their peers and with senior management because of global communication technology. Many CEOs e-mail periodic memos to all employees, updating strategic projects or simply sharing thoughts and thereby establishing a relationship, if only virtually, with a broader employee base than in the past.

Richard A. Goldstein, chairman and chief executive officer of International Flavors & Fragrances Inc., supplements his monthly memos to employees with quarterly global conference calls, held immediately following the company's earnings announcements. The calls are held at 7:30 a.m. New York time to accommodate employees in as many time zones as possible. Employees who prefer to ask questions anonymously can do so by fax or e-mail. The chairman and other senior executives field questions in their areas of responsibility. The global conference call serves multiple purposes:

> Of course, no amount of communication by telephone, video, or e-mail can replace face-to-face communication.

⇒ Employees who may rarely meet the chairman and the executive team can hear their voices and get a feel for how they work together.

⇒ Employees learn what is on their colleagues' minds in other countries. During a typical call, IFF may receive questions from over ten countries. As most of its employee base does little international travel, this is an effective way to get a sense of the breadth and diversity of the company and to feel part of something larger.

⇒ Anonymous questions ensure that difficult or negative issues being discussed in private or around the coffee machine are addressed publicly. Facing resentment head on—be it about executive compensation, benefits changes, or facility closings—is an invaluable step in allowing an organization to deal with change and move on. Employees are also more likely to trust leaders who tell the truth, however difficult it may be.

⇒ The calls are a high profile example of senior management's commitment to open, two-way communication with all employees.

⇒ Linking the employee calls with quarterly earnings announcements reminds employees that everything IFF does is to help the company grow and increase shareholder value.

Of course, no amount of communication by telephone, video, or e-mail can replace face-to-face communication. Site managers, local HR representatives, and front-line supervisors will always play a critical role in local communication.

For multinational companies, it is important that the CEO and other senior managers make periodic visits to as many affiliates as practical, understanding that too frequent travel can be prohibitively expensive and can take too much time away from day-to-day requirements. A town hall meeting with the CEO is always important, but in cultures that are more hierarchical than the United States, it takes on added weight. In India, it is not unusual for visiting high officials and company heads to be greeted by an elephant (a symbol of good luck) and a military marching band. In many cultures, the exchange of gifts is expected. The global corporate communication professional should learn such customs and brief the senior team in advance to avoid faux pas, embarrassments, or insults.

Because a visit from corporate headquarters can be costly and require extensive advance planning, it is important that the communication professional discourage unnecessary travel to avoid placing an undue burden on colleagues around the world. However, these visits can be very meaningful to employees in the host country. With boards of directors taking a greater interest in corporate governance due to the Sarbanes-Oxley Act, board members often travel with senior management.

Technology's enormous role in facilitating global employee communication is both good news and bad news, since it can make responding to e-mail a full-time job. In any large organization, the opportunity to communicate "too much" grows exponentially. As a result, communication and IT professionals often remind their colleagues to send fewer e-mails, copy fewer people, and remove attachments to avoid clogging up networks and distracting employees from more important matters.

Cascade Communication in Global Organizations

As mentioned earlier, organizational communication research suggests that employees prefer to get the most critical information from their immediate supervisors. This suggests that cascade communication should be an important part of global communication. Indeed, many communication departments and their agencies of record create "communication toolkits" with customizable PowerPoint® presentations and talking points, Q&As, assignments for breakout groups and discussion sessions, and feedback/evaluation forms to rate the effectiveness of the communication.

While managers need tools and information to discuss key issues with their teams, experience shows that effective use of global cascade communication is more difficult to achieve. Here is a vastly simplified example:

Chairman: Today is an important day in our company's history. We have decided to change our name from "One of the Great Spaghetti and Meatball Factories" to "The World's Best Meatball Factory." Why? Three reasons. First, we recently sold our spaghetti business, and our name should reflect that we're just meatballs now. Second, because we want to claim our spot as the best meatball company, not just one of the best meatball companies. And third, because we want to call attention to our global reach.

> Organizational communication research suggests that employees prefer to get the most critical information from their immediate supervisors.

Regional manager: Today is an important day in our company's history. We have decided to change our name from "One of the Great Spaghetti and Meatball Factories" to "The World's Best Meatball Factory." Why? Three reasons. First, we recently sold our spaghetti business, and our name should reflect that we're just meatballs now. Second, because we want to claim our spot as the best meatball company, not just one of the best meatball companies. And third ... well, I forgot the third reason.

Country manager: Today is an important day in our company's history. We have decided to change our name from "One of the Great Spaghetti and Meatball Factories" to "The World's Best Meatball Factory."

Line manager: Today, our company decided to change its name to "The World's Best Meatball Factory." Is that a stupid name or what?

Limited understanding of the language of a cascade toolkit only compounds the issue, increasing the chances that the manager will misinterpret the news and present it in a different, inaccurate, or negative light. With big news, there is rarely time to translate large quantities of communication materials, so it is important to use cascade communication carefully and discriminatingly in global organizations.

External Communication

The Global/Local Issue as a Message Strategy

Since globalization and consolidation are the rule in so many industries, it is a bit of a cliché to say that one's company is the ideal combination of global reach and local understanding. Nevertheless, global companies must address the issue and explain where they aspire to be on the global-local spectrum. Should they tout their scale, scope, and efficiency? Or is the personal touch paramount? Many companies make their position on the issue a key part of their branding, marketing, and advertising strategies. HSBC, for example, calls itself "The world's local bank." The May 2002 press release announcing the launch of an advertising campaign to support the new positioning said:

"Underpinning the advertising is HSBC's philosophy that the world is a rich and diverse place in which cultures and people should be treated with respect. Around the world, the group has built its businesses locally, and HSBC's 31 million customers can be confident that the service they receive has a world of experience behind it. HSBC's advertisements will demonstrate the importance of local knowledge by exploring distinctive national customs and practices. Carrying the strapline 'the world's local bank' the advertising will show that anyone who banks with HSBC can benefit from services and advice from a company with international experience, delivered by people sensitive to the customs and needs of their community."

HSBC's advertising campaign is supported by other corporate communication underscoring the bank's ability to help customers navigate cultural particularities, including messages on the Web site such as: "4 is an unlucky number in Japan. 13 is an unlucky number in the U.K. (the company's headquarters)."

Alternatively, messages can be structured for a geographic region, as illustrated in the Citigroup's 2002 Asian Centennial campaign, the first to include all the Citigroup businesses and Asian countries under one umbrella. The campaign, created and executed by Citigroup and Ruder Finn, spanned twelve countries in ten different languages. It targeted Asian stakeholders including customers, local government, the community and staff using a regional approach that allowed for tailored local market programs in local languages, while driving regional consistency and cost effectiveness.

Figure 9.1

In addition to unveiling a special Asian Centennial logo to appear with Citigroup's global branding, they created a book, "Citibank: A Century in Asia," which illustrated their history and achievements along with the region's history. Internally, they worked with each country to tailor major programs, such as a tour of the New York Philharmonic, for local businesses to use during the centennial in their marketing campaigns and drive revenue.[16]

Corporate communication executives need to evaluate on a case-by-case basis how best to balance the global or local message.

Global Networking

While the communication function may be centrally controlled, international public relations practitioners must have a thorough grounding in the regulatory issues, business practices, and media in their company's important markets. There are many ways to acquire this knowledge besides using the internal resources of the company.

One way to learn about another culture is to cultivate friendships with public relations colleagues overseas. Public relations associations in different countries are a great resource. Many of these, including the Public Relations Society of America (PRSA), are members of the Global Alliance for Public Relations and Communication Management (http://www.globalpr.org). The International Public Relations Association (IPRA) has members in one hundred countries and provides good networking opportunities. International public relations professionals should also take every opportunity to travel to important markets to visit corporate offices, to meet local public

> Public relations practitioners must have a thorough grounding in the regulatory issues, business practices, and media in their company's important markets.

relations resources, and to attend international industry or public relations conferences.

Katja Schroeder, a director at Burson-Marsteller Public Relations, emphasizes the value of local institutions, such as the chamber of commerce or the embassy commercial attaché as sources of valuable local information and networking. Agencies such as United States Information Technology Office (USITO, http://www.usito.org), a private, nonprofit trade association designed to promote trade and cooperation in the information technology industries of the United States and China, offer members valuable telecommunication updates through its newsletter and opportunities to network with other multinationals. [17]

Local relationships are not only important for information gathering, they are also key to establishing trust on a local level. Global corporate communication practitioners should strive to use the most credible and respected local sources to represent a business and deliver its message, whether it's a local or headquarters-based company spokesperson, a local government health official, or a celebrated sports or entertainment star.

Membership in international trade associations also provides a platform to meet government officials or potential business partners who can be influential in helping a company. Cultivating good working relationships with local media to understand what's important to them is key. This not only builds better working relations when there's news to communicate, but also allows global practitioners to more easily call on international journalists for inside information on their interests to effectively position news to meet the journalists' agenda.

Regulatory variances between countries can play a significant role in how messages are communicated internationally and can require a working knowledge of global regulations. For example, U.S. regulatory guidelines allow pharmaceutical companies to create messages raising awareness about a medical condition and advising consumers to see their doctors and to ask about a drug by name, while British regulatory guidelines cannot direct the consumer to ask for a drug explicitly by name (Bough 2005). Practitioners must be aware of these differences to create appropriate messages that are in compliance with regional guidelines.

Finally, international public relations practitioners must listen to local advice they receive. "In my experience, many of us learn about foreign cultures and hire local consultants to advise us, but then we often don't act on this advice if it differs too much from our own cultural way of doing things, sometimes much to our regret," said Barbara M. Burns, BBA Communications, New York, in her 2001 Atlas Award Lecture on International PR. "The art of bridging cultural differences in communications takes patience, trust of local advisors, and the courage and the wisdom to act in an effective and ethical manner."

Working with Media in Individual Countries

With the proliferation of global media through cable television, satellite, newspapers, and instant dissemination on the Internet, local news, especially bad news, can become global in seconds. Localizing the message is key, and practitioners need a thorough understanding of the local working language and environment to avoid costly gaffes. Working in Malaysia, for example, press releases must be translated into four languages to avoid alienating any segment of the media.[18]

Evolving National News Media

While media is one of the most powerful tools for reaching global audiences, it is certainly not a magic bullet for wide distribution of a message. In many developing countries, media reaches a relatively small, homogenous segment of the population because of illiteracy and poverty.[19] In communist or other countries where the media is or recently was government controlled, including China, the former Soviet Union, and certain South American nations, global media play by different rules—often requiring payment via advertising for news coverage. Government control of content and flow of information often erodes media's credibility, and therefore the company's credibility if that is the medium by which it communicates.

Do not underestimate the role that national pride plays in how media may respond to and report a story. For example, when a multinational company is sponsoring an event, local media will most likely approach it from a local angle—whether it is how a new plant opening will affect local employment or how a new hotel will help the local economy and tourism.

It is essential to understand the local media environment and send messages through the most credible channels. Key considerations include:

⇒ Private or public control of media
⇒ Alignment with political parties
⇒ Alignment with or control by theocracy
⇒ Extent of control over editorial freedom by media owners
⇒ Exercise of controls over editorial freedom
⇒ Journalists' professional standards
⇒ Media's ability to diffuse messages to a wide audience
⇒ Segments of the population receiving either print or electronic media
⇒ Local cultural media practices[20]

Due to differences in media between cultures or geographic areas—and because of the importance of developing relationships with individual journalists covering one's company—it is especially difficult to centralize global

> Do not underestimate the role that national pride plays in how media may respond to and report a story.

media relations. While continuing to use global electronic services to disseminate corporate messages, companies must implement media relations locally. If an organization does not have a local media insider, it is essential to hire either a global communication agency with local expertise in a particular market, or a local boutique agency.

The dramatic changes in China's media illustrate how local, cultural, and political values necessitate a localized approach. With China's acceptance into the World Trade Organization in 2001 and its exploding population and economy, China represents one of the greatest growth opportunities for multinational companies.

Mike H. He, PR manager at National Semiconductor Corporation in Santa Clara, California, notes in *Public Relations Tactics* (May 2003), "The Chinese government still maintains tight control over its major news outlets. [On the other hand,] trade media has experienced an unprecedented degree of freedom, especially in the technology area. Chinese readers are now turning more to trade publications than to government sponsored publications for technology news."

Burson-Marsteller's Schroeder, an expert in strategic public relations in China, notes that corporate messages for foreign companies in China must address six areas.

> Companies need to establish clear ethical guidelines about their commitment not to pay for editorial material.

1. Why is the company in China?
2. What is the company's global and local market presence? Who are the competitors?
3. What is the company's investment in China (for R&D, local staff, and local production facilities)?
4. What contributions will the company make to the region or country? (i.e., university donations, training centers, corporate responsibility programs, etc.)
5. How can the company help China/Chinese companies (the company's clients) to be globally competitive?
6. How important is China in the overall business plan?

While differences are apparent, traditional means of reaching media through releases, trade shows, press conferences, by-lined articles, and local spokespersons should be adapted for the local market.

Global Ethics

The blur between editorial and advertising is prevalent in many countries (including our own, in the case of certain publications). Publications frequently will not provide editorial coverage without a commitment to advertising or advertorial placement.

Companies need to establish clear ethical guidelines about their commitment not to pay for editorial material. Such a commitment establishes the credibility of the organization for the long term. The Charter on Media Transparency developed by the International Public Relations Association (IPRA) and available on their Web site (http://www.ipra.org) provides important guidelines. The initiative is supported by the International Press Institute, the International Federation of Journalists, Transparency International, the Global Alliance, and the Institute for Public Relations Research and Education, as well as IPRA.[21]

An additional global media relations challenge is when news crosses international time zones, such as the timing of news releases when a company headquarters is in one time zone, its stock is traded in another, and it is making news in yet a third. While the news should be issued from company headquarters, the timing of the release will need to reflect the target global market where the news has the most import and resonance. Of course, internal communication should be considered at the same time as the media strategy, so employees do not learn about something that might impact them from the press.

Virtual News Rooms

Web sites are an integral tool in managing global media relations. Virtual news rooms are essential in providing timely and archived information on a company, its products and services, and its policy issues. They are a key resource for global journalists to access internal media contacts. Global companies add additional value to their sites by including links to sites about relevant local or regional issues that can help the journalist do their job with greater ease.

Global Crisis Communication

During a crisis, an organization usually attempts to handle the media locally. Most crises are local in that they unfortunately often involve injuries or an accident at a facility. Even product quality issues usually, but not always, impact a limited number of shipments to a limited number of stores, cities, or countries. Therefore even if news travels globally through the Internet and other news outlets, an organization should keep perceptions of the issue localized where possible. Responding to a crisis far from its epicenter also sends the unwanted message that those at fault are evading responsibility. Regardless, a global crisis communication plan should be based on the same tried and true principles of any good crisis plan—rapid response, concern for those impacted, accepting responsibility, and taking action.

Time is of the essence in global crisis communication. If handling a crisis from the center means a slower response to local media, the greater the chance that someone else—a competitor, a hostile neighbor, an angry union—will tell the story first. Since the Internet is so pervasive, it is often where people will go first in a crisis. As a result, it is important for global communicators to use the Internet to gain control of messages in a crisis by posting phone numbers to call for information and by updating information regarding the crisis on a regular basis.

Perception often becomes reality, and managing perceptions on a global scale from afar and through different cultural lenses must be done with added planning and care.

Nongovernmental Organizations

Nongovernmental organizations (NGOs), such as Amnesty International, Greenpeace, and Human Rights Watch are increasingly influential in corporate reputation management. NGO "watchdog" or advocacy groups—numbering nearly 30,000[22]—often serve as consultants to governments and global organizations and have increasing influence in setting global agendas on individual issues. Companies must be increasingly alert and responsive to NGOs' agendas, especially in the areas of human rights, labor issues, the environment, and business practices.

According to Edelman Public Relation's Trust Barometer, NGOs are rated as the most trusted brands in Europe for the third consecutive year.[23] In many countries, media are increasingly turning to NGOs for their opinions on global issues and they are held as highly credible sources.[24]

In India, for example, Coca-Cola bottling plants require large amounts of water in a region where water can be scarce. The company is highly proactive in working with NGOs, local government, and the communities in which it operates to address environmental and resource issues. Partnering with local entities, Coke has established rainwater harvesting initiatives and shares its water management expertise with local communities to enhance local water collection. In April 2003, Coca-Cola India was honored by the government of Delhi in the State Government Bhagidari (partnership) program for its rainwater harvesting initiatives.[25]

Despite these initiatives, NGOs had a direct impact on the company's local operations. In March 2004, local officials shut down a Coca-Cola bottling plant in southern India over unsubstantiated claims by local residents and activists that it drained local water supplies. Beyond their increasing visibility and credibility in the global arena, Internet technology has enabled activist groups with limited financing to take their message to a global audience. A one-man NGO used a laptop computer, a Web site and a telephone calling card to build global alliances against Coca-Cola's environmental practices in India.[26]

For its part, Coca-Cola used its Web-based fact sheet to publicize its proactive work with the local community, counteracting the anticompany message.[27]

Corporate communication professionals must be vigilant in monitoring NGO agendas through the media and on the Web and must seek common ground to effectively address their concerns. As Coca-Cola did, communication professionals need to use their company Web sites as important proactive tools to advance their policies and agendas and to counteract misinformation.

Corporate Social Responsibility

When companies pursue global initiatives related to human rights, labor, the environment, and other "public goods," their corporate reputations can be significantly enhanced along with potentially positive effects on shareholder value, revenue, employee morale, and productivity.[28] This is known as Corporate Social Responsibility (CSR). The United Nations embraced CSR in its 1999 Global Compact, which makes the case for a new business model "that respects stakeholder and shareholder values simultaneously."[29] The compact advocates that global companies incorporate social responsibility into daily business practices related to human rights, labor standards, environment, and anticorruption and encourages companies and their CEOs to adhere to and promote the compact's principles.

Many stakeholders consider that companies have global responsibilities beyond normal business concerns. CSR thus has become a strategic issue for many organizations, especially those in Europe, because intangibles such as reputation and relationships have become important factors in value creation. Although American companies were the first to recognize the importance of philanthropy to build corporate trust, it is Europeans who have pioneered in the field of CSR.

When Deutsche Bank and Bankers Trust merged in mid-1999, the combined company reevaluated its corporate citizenship initiatives. In the process, the Deutsche Bank Americas Foundation shifted from a "Eurocentric institution to a global approach." Understanding that U.S. philanthropic values differed from those in Europe, the company created a corporate community relations campaign addressing core corporate values and resonating with audiences on both sides of the Atlantic. In the United States, the commitment built on the U.S. tradition of banks as important contributors to community development. In Europe, philanthropic initiatives focused on environmental issues. And in Latin America it focused on microcredit, a program of very small loans that enable impoverished people to buy tools to support themselves.

Gary Hattem, president of the Deutsche Bank Americas Foundation states, "The key to creating a corporate global program is picking the right issues. There's a lot of synergy between our core business as a bank and providing credit for self-employment as a way to alleviate poverty." The bank

> Corporate communication professionals must be vigilant in monitoring NGO agendas through the media and on the Web.

> The compact advocates that global companies incorporate social responsibility into daily business practices.

also launched its first corporate-wide U.S. volunteer program, providing school or youth service program supported by their employee volunteers. While volunteerism is not a European tradition, Hattem describes this initiative as a "culture building effort."[30]

Companies may also build philanthropic and employee volunteer activities into marketing campaigns, such as Lucent did in 1999 for an integrated Latin American branding initiative. In addition to an aggressive media relations effort in Mexico and Brazil, trade shows and events and regional employee communication outreach, the company created an annual "Day of Caring" in targeted Latin American countries involving employees in local causes and raising awareness of the company on a community level.

Starbucks conducts its global business to help communities and individuals who grow coffee and cocoa beans. Two such initiatives are providing low-interest loans to small farms in coffee-growing regions in Latin America and Africa and partnering with Ecologic Finance for financial literacy and capacity training projects for Latin American farmers. According to a news release, the company extends loans not only to Starbucks suppliers but also to coffee farmers throughout Latin America and Africa.[31]

Working with Public Relations Agencies

Companies, often with limited resources, have several options to communicate in many global markets via public relations agencies.

Global Agency of Record (AOR)

Because the talent and quality of global public relations agencies can vary greatly from location to location, corporate executives should choose carefully when considering bringing on a global agency of record (AOR):

⇒ Look at the agency's regional record of success for other clients in the market(s) and business closest to yours.
⇒ Consider the industry experience of the account managers and their involvement with your account. Some agencies may have a weakness in one practice area.
⇒ Consider selecting different agencies to handle your accounts depending on the product and geographic location.

If the corporate communication professional retains a global AOR, he/she should demand a "bulk purchase" discount. One benefit of an AOR is that the global account team should share information about its client's goals, projects, and issues. The client should not pay for each office to get up to speed. Global AORs may be best suited for a global product launch or for crisis communication, where it is most effective to have a standard set of communication processes globally.

Local PR Agencies

Some companies create their own networks of local PR agencies. There are several reasons for this decision. Some international corporate public relations directors prefer to work with agencies that are specialized in their industry, or have skills to address specific needs in a market.[32] An AOR's local office may not have the best expertise for the situation.

These private networks can include agencies belonging to a global group. It would be rare for a local PR agency to turn down an assignment because their global network has not been assigned as AOR. Sometimes, agencies can be identified and put on standby for situations as they arise, or for special projects. Most agencies will provide assistance on a project basis. In this way, the cost of outside agencies can be kept within budget, but top-level expertise is available when needed.

As noted earlier, whether the corporate communication professional hires an AOR or develops a network of local agencies, building trust between the corporate communication director and his/her department and the local public relations people is essential. Periodic public relations meetings to supplement ongoing communication is one proven method of building these relationships (see sidebar).

Getting Local Buy-In

The wise international public relations director will spend a great deal of time and effort getting the buy-in of local management. This requires persuading local management that corporate reputation is a valuable asset and that the resources spent on public relations will have a positive impact on the bottom line. These tasks require excellent spoken and written communication, interpersonal skills and a great deal of patience. Earning the support of regional and local managers for the global public relations program is challenging but it pays dividends as management passes the word down the line, easing some of the barriers to international and intercultural communications.

Barbara M. Burns, president
BBA Communications Inc.
New York

Measuring the Success of Global Communication

Periodically measuring the success of global public relations efforts is an essential aspect of any global communication strategy. Major criteria to measure success include:

⇒ Opinion research surveys and evaluation forms
⇒ Focus groups and one-to-one interviews

⇒ Content analysis of global news clips

⇒ Analysis of speaking engagements

⇒ Newsletter/video distribution

All are useful in determining how a company may continue to improve its success at delivering effective messages and achieving corporate communication goals.

Best Practices in Global Corporate Communication

Effective global corporate communication is a key component of any company's success in today's global marketplace. A good global corporate communication strategy will consider many of the best practices discussed in this chapter, including the following:

⇒ Global corporate communication staff and resources should be centralized for greatest efficiency and control of message.

⇒ Certain aspects of the global communication, most notably media relations, must be handled locally.

⇒ While maintaining the integrity of a global brand is paramount, practitioners must customize messages when necessary to make them understandable and relevant to local markets and audiences.

⇒ Since resources are limited, an informal global communication network is absolutely critical to ensure communication plans, tactics, and messages will work in different cultures, languages, and countries.

⇒ The Internet is invaluable for disseminating information rapidly, simultaneously, and inexpensively and for maintaining the integrity and consistency of a message.

⇒ Global companies must maintain positive relationships with local leaders and NGOs in the communities where they do business.

⇒ Corporate Social Responsibility and other philanthropic programs that address genuine local needs are important investments to enhance global reputation.

Resources for Further Study

Bartlett, Christopher A., and Ghoshal Sumantra. *Managing across borders: The transnational Solution*, 2nd ed. Boston: Harvard Business School Press, 1998.

Gesteland, Richard R., and George F. Seyk. *Marketing across cultures in Asia: A practical guide.* Copenhagen: Copenhagen Business Press, 2002.

How Do We Fit into the World. *Public Relations Strategist* (Winter 2004).

Howard, Carole M. Ten strategies to avoid global gaffes in media relations. *Public Relations Strategist* (Fall 2001):34–37.

Morley, Michael. *How to manage your global reputation: A guide to the dynamics of international public relations.* 2nd ed. New York: New York University Press, 2002.

Moss, Danny, and Barbara DeSanto. *Public relations cases: International perspectives*. New York: Routledge, 2002.

Sriramesh, Krishnamurthy, and Dejan Vercic. *The global public relations handbook: Theory, research, and practice*. Mahwah, NJ: Lawrence Erlbaum, 2003.

Taylor, Maureen. Cultural variance as a challenge to global public relations: A case study of the Coca Cola scare in Europe. *Public Relations Review* 26(3) (2000): 277–293.

Taylor, Maureen (2001): International public relations, opportunities and challenges for the 21st century. In Heath, Robert L.: *Handbook of public relations*. Thousand Oakes, CA: Sage Publications, (2001).

Tilson, Donn James, and Emmanuel C. Alozie. *Toward the common good: Perspectives in international public relations*. New York: Pearson, Allyn & Bacon, 2003.

Questions for Further Discussion

1. What does "Think global, act local" really mean?
2. Which is more important for a global company: A consistent look and feel and uniformity of positioning everywhere, or highly customized materials in each country that demonstrate alignment with that country's culture and values?
3. How important is it for a global company to have an "official company language"?
4. How important is state-of-the-art technology in effective global communication?
5. How can a company with far-flung communication staff measure the success of global communication efforts?

References

Amery, Elizabeth and Laura Turegano, Global philanthropy with a local flavor: A conversation with Gary Hattem, president of Deutsche Bank Americas Foundation, December 11, 2001. Retrieved July 20, 2005, from http://www.onphilanthropy.com/articles/print.aspx?cid=100.

Anderson, G. A global look at public relations. In *Experts in action: inside public relations*. 2nd ed. B. Cantor, Ed. New York: Longman, 1989, 412–422.

Are you reaching your intended audience? In *Public relations tactics*, June 1998, 5(6), 12.

Bough, Bonin, Personal interview, June 28, 2005.

Brinkerhoff, D.W. and M.D. Ingle. Integrating blueprint and process: A structured flexibility approach to development management. *Public Administration and Development* 9(1989): 487–503; qtd by Wakefield, *International public relations:A comparative analysis*. Eds. H. Culbertson and N. Chen. Hillsdale, NJ: Lawrence Erlbaum Associates, 1996, 17–28.

Burns, Barbara, Personal interview, July 15, 2005.

Burns, Barbara, PRSA international atlas award lecture, 2001.

Chen, N., Public relations in China: The introduction and development of an occupational field. In *International public relations: A comparative analysis*. Eds. H. Culbertson and N. Chen. Hillsdale, NJ: Lawrence Erlbaum Associates, 1996: 121–152.

CokeFacts.org Retrieved July 20, 2005, from http://cokefacts.org/citizenship/cit_in_environmental_p.shtml.

Culbertson, H., and N. Chen, Eds. *International public relations: A comparative analysis*. Hillsdale, NJ: Lawrence Erlbaum Associates, 1996: 17–28.

Drobis, David. The new global imperative for public relations: Building confidence to save globalization. *Public Relations Strategist*, Spring 2002. Retrieved July 20, 2005, from http://members.prsa.org/ScriptContent/resources/pdfpull.cfm?prcfile=6K-020236.pdf.

Drobis, David. Borderless believability: Building trust around the globe. Counselors Academy, Public Relations Society of America, *Monograph #9465*, July 1998.

Edelman Public Relations. Fifth annual Edelman trust barometer, January 20, 2004. Retrieved July 19, 2005, from http://www.edelman.com.

Ewing, A.P. Understanding the global compact human rights principles, and implementing the global compact human rights principles, in United Nations global compact and the office of high commissioner for human rights, embedding human rights into business practice, 2004. Retrieved July 20, 2005, from http://www.unglobalcompact.org.

Global Alliance for Public Relations and Communication Management. Position statement on corporate social responsibility, July 20, 2005. Retrieved from http://www.globalpr.org/news /features/csr_statement_280604.asp.

Grunig, J.E. and J. White. The effect of workviews on public relations theory and practice. In *Excellence in public relations and communication management*. Ed. J.E. Grunig. Hillsdale, NJ: Lawrence Erlbaum Associates, 1992: 31–64; qtd by Wakefield in *International public relations: A comparative analysis*. Eds. H. Culbertson and N. Chen. Hillsdale, NJ: Lawrence Erlbaum Associates. 1996: 17–28.

Grunig, J.E., L.A. Grunig, K. Sriramesh, Y.H. Huang, and A. Lyra. Models of public relations in an international setting. *Journal of Public Relations Research*, 1995: 163–186; qtd by Wakefield in *International public relations: A comparative analysis*. Eds. H. Culbertson and N. Chen. Hillsdale, NJ: Lawrence Erlbaum Associates, 1996: 17–28.

Grunig, L.A. (1992). Strategic public relations constituencies on a global scale. *Public Relations Review*, 18-127-136.

Harris, L., e-mail to author July 23, 2005.

He, Mike, H. Working with high tech media in China. *Public Relations Tactics*, May 2003. Retrieved July 15, 2005, from http://members.prsa.org/ScriptContent/resources/pdfpull.cfm?prcfile=6C-050323.pdf.

Hiebert, R.E. (1992). Global public relations in a post-Communist world: A new model. *Public Relations Review*. 18, 117-126.

Lesly, P. (1991). Public relations in the turbulent new human climate. *Public Relations Review*, 17, 1-8.

Manheim, J.B.,& Albritton, R.B. (1984). Changing national images: international public relations and media agenda setting. *The American Political Science Review*, 78, 641-657.

Morley, Michael. *How to manage your global reputation: A guide to the dynamics of international public relations.* 2nd ed. New York: New York University Press, 2002.

Robertson, R (1990). Mapping the global condition. Globalization as the central concept. In M. Featherstone (Ed.), *Global Culture: Nationalism, globalization and modernity* (p.p. 15-30).

Samuelson, Robert J. Time to toss the textbook. *Newsweek*, June 27, 2005.

Schroeder, Katja, Personal interview, June 28, 2005.

Seitel, Fraser. *The practice of public relations.* 9th ed. Upper Saddle River, NJ: Pearson Education Inc, 2004, 67–70, 378–394.

Sriramesh, Krishnamurthy, and Dejan Vercic. A theoretical framework for global public relations research and practice. In *The global public relations handbook*, Eds. K. Sriramesh, and D. Vercic. Hillsdale, NJ: Lawrence Erlbaum Associates, 2003, 1–17.

Starbucks invests additional $2.5 million in ecologic finance to assist smallholder farmers in Latin America and Africa, June 20, 2005. Retrieved July 15, 2005, from http://www.starbucks.com/aboutus/pressdesc.asp?id+517.

Stecklow, Steve. Virtual battle, how a global web of activists gives coke problems in India. *The Wall Street Journal*, A1, June 7, 2005.

Trissel, Edward, Personal interview, June 28, 2005.

United Nations Global Compact, December 1999. Retrieved July 20, 2005, from http://www.unglobalcompact.org/Portal/Default.asp?.

Vogl, Frank. International corporate ethics and the challenges to public relations. *Public Relations Strategist*, Spring 2001; Retrieved July 15, 2005, from http://members.prsa.org/ScriptContent/resources/pdfpull.cfm?prcfile=6K-020119.pdf.

Wakefield, Robert I. Interdisciplinary theoretical foundations for international public relations. In, *International public relations: A comparative analysis.* Eds. H. Culbertson and N. Chen. Hillsdale, NJ: Lawrence Erlbaum Associates, 1996, 17–28.

Wakefield, Robert I. What's wrong with multinational public relations? *Public Relations Strategist*, Spring 2000 Retrieved July 15, 2005, from http://members.prsa.org/ScriptContent/resources/pdfpull.cfm?prcfile=6K-010034 pdf.

Wilcox, Dennis, Ault, Phillip, Agee, Warren, and Cameron, Glen, *Essentials of public relations*, Addison-Wesley, 2001, 284.

CHAPTER 10

Integrated Communication

By Tim McMahon

> *Communication is a constant, interactive process*
> *aimed at (creating) consensus.*
> — Jack Welch

A-lo-ha Uh-oh!

In the early summer of 2002, I was in Honolulu with Pete Derzis, an ESPN executive. We were about to make the official announcement that ConAgra Foods would become the title sponsor of the Hawaii Bowl and as members of the media gathered at the outdoor press conference—with Waikiki Beach and Diamond Head as a backdrop—I took a call on my cell phone from our corporate counsel back home in Nebraska. The news was not good. Management at Swift & Co., at the time a part of ConAgra and one of the largest meat processing entities in the world, was concerned about the possible presence of e.coli O157:H7, a potentially deadly pathogen. We paid very close attention to food safety at ConAgra Foods. The subject occupied our daily conversations. It was a priority that started at the top with Chairman and CEO Bruce Rohde.

The governor of Hawaii beamed and told reporters that through its many famous brands ConAgra Foods had been a big part of his childhood on the island and "now they are going to become an official part of our holiday celebration." In this moment, with smiling faces on one end and a looming crisis on the other, I took comfort in the fact that the communication team was organized and that we had put together a framework to deal with such crises. However, the structure was new as were many of the players and we had not yet coalesced as a team. Further, the company's strategy had not yet fully developed, so its actual value in execution was not yet clear to all. As is often the case, at this moment we faced two reputation building moments of truth—one planned and one unplanned. And, while the framework for managing integrated communication was in place, the team was untested, and had not developed the knowledge, depth of relationships, trust, and interdependence needed to confidently manage through a crisis that would affect just about every constituency: employees, customers, consumers, vendors, investors, media, business partners, regulators, and special interest groups.

* * * * *

The chief marketing officer and the chief communication officer should be joined together at the hip. In some organizations this may be one and the same person, which is good. It doesn't matter; the first rule of integrated communication is to integrate the various ways a firm communicates, and that means pulling together all the people in the organization responsible for developing and communicating reputation and brand. In an article on Kodak's brand makeover, *The New York Times* wrote, "What they have come up with is a brand transformation program that encompasses not just advertising, but also product design, public relations, 'pretty much everything Kodak,'" (Deutsch, C.H., 2005). This reality that everything communicates is what drives a body of thought and actions called *integrated marketing communications.*

Integrated marketing communications (IMC) is a customer-centric, data-driven method of communicating with consumers. IMC—the management of all organized communications to build positive relationships with customers and other stakeholders—stresses marketing to the individual by understanding needs, motivations, attitudes and behaviors.

IMC is customer-centric, data-driven, (about) integration, and (about) effective branding.

Definition from *Journal of Integrated Marketing Communications* Web site. (Retrieved August 7, 2005, from http://jimc.medill. northwestern.edu/defined.htm.)

IMC stems from more than a decade of work by many professionals and academicians aimed at improving the effectiveness and reach of marketing. Top people responsible for communications and marketing see a convergence in this field. On one end is reputation, and at the other, branding. Reputations are based on perceptions of the company held by people inside and outside of the organization. Managing reputation requires putting to use the ideas, practices, and measures laid out in this book. Branding is the business discipline marketers use to define and manage the complex set of attributes, values, features, and character of products and services today. Their objective is to effectively position their brand in the mind of the consumer in a manner that results in more sales and profits.

Reputation building and branding rely on much of the same things: adopting a long-term view, gaining a deep understanding of the "customer," developing trusted relationships with key constituencies (often the same), and effective measurement and feedback.

To the chief communications officer the line between reputation and brand equity is blurred. Integration is essential to align brand—that stems from the company's products and services with reputation—the reflection of the values, character, and capabilities of the organization. Management researcher Charles Fombrun (1996, p. 9) writes, "Companies develop winning reputations by both creating and projecting a set of skills that their constituents recognize as unique." In marketing parlance, it is called positioning, and it is the way markets find their way into the prospect's mind so they will buy.

This chapter addresses this convergence and offers perspective and specific actions that will enable communicators to more effectively build a valued reputation and powerful brand equity. In doing so, it presents a framework to create effective integrated communication. It begins by presenting the underpinnings of the organization that affect its ability to stand out and effectively market—brand identity, leadership, vision, and culture; and finishes with the tactical treatment to make it happen—tools, working relationships, brand management, and best practices. The material pushes conventional thinking yet grounds all advanced thought in proven communication principles and practices.

Keep in mind, IMC is limited to marketing. What is covered here applies to the broader work of the enterprise and is called *integrated communication*.

Integrated communication (IC) is a dynamic communication practice aimed at advancing not just the marketing plan, but the overall operating or business plan of the firm and in so doing aligning brand with reputation.

This Chapter Covers

⇒ Foundational concepts
  - Creating enterprise value through strong brand identity
  - Leadership: The engine of effective integrated communication
  - A shared vision will replace a shelf full of policy manuals
  - Culture: The lever for transformation
⇒ Tactical tools
  - Communication toolbox: The devices used to move people to action
  - Marketing and sales: What is the difference? Does it matter?
  - The corporate brand: Differentiating the company's approach to business
⇒ Sidebar: Integrated communication—who should lead, by Louis Capozzi
⇒ Sidebar: A thirteen-step process for developing an agency proposal, by Mel Ehrlich
⇒ Best practices
⇒ Resources for further study
⇒ Questions for further discussion

Creating Enterprise Value through
Powerful Brand Identity

Simply put, marketing is about getting and keeping customers. Integrated marketing communication implies clear, consistent messaging devised to support a firm's marketing objectives. Marketers often abbreviate their complex craft by relying on mnemonic devices like, the four Ps—product, place, price, and promotion—shorthand to describe the tools used to position the product offering to a targeted segment. IMC arose to help communicate the point of difference of the brand within the framework of the four Ps. But, the practice of marketing has evolved and the four Ps may be too limiting to serve our purposes here.

Today marketers must focus on creating solutions. Solutions address prospects' needs for things they do not even know they need yet. Solutions often rely on innovation. Solutions are not delivered in a neat little package that rolls off the assembly line, but are part of a larger network of organizational resources. Consequently, solutions are only sustainable if there is active engagement between the firm and its customers at all levels and touch points. This requires true two-way communication and explains the reliance on relationship building, the stock-in-trade of communicators.

> Brand architecture produces a strategic marketing framework visible to the entire organization.

The second major challenge is sustaining competitive advantage. This begins with understanding the concept of brand. Brand is the vehicle marketers use to give meaning to the complex set of attributes, values, features, and character of products and services today. The objective of brand is not just about creating differentiation, which is motivating, but must create preference, which is crucial. One of the best characterizations, or definitions, of brand comes from Dave Sutton and Tom Klein (2003): "Like a person, a brand has individual values, physical features, personality, and character. Like a story, a brand has characters, setting, and a plot. Like a friend, a brand offers a personal relationship, one that—in the best-case scenario—evolves as you do."[1]

Brand Architecture: The Basis of Marketing Communication

Brand architecture is the output of gaining a deep understanding of the communication that causes customers to buy. There are three key dimensions: product features, functional benefits, and emotional benefits. These three parts and how they are crafted and communicated form the linkage between the brand and its customers. Grounded in a deep understanding of why customers buy, brand architecture "provides direction about which combination of specific emotional and functional benefits generate the greatest amount of customer purchase intent. Once completed, brand architecture produces a strategic marketing framework visible to the entire organization. You can then use this framework to begin communicating and delivering these benefits to your customers."[2]

This approach to marketing affirms that marketing success is increasingly more dependent on creating a cohesive corporate reputation—through vigorous two-way communication—that supports the brand architecture, and heightens the importance of a firm's employees being aligned with the firm's purpose, mission, vision, and benefits. Brand strength is a function of this alignment. The more that people on the outside believe, think, and feel about the brand the way the people on the inside do, the brand is considered strong, and if tied to a meaningful brand architecture, it creates value for the enterprise.

As it turns out then, transparency is necessary and not only describes the ability of the general public to view the organization, which is good, but also provides the opportunity to reflect the right attitude, receptiveness, reliability, credibility, and trustworthiness of an organization, that supports its marketing.

Moving People to Action

Richard Edelman, president and chief executive officer of Edelman, writes, "The future of business is not about selling, but about building relationships. The first step is to identify and build a core group of advocates who may not be grouped by traditional demographics such as education, income, age, or gender."[3] What Edelman refers to—building relationships—is the work of communicators. He refers to this as mobilizing catalysts—a group he describes as people who "share a personality trait, a missionary zeal. They are predisposed to taking positive action on issues close to their hearts."[4] Take comfort in the fact that the process of finding such people and converting them into zealots of the firm's brand has been a proven practice since the beginning of time.

In the late 1940s, there was a farmer in Otoe County, Nebraska, who fit the description of Edelman's catalyst. About that time, agronomists at the University of Nebraska were busy inventing new ways to work the soil to create greater productivity. But keep in mind, it is not as if the farming community was asking for it; postwar demand for crops was good. So, when the researchers at the university wanted to put into practice a radical new idea called terrace farming, there were no takers. However, people at the school had created a relationship with Otto Wirth, and that is all that was needed to launch a new brand of farming. Mr. Wirth listened to their story, immediately saw the wisdom, and put it into practice on his farm. It required moving a lot of earth and rearranging the look of the land. When his fellow farmers asked him why he was ruining his farm he had the answer: "I am not ruining it, I'm saving it," he would tell them. Once Otto put this innovation to work, and showed the benefits to his neighbors, the word spread and terrace farming was widely adopted soon thereafter.

In the language of marketing, terrace farming is the brand, the University of Nebraska is the company, and Otto Wirth is the customer. The customer had unique qualities to exploit (curiosity) and the concept of terrace farming held the potential to engage him emotionally, appealing to his missionary zeal. The university agronomist had developed a relationship built on trust. So, when the new brand of farming was presented, the first critical sale was made. Otto was a tough customer, but he was receptive, and saw something in it for him. It is difficult to imagine the total dollar value generated from the adoption of terrace farming, but it likely reaches into the billions in productivity gains, and land and water conservation. That is enormous value created through a crude but effective process of brand adoption.

Why It Takes More Than a Strong Brand to Realize the Full Value of an Innovation

This chapter centers on the concept of value creation, and provides a view of how it takes both brand equity and reputation to create value in organizations today. Being first is still important, but without relationships a firm may not extract maximum value from its brands. For example, TiVo® is the brand name to describe the simple and intuitive process for time-shifting programs, enabling viewers to view what they want when they want. This is a powerful concept with great value potential and powerful brand equity. TiVo even reached coveted verb status as in, "Could you TiVo Leno for me tonight?" Today, a few short years after introduction, the handwriting is on the wall: cable companies, offering generic digital video recording (DVR) devices to their regular monthly customers on a leased basis, have scooped up the value in digital time-shifting, leaving TiVo scrambling to cut deals with cable providers to preserve its market value, albeit with significantly diminished investor interest. In this case, cable providers' relationships with its customers captured the value of a well-branded innovation for lack of an established set of relationships with the target market (cable viewers).

Integrated Communication Drives a Broader Organizational Agenda

Suffice it to say, creating value begins by viewing communication in the larger context of the enterprise as cable operators viewed TiVo. So, too, communication must be integrated to support both marketing and the broader value-creating capabilities of the organizational plan. In other words, communicators must address both brand and reputation. In the long run, TiVo will survive, but, for lack of significant customer relationships, potential brand value leaked out.

In advising CEOs, business gurus Larry Bossidy and Ram Charan write, "Your ability to create fundamental value rests on how good you are at finding the right balance between your external and internal realities and your financial aspirations: in other words, how skillfully you develop and use your business model."[5] (The business model is composed of three components: the business environment, financial targets, and the activities of the business. This third area includes: "strategy formulation, operating activities, selection deployment, development of people, and organizational processes and structure."[6]) For most firms, growth will be a function of the members of the enterprise executing flawlessly on a clear-cut, value-producing strategy, through a business model that delivers customer satisfaction on demand. These actions are optimized through effective communications integrated throughout the organization. The model looks like this:

> ‹ *integrated communication,*
> > ‹ *working in concert with the organization's internal capabilities, and*
> > ‹ *honestly facing its external environment,*
> ‹ *enables a firm to reach its organizational (financial) targets.*

This is a workable model accomplished through disciplined development and rigorous execution of the *strategic communication plan* (SCP). The SCP is the planning and execution tool that serves to guide and drive effective integrated communication. Development of this plan begins with a deep understanding of the firm and then sets out to integrate the activities and functions related to communications; with strategy, objectives and goals of the organization's business plan. Success is predicated on leadership that is able to generate buy-in and create the emotional energy to drive the plan. While this process encompasses marketing, it does not stop at marketing. As we have illustrated, in today's environment, integrating communication with marketing is not enough, it must embrace advertising, public relations, customer service, anything in the firm that is capable of relationship building. What follows is a discussion of the underpinnings needed to create effective integrated communication across the enterprise. They are leadership, vision, and culture.

Leadership: The Engine of Effective Integrated Communication

Significant changes in the real world have altered the role of communication in most organizations. It can no longer be top-down or treated like an announcement, ad, or bulletin. As marketing legend Don Schultz wrote, "Senior managers are beginning to understand customers are acquired, retained, or lost based on brand experiences. And those come not just from products and services, but from inside the company."[7] In other words, people are the brand. So, a strong brand is dependent on having informed people who are engaged with customers. Enlightened managers have found that command-and-control tactics have lost their punch. Unilateral orders do not engage the hearts and minds of the people who execute the plan. There must be dialogue—give and take—and it must start at the top. Integrated communication must be "leader led" or it does not get done. In a speech in 1987, Jack Welch, CEO of General Electric, punctuated this point when he said, "Real communication is an attitude, an environment. It's the most interactive of all processes. It requires countless hours of eyeball-to-eyeball back and forth. It involves more listening than talking. It is a constant, interactive process aimed at [creating] consensus."[8] Welch describes the critical element that drives integrated communication: leader commitment. While Welch was addressing the employee constituency, his words apply to all constituencies—shareholders, regulators, customers, vendors, and all who come in contact with the enterprise. At its heart, communication must address the constituents involved in a manner that takes into account their fundamental concern: What's In It For Me (WII-FM).

Good to Great author Jim Collins dispels the myth that leadership must be charismatic, or dynamic, in order to develop followers. On the contrary, effective leaders, "channel their ego needs away from themselves and into the larger goal of building a great company."[9] Collins found the most important traits were humility and professional will. Effective leaders focus on others—hold themselves accountable for mistakes and others responsible for success. It is this kind of leader who will commit to communication because he or she recognizes the value they receive from the interchange: employees become and stay engaged.

> In other words, people are the brand.

It is possible to create successful and effective communication without committed, enlightened leaders but it is seldom lasting or meaningful. In their many years of studying the dynamic process of leadership, James Kouzes and Barry Posner uncovered five practices common to leaders who were able to get extraordinary things done: They (1) model the way; (2) inspire a shared vision; (3) challenge the process; (4) enable others to act; and (5) encourage the heart.[10]

These proven leader activities take root through communication that penetrates the skepticism and apathy that holds back greatness in many organizations. Change guru John Kotter said it best: "People change what they do less because they are given analysis that shifts their thinking than because they are shown a truth that influences their feeling."[11]

(See the sidebar article by Lou Capozzi, Chairman of the Publicis Public Relations and Corporate Communications Group.)

A Shared Vision Will Replace a Shelf Full of Policy Manuals

A vision is a roadmap for people in the company to follow. It is a reference point for decision making, and it is the fuel that drives emotional energy of individuals eager to be a part of something greater than they could be alone. More than ever, the vision is clarified from the bottom up, and when that happens, it is truly empowering and has the effect of setting the organization apart from all others—the desired outcome of integrated communication.

Organizational learning pioneer Peter Senge said, "A lot of people who became very successful throughout the Industrial Era had a deep, passionate, sense of personal vision and got a whole lot of people to follow their vision,"[12] and it worked. The question is: can an organization afford to rely on the vision of one charismatic leader? The answer is many of the value-creating ideas and visions in business today do not come from the top. More often, it is someone on the front line with a keen understanding of the capabilities of the organization, and seeing the needs of the customer, was afforded the opportunity to act on a vision shared by members of his or her organization. There is enormous emotional power when people in the organization bring their view of the vision into action.

Conversation is the fuel that creates understanding, clarity, and meaning.

Shared Vision Leads to Organizational Alignment

Several years ago, a salesperson for ConAgra Foods came away from a visit with a very large retail buyer who complained that his meal-maker customers needed a complete dinner that was inexpensive, easy-to-make, and gave her the feeling that she had created something special for her family. The sales rep took the challenge back to the culinary team who put a proven idea to use in a new package with fresh, new ingredients, and voila: a hot casserole prepared in minutes and baked in the time it took to change out of work clothes and set the table. Because it was baked, the house was filled with fresh-from-the-oven aromas, a user-valued benefit. The product was dubbed Banquet Homestyle Bakes, and it became a smash hit generating hundreds of millions of dollars in its first year on the market and redefining the home meal solutions category.

Visions provide direction and set an organization in motion with clarity of purpose and a sense of urgency. It often begins with a simple conversation between a customer and an employee.

Productive Communication Begins with Listening

Conversation is the fuel that creates understanding, clarity, and meaning. According to David Pottruck and Terry Pearce, executives who guided the growth of Charles Schwab, "Marketing is a conversation between a company, its employees, and its customers ... the beginning and renewing of this conversation happens not with talking but with listening—listening to employees and customers."[13] In the previous example, the sales rep, armed with the vision of creating a new mealtime solution, carried the conversation back to the culinary team, where dialogue ensued. Senge distinguishes dialogue as the process of thinking together. "The discipline of team learning starts with 'dialogue,' the capacity of members of a team to suspend assumptions and enter into genuine 'thinking together.'"[14] Rooted in the customer's vision, dialogue is the communication tool that enabled the magic to happen for Homestyle Bakes.

A vision points organizational energy in a meaningful direction consistent with the firm's strategy. When the vision is shared by all—the customer, the employees, and the broader entity of the company—value-creation soon follows. No manuals to consult, no bosses to bother, just satisfied customers and the uplifting feeling of a team of people coming together to create value for the organization.

Culture: The Lever for Transformation

Why is it then that even with a clear vision dialogue among its people does not follow? Or, why is it so hard for one part of the company, say the sales department, to communicate with another part of the company, say marketing? Culture expert Edgar Schein writes, "Culture will be most useful as a concept if it helps us better understand the hidden and complex issues of organizational life."[15] Culture explains why people resist change, why people and groups have trouble communicating, and why we see normally rational people behaving seemingly irrationally.

Change is a part of the landscape. How individuals and groups deal with it varies. In organizational development parlance, the way groups deal with change is related to the basic underlying assumptions that are held by its members. Often these assumptions are ingrained so deeply in the group that "members will find behavior based on any other premise inconceivable."[16]

Given this premise, it is clear that creating effective integrated communication to deal with a changing environment is a distinct challenge that must be based on a strategy that addresses the realities of organizational culture and works within it. "My way or the highway" may have effective short-term effect, but it is not likely to be effective in most cultures that populate organizations today.

The first step in creating effective communication within organizations is to recognize the nature of culture and how a deep understanding of it can be directed to help the organization create value. Organizational cultures and subcultures can have creative or destructive effects on an organization. Companies with strong cultures have a basis for generating buy-in of the ideas, strategies, and initiatives that create value. What is more, culture provides its members with the moral compass to make evaluations regarding personal behavior that will reflect favorably on the organization—a most coveted asset today. Most importantly, a strong culture brings life to communication efforts because beyond the words there is commitment, and genuine human understanding, and belief in the purpose, mission, and vision of the firm from the members of the firm. Culture is difficult and complex, however, and there is not nearly enough space in this chapter to deal with it fully. The SCP provides a framework to address the issues affected by culture in a meaningful and effective manner.

Dialogue Is the Base Medium of Change Management

Dialogue is the way people learn. It is the way they engage with each other to understand the fuzzy ambiguities. It is the way people at all levels of the organization—inside and out—decipher meaning in seemingly unrelated events. It is the way they make sense of things. Communicators are best served when they keep messages simple, ears open, and constituents fully engaged in dialogue.

> Most importantly, a strong culture brings life to communication efforts.

Too many organizations have a legacy of treating communications as if it were a company megaphone where corporate leaders on the bridge cast out messages deemed important. Communication can no longer be top-down and be effective because, when it comes to the important stuff, people no longer blindly follow orders. Communication gets filtered through their belief system and it is affirmed or denied when it is discussed with others in the organization. The subcultures within the organization may own a different set of assumptions about what creates success, or what they consider good for them. Force-feeding messages on organizations where its members have not worked out their differences is potentially destructive, and at the least, creates cynicism. Consider the way communication and culture is handled in most acquisitions and mergers:

> Communication can no longer be top-down and be effective.

X Bank buys Y Bank. The ensuing entity becomes The XY Bank. Simple as that. The only communication needed is a press release, maybe a letter from the new CEO to all the employees, some ads announcing the change, and of course signs and stationery need to be redesigned and printed. Everyone will love it, especially the analysts. They see savings when X wipes out all the duplicated functions of Y. They see taking the best of both leadership teams and forging one. Then they count up the cumulative transactions that XY will have together and what results is shareholder value. Too often, however, synergy fails to deliver value. Research indicates that change initiatives fail at a very high rate—70 percent![17]

Change initiative failures occur for a variety of reasons including poor strategy decisions, inappropriate choices, poor monitoring and control, lack of resources, leadership impatience, the lack of a unifying framework for action, a shift in conditions, the lack of holistic integration, poor execution or poor design, and communications.[18]

Broadly speaking all of these reasons could be addressed through a keen understanding of the cultural and communication aspects of the transaction. The fact is if two cultures are put together rarely will they find harmony on their own. One will become dominate and the other will die. So, instead of 1 + 1= 3, the equation becomes 1 + 1= something less than 2. It takes effective leader-led communication, assisted by capable communicators who understand the cultural aspects, to enable the X and the Y cultures to transition to the XY Bank. Done properly, it is a long-term process, five years or more, and requires a well-conceived strategic communication plan that accommodates the transition process. A transition, as William Bridges (2003, p. 3) writes, is a "process that people go through as they internalize and come to terms with the details of the new situation that the change brings about."

While this makes perfect sense, it seldom happens. There are examples every day of major mergers and acquisitions being executed with apparently little or no accommodation for the role of culture. The recent, disappointing Daimler-Chrysler merger stands out as just such an example, but there is still hope.

When Culture Works, It Is a Beautiful Thing

People rarely have trouble recognizing or appreciating successful, high-performing organizations with powerful, value-generating cultures at work. Southwest Airlines has a break-the-rules business model, the Mayo Clinic delivers unparalleled patient care, and Herman Miller operates through a liberated workforce. Each has a unique and value-generating "way of doing business" backed by years of superior financial performance. It likely reflects a conscious blend of reputation management and brand equity development and the disciplined communication each entails.

The Underpinnings Provide a Platform

This discussion of the parallels between reputation and brand, the changing nature of marketing, and the essential underpinnings for creating successful integrated communication (leadership, vision, and culture management) provides the foundation for offering proven tools and practices to create effective integrated communication in the organization. The second half of this chapter centers on the tactical aspects of IC.

Communication Toolbox: The Devices Used to Move People to Action

Along the way, communication professionals accumulate tools of the trade to be used to achieve an objective, create meaning, counter resistance, or simply move people in one direction or another. Here are some of the tools commonly used in the practice of integrated communication.

Integrated Communication Uncovers and Confronts Resistance

Organizational behavior professor Jay Conger points to four essential steps in creating effective persuasion. You must: (1) establish credibility; (2) frame your goals in a way that identifies common ground with your audience (positioning); (3) reinforce your position by using vivid language and compelling evidence; and (4) connect emotionally with your audience.[19]

Mass communication is pretty much a thing of the past. There is still a place to sound a general alarm like in terror code or hurricane warnings, for example, but effective communication today centers on the individual as much as possible and leads to developing a relationship. Relationships are built on trust. To be trusted, be trustworthy.

Fernando Bartolome writes that developing trust requires the three Cs: competency, caring, and character, and offers three questions to determine the presence of trustworthiness:

> Effective communication today centers on the individual as much as possible and leads to developing a relationship.

1. Is it likely that the receivers of the message will consider the sender someone who knows what he or she is talking about?
2. Does the person asking for trust really care? If so, he or she is probably fair and supportive.
3. Does this person have character and values, and is he or she predictable?

If there is a vacancy in any of these areas, all is not lost, consider filling in the gaps. Sometimes creating trust is simple. It may be a matter of who is chosen as the spokesperson to deliver a message, or it may involve drafting a recognized expert to corroborate the message, or appeal. People will respect competence, disregard incompetence, and respect the incompetent when they are honest about their lack of competence. Begin with a firm grip on reality, build small wins, and advance trust one step at a time, and use emissaries, if necessary.

Framing: The Basic Process of Managing Meaning

"People respond to the meanings they have for words and events rather than to the words and events themselves."[20] Framing is the tool communicators use to create appeal that will benefit an organization's position in the mind of the audience. Home Depot is an imposing place. But, properly framed it turns from a big, cavernous warehouse stacked with thousands of items into an old friend that makes "do-it-yourself" a rewarding reality. The company employs people who have experience with the products they sell. They then empower these people to hold in-store seminars to demonstrate their expertise. Customers discover these learning opportunities through in-store posters, ads, and by witnessing a live demonstration in the store. Home Depot knows its customers have varying levels of expertise and proactively offers to fill in any knowledge gaps an individual may have. In this fashion, Home Depot becomes a source of knowledge and personal empowerment, and that is how it manages meaning with regard to the contents of those big, cavernous stores. It relies on a conversation taking place between a company, its employees, and its customers. Sound familiar?

A Republican Cloth Coat

Metaphors help people learn by relating unknown concepts to known concepts. Lakoff & Johnson argue that metaphor creates coherence for people allowing them to understand something they do not know by relating it to something they know. With his back against the wall and a shot at the vice presidency on the line, Richard Nixon demonstrated a keen understanding of his audience, deft use of both framing and vivid, metaphorical language to wriggle out of a tight spot early in his career. As Dwight Eisenhower's running mate in 1952, Nixon found himself in the throes of a scandal—specifically that of taking $18,000 in campaign funds—that jeopardized his political future. Mustering uncommon political insight, Nixon booked network time and delivered a speech from an empty auditorium to millions of viewers in a high-profile attempt to set the record straight, and with an unwieldy 4,698 reasonably organized words recouped his good standing as a vice presidential candidate on the Eisenhower ticket.

The speech became known as "The Checkers Speech" because he told a story about one of the contributions he was accused of taking for personal use. It was a puppy sent to the family from a supporter in Texas. They named the little dog Checkers and he unabashedly told viewers that he had every intention of keeping it.

Nixon used language his audience understood. At one point he referred to his wife, sitting nearby, as wearing a Republican cloth coat, a positive conservative notion held by his audience. No furs or leather for this second lady to be! They showed Pat wearing the coat on TV, but Nixon created the metaphor by calling it out verbally.

There are many famous speeches with far-reaching effects where the specific words selected mattered greatly in their effect on the audience. Every one of them likely used metaphor. But, Nixon's speech proves that even uncharismatic speakers can use powerful words to get what they want. Following the speech the White House was inundated with pro-Nixon mail and he and Ike went on to victory.

Marketing and Sales, What Is the Difference? Does It Matter?

For the record, personal selling is a subset of the marketing mix. Neil Borden specified twelve mix elements: merchandising-product planning, pricing, branding, channels of distribution, personal selling, advertising, promotions, packaging, display, servicing, physical handling, and fact-finding and analysis-market research.[21] This eventually was boiled down to the "4 Ps" of product, price, promotion, and place. So, where in the 4 Ps is personal selling? You will find it under promotion, along with the other marketing communications elements. As Borden writes, "Effective marketing requires an integrated communication plan combining both personal selling efforts and nonpersonal ones such as advertising, sales promotion, and public relations."[22] But first, people in the company must get together on the value of collaboration and of bringing the elements listed here together to bear on the task of getting and keeping customers. By the way, this is not limited to IMC, as we have learned.

If Marketing Is about Value Creation, Should Not Everyone in the Organization Be a Marketer?

The answer to that question is an emphatic yes. In The Little Green Marketing Book, I open with the premise borrowed from marketing maven Theodore Levitt who set the record straight with respect to the purpose of a business: to create and keep customers. With that as the purpose, everyone in the organization must be a marketer—even the sales people!

Nirmalya Kumar brings this time-tested concept into sharp focus today when he writes that there are "three mutually reinforcing changes [that] are enabling faster and more coherent coordination of customer value creating activities within organizations."[23] Organizations are moving from functions to processes, from hierarchies to teams, and from transactions to partnerships. These changes stem from the need to better serve customers in a world where an abundance of choices and channels has overheated the environment.

The challenge in creating value in the marketplace today is not simply to create the product or service, but to create the networked organization that can deliver it on demand through the coordinated efforts of teams of multitalented employees who organize around the customer. This presents a significant opportunity to communicators, for it is inconceivable to think of creating such a group without effective integrated communication driving the process, creating meaning and understanding for all members of the firm. It begins with identifying the brand through brand architecture.

The Corporate Brand: Differentiating the Company's Approach to Business

"The first step to having a cohesive brand is to have a cohesive company."[24] The concept of a brand is not widely understood. But it begins with the idea that a brand is a promise. In the case of a bug killer, that means dead bugs when used. Easy to understand, easy to communicate. One famous branded bug killer, Raid®, still uses "Kills bugs dead" as its advertising slogan. While it is easier to consider the branding challenge of a tangible product with hard and fast features, functions, and benefits, the greater challenge is how does one communicate a corporate brand, especially if the corporate brand is really a holding company that owns many other brands? To do this, begin with a clear understanding of what the corporation values.

Does Virgin® mean records? Maybe when it stood over the door of a single record store it did, but not today. Richard Branson has created an organization that marches to the beat of a different drummer with a unique set of values different from its competitors. Its irreverent personality plays to its values (e.g., fun, innovative, value for the money, good quality, brilliant customer service, and competitively challenging) and it gives Virgin brand leverage because a significant subset of customers identify with it as a significant and unconventional refuge from the dark side of service sectors that are populated with a plethora of aloof and dispassionate providers. Virgin sees brand extension opportunities in underserved or poorly served industries. The company put its brand on everything from cell phones to airlines and trains to credit cards. (See http://www.virgin.com.) Virgin's Web site communicates in language that supports the brand and expresses its character. Would you expect to see the phrase, "Boredom Sucks" on the Verizon® Web site? Not likely. But it fits quite naturally with Virgin cell phones (or mobiles, as they are called in Great Britain).

> But it begins with the idea that a brand is a promise.

The Virgin brand appeals to customers and employees in a fresh way. There is alignment inside and out. With meaningful and recognizable values in place, brands can adapt and add value by holding forth more ethereal

Figure 10.1

benefits that often connect at a higher level of thought, or deeper level of commitment, with customers or anyone who comes in touch with the brand. This is the emotional benefit referred to earlier in this chapter. This level of brand equity is difficult for competitors to replicate, so it creates sustainable competitive advantage for those who can pull it off.

Creating the Umbrella Brand

In 1999, the chairman and the board of directors of ConAgra perceived that investors saw the company as "an agricultural giant" and that was incompatible with the direction the company was moving with respect to its role and purpose as management perceived. So, he directed that a campaign be developed that would clear up that misperception.

To create the campaign a single word became the common ground for the organization, and an award-winning campaign was born. The 2000 annual report featured a plain white cover with the word "Hungry?" featured front and center. It also carried the name ConAgra Foods, a small but meaningful name change from ConAgra Inc. The design of the book played a simple straightforward message to investors, employees, and customers: If you're hungry you've come to the right place™.

Communicating the Brand through Events, Activities and Partnerships

The following year the company partnered with Joe Gibbs, three-time Super Bowl winning coach and two-time NASCAR Cup champion team owner. Gibbs embodied the values of the company: honest, competitive, family-oriented, and committed to winning. The red and white #20 NASCAR Bush Series car carried the ConAgra Foods logo on the hood and displayed thirty of the company's brands on various parts of the car. To let everyone in on the act, a die cast scale model was created and distributed among customers, employees, and suppliers.

Additionally, the company's partnership arrangement put employees and customers in touch with the Joe Gibbs racing team at races across the country and in personal customer visits by the coach.

Taking It to the Streets

Activation is the term to describe the way a sponsorship pays off. So, the company put its message where its (customer's) mouth was through the ConAgra Foods mobile kitchen that crisscrossed the country sampling the many products of ConAgra Foods. Big Hungry, as the truck was dubbed, even made a special trip to lower Manhattan on Thanksgiving, 2001, to serve Thanksgiving meals featuring Butterball turkey and all the trimmings to 9/11 rescue and recovery workers. This event was put together by hundreds of employee volunteers throughout the company who felt compelled to do their part in paying tribute to the thousands of firefighters, police, and rescue workers at Ground Zero.

Corporate Responsibility through Partnerships

A company and its products can play a big role in the lives of its customers and in so doing support its corporate purpose and mission. As one of the largest food manufacturers in the world, ConAgra Foods focused on two issues with long-term programs aimed at demonstrating food safety and social responsibility.

The company forged a partnership with the American Dietetic Association and through its team of media-trained dietitians across the country launched Food Safety: It's in Your Hands˚ to communicate the important role consumers play in preparing foods safely in their own homes.

Home Food Safety...It's in Your Hands ˚ is dedicated to providing home food safety statistics, information about foodborne illness (also known as food poisoning), and safe food handling information and tips.

This alliance was invaluable in helping to mitigate the effects of the company's 2002 e. coli outbreak. Besides the outreach program, a Web site (http://www.homefoodsafety.org/index.jsp) serves as a ready-reference source for consumers and foodservice workers to educate and remind them of safe food handling procedures.

Social responsibility has become an expectation that many consumers have come to expect from companies that benefit from consumer trade. Marketing communications executive Carol Cone pioneered a discipline of communications called Cause Branding®, also known as cause-related marketing, that helps companies and nonprofits integrate values and social issues into brand equity and organizational identity. (See http://www.coneinc.com/Pages/cause_brand.html.) Cone seized on two findings in her study of ConAgra Foods' social responsibility issues. Through interviews with dozens of people in the organization it became apparent that employees were highly concerned about leveraging their expertise in sourcing, producing, and distributing food to benefit society in some way. Second, she discovered a U.S. Department of Agriculture statistic that pointed out twelve million American kids fight hunger each year. Studies show that hunger is a root cause for many of the problems young people face today, ranging from problems concentrating in school to conduct after school.

Acting on these findings Cone teamed her client with America's Second Harvest, a nonprofit group, and what ensued was Feeding Children Better, a multiyear commitment aimed at eliminating childhood hunger in America.

Leaders Use Communication to Create Clarity of Purpose

In Southwest Airlines' break-the-rules business model, enormous value is generated because management is dedicated to assuring members of the company see the vision and act on it. Printed below is the Mission Statement of Southwest Airlines. It is a meaningful statement at the company that supports all communication.

The Mission of Southwest Airlines

The mission of Southwest Airlines is dedication to the highest quality of Customer Service delivered with a sense of warmth, friendliness, individual pride, and Company Spirit.

To Our Employees

We are committed to provide our Employees a stable work environment with equal opportunity for learning and personal growth. Creativity and innovation are encouraged for improving the effectiveness of Southwest Airlines. Above all, Employees will be provided the same concern, respect, and caring attitude within the organization that they are expected to share externally with every Southwest Customer.

Source: http://www.southwest.com/about_swa/mission.html

Stories help people understand how beliefs are translated into behaviors.

The content of the airline's newsletter, called LUV Lines, helps draw members of the organization into a dialogue about relevant company news and information. As Kevin and Jackie Freiberg (1996, p. 125) write in their book about the company, "this dialogue almost always results in a better understanding of the implications of the information and its relevance to what people do." So, when a customer comes in touch with a front-line employee and discovers this person has a firm grasp on the issues that affect the company, it is magical because it so rarely happens in most firms.

Storytelling to Create Meaning and Clarity

Storytelling is another effective communication tool to breathe life into the culture. Stories help people understand how beliefs are translated into behaviors. One such story repeated frequently at Southwest is that of a flight attendant popping out of the overhead luggage bin. This is truly unconventional and at most airlines would be met with a reprimand. Not at Southwest where this story has become a symbol of company spirit. The airline business is highly stressful for all concerned. So, when customers and employees can laugh about something, the stress of travel is relieved somewhat. There are many stories like this one. For example, when a review of architectural firms failed to deliver the right design concept for its new corporate headquarters, the company hired a recent college architectural graduate to take a shot. It worked. What resulted was a design that supports the culture. Wall space became a display to express the history, values, and culture of the company. Artifacts of the company's history are posted on the walls everywhere. It is not uncommon for a veteran of the company to take a new person to a display on the wall to drive home one of the values of the company. In late 2005, the company experienced a disaster when one of its planes skidded off the runway onto a Chicago street and killed a youngster in a passing car. Within hours, the company had dispatched directly to the scene a team of ninety-four employees trained in managing such anticipated crises. The chairman of the company took responsibility for communicating and acting. The firm used its communication resources, including its Web site, to inform and assure its people, passengers, and the public in general. Culture is a powerful thing, and it is inconceivable to think of building it without effective communication.

The Strategic Communication Plan

The strategic communication plan (SCP) is the framework for integrating communication into the organization so as to support its business model. Its development serves to analyze environment, strategy, individuals, messages, media, measurement and feedback, structure and staffing, and budget. It is conducted parallel to the strategy development, marketing development, and any other significant processes conducted in the organization as it relates to managing the business model. Development and execution of the SCP is a disciplined process that connects the integrated communication to the organization's business plan. (For details regarding creation of an SCP for your organization, go to: http://www.mm-mkt.com.)

Integrated Communication: Who Should Lead? The Opportunity for Corporate Communications Professionals

By Louis Capozzi,
Chairman, Publicis PR and Corporate Communications Group

If you go to a podiatrist and complain of headaches, it is said, she is likely to find something wrong with your feet. The same holds true for communication. Ask an advertising executive for advice on a communications problem, and he is likely to recommend a thirty-second spot.

As integration has become the holy grail of communication, organizations desperately seek unbiased advice on how to deal with the increasingly difficult environment of the twenty-first century. The decline of advertising effectiveness, increasing audience skepticism, unbelievable noise levels, and the 24/7 realities of the Internet all fuel their frenzy.

There is plenty of agreement in the communications community about the need for unified strategies that form the foundation for all the elements in the communications mix. But who should lead the development of those strategies? After all, putting together a team with representatives from all the communication disciplines might lead to a strategy "without prejudice," but only if the team leader is truly objective.

Until recently, the "golden rule" has applied to leadership of these integrated teams: "he who has the gold, rules." On brands where there is $100 million in advertising on the table, along with a PR program and some "below the line" promotional work, there has been little doubt the advertising person would take the lead on the integration team.

But the current environment mandates that we reexamine this default model. We may understand the need for integration, but most communicators have not even scratched the surface on how to properly build an integrated program. Quite often we are starting from the wrong place and using the wrong terminology. Integration has to be more than picking the right tool from the toolbox. Our model needs to ensure that strategic business planning remains in the center. Hand in hand with strategic business planning is finding the best resource in the "mix" who will lead with a management orientation.

The answer: corporate communications professionals. Several trends have converged to make corporate communications professionals ideally suited to drive integrated communications in today's complex environment.

⇒ The Age of Transparency—The digital age has ushered in a new need for transparency for any successful organization. On the one hand, microsegmentation is a new option, on the other all of the audiences are interconnected and your interactions with them must assume full interaction and transparency among them. Everyone sees everything.

⇒ Advertising people are trained to communicate with a "bulls-eye" target audience—often called "consumers." Working with multiple audiences is like being a plate spinner in a circus—always hitting the wobbling plate. Sensitivity to multiple constituencies—employees, the community, government, and customers is part of a corporate communications professional's DNA.

⇒ Lack of Control—in the digital environment, you have to give up control to gain power. The analogy is that if you have a friend who is always telling you what to do, they will not be your friend for long. The same thing is true of brands. This is a disturbing notion to advertising people, who have controlled every word, every comma, and every pixel. But corporate communications professionals have always worked in an environment where their message passes through the filter of a third party. We need to embrace this new world and work with it.

⇒ Communication without prejudice—As anyone knows who has tried it, producing excellent advertising is a very tough job. Making a thirty-second spot that works, and selling it through a gauntlet of approvals is enormously challenging. And advertising people do it well. But honing that skill does not necessarily lead to expertise in other disciplines. Corporate communicators do not bring a bias toward any particular tool, and advertising is just that—a tool.

⇒ Globalization adds to the complexity, and to the need for a broader view. Look at the example Al Ries points to in his book. A global food company might be wrestling with the obesity issue in the U.S. while in Europe their big issue is genetically modified ingredients and in Africa the problem is malnutrition. The company needs to deal with all of these in an environment where all the global audiences are exposed to each other's messages.

⇒ Advertising, though, is not going away—because publishing is not going away and it needs advertising to support its business model. Look at all the big new buildings in New York—Time Warner Center, The Bloomberg Building, and so forth. So, advertising has to change. What has to change the most is the mentality of the people. We have to bring corporate communications thinking to the advertising business to change the mentality. Could corporate communications be the new face of advertising? Clients need communications programs that are "wisdom driven."

⇒ Time for a new model—Instead of competing for budgets, communications professionals from all disciplines need to learn how to work together. Corporate communications professionals can be the focal point for finding the right solution, implementing it flawlessly, and measuring the work, regardless of which discipline is employed.

⇒ The new model must be advice-centric. The organization's problem, analyzed and interpreted from the broadest possible communications perspective, must be at the hub of the effort. Team members from multiple disciplines can contribute to and enrich the advice, but in the end the disciplines support the advice, they do not drive it.

⇒ Look to China for the new model—Developing nations are jumping over old technologies to new models—jumping over wired telephone networks to wireless, jumping over gasoline directly to hybrids or hydrogen. Maybe communications in China will jump over the old model—miss completely the bad days of disjointed communications—and go right to some new model. If they do, bet on corporate communications professionals—particularly PR and Public Affairs—to play a major role. After all, in a communist country the role of the government is disproportionately important.

⇒ Time for a new tone as well – from selling to factual. From big bang to continuous conversation. From "shovel ware" to tailored. As Richard Edelman has said, "we need to admit complexity and contradiction."

The bottom line is this: the training and skills required to deal with this complexity make corporate communications professionals very well suited to the job of creating total communication strategies. Advertising and the media need our guidance and expertise to manage the change. This is the dawn of the age of the corporate communications counselor.

What do corporate communications professionals need to do to make the most of this opportunity?

First, step up to the need for measurement and accountability. New models are needed for tracking, evaluating, and analyzing the results of corporate communications programs. We need to understand the impact and influence our work has on audience attitudes and behavior, and the factors that drive the change. As Jack Welch, the venerable former chairman of General Electric, is famous for saying, "if you can't measure it you can't do it."

Second, corporate communicators need to attract more and better talent to the profession. Future leaders in corporate communications must be:

⇒ Business people—capable of handling higher-level business relationships and understanding the businesses and industries they serve
⇒ Strategists—whose work is rooted in strategic audience insights that align with overall business objectives and goals
⇒ Marketers—who understand all aspects of the marketing mix in order to seize opportunities and leverage the elements
⇒ Scientists—who fully understand the importance of research and know how to measure a program's value and impact
⇒ Globalists—who are accustomed to and appreciative of the differences across cultures and geographies

Corporate communications professionals have an enormous opportunity ahead of them to lead the next generation of marketing and communications activities around the world. Maintaining a broad view, building experience, staying on top of technological change, and recruiting the best people with next-generation skills will take the profession where it has the potential to grow.

A 13-Step Process for Developing an Agency Proposal

By Mel Ehrlich,
Communications Consultant

Step 1: Phone call from the prospect

A prospective client has asked you to participate in a competitive bid for a PR assignment. Assuming you have no existing clients that compete with this prospect and therefore present no conflicts, your first step after accepting the challenge is to ask for a client briefing—an input session in which your prospect gives you (and your competitors) information about the company, its products and services, and existing communications vehicles and activities.

Before the briefing, conduct basic research on the company and the product or service you are being asked to support. Do not participate in the briefing without doing advance backgrounding. Be prepared to ask questions that will guide your eventual program strategy. Clarify these items:

⇒ Prospect's target audiences for the PR initiative: women? teenagers? senior citizens? ethnic or special communities? physicians? patients ? politicians? analysts? potential investors?

⇒ Audience for your presentation: the company's marketing team? an in-house PR professional? Who are the decision makers?

⇒ Presentation style your prospect prefers: formal and speech-like or casual and conversational, PowerPoint slides or presentation boards—or both?

⇒ Prospect's in-house spokesperson: CEO? Marketing director? Has he or she been media trained?

⇒ Prospect's third-party allies: Consumer groups? Patient support groups? Physicians and their professional associations? Analysts? Can you contact them to prepare your program?

⇒ How will success be measured: media placements; placements converted to advertising costs; surveys conducted in key markets before your program is implemented, then again when it has been completed to determine if it has changed perceptions of the company and/or its product(s); response mechanisms such as Web site hits, calls to a toll-free number, Business Reply Cards, or, if you are pitching for a health-care assignment, physician visits, dialogues with doctors about the product, an increase in prescriptions, an increase in sales—or some or all of the above?

After the briefing, ask your prospect for the company's (or the product's) marketing plan and its advertising campaign (if one is in place); they will help you determine the prospective client's PR positioning and strategy—and your program must support the marketing strategy and the ad campaign.

Assuming you are working with an agency team or with other consultants, move into Step 2.

Step 2: Understanding the assignment

Make sure the team you have assembled to work with you understands what the prospect expects. A company's business objectives (an increase in product sales or rapid uptake of a newly launched product, for example) can be different from its communications objectives, such as conditioning the market for a new product launch or raising awareness of a problem (an existing or impending public-health crisis, for example) for which the prospect or its product is a solution. You need to know what the prospective client expects PR to accomplish and when those objectives must be achieved. Invariably, your program should communicate the company's benefits, or its products', to its target audiences, its stakeholders.

Step 3: Time-and-Events Schedule

Develop a timeline highlighting critical dates:

⇒ When research must be completed
⇒ When the creative part (visuals) of your presentation must be completed and reviewed
⇒ PowerPoint slides and/or presentation boards
⇒ Appropriate props—"toys" that can be left behind after the presentation
⇒ Printed or CD-ROM version of the presentation to be left behind after the presentation
⇒ Rehearsals

Step 4: Research

Thorough research is the most important part of this process. Decide on a research plan that specifies your research objectives and areas of interest; draft questionnaires to help team members who are conducting research ask succinct questions in order to get useful answers. You need to know as much about the company and its product(s) as its marketing team does. You must know and have an in-depth understanding of:

⇒ the prospect's market (consumer products, for example)
⇒ the category this particular product or product line (skin care, for example) is in
⇒ market issues, product issues
⇒ the company's competitors and their products and services
⇒ how its stakeholders perceive the prospect

Consequently:

⇒ A lit search, including consumer and trade media coverage of the company and its products and services

⇒ Online searches, including the blogosphere

⇒ Third-party interviews: how do they perceive this prospect?

⇒ One-on-one telephone or face-to-face interviews with consumers who use (or could use) the company's product(s)

⇒ Professionals—key opinion leaders (KOLs) such as physicians, if appropriate

⇒ Retailers

⇒ Investors, analysts

⇒ Media (if possible)

While you are conducting research, build a relationship with the prospect. Call with questions and updates; let your prospect know about the progress you are making on the program. Do not be afraid to ask if you are on the right track.

Step 5: Analyzing the research

When you have completed the research, analyze it. What is missing? "Interrogate" the research: What is it telling you? Thorough analysis of research leads to a situation or SWOT—strengths, weaknesses, opportunities, threats—analysis that will be incorporated into your final program. It should isolate weaknesses that your program must address, opportunities it must recognize and capitalize on, threats it must foresee and blunt (a similar upcoming competitive product, for example), strengths it needs to trumpet. Market or product issues could necessitate your including an issues or crisis management section in your program. Research will also give you a picture of the competitive landscape. And it will lead to a strategy.

Step 6: Immersion meeting

You are now ready to finalize strategy and develop positioning statements and messages.

Step 7: Creative brainstorming

Based on your research, including the insights you have gained by contacting the prospect's third-party allies (Step 1), conduct a brainstorming session with your team and with colleagues who have not been working on this project; they may have valuable insights. The brainstorm's purpose is to produce tactics—the creative activities and vehicles you will undertake to implement your campaign.

Step 8: Produce the presentation "deck" and leave-behind (binder and/or CD-ROM)

Make sure that your:

⇒ Strategy supports your program's objectives

⇒ Tactics support strategy and objectives and respond to your SWOT/ situation analysis

⇒ Program addresses measurement (metrics)

⇒ Program includes an appendix—a compilation of the research you have conducted, including verbatims of telephone conversations you have had with third parties

⇒ Program demonstrates how it will benefit the company and/or its products and services

Also, include a budget estimate and an organizational chart that includes everyone who will work on this assignment if you win it, and their titles.

Step 9: Rehearse

Rehearsals should be conducted two to three days before the actual presentation—and more than once. Your presentation will inevitably change somewhat during rehearsals as you hear the program unfold. Rehearsals also give you the opportunity to anticipate prospective questions and rehearse appropriate answers. Role-playing is strongly encouraged. Rehearse with colleagues not involved in the programming process to get objective feedback and constructive criticism. Then finalize the deck.

Step 10: Scoping the scene

Find out about the venue and room you will be presenting in. If possible, do a site-check. Will audiovisual equipment—a computer, a projector, a screen—be available? Will a technician be available if a problem arises?

Step 11: The "what if …?" stage

Think like a crisis planner: What if the presentation starts late, thereby depriving you of presentation time? What if the prospect has an internal crisis and can give you only ten minutes to present? What if the computer/ projector does not work and you have to present without visuals? Will you be prepared for these exigencies?

Step 12: Showtime

Arrive at the room you are presenting in about twenty to thirty minutes before the meeting begins to "size up" the environment. Rehearse the opening—the introduction to your program—aloud in the room. The opening is often the most difficult part of a presentation; once you get past it, you are very likely to continue smoothly and professionally.

Presentations, ideally, should be interactive so that your prospect can ask questions during your presentation.

Step 13: Curtain call

When you have finished presenting, ask for the assignment and encourage your prospect to discuss next steps. In other words, move from the presentation to an action plan.

Best Practices in Integrated Communication

As we have seen in this chapter, integrated communication allows communicators to more effectively build a valued reputation and powerful brand equity. The best practices of integrated communication include:

1. Evaluate your organization's communication to ensure that it parallels your strategy and supports the business model. This entails use of an effective audit of communication, both inside and out, and at the very least a SWOT analysis.
2. Marshal communication tools, practices, and resources to reach your organization's business goals and objectives, and make certain communication professionals who deeply understand these resources are actively involved in the organization.
3. View communication as two-way and in the larger context of the enterprise, not just its marketing activities.
4. Create an environment for a shared vision to surface. Begin with articulating and communicating the values of the firm.
5. Empower employees to listen to customers and dialogue with their colleagues to learn new ways to satisfy and delight customers.
6. Dialogue unlocks the value in communication. Listen to the environment and develop relationships through integrated communication to create an open environment of trust and accountability.
7. Utilize effective, integrated communication to create and manage change. By envisioning a future state—where organizational value is created through a shared vision, a common understanding of the overarching purpose of the firm, the importance of customers, and assumptions about what works—members of the organization can be brought to recognize the need for cultural revolution.
8. Integrated communication relies on engaging the intended receiver in a more meaningful way that leads to developing a relationship.
9. Corporate branding must reflect values. Brands are living, breathing entities made up of people and the products and services they provide. With values in place, brands can take root and add value.
10. Employ a strategic communication plan and update it regularly.

Resources for Further Study

See References, below, and the following Web sites.

The Website of the Journal of Integrated Marketing Communication: http://jimc. medill.northwestern.edu/defined.htm.

The Website of the American Marketing Association: http://www.marketingpower. com/.

McMahon, T.P. *The little green marketing book*. New York: Spring Rain Publishing, 2004.

Questions for Further Discussion

1. *Integrated marketing communication* focuses on selling the product and building customer relationships through marketing and public relations, whereas *integrated communication* focuses on all the organization's relationships. IMC cares about marketing the brand and IC markets the entire company. IC cares about the product and sales but also about philanthropy, the environment, and public policy. Is the distinction important?
2. How is it that a strong organizational culture can "bring life to communication efforts"?
3. What is it that makes Southwest Airlines so successful?
4. What is meant by the phrase "listening to the environment"?
5. Can you think of an example of cause-related marketing that might help your organization as well as a particular cause?

References

Bartolome, F. Nobody trusts the boss completely – now what? *Harvard Business Review,* (March–April, 1989): 135–142.

Borden, N. The concept of the marketing mix. *Journal of Advertising Research,* v.4, June, 1964, pp.2-7.

Bossidy, L., and R. Charan. *Confronting reality: doing what matters to get things right.* New York: Crown Business, 2004.

Bridges, W. *Managing transitions.* 2nd ed. Cambridge, MA: De Capo Press, 2003.

Collins, J. *Good to great.* New York: HarperCollins, 2001.

Conger, J. A. The necessary art of persuasion. *Harvard Business Review.* (May–June 1998): 85.

Deetz, S.A., S.J. Tracy, and J.L. Simpson. *Leading organizations through transition.* Thousand Oaks, CA: Sage Publications, 2000.

Deutsch, C.H. The new Kodak moment: Is it warm or is it cool? *The New York Times,* August 28, 2005. Retrieved August 28, 2005, from http://www.nytimes.com/2005/08/26/business/media/26adco.html?pagewanted=1.

Edelman, R. The relationship imperative. *Journal of Integrated Communications* (2003): 7–13. Retrieved August 8, 2005, from http://www.medill.northwestern.edu/imc/studentwork/pubs/jic/journal/2004/JIC2004.pdf.

Fombrun, C. *Reputation: Realizing value from the corporate image.* Boston: Harvard Business School Press, 1996.

Freiberg, K., and J. Freiberg. *Nuts! Southwest Airlines' crazy recipe for business and personal success.* Austin, TX: Bard Books, 1996.

Garvin, D. Building a learning organization. *Harvard Business Review* (July–August, 1993): 78–91.

Gill, J., and S. Whittle. Management by panacea: Accounting for transience. *Journal of Management Studies* 30(2) (1993): 281–196.

Higgs, M., and D. Rowland. Building change leadership capability: The quest for change competence. *Journal of Change Management* 1(2) (2000): 116–130.

Kotter, J.P., and D.S. Cohen. *The heart of change.* Boston: Harvard Business School Press, 2002.

Kouzes, J.M., and B.Z. Posner. *The leadership challenge.* San Francisco: Jossey-Bass, 2002.

Kumar, N. *Marketing as strategy.* Boston: Harvard Business Press, 2004.

Lakoff, G., and M. Johnson. *Metaphors we live by.* Chicago: University of Chicago Press, 2003.

McMahon, T.P. *The little green marketing book.* New York: Spring Rain Publishing, 2004.

Miller, D. Successful change leaders: What makes them? What do they do that is different. *Journal of Change Management* 2(4) (2002): 359–369.

Moser, M. *United we brand.* Boston: Harvard Business School Press, 2003.

Pottruck, D. S., and T. Pearce. *Clicks and mortar.* San Francisco: Jossey-Bass, 2001.

Schein, E.H. *Organizational culture and leadership.* 2nd ed. San Francisco: Jossey-Bass, 1997.

Schultz, D. The 21st century roller-coaster ride continues. *B-to-B Chicago* 90(7) (June 13, 2005): 45.

Senge, P. (Author and Speaker). *The fifth discipline field book* [Audio tape]. New York: Bantam Doubleday Dell Audio Publishing, a division of Random House, 1999.

Senge, P.M. *The fifth discipline: The art and practice of the learning organization.* New York: Currency Doubleday, 1994.

Sutton, D., and T. Klein. *Enterprise marketing management: The new science of marketing.* New York: John Wiley & Sons, 2003.

Tichy, N.M., and S. Sherman. *Control your destiny or someone else will.* New York: Harper Business, 2001.

CHAPTER 11

Issues Management

> *Plan for what is difficult when it is most easy,*
> *do what is great while it is small.*
> *The most difficult things in the world must be done*
> *while they are still easy, the greatest things*
> *in the world must be done while they are still small.*
>
> —*The Tao-te Ching*, or *The Way and Its Power*,
> Lao Tzu (604–581 BC)

When Merck began its AIDS research in 1986, pharmaceutical companies had been savaged by activists, patient advocates, the research community, the government, and the news media for failing to do enough research and for pricing their drugs too high. Demonstrations were held at several company headquarters. There was violence.

Merck public affairs began meeting with AIDS activists and patient advocates in late 1990, by which time the company had begun to make progress with its research, but was nowhere near introducing a drug to market. The pharmaceutical industry had never before faced such a powerful consumer group as people with HIV, and in the decade following the first cases of AIDS in 1980, the industry had not reacted well. Business people and scientists were not used to dealing with sensitive issues like those surrounding sexual practices and illicit drug use, or with people who were often angry and aggressive. The activists' primary concern was both the availability and affordability of potentially life-saving medicines.

In those early days, Albert Angel, Linda Distlerath, John Doorley, and several others in Merck public affairs believed strongly that Merck had every reason to be forthright and proactive with the activist community as the company battled to develop effective medicines that could be made widely available. An issues management strategy of engagement, consisting of aggressive internal and external initiatives, was adopted. For example, hundreds of employees and company researchers in the United States and abroad were trained to understand and meet with the activist community. Activists were invited to speak at several Merck sites, and they routinely toured the research facilities and met with the researchers. In a six-year period (1990–1996), public affairs held over one hundred meetings to listen to activist needs and relay Merck's plans and positions. The company made several changes in policies and research protocols based on activist input.

By late 1994, after having tested thousands of compounds that failed because of safety issues or viral resistance, it looked like one compound, later known as Crixivan, might make it to market. But the chemistry was extraordinarily complex and the production process was difficult.

In January 1995, several leading activists let the company know that they did not believe that Merck could not produce enough Crixivan to expand clinical (human) trials and provide a compassionate (premarketing) use program. To manage this issue, Merck public affairs recommended that activists bring their own chemist consultant to Merck to discuss the complex chemistry of Crixivan. Public affairs assured the community—and its chemist—that it could decide for itself. Understandably, Merck lawyers were not happy, but after confidentiality agreements were signed, the meeting took place at the company's Rahway, New Jersey, research facility in January 1995. Activist Tom Blount, upon hearing his own consultant praise what Merck had achieved, began to cry and walked from the room. He knew there would be no quick solutions.

John Doorley followed Tom into the hallway, and Tom apologized for having been so skeptical about the company's efforts to date. This was not the first or last time that Merck's relationship with AIDS activists—which ABC-TV's Nightline *news program later called "remarkable"—would be tested. But the relationship proved strong and successful in terms of permitting the research effort to proceed unimpeded, in a scientifically valid way.*

When Crixivan reached the market in March 1996, Martin Delaney, founding director of Project Inform, one of the most respected activist organizations, wrote to the company saying its behavior "demonstrates that Merck is responsive to the public and holding true to the traditions of its founders. In my 11 years of AIDS activism, neither I nor my cohorts have ever been motivated to write another letter like this. Our congratulations to all of your team."[1]

* * * * *

This Chapter Covers

⇒ Issues management overview
⇒ Establishing an issues management function
⇒ Prioritizing issues
⇒ Issues management planning process
⇒ Developing an issues management plan
⇒ Issues management analysis and planning template
⇒ What elements of the issues management analysis and planning template mean
⇒ Best practices
⇒ Resources for further study
⇒ Questions for further discussion

Issues management is a corporate process that helps organizations identify challenges in the business environment—both internal and external—before they become crises, and mobilizes corporate resources to help protect the company from the harm to reputation, operations, and financial condition that the issue may provoke. Issues management is a subset of risk management, but the risks it deals with involve public visibility and possible reputational harm.

Issues Management Overview

Enlightened companies have formal issues management processes, at the enterprisewide level and in individual business units or geographically dispersed locations. Sometimes the corporate communication department runs the function, but often the function is run from the legal, quality assurance, government relations, or risk management departments. Wherever issues management may reside in an organization, typically it is an interdisciplinary function involving multiple corporate perspectives and several communication functions.

Establishing an Issues Management Function

A formal issues management function involves establishing a multidisciplinary issues management team consisting of all major business functions.

Initial tasks for the team include identifying issues that matter to the company. Typical issues are:

> Enlightened companies have formal issues management processes, at the enterprise-wide level and in individual business units or geographically dispersed locations.

⇒ Possible legislative activity impacting the company, its competitors, its products, its pricing, or its marketplace.

⇒ Regulatory events and business climate changes. For example, between 2001 and 2005 there were significant changes in the regulatory climate in the United States for the public accounting, investment banking, pharmaceuticals, and insurance industries.

⇒ Changes in social trends that make previously accepted practices unacceptable. After nationally televised U.S. Senate hearings on the 1991 nomination of Clarence Thomas to the U.S. Supreme Court made the issue of sexual harassment highly visible, workplace standards for many companies were revised.

⇒ Competitors' activities, both positive and negative. For example, in 2004 Marsh Inc., an insurance brokerage, mutual fund, and consulting organization, suffered a series of setbacks in the wake of investigations by New York State Attorney General Elliot Spitzer. This called into question the integrity and soundness of many other insurance companies, and the insurance industry as a whole was cast in a negative light. So even insurance companies that had nothing to do with Marsh's scandal suffered collateral damage, and needed to manage the negative perception of their sector.

⇒ Lawsuits, including class action lawsuits where a large number of people claim to have been harmed by a company's products or business practices.

⇒ Product quality and safety issues, especially issues that require the recall of defective products or put customers' lives, health, safety, or financial condition at risk.

⇒ Internal problems, such as the need to restate earnings or change accounting treatment of previously disclosed earnings.

⇒ Activities by groups with specific agendas, such as the AIDS advocacy organization mentioned above.

Prioritizing Issues

Once an issue is identified, it is important to understand how significant it is and what corporate resources will be needed to manage the issue effectively.

The two critical factors in assessing the importance of an issue are: likelihood—how likely is it that this issue will play out to the company's disadvantage; and magnitude—if it does play out to our disadvantage, how significant could the harm be?

Any given issue can be measured on a likelihood/magnitude matrix:

On a scale from zero to ten, the matrix is divided into four quadrants. The upper right contains issues with high magnitude and high likelihood; the upper left, issues with high likelihood and low magnitude; the lower right, low likelihood and high magnitude, and the lower left for issues where both magnitude and likelihood are low.

Single issues can be plotted on this matrix, which functions as a tool to allocate resources and management attention to a given issue. High likelihood/high magnitude issues would get primary attention. Various scenarios of how issues might play out can also be plotted on the matrix to help give a sense of the relative resources required to manage an issue in dynamic circumstances. Multiple issues can be plotted to help the issues management group prioritize its work based on the relative magnitude/likelihood of each issue:

> Any given issue can be measured on a likelihood/ magnitude matrix.

Likelihood/Magnitude Matrix

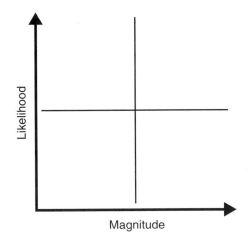

Figure 11.1

Prioritizing Issues

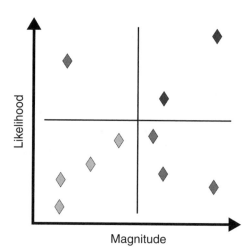

Figure 11.2

If an issues management team considered a range of issues plotted on the graph above, it would focus on the two issues in the upper right quadrant. Second, it would appraise the single issue with high likelihood but low magnitude and the three issues with low magnitude but high likelihood. The four issues where both magnitude and likelihood are low would be put on a watch list and periodically reviewed.

For each issue identified, the issues management team would next develop a plan to analyze it, allocate resources to influence events to lessen its impact, and engage stakeholders in support.

Issues Management Planning Process

Three First Steps

⇒ Establish a mechanism (e.g., regularly scheduled meetings, ongoing research, periodic discussion with key stakeholders) to identify potential issues or crises before they occur.

⇒ Prepare background documents and analysis. The longer the document, the more important the executive summary.

⇒ Empower the communications team to advise lawyers, business heads, and company members who might not see the connections between discrete issues and the business interests of the enterprise.

Develop an Action Plan

⇒ Develop an issues management and communication plan with objectives, strategies, tactics, messages, budgets, timelines, and an evaluation mechanism.

Enlist or Adapt the Current Communications Program

⇒ Aggressively manage the communication program.

Evaluate and Review

⇒ Periodically assess results.

Developing an Issues Management Plan

The starting point of an issues management plan is an analysis that identifies both the problem to be solved and the organization's ability to provide meaningful impact on the issue. Effective analysis attempts to develop understanding of the external environment and the company's internal state, as well as ways the company might adapt operations, practices, procedures, or structure. In other words, the analysis is intended to develop both situational awareness and self-awareness.

All too often companies focus on understanding and trying to manage external issues without acknowledging the internal realities of the company. Issues management then becomes ineffective because the company is constrained throughout the process by internal obstacles such as lack of buy-in or sufficient resources. Over 2,000 years ago the Chinese philosopher-warrior Sun Tzu identified the need for both situational awareness and self-awareness in navigating through perilous times. He wrote: "If you know others and know yourself, you will not be imperiled in a hundred battles; if you do not know others but know yourself, you win one and you lose one; if you do not know others and do not know yourself, you will be imperiled in every single battle."[2]

This chapter describes an approach to issues management planning that has been field-tested by dozens of companies and organizations from Fortune-25-size financial firms and small not-for-profit advocacy groups; publicly traded companies and private concerns; and by U.S. corporations and companies based abroad. It has been applied to issues that threatened a company's survival, and to minor bumps that merely caused embarrassment; to issues that were planned for and expected well in advance, and to those that arose suddenly and became public quickly. The planning process allowed these companies to respond effectively, quickly, and definitively and to protect their reputations, operations, and financial conditions.

The plan should consist of two key sections:

⇒ An analysis identifies the issue, event, or potential crisis and assesses the scope and likelihood of operational or reputational damage. The analysis section names the problem and elucidates how it is likely to affect the organization and constituencies which matter to the organization.

> Issues management then becomes ineffective because the company is constrained throughout the process by internal obstacles such as lack of buy-in or sufficient resources.

⇒ The plan prescribes the steps to take to protect the company from operational harm and protect or restore the company's reputation. Bear in mind that drafting the plan—the proposed solution—without a clear understanding of the problem can be highly counterproductive. It is possible to craft at least an outline of an analysis quickly. An analysis can catalyze an entire management team into a common understanding of the problem and of the ramifications if the issue remains unaddressed.

The issues management analysis and plan may be written in complete sentences or paragraphs, in bullet points, in presentation slide format, or in any other medium that works for the company in question. The style of the written document is less important than the quality of the thinking and the level of engagement by management in the issues raised in the plan.

"Issue" Versus "Event"

Below is a quick summary of the Issues Management Analysis and Planning Template, followed by a detailed description of each element. Note the template is similar to the actions mandated in handling crisis communications. The major difference is that an "issue" is more typically a situation played out over a period of time instead of a singular incident or event.

Issue Management Analysis and Planning Template

The Issues Management Analysis and Planning Template provides a structured way to think about solutions to a problem. It provides an ordered, outlined overview of a basic, viable, and strategic issue-management approach. It is a predictable, goal-oriented process which clarifies actions and messages in support of business goals.

Issue Analysis

⇒ Threat Assessment
⇒ Magnitude
⇒ Likelihood
⇒ Define affected constituencies
⇒ Research additional information

Issue Management Plan

⇒ Business Decisions /Actions
⇒ Business Objectives
⇒ Issues Management Strategies

⇒ Actions to Take (Tactics)

⇒ Staffing

⇒ Logistics

⇒ Budget

⇒ Communications Plan

  - Communication Objectives
  - Communication Strategies
  - Target Audience(s)
  - External
  - Internal
  - Tactics
  - Targeted Messages
  - Documents
  - Logistics

What the Elements of the Issues Management Analysis and Planning Template Mean

Issue Analysis. Issue analysis is descriptive: It answers the question "what?" It addresses what happened, and what could happen if the issue is not handled properly. It helps to establish both self-awareness and situational awareness.

> It helps to establish both self-awareness and situational awareness.

This establishes the context in which an issue is to be understood and the challenges it presents. It leads management toward a crisis response action plan and communication plan calibrated to the magnitude and likelihood of the event or threat. The analysis is intended to provide management, internal and external staff, and other company employees with a common understanding of the nature of the threat and the possible consequences. The subsequent action plan should be crafted to neutralize damage resulting from the threat identified in the analysis.

The key elements of the analysis are:

Threat Assessment

The analysis begins by naming the problem: It presents a clear description of the threat and the various ways it could play out. There are many kinds of threat:

⇒ A negative event within the company, such as termination of key employees, discovery of malfeasance, abrupt departure of key leaders, filing a lawsuit, or the verdict in a lawsuit.

⇒ A negative event outside the company but directed at it, such as litigation, a competitor's triumph, or regulatory activity.

⇒ A routine business process or decision that risks being misunderstood or will be the subject of opposition.

⇒ An accepted business practice that becomes controversial because the political, social, or business environment has changed.

⇒ An event or change in the business environment that affects the company's competitiveness, financial stability, or operations. These could include natural disasters, new legislation, acts of terrorism, or similar issues not directed at the company but from which the company suffers collateral damage.

In addition to naming the threat, the analysis should address why the threat is something to be managed:

⇒ What is the likely impact on the company, its constituencies, and its operational and financial health?

⇒ What is the likelihood that the issue, left unmanaged, will cause harm?

⇒ What is the likelihood the company can minimize or prevent that harm?

⇒ What is the likelihood the company will make matters worse?

Sample Threat Assessment: An Embezzlement

The threat assessment should assess the specific business processes, business relationships, and elements of the business environment that might be affected. For example, a company discovering employee embezzlement might identify the following as areas of concern:

⇒ Reasons existing control structures did not detect the embezzlement earlier

⇒ Facilitation by or participation of other employees

⇒ Vulnerability of other areas (financial reporting, physical property theft, accuracy of preemployment data, etc.)

⇒ History of similar events

⇒ Advisability of involving law enforcement

⇒ The need to dismiss the employee; and what to say internally upon the employee's dismissal

⇒ Desirability of investigating via internal or external legal and accounting resources

⇒ Likelihood of news of the embezzlement leaking

⇒ Advisability of proactive disclosure of discovery and steps taken to identify scope and prevent recurrence

⇒ Materiality of the dollar amount and the need to disclose into the financial markets

The threat assessment should assess the specific business processes, business relationships, and elements of the business environment that might be affected.

⇒ Connections between the embezzlement and seemingly unrelated problems that might become public in the same timeframe

⇒ The probability that competitors, adversaries, activists, regulators, or others may use the event to agitate against or embarrass the company

In addition to the business processes, relationships, and environmental challenges, the threat assessment should also identify the likely visibility that the threat represents, either left to itself or if mishandled, including visibility in the news media and likely public comment by investors, adversaries, regulators, legislators, ratings agencies, securities analysts, employees, and others.

To the degree that the issue is caused or may be inflamed by an adversary, the threat assessment should also anticipate the adversary's likely plan of attack and its next moves.

Alternative Scenarios

It may also be useful for the threat assessment to include a number of possible scenarios, particularly when the threat is outside the control of the company. For example, if a regulatory investigation is underway, there may be several scenarios including:

⇒ The investigation concludes that there was no malfeasance on the part of the company or its officers

⇒ The investigation concludes that there was malfeasance on the part of a single or limited number of employees of the company

⇒ The investigation concludes that malfeasance was widespread and endemic within the company.

Similarly, in the case of a pending verdict in litigation, the scenarios could include:

⇒ The company has a major victory

⇒ The company has a major defeat

⇒ An ambiguous verdict that finds for the company in some elements of the case, but against the company in others

⇒ The company settles on favorable terms that are publicly disclosable

⇒ The company settles on confidential terms

For each scenario, there would be a corresponding list of considerations, including an assessment of the likely response to each outcome among those who matter to the company, and the company's and adversary's likely next steps (appeal, settlement discussion, initiation of new litigation, etc.).

Magnitude Analysis

The magnitude analysis assesses the relative magnitude of the threat's impact on the company's reputation and operations. If the threat could play out according to several scenarios, the reputational and operational impact of each scenario should be assessed. This assessment involves the same process as was described above, in the discussion of prioritizing various issues.

Likelihood Analysis

The likelihood analysis assesses the relative certainty or probability that any particular event will take place and will cause operational or reputational damage. As with the magnitude analysis, the likelihood analysis should take account of different scenarios.

The likelihood/magnitude matrix described earlier in this chapter should be used to plot the relative impact of an issue or set of scenarios.

Affected Constituencies

The constituency analysis creates an inventory of the constituencies likely to be most affected by the issue and their likely attitudinal or behavioral predispositions. These constituencies could include internal groups such as employees, specific internal functions or departments, or affiliated groups who function as internal resources, such as contractors, agents, brokers, or an independent sales force; or external groups such as regulators, customers, investors, allies, or adversaries.

> Whereas the issue analysis is descriptive, the issue management plan is prescriptive.

For each constituency named, the analysis should assess the likely attitudinal or behavioral outcome of the event, under each likely scenario.

What Additional Information Is Required?

The analysis should also identify additional specific information that needs to be obtained in order to either fully assess the threat or to begin the planning process. It also identifies the internal and external resource persons who need to be consulted or involved in the planning process.

The Issue Management Plan

Once the issue or event has been analyzed, the issue management plan can be constructed. Whereas the issue analysis is descriptive, the issue management plan is prescriptive: it prescribes a course of action to deal with the situation as presented in the analysis. Not all of the following categories may apply in every case. However, each category should be considered for each issue, event, or crisis, and the decision not to include one or more categories in any particular written plan should be made based on the issue in question.

At the very least, every plan should include business objectives, issues management strategies, actions to take, communication objectives, communication strategies, messages, and tactics.

Business Decisions and Actions

Business Objectives. Business objectives describe what will be or what ought to be done if the company's management of the issue is effective. These objectives define the business goals that the actions and communications will accomplish. They are formulated as desired outcomes: the resulting status or change in the business environment that action and communication is intended to create.

For example, business goals could include:

⇒ Maintain market share despite a product recall or pricing pressures
⇒ Prevent regulators from taking action against the company in the wake of discovering problems
⇒ Prevent proposed legislation from restricting a company's ability to operate in its marketplace profitably
⇒ Sustain productivity during a management shakeup
⇒ Protect the company's independence in an environment of consolidation
⇒ Preserve the ability to raise capital in the wake of a financial scandal
⇒ Avoid involuntary bankruptcy

Issue Management Strategies

The issue management strategies describe how the business objectives will be achieved. They delineate the conceptual frameworks which a company will use to organize its energies and deploy its resources to influence the business environment and protect the company's operations and reputation, and to remedy any damage. They further describe ways the problems identified in the analysis will be fixed.

Strategies are not actions to take. It is easy to confuse the two, and the difference between strategies and actions to take (tactics) is described in greater detail below. In general terms, though, strategies will be the constant processes to be employed using many changing tactics.

Actions to Take (Tactics). Actions to Take describes the specific business decisions that need to be made. These are the tactics to implement in response to or in anticipation of an issue. The actions could be changes to an operating process, convening of a team of people designated to handle the company's response to an issue, articulation of steps to take to reach various constituencies, or any other concrete step. For the plan to work well, the actions to take should each put into operation at least one of the issue management strategies. An action that does not derive from one of the issue management strategies is likely to be counterproductive in at least three ways: first, it may not help solve the problem and could even make it worse; second, it expends resources that could otherwise be directed to solving the problem; third, the misguided action makes management believe that it is taking effective steps to solve the problem. The Actions to Take section could also include a menu of possible actions to be considered under various scenarios, as well as timelines of events known or expected to take place in the future, or targets for certain company-initiated activities to take place. The timetable may also prescribe regularly scheduled meetings or conference calls for the core team, its advisors, and management to review progress and facilitate decision making.

Secure Area. Depending on the scope and duration of an issue, a company may consider establishing a secure room or suite of rooms (known informally as a "war room" or "operations center") to serve as a location for the issues management team to work. Such a facility usually has restricted access and robust technological capability including phone lines, conference call capability, secure computers, printers, fax, and copiers, plus cable television, presentation slide projection capability, and a shredder. Much of the work product generated by the team can be produced in the room, and meetings of the core team can take place there, which will reduce distraction and curiosity in normal operating areas of the company and diminish the flow of rumors.

> Depending on the scope and duration of an issue, a company may consider establishing a secure room.

The Difference between Issue Management Strategies and Tactics (Actions to Take)

It is easy but counterproductive to confuse strategies and tactics. The two must be kept clear and distinct. The tactics serve the strategies, which in turn serve the business objectives.

Issue management strategies describe in conceptual terms how the objectives will be accomplished. The strategies are unlikely to change as the issue unfolds. But the actions to take—the tactics—are likely to change. Multiple actions can support a single strategy. And as the circumstances evolve, some actions may be discontinued and others begun, all in the service of a single strategy.

For example, a strategy could be: Identify the scope and severity of an embezzlement. For that single strategy there could be a number of actions to consider. These could include:

⇒ Retain a forensic accountant to review the books and determine whether other funds were stolen, as well as how the embezzlement took place

⇒ Retain an outside law firm to conduct a thorough investigation

⇒ Review whether there were any other instances of dishonesty by the employee, including expense reports, prior employment and educational data, vendor relationships, and the like

⇒ Cooperate with law enforcement authorities investigating the criminal elements of the embezzlement

These actions are not mutually exclusive, but all or part could be conducted simultaneously or in sequence. New tactics may arise as the issue unfolds, as the company learns more about the embezzlement, and as the constituencies who matter to the company react to the issue and to the company's initial responses. All proposed tactics should be compared to the strategies to determine whether each possible tactic serves an existing strategy. No tactic should be embraced unless it demonstrably supports at least one strategy. And the totality of tactics need demonstrably to support the totality of the strategies. If there is a strategy that is not supported by at least one tactic, the tactics list is not sufficiently developed.

If it becomes difficult to differentiate between strategies and tactics, a simple rule of thumb could help: Strategies are conceptual, tactics are tangible. You can assign a precise cost or date for the tactics, whereas the strategies transcend such tangible precision. In the embezzlement example above, the strategy is to identify the scope and severity of an embezzlement. However tempting, it is difficult to assign a particular cost or date to that strategy. The tactics, on the other hand, are more concrete. The first tactic is to retain a forensic accountant to review the books. This is tangible. You can point to a particular accountant to be hired for a particular fee to deliver a report on a particular date. The other tactics are similarly concrete, and each could be quantified if necessary.

Staffing. The issues management plan should designate the team or teams who will work on issues day-to-day. Most plans identify a core team that is accountable for results. That team is often empowered to prepare the plan for management review and approval, and to implement the plan once approved. Some plans identify both the core team and a governing group of managers to whom the core team will report and who can facilitate the allocation of resources quickly.

The plan should also identify other resources, both internal and external, that the team can draw upon or who may be asked to join the core team. These can include legal counsel, accounting or investment banking counsel, crisis communication counsel, operations, security, human resources, and other functional experts who can contribute based on the company's needs and the specifics of the crisis.

Part of organizing the core team is developing a complete and up-to-date working group list of all the people involved in the crisis. This should include names, titles, assistants' names, and all relevant addresses and numbers, phone, mobile phone, e-mail, pager, and other contact information.

The staffing section of the plan may also describe the frequency of core team or management team meetings, conference calls, and other contact, as well as an expedited process for review and approval of documents.

Logistics. The logistics section of the plan, which is optional, identifies the operational details that need to be addressed for the plan to work. The logistics section covers everything from who will be responsible for what work product, to the number of desks, printers, photocopiers, phone lines, and so forth, that will be required for the secure "war room," to ensuring access to the building after hours, to making certain that teams working late are fed and have transportation home at night or a place to sleep. The logistics section of the plan can range from a single piece of paper to a large three-ring binder to a computerized database. This helps the core team or its leaders understand how to operationalize the tactics they recommend and the day-to-day procedures of the crisis team.

> The logistics section of the plan can range from a single piece of paper to a large three-ring binder to a computerized database.

Budget. The budget section is also optional, and addresses the costs of managing the issue, including the retention of outside experts, out-of-pocket expenses, and remediation of the underlying issue, including possible costs of litigation, medical care, reconstruction of facilities, and so forth. Very often cost is the least important consideration with a severe issue. But it is useful to have some accountability and predictability in cost; at the very least to have a mechanism to assure that resources are properly allocated and to understand the consequences of assigning additional resources to an issue. But in general terms, issues management should not be driven by a budget, and certainly should not be held up while a budget is being developed and approved.

Communication Planning. Because most issues are or could become public, and because much damage to a company's operations and reputation is based on public reaction and criticism of the company, each issue management plan should include a communication section. The communication section is intended to support the business strategies and actions to take. It should be written following the establishment of the business strategies and specification of the actions to take. Because speed is a factor in a crisis, it may not be necessary to wait until the logistics and budget sections are completed before beginning communication planning. Ideally, the communications plan should be written as an integral part of the crisis response action plan.

Communication Objectives. Communication objectives answer the "conceptual what" questions. What will be the end result of our communications efforts, effectively implemented? Objectives describe desired outcomes, not the processes by which these outcomes will be accomplished. Whereas business objectives describe the desired change in the business environment, communication objectives describe the attitudes, emotions, or behaviors to be exhibited by your constituencies as a result of your communications program. Communications objectives could include:

⇒ Changes in knowledge, awareness, understanding, support, or feelings
⇒ Steps we expect our audiences to take, such as approving a course of action, supporting a point of view, or trying a new product
⇒ Neutralizing or minimizing the impact of negative visibility on audiences' thinking
⇒ For example, if a business objective is to maintain the company's stock price, the communication objective may be to maintain investor confidence in the company's management team and prospects for future success.

Communication Strategies. Communication strategies are ways in which the communication goals will be achieved. Communication strategies answer the "conceptual how" questions. In broad overview, how will the communications objectives be accomplished? As with business strategies and actions to take, it is common to confuse communication strategies, which answer "conceptual how" questions, with communication tactics, which answer "operational how" questions. The difference between business strategies, communication strategies, and communication tactics is critical.

The communication strategies provide conceptual frameworks for accomplishing the communications objectives. They provide the broad game plan for all communications activities. For example:

⇒ A business objective could be: Maintain the company's stock price
⇒ A communication objective to support the business objective may be: Maintain investor confidence in the company's management team and prospects for future success
⇒ A communication strategy to support that communication objective may be: Keep analysts and investors aware of progress being made to solve problems
⇒ Among the many communication tactics to support that communication strategy could be:

– Send an e-mail to all analysts with an update
– Hold a conference call with analysts and investors
– Post regular updates on the Web site
– Be prepared to field inquiries from analysts and investors
– Conduct an interview with a financial newspaper that is read by investors

Audiences. The audiences section lists the constituencies to whom the communications will be directed. While not every communications plan needs an audience section, it provides a reality check in the form of an inventory of the groups who matter and to whom communications will be directed. The audience inventory, in turn, informs the balance of the plan. In general, the tactics section ought to include at least one mechanism for reaching each audience, either directly or indirectly.

It is common for audiences to be prioritized in a number of ways. A typical prioritization order is:

⇒ Internal: Board of Directors, all employees, departmental, regional, or specific-level employees; senior management; and so forth.
⇒ External: Current shareholders; the market as a whole; governments, academics, activists, and so forth.

It is also common to differentiate *ultimate audiences*, those you ultimately want to reach and who matter directly to the success of the organization, and indirect or *influencer* audiences, who are not necessarily your constituents but through whom you reach your constituents. Examples include:

⇒ Ultimate audiences: employees, shareholders, regulators, the general public
⇒ Influencer audiences: Media, analysts, academics, consumer advocates, and so forth.

Ultimate Audience or Influencer Audience

A constituency that in some circumstances is an ultimate audience in others may be an influencer audience. For example, if we are seeking initial analyst coverage of our stock, analysts are an ultimate audience. However, if we wish to persuade shareholders to accept a point of view, we may consider the analyst to be an intermediary audience, to whom we communicate in order for the analyst to then communicate our message to shareholders.

The list of audiences in the plan may or may not be identical to the list of affected constituencies in the analysis portion of the template. The difference is this: For purposes of analysis it is useful to identify those constituencies who are affected by the issue in question. However, not every affected constituency would necessarily be an audience of communication. Similarly, some audiences (e.g., the media) may not be an affected constituency, but may be instrumental in reaching an affected constituency (such as customers) to whom direct communication will not be attempted.

Messages. Messages are the critical thoughts we wish the constituents to internalize; the core themes we wish to reinforce in all communications. The word "message" has many possible meanings, but for the purposes of developing an issues management plan, it should be understood to mean what you want those constituencies who matter to the company to think, feel, know, or do—and what you need to say in order for those groups to think, feel, know, and do those things. As a general rule, the messages can be determined by focusing on the communications objectives: the desired attitudinal, emotional, or behavioral outcomes among ultimate audiences.

One way to determine the messages is to undertake the following process:

1. Assume your ultimate audiences. What do you want them to know, think, or feel about either the company or the issue in question? What is the strongest credible thing you can say that, if believed, will cause them to know, think, or feel this way? This becomes your first message.
2. Assume that your audience has fully internalized the first message. What is the second thing you want them to know, think, or feel about either the company or the issue in question? This becomes your second message.
3. Assume that your audience has fully internalized the first two messages. What is the third thing you want them to know, think, or feel about either the company or the issue in question? This becomes your third message. As a general principle, three messages are the maximum you can expect any audience to internalize.

> The three core messages stand by themselves, and should be included in each communication the company makes.

These three sentences become the three topic sentences that drive all substantive communication about the issue. Just as tactics may change but strategies usually will not, the factual support to a particular message may change as the issue unfolds, but the message usually will not. And different support statements may be used with different audiences, or with the same audience at different times, while the message remains unchanged.

Using Core Messages. The three core messages stand by themselves, and should be included in each communication the company makes: These three messages become the quote in the press release; they become the topic sentence in employee meetings; they become the outline of presentations to the investment community; they become the three themes in letters to regulators or to customers; they serve as hyperlinks on the company's Web site, driving a visitor deeper into the supporting detail of each. The three messages need to be repeated every time the company communicates, requiring a very high tolerance for repetition. The ability to consistently articulate the top three things a company wants its constituencies to know is a critical attribute of leadership and essential to effective management of issues. General Electric's CEO Jeff Immelt has said, "Every leader needs to clearly explain the top three things the organization is doing. If you can't, you're not leading well."[3]

It is only at this point in the planning process that attention should turn to the tactics. Paradoxically, most companies reflexively default to tactics as a first resort: "We need to hold a press conference …" or "We need to send out a press release …" This is the rookie's mistake in issues management and crisis avoidance. It is impulsive, unthoughtful activity, and it is often both self-indulgent and self-destructive. But once the plan is in place, a framework for using the tactics effectively can be established, and the implementation of the plan can be accomplished in a flexible, effective, and cost-effective way.

Communication Tactics. Communication tactics are the specific communications techniques that will be employed to convey the messages to the ultimate audiences. The tactics part of the plan is a substantive inventory of the communications activities to be undertaken. It is what will actually be done to send the messages. As a result, it tends to get the most attention. Because communication tactics involve what people actually do, they may tend to drive the communications planning process. It is easy for people to focus on interesting tactics ("let's hold a press conference" or "let's do a DVD") regardless of the purpose or whether sufficient resources are available for effective execution.

Choice of tactics should be driven by two general considerations, each of which requires a degree of discipline.

⇒ First, communication tactics should be driven by the communication strategies: The tactics should not be determined until after there is a clear articulation of the analysis, the business objectives and strategies, and the communication objectives and strategies. There should be at least one strategy that demonstrably accomplishes each objective. And each tactic should demonstrably support at least one strategy.

⇒ Second, tactics should be do-able. Napoleon once remarked, "Amateurs worry about tactics, professionals worry about logistics." What is sustainable should govern tactics. The plan should not, for example, include labor-intensive tactics unless it also addresses staffing and other resources. And it should not promote "gee-whiz" technologies unless it also addresses how those technologies will be obtained and delivered.

There should be specific communication tactics listed to support each strategy (and, as appropriate, each audience).

Communication tactics are deliverable items. They may include:

⇒ Employee memoranda or e-mails
⇒ Press releases
⇒ Web site postings
⇒ Press conferences
⇒ Op-ed articles in newspapers
⇒ Advertisements
⇒ Investment community conference calls

Because each tactic is subordinate to a specific strategy to achieve a known objective, it is easy to discard tactics that are not working and replace them with new tactics that are more likely to work.

One virtue of the systematic planning process that this template represents is that it allows for prompt midcourse correction without losing sight of objectives. If the objectives, strategies, audiences, and messages are clear, it is easy to adapt the plan to assure it is accomplishing its purpose.

> One virtue of the systematic planning process that this template represents is that it allows for prompt midcourse correction without losing sight of objectives.

Documents. The documents section of the plan is optional. It is intended to serve as an inventory of specific pieces of writing necessary to execute the communication tactics. The documents section identifies each individual communication required to implement the tactics. Since each piece of communication needs to be drafted, and since all need to be consistent and mutually reinforcing, this section constitutes a work list of documents to be produced before tactics can be executed.

These documents will include:

⇒ Press releases
⇒ Media Q&A
⇒ Employee e-mails
⇒ Employee Q&A
⇒ Call center scripts
⇒ Call center Q&A

Note three different Q&A documents are called out above. Since each is a Q&A format, a document inventory makes it clear that a separate Q&A is needed for three separate constituencies. The three Q&As will provide different emphases and different levels of detail, but all three will be consistent with and mutually supportive of each other.

Communication Logistics. The communication logistics section identifies the resources and tools necessary to implement strategies and execute tactics. Like the documents section, it is optional. Like the documents section, it serves as a kind of reality check against tactics. It may include timeline of preparation and execution of tactics. It may also include the resources necessary to prepare the tactics for execution, or the individuals tasked to draft documents, seek approvals, or perform other tasks.

Best Practices in Issues Management

Effective anticipation of issues, and planning for and managing issues, can help a company protect its reputation and its competitiveness. Among the best practices to embrace are:

1. Focus on the goal, not just on the processes
2. Get management buy-in
3. Name an accountable leader
4. Involve all relevant business functions
5. Set tangible communication objectives and measure success against them
6. Follow the plan, focusing on the goal; adapt the tactics to changes in the environment, but keep the emphasis on the goal.

Resources for Further Study

Issue Action Publications

Issue Action Publications, affiliated with the Issues Management Council, publishes a range of resources for those with issues management responsibility. It publishes two monthly newsletters:

⇒ Corporate Public Issues and their Management
⇒ The Issue Barometer

It also publishes a range of issues management books, including:

⇒ *The Critical Issues Audit*, by Eli Sopow, 1994.
⇒ *Don't Just Stand There: The Do-It Plan ™ for Effective Issue Management*, 2000,
⇒ *Strategic Issues Management: Organizations and Public Policy Challenges*, by Robert L. Heath, 1997.
⇒ *Strategic Reputation Risk Management*, by Judy Larkin, 2003.
⇒ *Influencing Public Attitudes: Strategies that Reduce the Media's Power*, by James E. Lukaszewski, 1992.

It also publishes reports that are useful to issues managers, including:

⇒ Building an Integrated Issue Management Process as a Source of Sustainable Competitive Advantage, by Michael Palese and Teresa Yancey Crane

⇒ Issue Management: Activator for Integrated Corporate Strategy, by Michael Palese and Teresa Yancey Crane

⇒ A Global Perspective on Issue Management Best Practice, by Teresa Yancey Crane and Michael Palese

Each of these newsletters, books, and reports may be found at http://www.issueaction-publications.com/documents/products.htm.

Issues Management Council

The Issues Management Council is a professional membership organization for people whose job includes managing issues. It offers conferences, publications, and other resources. It can be found at http://www.issuemanagement.org/index.html.

Public Affairs Council

The Public Affairs Council, based in Washington, D.C., is a leading association of public affairs professionals. It offers conferences, seminars, training, and other resources on a range of topics, including an extensive issues management section. It can be found at http://www.pac.org/public/issues_management.shtml.

Questions for Further Discussion

1. Why is it so important to get management buy-in for an issues management process?
2. What is the optimal relationship between the issues management process and media relations and employee communications?
3. How can an effective plan make issues management more effective?
4. What is the difference between ultimate audiences and intermediate audiences?
5. Why is message discipline so important in issues management?

CHAPTER 12

Crisis Communication

> *Our greatest glory is not in never falling,*
> *but in rising every time we fall.*
>
> — Confucius

It was a Monday morning in the spring of 1990, and Fred Garcia, head of public relations for the global investment bank CS First Boston, had just gotten a call from a business reporter for The New York Times. *The reporter, with whom Fred had worked for several years, said that he had it from an impeccable source within First Boston that a young stock trader had just committed suicide because he was being investigated for insider trading. The reporter said he was calling for a statement, but that he did not need confirmation; the story would surely run in* The New York Times *the next day. Fred said, "I'll look into it and get right back to you."*

If the story was true, it was bad news for the company. Insider trading was the corporate scandal of the era, and the movie "Wall Street," with insider trading as the plot line, had elevated the once-obscure crime to the level of popular culture. An insider-trading scandal at First Boston would set off alarm bells. The company's reputation would suffer, its operations would be disrupted by distraction, personnel changes, customer unrest or defections, and possibly even by arrests.

If the story was false, a typical corporate response—for example, "as a matter of policy we don't comment on personnel matters or investigations"—would not have prevented the story from appearing. It would have appeared, with Fred's "no comment" statement in the second or third paragraph.

A New York Times *story about a suicide provoked by an insider trading investigation would be believed by most people who read it. Other media—both print and broadcast—would follow the story, and a proverbial journalistic feeding frenzy would ensure that the firm would be in the headlines for days, if not weeks. And just as in the case of a true story, the firm could expect reputational harm as well as operational and financial disruptions.*

One thing was clear: First Boston had to get ahead of the story so that if true, the firm would proactively announce it, and if false, The New York Times *might be persuaded not to run it.*

On the firm's sixth floor trading room, the head of trading was sitting by himself in a glass-enclosed conference room, rather than at his usual open desk on the trading floor. He seemed surprised when Fred arrived and asked him about the young trader. "How did you hear about this so fast? Well, it's a tragic situation. Yes, he did commit suicide. He has been with us for about a year, and was a very good trader. Friday he went to his family's home in Chicago. I just got off the phone with his father, who said that the young man took his own life over the weekend, after what the father described as 'an emotional family encounter.' I'm just now breaking the news to his colleagues on the trading floor."

Fred asked, "Was he under investigation for insider trading?" The head of trading said unequivocally that he was not. Fred asked why The New York Times would think he was. The head of trading pondered a moment, and offered, "The only thing I can imagine is that on Friday his trading desk was the subject of a routine compliance department audit. Maybe someone heard about the audit and assumed that the suicide and the audit were related. But the audit was routine. There's no suggestion of any impropriety. And the suicide seems to have been prompted by whatever happened at home, not here."

Fred had most of what he needed, but had to ask one more question. "Was the young man, his department, or the firm under investigation for insider trading or anything else?" The reply was unequivocal. "No. As far as we know everything is fine."

Although the tragic event apparently had nothing to do with company behavior or performance, the routine ways of speaking with the media would not be persuasive. Such routine communication would predictably result in severe reputational, operational, and financial harm. Fortunately, Fred had standing permission from his bosses to use his judgment when dealing with reporters. By the time he got back to his desk, his plan was clear. He called the reporter, and said, "For the record, First Boston does not comment on either personnel matters or investigations. I can offer more information, but it would have to be on background, meaning you can use what I tell you but you cannot attribute it to me or to any official at the firm." The reporter agreed to that ground rule. Fred corroborated the young man's employment and suicide, as well as the discussion with the father. Fred said, "I have no idea what the emotional family encounter was about, and I leave it to your sense of decency whether to call the father and ask about it. I can tell you that he was not under investigation for anything, nor suspected of any improper activity. I can further tell you that on Friday the compliance department conducted a routine audit of the desk on which he worked. So let me ask you, before you damage the memory of this young man and cause his family unnecessary pain, and before you put the firm's reputation at risk, please go back to your source and confirm whether what you heard was an accurate account of what happened, or a rumor or speculation about two unrelated events."

A half-hour later the reporter called back. He said, "I have looked into this further, and now believe that the suicide was unrelated to the person's duties at your firm. So this is a personal tragedy, not a business event, and doesn't rise to the level of a story in The New York Times."

* * * * *

This Chapter Covers

⇒ Introduction
⇒ What is a crisis?
  A crisis is a crisis because …
  If it smells and feels like a crisis …
⇒ Timeliness of response: the need for speed
  Ten avoidable mis-steps
  The golden hour of crisis response
  The golden hour and the golden arches
⇒ Control the communication agenda
⇒ Dealing with rumors
  Rumors, uncertainty, and relief of emotional distress
  The morphing of rumors: How they change over time
  Preventing rumors
⇒ Controlling rumors: A mathematical formula
  Dynamics of controlling a rumor in the news cycle
⇒ Best practices
⇒ Resources for further study
⇒ Questions for further discussion

Introduction

One of the core roles of the corporate communication function is to help companies make decisions and communicate clearly when something goes wrong.

Every organization, at some point, will be on the receiving end of an event that risks reputational damage. And the epidemic of crises following the Enron, Arthur Andersen, Martha Stewart, and Roman Catholic Church scandals of recent years showed that a sterling track record, a respected management team, political connections, and financial clout are not sufficient to protect an organization from major reputational, operational, or financial harm.

Effective crisis response—including both in what a company does and what it says—provides companies with a competitive advantage and can even enhance reputation. Ineffective crisis response can cause significant harm to a company's operations, reputation, and competitive position. And because time is one's enemy in a crisis, the sooner a company recognizes that business as usual does not apply, the sooner it is likely to mobilize its resources to respond effectively in a crisis.

Whether a company survives a crisis with its reputation, operations, and financial condition intact is determined less by the severity of the crisis—the underlying event—than by the timeliness and quality of its response to the crisis. Institutions that suffer the same very severe crisis can experience dramatically different outcomes based on the timeliness and quality of their respective responses.

Take, for example, what was for years the paragon of ineffective crisis response: Exxon's March 1989 spill of crude oil in Alaska's Prince William Sound. In prior years dozens of ships had hit rocks and spilled crude oil into pristine waters. But there is only one ship—the Exxon Valdez—and one company that people remember years later. Moreover, people remember the Exxon spill not because the oil was any dirtier than any other oil spilled by any other ship; not because Prince William Sound was any more pristine than any other body of water into which oil spilled. Rather, people remember the Exxon Valdez because in the weeks immediately following the spill Exxon was perceived to be indifferent to the damage the spill caused. Fifteen years after the spill a federal appeals court upheld a lower court judgment of $4.5 billion against the company (in addition to the more than $3 billion it had previously paid for cleanup and related costs). The court said its purpose in upholding the award was to achieve "retribution and justice." *The New York Times* opined that such a judgment and such a purpose were entirely appropriate, given Exxon's indifference in the initial phase of the spill. [1]

The new paragon of ineffective crisis response is the U.S. government's delay in marshalling resources to help the victims of the New Orleans flood in late August 2005. President George W. Bush had been seen to rise to the occasion after the attacks on the World Trade Center and Pentagon on 9/11/2001. But in the days immediately after the flood he seemed disengaged, uninformed, and unconcerned about the plight of New Orleans citizens. On Day Three after the flood Federal Emergency Management Agency chief Michael Brown appeared on CNN and other television networks and admitted that the government had been unaware of thousands of people stranded in the New Orleans convention center without food and water for days—a fact that had been widely reported on television—until told about the situation in an interview. Two days later the President, invoking the FEMA chief's nickname, told him on television, "Brownie, you're doing a heck of a job ..." Two weeks after the flood President Bush's approval ratings fell to then-record lows. [2]

Whether a company survives a crisis with its reputation, operations, and financial condition intact is determined less by the severity of the crisis than by the timeliness and quality of its response.

Fifteen days after New Orleans flooded, as the federal response was finally getting into full swing, *Time* magazine's Web site published a cartoon of a man standing waist-deep in water, holding a sign that implored, "Leadership Please."[3] The next day FEMA chief Brown resigned.

It is the perception of indifference, not the severity of the problem, that is a common denominator in many of the well-known crises of the early 2000s—from the priest sexual abuse scandal in the Roman Catholic Church to the early phases of the Ford Explorer/Firestone Tire recall to scandals involving market timing in mutual funds.

This chapter lays out some of the disciplines of crisis communication, crisis management, and effective crisis response.

What Is a Crisis?

A Crisis Is a Crisis Because ...

> A crisis is not necessarily a catastrophic event, but rather an event that, left to usual business processes and velocities, causes significant reputational, operational, or financial harm.

The suicide example that opened this chapter is such an event: left to usual business processes, velocities, and ways of speaking, the harm to the company could have been significant.

But how does a professional communicator know whether his or her company faces a crisis? The question is important because in a crisis timing is critical: Actions that could effectively prevent any harm to a company's reputation on Day One may be completely ineffective on Days Two, Five, or Ten.

When a company is in a crisis or approaching one, business as usual needs to be suspended, especially the sometimes ponderous ways decisions get made in complex organizations. Knowing whether such a suspension is necessary is often the first and most difficult decision. The risk for companies and other complex organizations is in failing to recognize that business as usual must cease.

It is all too easy for companies to recognize too late that they are in a crisis, because often the organization itself does not recognize it until people outside the organization are already feeling the effects. There is a natural tendency to assume that a crisis is by definition a catastrophe; that a crisis exists only when damage has already been done or only when the event in question is potentially catastrophic. That is much too narrow a view. Many crises are not catastrophes, but small-scale interruptions in routine business that, if ignored or handled poorly, can easily escalate to cause significant operational or reputational harm.

The American sociologist Tamotsu Shibutani defines a crisis as "any situation in which the previously established social machinery breaks down, a point at which some kind of readjustment is required ... A crisis is a crisis precisely because [people] cannot act effectively together. When previously accepted norms prove inadequate guides for conduct, a situation becomes problematic, and some kind of emergency action is required. Since activity is temporarily blocked, a sense of frustration arises; if the crisis persists, tension mounts, and an increasing sense of urgency for doing something develops."[4]

So companies need to be prepared in two ways for crises: they need to understand what constitutes a crisis in the first place; and they need an early warning system that helps them understand when business as usual has ceased to exist—or is likely to cease to exist—and that therefore business-as-usual practices need to be suspended. The corporate communication function is often an important part of that early warning system.

One way to think about crises is suggested by Steven Fink in his book *Crisis Management: Planning for the Inevitable*. Fink describes a crisis as a "turning point," not a necessarily negative event or bad thing. "It is merely characterized by a certain degree of risk and uncertainty."[5] Fink refers to crises as "prodromal," or as precursors or predictors of something yet to come: "From a practical, business-oriented point of view, a crisis (a turning point) is any prodromal situation that runs the risk of:

1. Escalating in intensity.
2. Falling under close media or government scrutiny.
3. Interfering with the normal operations of business.
4. Jeopardizing the positive public image presently enjoyed by a company or its officers.
5. Damaging a company's bottom line in any way."[6]

Fink points out that as a turning point the crisis could go either way: "If any or all of these developments occur, the turning point most likely will take a turn for the worse ... Therefore, there is every reason to assume that if a situation runs the risk of escalating in intensity, that same situa-

> *A crisis is a nonroutine event that risks undesired visibility that in turn threatens significant reputational damage.*

tion—caught and dealt with in time—may not escalate. Instead, it may very conveniently dissipate, be resolved."[7]

Fink's approach to crises anticipates both catastrophic events and also routine dealings that are suddenly the subject of attention. It finds merit in early intervention and affirmative management of business processes as well as the communications about the event.

Our own definition of a crisis integrates much of what Fink and others have suggested:

This "nonroutine event" may be the result of a normal business practice that suddenly becomes controversial, or it may be an attack from outside the organization. The crisis consists not in the fact that the event is non-routine, but in the possible consequence of the event: visibility that could threaten damage to the organization's reputation.

If It Smells and Feels Like a Crisis ...

One quick way to determine whether something that just happened or is about to happen is likely to become a crisis is to convert the descriptions of crises summarized above into questions.

For example, to use Fink's definition, ask:

⇒ Is this situation a precursor that risks escalating in intensity?
⇒ Does it risk coming under close scrutiny?
⇒ Will it interfere with normal business operations?
⇒ Will it jeopardize our public image or bottom line?

If the answer to one or more of these is yes, a crisis exists.

To use our own definition, ask:

⇒ Is this a nonroutine event?
⇒ Does it risk undesired visibility?
⇒ Would that undesired visibility in turn threaten reputational damage?

> The company needs to recognize that the situation is anything but business as usual.

If not, then a company probably does not need to do anything out of the ordinary. But if the answer is yes, the company needs to recognize that the situation is anything but business as usual, and that the company needs to behave and communicate in different ways.

One virtue of these definitions of crisis is that they focus on outcomes: on the effect that the crisis may have on the stakeholders who matter to a company, and how the company can maintain the trust and confidence of those stakeholders as the event plays out.

One problem, of course, is the word "crisis." The very word can cause alarm and even panic. But the original meanings of the word are not nearly

Figure 12.1

as dire. The original Greek word from which our "crisis" is derived, Κρισισ (krisis), originally meant decision, choice, event to be decided, sudden change for better or worse, turning point, and the power of judgment. So a crisis, originally, was a decision that would determine whether a course of events would unfold one way or another, for better or worse—very similar to Fink's view of crisis as turning point.

In Chinese, the character that translates into the English word crisis is wei ji, a combination of two ideograms. Wei means danger or fear. Ji means opportunity or desire. So the short-hand meaning of wei ji is danger plus opportunity. There is some dispute as to whether the two ideograms mean "danger plus opportunity," "dangerous opportunity," or "opportunity for danger." But whatever the syntax or grammar, the thoughts suggest something less clear-cut than a catastrophe.

Timeliness of Response: The Need for Speed

The first determinant of success in protecting reputation in a crisis is the speed with which an organization reacts.

For example, New York City Mayor Rudolf Giuliani's immediate response to the 9/11 attacks on the World Trade Center in 2001 propelled his reputation—which had suffered in the months before the attacks—to near rock-star proportions.

Crises require special handling. Most routine corporate events can be handled by normal communications methods through traditional channels following usual procedures. But when a company determines that it faces a crisis it is important to recognize that routine decision-making processes, routine communications, and routine timeframes can be counterproductive.

In particular, time is an enemy in a crisis. The sooner a company is seen as taking the event seriously, acting responsibly, and communicating clearly, the more likely it is that the company will emerge with its reputation and operations intact. *The Wall Street Journal's* Ronald Alsop states that: "Crises aren't like fine wines; they don't improve with age. A communications void is highly dangerous during a time of crisis. Silence gives critics time to gain the upper hand and reinforces the public's suspicion that a company must be guilty. Without information from the company, rumors and misinformation can proliferate fast."[8]

A delay in responding to a crisis can be perceived not just as indifference, but as arrogance, and even an evasion that confirms dishonesty.

One reason companies often respond too slowly to a crisis is that they do not believe they are likely to suffer a crisis. Indeed, Alsop describes an all-too-typical corporate behavior: "Too often companies become complacent. They begin to feel almost invincible. Their financial performance is strong, and they fall into the trap of believing they have little to worry about. Then they're blindsided by a crisis and don't have a response plan in place. Flailing around and looking helpless aren't inspiring to your stakeholders."[9]

> A delay in responding to a crisis can be perceived not just as indifference, but as arrogance, and even an evasion that confirms dishonesty.

One of the critical roles for corporate communication professionals is to help their organizations understand how core stakeholders are likely to perceive a company's silence or inaction in the wake of a crisis. As the keepers of corporate reputation—and in many cases also keepers of a corporation's conscience—corporate communication professionals need to be on guard to the common institutional barriers to taking crises seriously.

Ten Avoidable Mis-Steps

There are ten predictable, avoidable behaviors that organizations typically engage in when a crisis breaks that get in the way of effective and rapid response. The behaviors have two negative effects. First, they make the crisis worse; second, they distract attention from solving the underlying problem, while lulling management into a false sense that the crisis is being dealt with.

The ten mis-steps are:

1. Ignore the problem: Management seems unaware and is surprised by a crisis that others saw coming, or that they themselves were warned about but chose not to take seriously.
2. Deny the severity of the problem: Management takes only minimal steps to address a problem, or downplays its significance, resulting in an inadequate response.
3. Compartmentalize the problem or solution: Management mistakenly assumes that others will appreciate its own functional division of labor, and defines the crisis or its solution as specific to a department, division, geographic region, or other compartment, while the constituencies who matter most view the problem as an enterprisewide crisis and expect an enterprisewide response.
4. Tell misleading half-truths: Management tries to misdirect attention by speaking literally true statements with the intention of misleading, which challenge adversaries or whistleblowers to uncover the full story.
5. Lie: Management tells a deliberate untruth with the intention of deceiving.
6. Tell only part of the story; let the story dribble out: Management reveals only the smallest amount of bad news it feels compelled to on any given day, but repeats the cycle on subsequent days, leading to multiple bad news cycles. The operative principle of telling bad news is to bundle bad news into as few news cycles as possible, preferably just one.
7. Assign blame: Rather than taking meaningful steps to solve the problem, management tries to redirect attention away from itself and to someone else.

8. Over-confess: Managements unaccustomed to criticism often implode publicly and turn public statements into private therapeutic sessions in which they unburden themselves of pent-up frustrations.

9. Panic and undergo paralysis: Work grinds to a halt as management and employees focus exclusively on the fear or the thrill of the crisis, and companies suffer operational or financial harm from reduced productivity.

10. Shoot the messenger: Management creates a culture of punishing those who bring problems to their attention, resulting in problems being buried and compounded.[10]

Corporate communication professionals need to be on guard against these behaviors, and find ways to overcome them quickly.

The Golden Hour of Crisis Response

Crisis communicators speak of the "Golden Hour" of crisis response: the early phases when the opportunity to influence the outcome is the greatest. The golden hour is a metaphor from emergency medicine, first coined by Dr. R. Adam Cowley, a veteran of the U.S. Army Medical Corps, who discovered that wounded soldiers who were brought to a field hospital within an hour of suffering their wounds had a very high likelihood of survival. Soldiers with the same wounds brought in just a half-hour later had a significantly lower probability of survival. The difference was literally a matter of life and death. Dr. Cowley applied this lesson to civilian emergency medicine, and coined the term golden hour in 1961.[11] It is now an accepted standard in trauma care in dealing with, for instance, heart attacks. The golden hour refers not to a precise duration but rather to the observation that incremental delays have a greater than incremental impact on the likelihood of success.

This has translated into a relatively well-established principle in dealing with the news media: fielding an inquiry from a newspaper reporter at 10 AM and responding definitively by 11 AM can allow one to prevent a story from being published, or to significantly shape what the story will look like. But waiting until 5:30 PM to respond to a 10 AM inquiry significantly diminishes the likelihood that a story can be shaped: by then the story has already been written and edited, and at best a company can insert a paragraph refuting the central accusation. But the accusation and all the commentary based on it will be in the story.

A similar principle applies beyond the media, where incremental delays can result in greater than incremental setbacks with other critical constituencies, from employees to investors to customers. And in a world of twenty-four-hour news and instantaneous Internet communication, and where seemingly disparate constituencies are linked electronically, a set-

334 Reputation Management

back with one constituency can quickly cascade to setbacks with others. This is especially the case when the crisis is being fed by an adversary who can embarrass the organization. Whether the adversary is a lawyer bringing suit, a union organizer, a community activist, or an ambitious regulator, the adversary often counts on organizations taking excessive time to respond. This makes the adversary's job much easier, and allowing the adversary to begin a cascade of negative news among many constituencies before the company can develop a sufficient response, at which point it may be too late for the company.

This need for speed is not intended to suggest that a company should communicate reflexively or without careful thought. But it is an argument for establishing a quick response capability with preauthorization to suspend business as usual in order to be able to respond quickly in the aftermath of a nonroutine event that risks undesired visibility.

In many ways, the perfect is the enemy of the good-enough: companies often want to be certain of every fact, to dot every I and cross every T, before making any statement. This abundance of caution can be a healthy impulse in normal times. But in the earliest phases of a crisis, something less than perfect, so long as it is accurate, is better than silence. Sometimes just an acknowledgement that the company is aware of a problem, is studying it, and will take appropriate action is sufficient.

One quick test of when to respond in a crisis is to ask these questions:

⇒ Are others speaking about us now, shaping the perception of us among those who matter to us? Will they be soon?

⇒ Will those who matter to us expect us to do or say something now? Will silence be seen as indifference to the harm caused, as arrogance, or as guilt?

⇒ If we wait, will we lose the ability to determine the outcome compared to acting or communicating now?

⇒ What is the minimum amount we can say now that shows we are taking this problem seriously? That we are not indifferent to the harm caused?

The Golden Hour and the Golden Arches

The effectiveness of rapid response in a crisis was illustrated by McDonald's Corporation, whose CEO died of a heart attack the morning of April 19, 2004, while attending McDonald's worldwide owner/operator convention in Orlando, Florida. The sixty-year old chairman and CEO, James Cantalupo, had been instrumental in reconfiguring McDonald's menu away from the seemingly unhealthy focus on fats and super-sized portions to more healthy alternatives such as salads and grilled chicken.

At 8:07 that morning (East Coast time) the company issued a press release announcing his death. When the stock market opened at 9:30 the stock traded down on heavy volume. There was a significant risk that attention would be drawn to the irony of Mr. Cantalupo's suffering a fatal heart attack while spearheading the move away from McDonald's fat-rich menu. Indeed, some early news accounts made just that point.

But at 10:42 AM, just over two-and-a-half hours after announcing Mr. Cantalupo's death, and just seventy-two minutes after the stock market opened, McDonald's announced that Charlie Bell, who had been president and chief operating officer, would be the new CEO, and Andrew J. McKenna, who had been the board's presiding director, would be the nonexecutive chairman of the board. The analysts focused on McDonald's' future rather than its tragedy, the media coverage was factual and forward looking, and the stock quickly recovered.

Indeed, the next morning's *The Wall Street Journal* praised McDonald's' ability to make and announce its decision quickly: "The swift decision gave immediate reassurance to employees, franchisees, and investors that the fast-food giant had a knowledgeable leader in place who can provide continuity and carry out the company's strategies. It may also shift any spotlight away from McDonald's high-cholesterol, fat-rich foods and prove a savvy public relations move."[12]

The Wall Street Journal noted that such quick action is uncharacteristic of large companies. It quoted Jay Lorch, a Harvard Business School professor, who said, "The speed with which they moved is exactly what you would expect to happen, but few companies are as prepared as McDonald's appears to have been for this calamity."[13]

McDonald's had a clear succession plan in place. Its directors moved quickly to implement the plan and announce the new CEO. If they had delayed, the company would have been subject to continued stock volatility as well as speculation about its future and its strategy of emphasizing more healthy choices in its restaurants, and would even have risked late-night comics' pointing out the irony of the manner of Mr. Cantalupo's death. Worse, its worldwide franchisees, gathered at the convention where Mr. Cantalupo had died, would have seen a leaderless organization. McDonald's prompt actions and announcements prevented the turmoil that a delayed appointment and announcement would have caused, and allowed the company and its stakeholders to focus on the future.

Control the Communication Agenda

Speed is one ingredient of effective communication; robust content and effective distribution of the messages are others. One of the goals of crisis communication is to influence the way key stakeholders think and feel, and what those stakeholders know and do. To do so requires controlling the communication agenda, and not allowing the media, adversaries, or the rumor mill to define a company's situation.

So crisis communication needs to be grounded in the desired outcome: the end state in the audiences to whom you are communicating.

Content needs to be crafted to sufficiently influence the audience's frames of reference. And the channels through which communication takes place needs to be sufficient to reach audiences effectively.

Once you have determined the goals of communicating and the core messages, the process of communicating is relatively straightforward. Once you have decided what you want to say, the rule for doing so is the following:

⇒ Tell it all;
⇒ Tell it fast;
⇒ Tell them what you're doing about it;
⇒ Tell them when it is over;
⇒ Get back to work.

> Once you have determined the goals of communicating and the core messages, the process of communicating is relatively straightforward.

Tell it all. This admonition should not be confused with an instruction to bare the corporate soul and confess every sin and weakness you know of.

"Tell it all" means bundle everything that will inevitably be known into the smallest number of news cycles possible. Rather than letting bad news drip out over time, take all the pain all at once.

Further, "tell it all" should not be confused with saying more than you know, are legally permitted to say, or find it prudent to say. For example, if the crisis is still unfolding, tell only what you know, but all of what you know. If the extent of damage has not been determined, do not speculate; say that the extent of damage has not been determined. If you have a contractual obligation to keep certain information confidential, do not break the contract. If you know the names of people killed or injured, but the next of kin have not been notified, do not disclose the names. But in each case you will be advantaged by saying what you do know and the reasons you are not disclosing; for example, "The extent of damage is still being investigated by the fire marshal, and we will let you know as soon as the investigation is concluded;" or "The identities of those killed are known, but we will not release the names until next of kin have been notified."

Tell it fast. It is common for companies to want to delay disclosure of bad news until the last possible moment. The risk, of course, is that others will be talking about the problems before the company does, and that the negative news can take on a life of its own.

"Tell it fast" says that to the degree possible, it is better to be the one who brings the news to the public's attention, rather than reacting to someone else's account of the news. Even when the company is not the first to disclose, "tell it fast" suggests that speed of communications throughout a crisis is critical: it keeps the company in the driver's seat and prevents the story from getting out of hand. And to the degree that you are susceptible to rumors—which, in a crisis, is often,"tell it fast"—allows you to control or eliminate damaging rumors.

The manner in which one communicates quickly should be based on the specifics of the particular crisis. It could include a press release; it could be an employee meeting or memo; it could be an interview with a reporter. Or it could be all or none of these. But whatever the specific communications vehicle (or combination of several), the tactical goal is to speak completely and quickly so as to take the high ground and control the communications agenda.

Tell them what you are doing about it. It is important, as early in the communication process as possible, to outline the remedial steps that are underway to resolve the underlying issues in the crisis. If such steps have not yet been determined, it is sufficient to outline the processes being put in place; for example, "We have launched an investigation, which we expect to be completed soon, to discover the cause of the problem and to identify solutions."

Many companies (and many lawyers) are reluctant to talk about steps the company is taking because there is so much uncertainty in the early phases of a crisis. They need to overcome this reticence, and to know that the public will expect to be told not only what happened, but what is being done about it.

Tell them when it is over. Similarly, many companies are reluctant to open old wounds when a crisis is resolved. This instinct, while understandable, is counterproductive. There will always be some people whose last interaction with the company was in the context of a crisis. If the crisis is past, and the company has recovered, it needs to update those who matter (and the databases) to let the world know that the crisis has been solved.

Get back to work. Once the crisis team has been assembled and communication is being handled, do not let the crisis distract attention from the important work of running the company. Too many people want to be crisis managers. The tasks should be clearly assigned; people not directly involved in the crisis communication should be directed to return to prior duties.

Even those who are needed in some element of crisis communication, such as senior executives, eventually need to stop communicating and get back to work. This includes the CEO, who has many other claims on his or her time than an exclusive focus on the crisis.

Dealing with Rumors

A challenge facing nearly every organization in a crisis is the circulation of rumors that, unaddressed, can cause significant reputational harm, sometimes even more damage than the crisis event itself. (The suicide example that began this chapter is an example of such a rumor.)

> A challenge facing nearly every organization in a crisis is the circulation of rumors that, unaddressed, can cause significant reputational harm.

Rumors are particularly damaging because they often seem nebulous. It is hard to figure out where a rumor started, how it is building momentum, and where it might end. And people tend to pass rumors along, whether or not they actually believe them.

Sometimes rumors are deliberately planted by people who are out to hurt a company or to profit from its distress, such as Wall Street short-sellers, disgruntled former employees, community activists, competitors, and people suing a company.

Once started, rumors can spread among employees, customers, suppliers, lenders, investors, and regulators. Rumors can feed other rumors, and rumors from several different sources can be combined in the retelling from one person to another. And when rumors hit the newspapers, television news programs, radio, or the Internet, they get formalized and are then seen to be an accurate rendering of reality. Worse, people who may have been skeptical of the original rumor, on seeing or hearing the same thing in the newspapers or on television, often conclude that the news account proves the accuracy of the rumor.

Rumors can also become self-fulfilling. For example, a bank that is completely sound can quickly get into trouble if rumors circulate that it is in financial distress. Depositors can cause a run; customers can avoid dealing with the bank, and eventually it will find itself in financial distress.

And if the rumor is about some kind of malfeasance or inappropriate activity, it commands a high level of credibility. As noted in the best-selling book *A Civil Action* by Jonathan Harr, "It is the nature of disputes that a forceful accusation by an injured party often has more rhetorical power than a denial."[14]

The sociologist Tomatsu Shibutani notes that rumors arise from uncertainty, from the absence of context and concrete information by which those affected by a crisis may understand its significance. Whenever an information vacuum exists, rumors will arise to fill the void. Shibutani elaborates:

> The discrepancy between information needed to come to terms with a changing environment and what is provided by formal … channels constitutes the critical condition of rumor construction. Demand for news may arise in an effort to cope with an unexpected event or in sustained collective tension, when [people] are mobilized to act but have no clear-cut goals … When activity is interrupted for want of adequate information, frustrated [people] must piece together some kind of definition, and rumor is the collective transaction through which they try to fill this gap. Far from being pathological, rumor is part and parcel of the efforts of [people] to come to terms with the exigencies of life.[15]

Rumors, Uncertainty, and Relief of Emotional Distress

Rumors often ameliorate anxiety, uncertainty, and fear, especially when people feel that a crisis directly affects them. This is commonly the case in employee populations when rumors about layoffs, cutbacks, restructuring, hiring freezes, benefit reductions, or other changes arise. Rumors allow employees to express collective frustration and validate each other's fears. Rumors can also be subversive, providing an alternative communication channel and establishing an unofficial culture.

Because crises are by nature characterized by uncertainty, rumors are a fact of life in crises. The good news is that preventive and remedial actions are possible, allowing professional communicators to minimize the damage from rumors, or even to stop them in their tracks (as happened in the suicide example that opened this chapter).

One of the important roles corporate communication professionals fill is to be an early-warning and rapid-response mechanism for rumor control. But being effective in preventing or controlling rumors requires an understanding of the psychological and sociological factors that drive people to listen to, pass along, and believe rumors. More important, being effective requires companies to act in counterinstinctive ways: to make and communicate decisions faster than they may be accustomed to making them, and to be more forthcoming with information than they otherwise would be.

> Paradoxically, telling more and telling it faster has the effect of eliminating a rumor.

Paradoxically, telling more and telling it faster has the effect of eliminating a rumor. Most executives are uncomfortable with the notion that they must affirmatively disclose information in order to stop the flow of information. It is a paradoxical situation, but the results will pay off.

Fighting forest fires is a good analogy. Sometimes it is impossible to fight a forest fire using direct methods such as building a firebreak—a cleared area around the area that is in flames in order to stop a fire from spreading. Firefighters may then engage in a practice called "backburning," where they set a fire to remove fuel (for example, brush) between the spreading edge of a wildfire and the control line established by the fire commanders on the scene.[16]

Just as it is paradoxical to start a fire to put out a fire, so too is communicating to shut down communication. But as with fighting a forest fire, it works, and sometimes it is the only thing that works. The backburn removes the fuel that would feed a fire, just as timely and robust communication removes the fuel—uncertainty and fear—that feeds a rumor. But like a backburn, the communication must be done at the right time and in the right way. Therefore, effective rumor control requires a high degree of both courage and discipline to recognize that counterinstinctive actions in the short term have a predictable, though paradoxical, long-term benefit of preventing rumors from proliferating.

The Morphing of Rumors: How They Change over Time

One of the defining elements of rumors is that they are not static. As a rumor passes from person to person, it tends to change in predictable ways, through a process that social psychologists call leveling, sharpening, and assimilation.

In the 1940s two Harvard University psychologists, Gordon W. Allport and Leo Postman, conducted experiments on how the content of rumors changes as the rumor passes from person to person. They concluded that as a rumor travels, it tends to grow shorter, more concise, and more easily grasped and told: In subsequent versions, more and more original details are leveled out, fewer words are used, and fewer items are mentioned.

> As leveling of details proceeds, the remaining details are necessarily sharpened. Sharpening refers to the selective perception, retention, and reporting of a few details from the originally larger context. Although sharpening, like leveling, occurs in every series of reproductions, the same items are not always emphasized. Much depends on the constitution of the group in which the tale is transmitted. Those items will be selected for sharpening which are of particular interest to the reporter …
>
> Assimilation … has to do with the powerful attractive force exerted upon the rumor by habits, interests, and sentiments existing in the reader's mind … Items become sharpened or leveled to fit the leading motif of the story, and they become consistent with this motif in such a way as to make the resultant story more coherent.[17]

Allport and Postman emphasize that while leveling, sharpening, and assimilation are independent mechanisms, they function simultaneously. The result is that a story becomes more coherent, more interesting, and therefore more believable with each retelling. But like a game of "telephone," later participants in the chain are likely to experience the rumor differently than earlier participants. Indeed, Allport and Postman's conclusions were based, in part, on their own experiments on the "telephone" phenomenon.

But unlike the game of "telephone," rumors do more than simply level, sharpen, and assimilate the stories contained in them. Participants in rumor transmission have an investment both in the content of the rumor and in the status that transmitting the rumor conveys. In particular, some people see retelling a rumor as a status-enhancing activity. Sociologists refer to this as a process of exchange, where information is a commodity with value, and the sender derives status from being seen to be "in the know."

The French sociologist Jean-Nöel Kapferer explains: "By taking others into his confidence and sharing a secret with them, the transmitter's personal importance is magnified. He comes across as the holder of precious knowledge, a sort of front-runner scout—creating a favorable impression in the minds of those he informs."[18]

The sender therefore has an interest not merely in passing the information along, but also in persuading the receiver to believe and act on the rumor. But often in order to achieve desired status the transmitter needs to enhance the details even more than the leveling and sharpening that Allport and Postman found.

And as a rumor changes with each telling, there is a reason for each transmitter to modify, or assimilate, the details of the rumor in ways that increase his or her status. Indeed, rumors cannot continue without exaggeration. This is a process known as snowballing, where the rumor's importance seems to grow with each telling. According to Kapferer, "Exaggeration is common when it comes to rumors. It is not some kind of pathological or aberrant phenomenon, but rather a logical consequence of communication. Rumors can be viewed as a process of commodity exchange. In the rumor process, once information is shared among too many people, its value seriously diminishes, and the rumor thus stops short. The end of the rumor does not mean disbelief: it means silence."

> Snowballing is the only way for a rumor to last. It is a necessary condition of rumor persistence. Indeed, identical repetition kills the news value of all information. Were a rumor repeated word for word, without any modification whatsoever, throughout its diffusion process, its death would be thereby accelerated. If everyone's friends have already heard it, or everyone imagines that they have, nobody would then dare speak of it again: for there would be a high risk of receiving no reward, or worse, of receiving negative reinforcement.
>
> On the contrary, the permanent addition of new details, the systematic inflation of figures (at the outset, one dead man; then five; then one hundred, etc.), amplification, and exaggeration are value-boosting devices. They make possible the continuation of communication within a group. Snowballing is not some innate or odd trait that rumors have: a rumor, that is, a contagious process of information exchange, would not last long without this value-added process.[19]

It is regrettably common for management teams in a crisis simply to dismiss the rumor mill's significance, or to insist that employees get back to work and pay no attention to rumors. This is counterproductive. It is precisely when people are feeling vulnerable that they seek reassurance.

And if management does not take their concerns seriously, people will find reassurance from those around them.

The result of inattention to the emotional needs of external stakeholders can be reduced demand for a company's products, decline in stock price, negative media coverage, and increased regulatory scrutiny. Inattention to the emotional needs of employees can include significant distraction, reduced productivity, and—through leveling, sharpening, assimilating, and snowballing—the transmission of ever-more damaging, distracting, and counterproductive rumors. Being a closed environment, employee populations tend to be rumor-incubators, especially when management tends to withhold important information. Such internal rumor processes are sometimes seen by employees to be the only credible sources of information about the company, in contrast to what employees consider to be propaganda from official sources.

Preventing Rumors

Rumors arise and are believed when official information is lacking or is not believed. Rumors can be avoided—along with their attendant negative consequences—if companies recognize the need to provide sufficient clarifying detail and information as early as possible in life of a disruptive event. Kapferer makes this point dramatically: "They constitute an informational black market."[20] And the way to prevent a black market is to create a robust legitimate market: in the case of rumors, by diminishing the demand for information, and diminishing its value, by increasing its supply.

So what is a rumor? In *The Psychology of Rumor* Allport and Postman define it as follows: "A rumor, as we shall use the term, is a specific (or topical) proposition for belief, passed along from person to person, usually by word of mouth, without secure standards of evidence being present ... The implication in any rumor is always that some truth is being communicated. This implication holds even though the teller prefaces his tidbit with the warning, 'it is only a rumor, but I heard ...'"[21]

The most important element of this definition is that a rumor exists in the absence of secure standards of evidence, but is taken by the recipient to be true. But in the presence of secure standards of evidence a rumor will not arise. Allport and Postman elaborate: "Rumor thrives only in the absence of 'secure standards of evidence.' This criterion marks off rumor from news, distinguishes 'old wives' tales' from science, and separates gullibility from knowledge. True, we cannot always decide easily when it is that secure standards of evidence are present. For this reason we cannot always tell whether we are listening to fact or fantasy."[22]

Allport and Postman give a compelling, if now somewhat out of date, example of how a rumor can be prevented by providing verifiable factual

> Rumors arise and are believed when official information is lacking or is not believed.

information before rumors have a chance to start: "Rumors thrive on the lack of news. The almost total absence of fear-inspired rumors in Britain during the darkest days of the blitz was due to the people's conviction that the government was giving full and accurate news of the destruction and that they, therefore, knew the worst. When people are sure they know the worst, they are unlikely to darken the picture further by inventing unnecessary bogies to explain their anxieties to themselves."[23]

This latter concept—that when people are convinced they know the worst they are unlikely to darken the picture further in order to justify their own anxieties to themselves—can be of critical importance in situations that affect people over time. When people—whether as employees facing corporate downsizing or whose company is for sale, or investors in a corporation under investigation—do not believe they know the worst, they look for the slightest scrap of information to validate their fears. But when employees know what will happen next, what the worst case is likely to be, or that the worst is in fact over, they are less likely to be driven by rumors or look for hidden meanings.

In short, ambiguity provokes anxiety, and anxiety prompts rumors. Conversely, absence of ambiguity reduces anxiety, and in turn diminishes the strength of rumors. Allport and Postman observe: "Unguided by objective evidence, most people will make their prediction in accordance with their subjective preference."[24] And in the presence of objective evidence, it is possible for people to move beyond their subjective preference, even their subjective fears.

For crisis communicators, the challenge is to help clients and employers summon the courage to disclose what is necessary to provide objective evidence that helps people move beyond their subjective preferences. The good news is that Allport and Postman provide a way to do so.

> In short, ambiguity provokes anxiety, and anxiety prompts rumors.

Controlling Rumors: A Mathematical Formula

Fortunately, rumors tend to follow predictable patterns, and intervention in specific ways can help an organization overcome, or even kill, a rumor.

The breakthrough work on rumors—including how to kill false rumors—was conducted during World War II by Allport and Postman. Much of their work was classified, but after the war it was published, first in *Public Opinion Quarterly* in 1946, and then in their 1947 book, *The Psychology of Rumor*. One of their most significant contributions to the study of rumors was a mathematical formula that described the way a rumor works. The formula further suggests ways to control or eliminate a rumor.

The two factors that influence a rumor are (1) its importance to the listener and (2) its ambiguity. In order to control a rumor one must either diminish the level of importance one assigns to the rumor if true, or eliminate the ambiguity around the factual basis of the rumor, or both. Eliminating ambiguity is particularly important if the rumor is in fact completely false. But even where the rumor has some mixture of truth and fiction, eliminating ambiguity about the fiction can help control the rumor and ground it in reality. Once an unambiguous reality is established, it may be possible to reduce the level of importance of the content of the rumor, thereby diminishing its transmission to others.

Take, for example, the suicide story that began this chapter. Through a process of leveling, sharpening, assimilation, and snowballing, *The New York Times* reporter had presented Fred with a rumor: that a trader had committed suicide because he was being investigated for insider trading. Simply denying the rumor would not have been persuasive to the reporter. But Fred was able to provide an unambiguous alternative explanation: that there had been a routine compliance audit of the trader's department, and that the trader's father had described the suicide as following an "emotional family encounter." Both those pieces of specific detail reduced ambiguity about the cause of the suicide. And because the link between job performance and the suicide was effectively broken, the importance of the rumor declined significantly.

Allport and Postman summarize these two factors of importance and ambiguity: "Rumor travels when events have importance in the lives of individuals, and when the news received about them is either lacking or subjectively ambiguous. The ambiguity may arise from the fact that the news is not clearly reported, or from the fact that conflicting versions of the news have reached the individual, or from his incapacity to comprehend the news he receives."[25]

The ambiguity can further arise when a company's credibility is weak, when the company sends mixed messages, and when people have become conditioned to distrust what the company says. In such cases, even when the company is telling the truth, people are disinclined to believe it. Allport and Postman observe, "Most important of all ... rumor will race when individuals distrust the news that reaches them."[26]

Allport and Postman elaborate how the two factors of importance and ambiguity work together, and note that there is a mathematical relationship:

The Basic Law of Rumor

The two essential conditions of importance and ambiguity seem to be related to rumor transmission in a roughly quantitative manner. A formula for the intensity of rumor might be written as follows:

$$R \sim i \times a,$$

In words this formula means that the amount of rumor in circulation will vary with the *importance* of the subject to the individuals concerned

(i) times the *ambiguity* of the evidence pertaining to the topic at issue (a). The relation between importance and ambiguity is not additive but multiplicative, for if either importance or ambiguity is zero, there is no rumor. Ambiguity alone does not sustain rumor. Nor does importance.[27]

Because the relationship between importance and ambiguity is multiplicative, an incremental decline in either can result in a greater than incremental decline in the scope of the rumor.

Here are some ways to think about the model quantitatively. The elements of the Allport and Postman model of rumor dynamics are:

$$R \sim i \times a,$$

   where:

⇒ R is the rumor: its reach, intensity, duration, and the degree that people will rely upon it.

⇒ i is the *importance* of the rumor to the hearer or reader, if true;

⇒ and a is the level of *ambiguity* or uncertainty surrounding the rumor.

In other words, the reach, intensity, duration, and reliance on a rumor is roughly equivalent to the importance one attaches to the rumor if true, multiplied by ambiguity surrounding the rumor, especially surrounding its denial. Note that simply denying a rumor does not eliminate ambiguity; it may even increase it. Rather, eliminating ambiguity requires giving an affirmative factual demonstration that gives people a basis for not relying on the rumor; in Allport and Postman's words, providing objective evidence sufficient to overcome people's subjective preference.

Here is how the math works. Assume a scale of zero to ten, zero being nonexistent and ten being certainty. If both importance and ambiguity are high, say ten, the scope of the rumor will be quite strong:

$$R \sim i \times a$$
$$R \sim 10 \times 10$$
$$R \sim 100$$

In other words, when both the importance and ambiguity are at their highest, ten, the scope of the rumor will be at its highest, one hundred. But reduce just one of the factors and the scope of the rumor declines considerably. Assume that importance remains high, ten, but that ambiguity can be reduced to three. Apply the model as follows:

$$R \sim i \times a$$
$$R \sim 10 \times 3$$
$$R \sim 30$$

The scope of the rumor has declined from one hundred to thirty, or by more than two thirds. Reduce both factors and the decline is even more dramatic. Say both are three:

$$R \sim i \times a$$
$$R \sim 3 \times 3$$
$$R \sim 9$$

The scope of the rumor has reduced from one hundred when importance and ambiguity were at ten, to just nine when each is reduced to three.

Because anything multiplied by zero equals zero, if either ambiguity or importance is reduced to zero the rumor disappears. Assume that importance is still ten, but ambiguity is completely eliminated, at zero:

$$R \sim i \times a$$
$$R \sim 10 \times 0$$
$$R \sim 0$$

The scope of the rumor is zero, and the rumor disappears. In practical terms, this formula lets a professional communicator and a management team do several powerful things. Knowing that importance and ambiguity drive a rumor, a company can be far more efficient in identifying what it needs to do and say than if it was not so aware. Second, knowing the formula gives clients and bosses confidence that they can influence the interpretation of events. The formula empowers management to focus communications in ways that can have impact on how the company is being perceived. Best of all, the formula can disarm negative information, killing a rumor and preventing further damage.

> The scope of the rumor is zero, and the rumor disappears.

Dynamics of Controlling a Rumor in the News Cycle

When applying the $R \sim i \times a$ formula, one critical element of success is how early one can influence the two factors that drive rumors, importance, and ambiguity. Corporate managements, however, have little appreciation for the need to preempt rumors, or for the seemingly arbitrary and somewhat confusing deadlines under which journalists work. The Allport and Postman model empowers crisis communicators and companies to disclose more sooner, thereby controlling the rumor and decreasing the likelihood of a negative story.

The Rule of Forty-Five Minutes, Six Hours, Three Days, and Two Weeks

But it is possible to persuade management to make decisions and to communicate quickly. There are specific points in a news cycle where it is possible to kill a negative story or control a partially accurate story. Miss one of these points and you will suffer reputational damage. Worse, the distance between the points, the intensity of the crisis, and the potential for reputational harm grow in almost an exponential fashion as bad news spreads. And while these points result from careful observation of how the news cycles and the rumor formula interact, the same orders of magnitude apply beyond the media, when progressively larger groups of people, over time, become invested in a rumor.

The First Forty-Five Minutes. Give or take, you have maximum influence on the outcome of a story in the first moments after the rumor arises. During this time, only a small number of people, and possibly only one reporter, know about a rumor or are working on a story. If you follow the R ~ i × a formula to convince a reporter not to pursue a story in those first forty-five minutes or so, the chances are high that the story will disappear. If, on the other hand, you are unable to respond to the reporter within that forty-five minute time frame, a number of powerful and negative things happen. First, the original reporter is likely to be working the phones trying to confirm the rumor, retelling it to sources who themselves can pass it along to other reporters. Second, given the proliferation of all-news television, radio, and the Internet, the chances are high that the story will break quickly. Third, in the retelling of the rumor from the first reporter to other sources and other reporters, the substance of the rumor will change. As the rumor becomes known in slightly different forms by many different people, it will become harder to find a definitive demonstration that unambiguously puts the rumor to rest.

Once the story breaks, many more reporters become aware of and pursue it. It becomes much more difficult to control the story, if only because you now do not know precisely which reporters have heard the rumor. Controlling the rumor now becomes less a function of persuasion—a private intervention with a single reporter—than of a public statement to influence your ultimate constituencies. Because the original rumor has become a matter of public record, refuting it may require going public with the media and all your constituencies, including direct communication with employees, customers, and regulators, among others.

Six Hours. Once a story crosses a wire service, is broadcast on television or radio, or appears on the Internet, it is, at least for the moment, out of your control. It may still be possible eventually to control the rumor and even to kill the story. But now it will be much more difficult. And it takes much longer. As a general rule, once a story is broadcast you can expect to have at least six hours of negative coverage.

During these six hours, more and more reporters are coming to the story, and the story is being rebroadcast on competing media outlets. More and more people become aware of the rumor, and it grows exponentially. If a story appeared on one all-news cable television, the odds are high that it will appear on others and on the regular network or local TV news stations that night, and in drive time radio. Your customers, employees, suppliers, competitors, regulators, and local community are made aware of the rumor and can begin to act on it, to your reputational and business disadvantage.

If, during this part of the cycle, you succeed in following the R ~ i × a formula in your public statements, the chances are high that the rumor can be controlled and the story will fade away. But by then the reputational damage may have been done.

If you are unable to control the story during this phase of the cycle, however, expect several days of negative news. And all the while, the processes of leveling, sharpening, assimilation, and snowballing are morphing the rumor into something far less manageable. And as more and more people learn about the rumor and become invested in it, it becomes harder and harder to reach them with the demonstration that puts the rumor to bed.

Three Days. Once a story hits the daily newspapers, you can expect it to be alive for several days. During the day the story appears there is likely to be television and radio commentary about the story, as well as gossip among your customers, employees, and competitors, with all the attendant distortion. The day following publication, newspapers that missed the story on day one are likely to pick it up as their own day one story. Even newspapers that carried the story on day one can carry a second-day story of reaction to the first story. And those who come late will themselves carry their own second-day stories on day three.

During this period it is still possible to invoke the R ~ i × a formula successfully. But by this time you will have suffered several days of reputational damage and will have seen a much wider range of people exposed to the negative rumor, and many more versions of the rumor that may be inconsistent with each other. It becomes much harder to refute.

If you cannot control the story during these three days, expect at least two weeks of negative coverage.

Two Weeks. After the daily newspapers have had their run, there is still a further news cycle that includes weekly and semimonthly magazines, industry trade publications, weekend newspaper wrap-up sections, and the Sunday morning talk shows. If a story has been alive for three days in the daily press it is unlikely to escape some notice from the weeklies and semimonthlies. During this period you can still invoke the R ~ i × a formula to kill the rumor and prevent its further spread. But by then you will have suffered several weeks of negative coverage and reputational harm. And, as noted above, Kapferer points out that snowballing is the only way for a rumor to last. It is a necessary condition of rumor persistence. Identical repetition kills the news value of all information.

So for rumors to remain alive they need to constantly grow in strength and importance. The rumor in the second week of its life may bear no relationship to the rumor as it existed in the first forty-five minutes, when only a few people knew about it and when the processes of exaggeration had not begun.

If, however, you are unable to control the story in this timeframe, expect continuous coverage, coverage of Clinton-Lewinsky or OJ Simpson proportions. A company is unlikely to recover quickly from this kind of scrutiny.

All of this suggests that it is a fundamental mistake for corporations to make decisions about crisis communications on their own routine timelines. They need to recognize that however arbitrary and at times irrational news media deadlines may seem, companies can control their own destinies better if they can kill rumors as early in a news cycle as possible.

Successfully employing both the R ~ i × a formula and the Rule of Forty-Five Minutes, Six Hours, Three Days, and Two Weeks can help prevent reputational damage and keep the company focused on its own agenda. Failure to recognize the power of these two formulas puts the company at the mercy of the rumor mill, gossip mongers, and the irrational-seeming dynamics of the news media.

However arbitrary and at times irrational news media deadlines may seem, companies can control their own destinies better if they can kill rumors as early in a news cycle as possible.

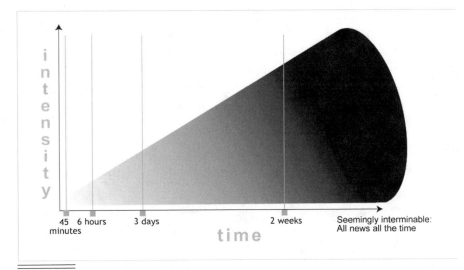

Figure 12.2

Best Practices in Crisis Management

Effective crisis communication requires both discipline and flexibility, and a keen focus on the desired outcome of communication. Among the best practices are:

1. Know when to suspend business as usual: have a clear sense of what constitutes a crisis, and how to mobilize energy and resources quickly.
2. Get preauthorization to use judgment quickly when dealing with incoming media inquiries.
3. Keep in mind the golden hour of crisis response: incremental delays cause greater-than-incremental harm to reputation.
4. Control the agenda: do not let the media, adversaries, or the rumor mill define your situation.
5. Develop messages and plan tactics with a goal in mind: how do you want your key constituencies to think and feel, and what do you want them to know and do? When you have determined this, follow this process:
   Tell it all
   Tell it fast
   Tell them what you are doing about it
   Tell them when it is over
   Get back to work

6. Be attentive to rumors, and work to eliminate them as quickly as possible. Follow the formula for diminishing or eliminating rumors: $R \sim i \times a$.
7. Note that there are particular points in the cycle of bad news where you can take control of your destiny. The most powerful point is the first:
   Forty-five minutes
   Six hours
   Three days
   Two weeks

Resources for Further Study

Logos Institute for Crisis Management & Executive Leadership

This resource on crisis communication and related topics is run by co-author Fred Garcia, provides a number of publications, articles, best practices guides, and other tools for helping professional communicators and managers plan for, manage through, and recover from crises. Its Web site is http://www.logosinstitute.net.

Publications that expand upon the information in this chapter include:

⇒ *Avoiding Crisis Mis-Steps*, by Helio Fred Garcia, Logos Consulting Group Crisis Monograph Series, 2004.
⇒ *Crisis Response and Competitive Advantage*, by Helio Fred Garcia, Logos Consulting Group Crisis Monograph Series, 2004.

⇒ *Elements of Strategy in Crisis Planning: How to Become Habitually Strategic in Managing a Crisis*, by Helio Fred Garcia, Logos Consulting Group Crisis Monograph Series, 2005.

⇒ *Introduction to Crisis Communication*, by Helio Fred Garcia, Logos Consulting Group Crisis Monograph Series, 2004.

⇒ *Preventing and Overcoming Rumors*, by Helio Fred Garcia, Logos Consulting Group Crisis Monograph Series, 2004.

The Lukaszewski Group

Run by crisis guru Jim Lukaszewski, the Lukaszewski Group's Web site (http://www.e911.com) includes a broad range of resources available to professional communicators. These include a free newsletter, Executive Action: Urgent Information for Executive Decision-making. The following publications are particularly useful:

⇒ *Crisis Communication Planning Strategies: A Crisis Communication Management Workbook*, by James E. Lukaszewski, The Lukaszewski Group/Public Relations Society of America, 2000.

⇒ *Media Relations Strategies During Emergencies: A Crisis Communication Management Guide*, by James E. Lukaszewski, The Lukaszewski Group/Public Relations Society of America, 2000.

⇒ *War Stories and Crisis Communication Strategies: A Crisis Communication Management Anthology*, by James E. Lukaszewski, The Lukaszewski Group/Public Relations Society of America, 2000.

New York University Programs in Law and Business

Housed in NYU's School of Continuing and Professional Studies, this program includes courses on crisis management, crisis communication, crisis strategies, and a certificate program in disaster recovery and business continuity. Its Web site is http://scps.nyu.edu/departments.

Books

The following books are recommended for anyone interested in crisis management:

⇒ *Clausewitz on Strategy: Inspiration and Insight from a Master Strategist*, by Tiha von Ghyczy, Bolko von Oetinger, and Christopher Bassford, A Publication of the Strategy Institute of the Boston Consulting Group, Wiley, 2001.

⇒ *Crisis Communications*, by Helio Fred Garcia, two volumes, AAAA Press, 1999.

⇒ *Crisis Management: Planning for the Inevitable*, by Steven Fink, American Management Association, 1986.

⇒ *Don't Think of an Elephant!: Know Your Values and Frame the Debate*, by George Lakoff, Chelsea Green, 2004.

⇒ *Harvard Business Review on Crisis Management*, Harvard Business Review Press, 2000.

⇒ *Managing Crises Before they Happen: What Every Executive Needs to Know About Crisis Management*, by Ian I Mitroff, Gus Anagnos, AMACOM, 2000.

⇒ *On War*, by Carl von Clausewitz, edited and translated by Michael Howard and Peter Paret, Princeton University Press, 1984.

⇒ *Rumor in the Marketplace: The Social Psychology of Commercial Hearsay*, by Frederick Koenig, Auburn House Publishing, 1985.

⇒ *Rumors: Uses, Interpretations, & Images,* by Jean-Noël Kapferer, Transaction Publishers, 1990.

⇒ *Will Your Next Mistake Be Fatal: Avoiding the Chain of Mistakes That Can Destroy Your Organization*, by Robert E. Mittelstaedt, Jr., Wharton School Publishing, 2005.

Questions for Further Discussion

1. If a crisis requires accelerating the decision-making processes, how can a communicator get management's attention early enough to suspend business as usual?
2. Why do incremental delays in managing and communicating in a crisis have greater-than-incremental impact on the result?
3. How do rumors affect employee morale and customer demand for a company's products or services in a crisis?
4. What is the optimal role of corporate communication professionals in a crisis?
5. If a crisis is a turning point, how can a company act promptly enough to prevent the turning point moment from turning negative?

CHAPTER 13

Corporate Responsibility

By Anthony P. Ewing,
Partner, Logo Consulting Group

> *You cannot escape the responsibility of tomorrow by evading it today.*
>
> – Abraham Lincoln

Nike's Journey

Nike, by 1996, had built a $5 billion sporting goods business and its "swoosh" logo embodied the celebrity-fuelled American sports culture worldwide. But the global brand that symbolized performance and excellence to millions would soon acquire some truly frightening attributes— greed, exploitation, and indifference to human suffering.

Warning signs had appeared as early as 1992, with a two-page story in Harper's *magazine criticizing Nike labor practices in Indonesia. However, the storm of anti-Nike publicity and activism which had the potential to inflict lasting damage on the company's reputation did not gather fully until 1995, when concerns over globalization and sweatshops converged, capturing the attention of activists, consumers, and policymakers. Between April and August 1995, the CBS television news magazine* Eye to Eye *ran a segment portraying Pakistani children as young as six stitching Adidas and Reebok soccer balls; United States-based labor activists publicized the plight of workers fired for organizing a union in a Salvadoran apparel factory supplying Gap and Eddie Bauer; and state officials freed enslaved immigrants from an El Monte, California, garment sweatshop.*

It did not take long for Nike's business practices to become the focus of intense scrutiny. By 1996, media coverage of working conditions in Asian factories had turned Nike into the corporate poster child for the inequities of the global economy. The allegations were serious and attention grabbing. Indonesian factory workers making Nike sneakers were paid less than the local minimum wage and required to work excessive overtime. Pakistani children were stitching Nike soccer balls. Factory managers in Vietnam subjected workers to physical, verbal, and sexual abuse and exposed workers to toxic chemicals.

Negative press coverage prompted a broad range of constituencies important to Nike to question the company's motives and business practices. Columnists pointed out the enormous disparities between the price of celebrity-endorsed sneakers sold in the United States and the wages earned by the Indonesian women who made them. Activists accused Nike of ruthlessly exploiting workers and the environment in the company's global pursuit of profit at any cost. Students organized campus protests and boycotts of Nike products, demanding that Nike disclose the location of its subcontracted factories worldwide. Government officials in North America and Europe introduced measures to ban imports of apparel and sporting goods made with child labor. Socially responsible investment funds, using the same strategies they had applied a decade earlier to encourage corporate divestment from Apartheid South Africa, began to screen their investment portfolios for labor and environmental policies, and submit shareholder resolutions urging companies to adopt codes of conduct for their suppliers. Meanwhile, the plaintiffs' bar in the United States began testing novel legal strategies to hold companies accountable in U.S. courts for the abusive treatment of workers in foreign markets.

Nike's initial response to the rising tide of criticism was instinctively defensive. At first, Nike spokespeople denied knowledge of specific instances of abuse and asserted no responsibility for the conduct of the company's suppliers. Nike's public statements sought to discredit critics and deflect responsibility.

"One has to question the credibility of an individual whose organization is largely financed by labor unions opposed to free trade with developing nations. It's also too bad that Kathie Lee Gifford has found it necessary to avoid the media spotlight by pushing Michael Jordan into it." – Excerpt of Nike press release (June 6, 1996, responding to an allegation that Nike Air Jordan shoes were made in Indonesia for fourteen cents an hour).

Nike's high profile founder and chairman, Philip Knight, vehemently responded to criticism of Nike's business practices through letters, press statements, speeches, and other public communications, arguing that Nike's presence in developing markets contributes to higher standards of living and that the company does its best to ensure that labor abuses do not occur. In the midst of growing pressure from universities to ensure minimum labor standards in the production of university-licensed apparel and heated anti-Nike rhetoric on college campuses, Nike cancelled a contract with the University of Michigan in a dispute over applicable codes of conduct. Knight went so far as to withdraw a personal donation to his alma mater, the University of Oregon, publicly linking his decision to the university's criticism of Nike's labor practices.

But under steady pressure from stakeholders to take meaningful steps to address labor practices in its supply chain, Nike's approach began to change. By necessity and through much trial and error, Nike has become a corporate responsibility leader.

Nike's efforts over the past decade to restore its reputation and demonstrate responsible practices parallel the emergence of corporate responsibility as a corporate discipline. Nike has implemented almost every innovation in the field. In 1992, the company adopted a code of conduct and set minimum labor standards for its suppliers. Since then, Nike has acknowl-edged responsibility for social and environmental conditions in its supply chain and changed the way it sources certain products to improve envi-ronmental performance and reduce the risk of labor violations. Executives have engaged in the public debate over globalization and in conversations with the company's critics. Nike joined governmental and industrywide efforts to eliminate sweatshops and participates actively in multistake-holder partnerships to develop factory standard-setting and monitoring mechanisms, and to support programs for workers and communities. Nike created the position of vice president for corporate responsibility to lead the company's efforts and signal the issue's importance. The company launched internal monitoring of its supply chain, expanded its compliance to include external third-party monitoring, and made its audit results public. Nike signed on to international corporate responsibility initiatives like the United Nations Global Compact and references international human rights, labor and environmental standards in its own standards. Nike began issuing a Corporate Responsibility Report on its social and environmental performance in 2001 and has become an advocate for common standards and reporting guidelines.

Communication has played a key role in every step of Nike's journey through the frequently hostile and always complicated terrain of corpo-rate responsibility. At first, Nike did a poor job communicating corporate responsibility. In 1997, a Wall Street Journal *article questioned whether Nike's public relations efforts on employment practices had done any good at all. By 1998, in a speech to the National Press Club, Nike CEO and Chairman Philip Knight was acknowledging the company's accountabil-ity for the business practices of Asian manufacturers and announcing a number of unilateral initiatives to adopt United States air quality stan-dards for foreign factories, raise the minimum working age to eighteen for all footwear manufacturing workers, and permit the external monitor-ing of Nike suppliers. Nike's response to stakeholder pressure shifted from merely asserting, to actively demonstrating corporate responsibility.*

The cultural change at Nike has been dramatic, a point the company readily acknowledges:

"From our early years up to the 1990s, the stakeholders we thought most about were athletes and consumers. In the 1990s, we ignored an emerg-ing group of stakeholders. We learned a hard lesson . . . Nongovernmen-tal organizations, trade unions, and others have opened our eyes to new issues and viewpoints, and have enabled us to draw on their experience and expertise. This does not mean that we will always agree with our

stakeholders, but we know from experience that constructive engagement is usually the approach that brings about the best insight to the challenges we all have an interest in addressing." – Nike FY04 Corporate Responsibility Report[1]

In April 2005, Nike announced that it would disclose every contract factory worldwide where its products are made. Nike's announcement, which reversed the company's longstanding position against factory disclosure, has the potential to change the way an entire industry sector manages compliance issues in its global supply chain and marks a major step in the evolution of corporate responsibility best practices.

* * * * *

Effectively demonstrating corporate responsibility is a key challenge for business managers. Decisions about what, how, and to whom a company must communicate are a central element of any corporate responsibility program. Most companies have not had the benefit of spending years at the center of the corporate responsibility debate, like Nike, learning what works and what does not.

This chapter is intended to provide an overview and practical guidance to business leaders, managers, and others who seek to better understand corporate responsibility and the challenges of communicating it.

> Corporate responsibility encompasses corporate efforts to meet the financial and non-financial expectations of various stakeholder groups. Corporate responsibility goes beyond philanthropy and legal compliance.

This Chapter Covers

⇒ Corporate responsibility
- Definition
- The business case
- Corporate initiatives
- Key issues
  - How should a company respond to critics?
  - How much responsibility is too much responsibility?
  - How can a company connect corporate responsibility to business strategy?

⇒ Communicating corporate responsibility
- Audiences
- Principles

- Accuracy
- Transparency
- Credibility

⇒ Tools
- Codes of conduct
- Monitoring and certification
- Training and education
- Corporate responsibility reporting

⇒ Legal considerations
⇒ Best practices for communicating corporate responsibility
⇒ Resources for further studies
⇒ Questions for further discussion

Corporate Responsibility

Definition

The first challenge is defining corporate responsibility.

According to economic theory, the sole responsibility of business is to maximize profits. As long as companies obey the law, there are no requirements or duties beyond the financial imperatives of the corporation. Any corporate activity that elevates societal interests above the interests of shareholders is an inappropriate use of corporate resources. In this orthodox view of the world, there is a strict separation of governmental and corporate responsibilities. Business benefits society by generating profits for its owners, providing employment, and delivering goods and services. It is the distinct role of government, and not the business of business, to legislate, to tax for public purposes, and to enforce societal standards. An economist might argue that Nike has no responsibility for the activities of its independently owned suppliers and Nike's efforts to improve working conditions in its supply chain constitute mismanagement. Only the governments of Indonesia, Pakistan, and Vietnam should set and enforce local labor standards.

Few companies articulate such a narrow view. The history of the corporate responsibility movement illustrates an evolving definition of the role and responsibilities of business in society, from a focus exclusively on shareholder returns or other financial measures, to the acknowledgment by business of a much broader group of corporate stakeholders and responsibilities.[2]

Defining corporate responsibilities and stakeholders is not easy. Companies use the terms "corporate responsibility," "corporate social responsibility," "corporate citizenship," "business ethics," and "sustainability" interchangeably to describe corporate initiatives ranging from philanthropy, to legal compliance, to social and environmental programs.

For many corporate observers, particularly those who view corporate motives suspiciously, corporate responsibility means companies simply follow the rules. Corporate responsibility comprises the corporate ethics programs, codes of conduct, and compliance programs necessary to meet legal and regulatory requirements.

But compliance is just the starting point for any discussion of corporate responsibility. Corporate stakeholders expect legal compliance; increasingly they demand voluntary standard setting beyond the legal minimum. When U.S. companies manufacture products in developing countries, for example, advocates and customers expect the companies to adhere to U.S. levels of health and safety and environmental protection in their foreign factories, even if local standards are lower or unenforced.

When apparel companies were accused of running sweatshops in the early 1990s, a common corporate response was to deny any legal responsibility over factories the companies did not own. Legal precision did nothing to improve conditions for workers, however, and stakeholders were not satisfied. Smart companies realized that irrespective of legal liability, their credibility was tied to acknowledging responsibility for working conditions in their supply chain and setting standards that exceeded legal minimums. In 1998, for example, Nike raised its minimum age for footwear factory workers to eighteen, well above the international standard of fourteen, and adopted U.S. air quality standards for all footwear factories.

Many corporate responsibility initiatives go beyond compliance to set minimum standards for business conduct, and for social and environmental performance within a company's "sphere of influence," even in the absence of legal requirements or enforcement.

> Many corporate responsibility initiatives go beyond compliance.

Companies also act responsibly by meeting unmet needs. As the influence and relative power of government has declined, companies are frequently the best-suited organs of society to tackle major social challenges.[3] Private sector efforts to advance the United Nations Millennium Development Goals,[4] such as the Global Business Coalition on HIV/AIDS and the World Business Council for Sustainable Development, are examples of the private sector assuming roles traditionally carried out by government.

The U.S. conglomerate General Electric (GE) recently defined corporate responsibility for its own operations by combining the traditional financial notion with compliance and a broader concept of ethical decision making: "Good corporate citizenship comprises strong economic performance over time, rigorous legal and accounting compliance, and going beyond compliance when there are opportunities to create benefit for society and the long-term health of the enterprise." – GE 2005 Citizenship Report[5]

For the purposes of this chapter, corporate responsibility encompasses corporate efforts to meet the nonfinancial expectations of stakeholders.[6]

Under this definition, corporate responsibility goes beyond philanthropy and legal compliance. Stakeholders may include investors, employees, business partners, suppliers, customers, governments, regulators, international organizations, nongovernmental organizations, and the communities where businesses operate.[7] Most of the examples in this chapter are of companies seeking to set minimum social and environmental standards for their operations or in their supply chain.

The Business Case

Companies face growing pressure to act responsibly. Sources of pressure for greater corporate responsibility can be market based (investors and customers); legal (the threat of regulation or litigation); and public (advocacy campaigns and media coverage).

The globalization of media and communications powered by the Internet means that the activities of companies at home and in foreign markets are no longer invisible to stakeholders. Business practices are a particular focus of scrutiny.

Human rights are now a business concern.

Human rights are now a business concern.[8] Today, alongside governments, companies often are viewed as a source or cause of human rights abuse, as well as an international actor with the capacity to promote human rights.[9] Over the last ten years, human rights advocates and the media have shined a spotlight on human rights conditions in a wide range of transnational industries, including oil and mining; the manufacturing of apparel, carpets, footwear, sporting goods, and toys; and the pharmaceutical and other high technology sectors. More recently, human rights activists have focused attention on human rights conditions in agriculture on farms that produce coffee, tea, cocoa, and bananas for global markets, demanding "fair trade" practices.[10]

Environmental performance is another focus of corporate responsibility efforts.

Environmental performance is another focus of corporate responsibility efforts. Following the 1989 Exxon Valdez oil spill in Alaska, environmental groups and institutional investors came together to promote principles for corporate environmental conduct.[11] Since then, in a number of companies, environmental sustainability has become an element of corporate strategy. In response to sustained pressure from stakeholders, companies are beginning to articulate policies on climate change, natural resource management, and environmental stewardship.

Stakeholders are calling attention to the broader social impact of corporate activities on the communities and societies where they operate. The fair trade movement seeks to improve living standards for small farmers worldwide by creating a market for agricultural products purchased at fixed prices directly from farmer cooperatives.[12] Anticorruption initiatives like the Publish What You Pay Campaign advocate corporate disclosure as a tool for tracking government management of revenues from foreign direct investment.[13] Sustainability advocates promote "triple bottom line" reporting that accounts for a company's economic, social, and environmental performance.[14]

Corporate ethics and compliance programs are now common among public companies in response to regulations such as the U.S. Sentencing Guidelines, the Foreign Corrupt Practices Act, and most recently, the Sarbanes-Oxley Act.

For many years, companies have used corporate philanthropy to burnish corporate reputation, improve corporate relationships, and support good works. Today, stakeholders are calling on the private sector to go beyond traditional corporate giving to more closely align philanthropy with business strategy and use the considerable resources and expertise of business to tackle social problems. Calls for pharmaceutical companies to provide universal access to life-saving drugs are just one example.

In response to these pressures, companies are taking a broader view of corporate responsibility and making the business case for their efforts.

> Social responsibility is a matter of hardheaded business logic. It's about performance and profits, and attracting the best people to work for you . . . To work effectively we need trust and the confidence of the society in which we are operating.
>
> — John Browne, chief executive, BP[15]

Effective corporate responsibility improves and protects the bottom line by managing risk.

> To me, opportunities to do business and do good are not mutually exclusive, nor are they less valuable for having a positive business impact. This marriage of business opportunity with global need can create a model that our Company and others will see as an opportunity to deliver more than financial performance and have a far-reaching impact.
>
> — Jeffrey R. Immelt, chairman and CEO, GE[16]

According to a recent survey of corporate leaders, business reasons for adopting responsible corporate practices include:

⇒ Protecting and enhancing reputation, brand equity, and trust
⇒ Attracting, motivating, and retaining talent
⇒ Managing and mitigating risk
⇒ Improving operational and cost efficiency
⇒ Ensuring a license to operate
⇒ Developing new business opportunities
⇒ Creating a more secure and prosperous operating environment[17]

Effective corporate responsibility improves and protects the bottom line by managing risk. Each kind of pressure for greater corporate responsibility presents a risk to be managed. Market-based pressure poses the risk of lower sales and a higher cost of capital. Legal pressure presents the risk of corporate liability and less operating flexibility. Public pressure puts at risk a company's most valuable intangible assets—corporate reputation and brand equity. All of these risks ultimately affect company financials.

Corporate responsibility can also create competitive advantage. By joining the multistakeholder Fair Labor Association, the apparel brand Phillips-Van Heusen taps into an early warning system that can alert the company to labor abuses in factories manufacturing its apparel before an activist campaign cuts into sales through boycotts, or socially responsible investment funds screen the company from its holdings.[18] By adopting sustainable water management practices, Central American coffee suppliers make themselves more attractive to leading global coffee buyers like Starbucks, whose customers, shareholders, and other constituencies demand minimum environmental standards. By providing incentives for its suppliers to improve environmental performance, Starbucks helps to ensure its future coffee supply.

While there is much debate over the quantifiable impact of corporate responsibility initiatives, efforts that are perceived by corporate managers to enhance shareholder value over time are likely to become best practices for leading companies, creating more pressure for their widespread adoption.[19] The proliferation of domestic partner benefits offered to employees by Fortune 500 companies is one example of a voluntary corporate initiative now widely recognized as necessary to attract and retain employees competitively.

Corporate Initiatives

Companies have responded to increased scrutiny of business practices, calls for greater corporate accountability, and the expanding definition of corporate stakeholders and responsibilities in many different ways, ranging from hostility and inaction to acknowledgement, engagement, and the transformation of business strategy. For some companies, corporate responsibility efforts are simply a means to meet minimum requirements or silence critics.

Companies that take corporate responsibility seriously, however, have developed a variety of new tools for managing their efforts.

Industries targeted by human rights, labor, and environmental activists have responded through voluntary standard-setting initiatives, codes of conduct, monitoring and certification programs, multistakeholder partnerships, and corporate responsibility reporting. The newest generation of initiatives focuses less on standards enforcement and more on education and training to improve corporate responsibility performance.

Companies in targeted industries and companies with well-known, valuable brands in global markets have led efforts to set standards for social and environmental performance. Nike, Starbucks, and BP, have all been thrust into leadership positions.

In some instances, corporate responsibility is part of the brand. Ben & Jerry's and the Body Shop built their businesses by emphasizing their corporate commitment to community involvement and sustainable development, respectively. Reebok publicly associated its brand with the human rights movement in 1988 by sponsoring Amnesty International and establishing a Reebok Human Rights Award that recognizes young human rights activists worldwide. Starbucks has marketed its commitment to employees and the environment. BP was one of the first companies in the energy sector to take up human rights issues and address climate change as part of its corporate policy. Arguably, Nike has transformed itself from the corporate poster child for corporate irresponsibility into a corporate responsibility leader.

Pressure frequently spreads from the high-profile easily targeted brands to an entire industry sector. Specialty coffee company Starbucks was the first major company to respond to pressure to offer Fair Trade Certified coffee, for example, but since then the largest coffee retailers—companies including Sara Lee and Proctor & Gamble—have purchased Fair Trade coffee and adopted or enforced a voluntary code of conduct for coffee production.

The experience of companies in the apparel, sporting goods, extractive, and agricultural industries have shaped second generation corporate responsibility strategies in healthcare, technology, and financial services.

> Pressure frequently spreads from the high-profile easily targeted brands to an entire industry sector.

Key Issues

A number of difficult questions are shaping the emerging field of corporate responsibility.

How Should a Company Respond to Critics? The catalyst for a company to address corporate responsibility, more often than not, is public criticism. The first instinct of corporate managers accused of corporate irresponsibility is to defend the organization and ignore or attack its critics. Both tactics can do more harm than good.

In December 1995, *The New York Times* ran an editorial arguing that the world's largest oil company, Royal Dutch/Shell, had failed to shoulder its responsibility to intervene with the military government of Nigeria on behalf of the activist Ken Saro-Wiwa.[20] In 1994, Shell had called in Nigerian government security forces to protect its facilities from violent attacks and quell unrest in the area of its oilfields. Saro-Wiwa, a prominent political opponent of the Nigerian dictatorship and of Shell's operations in Nigeria, was arrested by government security forces for allegedly inciting a riot and sentenced to hang in a trial widely criticized as corrupt and politically motivated. Initially, after Saro-Wiwa was found guilty, Shell argued that it was "not for a commercial organization to interfere with the legal processes of a sovereign state." After the storm of public criticism following Saro-Wiwa's execution, Shell eventually changed its policy on human rights engagement, asserting its right and responsibility to make its position known on any matter which affects the company, its employees, customers, shareholders, or community.[21] Learning from its experience as the focus of intense criticism, Shell now regularly engages critics, participates in multistakeholder initiatives like the Voluntary Standards on Security and Human Rights and the UN Global Compact, and actively monitors human rights risks wherever the company operates.

In 1998, Shell's competitor BP faced a similar issue in Colombia. The United States-based advocacy group Human Rights Watch accused BP of complicity with Colombian security forces that had a record of human rights abuse.[22] Rather than adopt an exclusively defensive posture, BP entered into dialogue with critics and ultimately, along with Shell, other energy companies, and human rights advocates, participated in a process convened by the U.S. and British governments to develop the Voluntary Standards on Security and Human Rights.[23] More recently, BP has made engaging critics a key element of its business strategy as the lead partner in a consortium building a natural gas pipeline from Georgia to Turkey. The pipeline project generated opposition from human rights and environmental groups. When Amnesty International released a report critical of BP and the human rights impact of the pipeline,[24] BP engaged Amnesty in dialogue, and sought to address some of the human rights concerns by incorporating international human standards in the legal agreements governing the project. According to one BP executive, "Our work with Amnesty International was an eye-opener; they viewed things in a way we never would have."[25] Engaging its main critic and taking stakeholder concerns seriously earned the company credibility.

> Most companies, however, are exceedingly cautious and reluctant to engage corporate critics.

Most companies, however, are exceedingly cautious and reluctant to engage corporate critics. In 2003, The Coca Cola Company received a letter from Human Rights Watch (HRW) expressing concern over hazardous child labor in the production of sugar cane in El Salvador, sugar that is purchased to make Coke.[26] In a series of communications with HRW, Coca Cola sought to distance itself from the issue of working conditions in the sugar cane fields by asserting its responsibility only for conditions at its direct supplier, the large processing mill covered by Coca Cola's Guiding Principles for Suppliers. While Coca Cola deserves credit for a certain level of engagement, the company's response is reminiscent of Nike's initial response to allegations of child labor and Shell's original position on raising issues with host governments. By adopting a legalistic approach and distancing itself rather than engaging critics and exploring possible remedies, Coca Cola may have missed an opportunity to manage a supply chain risk to its reputation, gather accurate information, and promote human rights in the communities where it both sources and sells its product.

Leading companies also think carefully about the expertise their organization can and cannot provide, and seek expert partners when appropriate. When the international sporting goods industry addressed child labor in the production of soccer balls, the industry partnered with the International Labor Organization for its expertise monitoring workplace standards and with the humanitarian organizations UNICEF and Save the Children for their expertise devising social protection programs for displaced child workers.

To be sure, the main objective of many corporate critics is publicity and not improved corporate performance, but when an issue raised by critics is likely to be a concern shared by reasonable corporate stakeholders, it is in the company's interest to engage critics and seek out credible experts.

How Much Responsibility Is Too Much Responsibility?   No company can, or should, assume responsibility for all the issues of concern to its stakeholders. Leading companies evaluate and prioritize the corporate responsibility issues they face and devote corporate responsibility resources accordingly.

Corporate responsibility programs are an opportunity for a company to define its responsibilities consistent with the firm's "sphere of influence." The sphere of influence concept is based on the notion that a high degree of influence carries a high degree of responsibility. Conversely, where a company has little impact or control, its responsibility is correspondingly small.

The influence a company has over social and environmental conditions varies depending on the company's industry, operations, geography, relationships, and products. An apparel brand sourcing products from independently owned factories may have little influence over local government human rights policies, whereas an oil company that represents substantial direct foreign investment in that same country may have a great deal of influence over government policies and therefore a much higher degree of responsibility. Working conditions for a company's own employees are at the center of the company's sphere of influence, as are the environmental impacts of a company's own facilities.

Beyond the workplace, a company's sphere of influence may extend to its suppliers, the communities where it operates, the government, or even its customers or those who use its products. Shell, for example, defines its human rights sphere of influence to include the human rights conditions of its own employees, of the employees of Shell's principal suppliers and business partners, and in the communities and markets where Shell operates.[27] A company's sphere of influence is also a function of the conditions at issue. Agricultural and heavy manufacturing companies have environmental impacts that technology companies do not. Arms manufacturers and tobacco companies produce products that raise stakeholder concerns about their end use. Drug companies face issues of access to healthcare and the role of the private sector addressing global health threats such as HIV/AIDS.

Companies can fall into the trap of accepting too much responsibility when it is other actors—local governments, for example—that must act to achieve lasting improvements. The issue of freedom of association in China illustrates the limits of corporate influence. Companies operating in China, such as Nike, Mattel, and Gap, all have codes of conduct for employees and suppliers that protect the fundamental right of free association. But no such right is protected in China, where independent organizations are illegal and the government restricts most forms of association. Companies have experimented with parallel means of achieving authentic worker representation in Chinese factories, but true freedom of association can only come when government acts to ensure it. Freedom of association is a human rights expectation of stakeholders that companies can influence within their own operations, but not necessarily beyond the factory walls.

An appropriate and clearly articulated definition of a company's sphere of influence, consistent with a company's business, can go a long way toward meeting the nonfinancial expectations of stakeholders.

Conversely, companies that seek to define their influence and responsibilities too narrowly risk a stakeholder backlash. The energy company, Unocal's attempts to reframe fundamental human rights issues as something more innocuous and beyond corporate control for example—apparently coordinated messaging analogizing the abusive actions of the Burmese military protecting its pipeline to domestic law enforcement activity (or even more absurdly, firefighters)[28]—at best confused stakeholders, and at worst was perceived to be so offensive that it energized corporate critics. Notably, Unocal chose to settle the suits against it alleging complicity in human rights violations less than two weeks before it reached an agreement to be acquired by ChevronTexaco in 2005.

The way a company defines its sphere of influence will determine the appropriate scope for any corporate responsibility program. Given the wide-ranging definitions of the appropriate role of business, if a company remains silent, the terms of its responsibility will be provided by others.

How Can a Company Connect Corporate Responsibility to Business Strategy?   Stakeholders expect corporate responsibility to be an integral part of business strategy. Investors who value information on social and environmental performance want a company to explain what it is doing to incorporate sustainable practices in the company's long-term business strategy. Customers, employees, and partners look for signals that initiatives reflect an ongoing organizational commitment rather than an ad hoc response to an isolated issue.

Every business function should understand and be equipped to articulate the business case for corporate responsibility. As with all corporate strategy, corporate responsibility initiatives carry the greatest weight when led by the company's CEO and most senior executives. But unlike traditional business disciplines such as marketing and investor relations, there is no well-defined way to conduct corporate responsibility throughout the rest of the organization. Functional responsibility for corporate responsibility initiatives can be found in legal departments, operations, sourcing, government relations, investor relations, and corporate communications. Corporate responsibility efforts are most effective when they are integrated, well-understood, and rewarded at all levels of an organization, from the board to the factory floor.

Leading companies adopt initiatives that align business and corporate responsibility objectives.

> Companies need to move away from defensive actions into a proactive integration of social initiatives into business competitive strategy.
> — Michael Porter

Nike is using its corporate responsibility strategy to level the playing field among well-known apparel brands.

In 2001, Starbucks developed a preferred supplier program that provides financial incentives to coffee producers that meet minimum standards for financial transparency, social, and environmental conditions.[29] Starbucks' efforts to improve conditions and ensure sustainable supplies of coffee are an attempt to link labor standards and quality improvements, reflecting the company's concern over the future availability of coffee.

> [B]ecause of Starbucks' exceptionally high standards for quality coffee, one of our most critical needs is to secure a long-term supply of unroasted green coffee from the farmers we know and trust. The sustainability of their farms is intrinsically linked to our success.
> — Starbuck's 2001 Corporate Social Responsibility Report[30]

Starbucks expects that in five years, 70 percent of its coffee will come from Preferred Suppliers under the Program.[31]

By unilaterally disclosing all of its contract factory locations and calling for industrywide approaches to improve working conditions in apparel factories, Nike is using its corporate responsibility strategy to level the playing field among well-known apparel brands. Levi Strauss followed Nike's lead by disclosing the locations of its own suppliers in October 2005.

Communicating Corporate Responsibility

For companies in industries ranging from consumer products to energy to financial services, demonstrating corporate responsibility has become an increasingly important performance goal. Successfully communicating the ways a company maintains labor standards in its supply chain, contributes to the communities where it operates, or minimizes its environmental impact can enhance a company's reputation, protect existing operations, generate new business, and create a competitive advantage in the marketplace. Failing to meet expectations of corporate responsibility can prompt public criticism, raise the costs of doing business, and even threaten the viability of the organization itself.

As in all corporate disciplines, actions speak louder than words when communicating corporate responsibility. Managers should resist the temptation to try to demonstrate corporate responsibility via press release or advertising. Corporate communications and marketing should support, not drive, corporate responsibility programs. The most effective corporate responsibility communications are corporate actions that address the concerns of stakeholders. Enforcing minimum labor standards in your supply chain is more effective than issuing a statement to explain why the company was unaware that its main supplier fired employees for attempting to organize or routinely administered pregnancy tests to prospective employees.

> As in all corporate disciplines, actions speak louder than words when communicating corporate responsibility.

Attempting to "spin" issues of corporate responsibility is even worse. In the 1990s, the U.S. energy company Unocal faced intense criticism over its pipeline project in Burma from activists who alleged that the company was complicit in human rights abuses committed by the military to clear the pipeline route. In a 1996 internal e-mail to a Unocal spokesperson, a company executive advised a colleague how not to answer difficult questions: "By saying we influenced the army not to move a village, you introduce the concept that they would do such a thing; whereas, by saying that no villages have been moved, you skirt the issue of whether it could happen or not."[32]

Communication that avoids or hides the underlying facts never meets the expectations of stakeholders. In fact, Unocal had known of the Burmese government's poor human rights record and common use of forced labor in support of infrastructure projects since before the company invested in Burma in 1992. Recently, Unocal settled a lawsuit that accused the company of complicity with government security forces that used forced labor to clear the pipeline route. In 2005, facing various lawsuits brought by Burmese villagers at the same time it was engaged in merger discussions, Unocal ultimately agreed to compensate the villagers who had sued the company for complicity in forced labor and other human rights abuses.

Companies that view corporate responsibility as simply a public relations issue, or that fail to take any meaningful action to improve performance or address deficiencies, unnecessarily increase their legal, regulatory, and reputational exposure.

Assertions of corporate responsibility without the appropriate due diligence, policies, and procedures in place to back them up will do more harm than good. Critical stakeholders will quickly point out any inconsistencies between word and deed. Given the inherent news value to journalists of stories of corporate misdeeds and mistakes, encouraging media coverage before the underlying corporate actions are in place is likely to backfire. Stakeholders who are not otherwise focused on the company may then become concerned based on the company's own communications.

As with all corporate communication, you must understand your audiences and available communications tools to effectively communicate corporate responsibility.

Audiences

The audiences for corporate responsibility include every traditional constituency—customers, employees and investors—and extend beyond a company's direct relationships to include the media, investment analysts, regulators, policymakers, international organizations, and the vast array of "civil society" groups active on corporate responsibility issues. The number of these organizations is growing rapidly. Nongovernmental organizations engaged in the corporate responsibility debate include human rights organizations, environmental groups, labor unions, and development organizations. International organizations including the United Nations, the International Labor Organization (ILO), the World Bank, and the Organization for Economic Cooperation and Development (OECD) are active in the corporate responsibility field. Trade groups devoted to corporate responsibility support the emerging discipline, conduct research, and promote the sharing of best practices.[33]

Leading companies take into account the expectations of each of these audiences and make sure that stakeholders understand their corporate responsibility efforts. Effectively communicating to these audiences draws on resources throughout the firm, which may include investor, government, media and community relations; sales and marketing; product development and sourcing; the legal department and human resources.

Communicating to internal audiences is just as important as reaching external audiences. Employees need to understand a company's corporate responsibility policies and practices. A recent survey found that senior executives hold more optimistic views of the success and impact of these programs than corporate responsibility managers, suggesting that senior executives could do a better job communicating corporate responsibility objectives to their managers, and managers can do a better job setting expectations for senior executives [34]

Choosing language carefully is particularly important. The topics may be unfamiliar both for the audience and for the spokespeople. An abstract concept like human rights, for example, may be difficult to explain in corporate settings, but employees and other corporate audiences will easily understand the importance of adequate working conditions, nondiscriminatory treatment, and protections against abusive treatment.

Although the audiences are diverse, they all share the expectation that corporate responsibility communications embrace common principles.

Principles

The most effective communications are accurate, transparent, and credible.

Accuracy. Responsibility begins with accurate information. Companies often find themselves in crisis mode when they first publicly address corporate responsibility. Facing accusations of irresponsible practices—sweatshop working conditions, complicity with human rights violations, poor environmental practices—companies must first provide accurate information.

> When challenged, the industry could not say confidently that its supply chain was free of child labor.

Without a clear understanding of conditions on the ground, companies cannot respond to critics or improve performance. Sporting goods manufacturers were caught flat-footed in 1995 when media accounts portrayed thousands of children stitching soccer balls in Pakistan. Nike, Reebok, and other companies had codes of conduct that prohibited child labor, but had failed to implement the standards beyond their principal Pakistani suppliers. When challenged, the industry could not say confidently that its supply chain was free of child labor. In fact, children were stitching soccer balls at home in an extensive subcontracting network.

The critical first step for the sporting goods industry to demonstrate corporate responsibility was to commission local experts to survey the role of child workers in soccer ball production. Contrary to the most sensational media accounts, the survey found that the worst forms of child labor were not prevalent and the number of young children affected was smaller than originally reported. Sporting goods brands, once they understood the reality on the ground, convinced their suppliers to eliminate home stitching and monitor the age of workers.[35]

Accurate information not only informs smart business decisions, it minimizes the legal and regulatory risks associated with public communications. Nike, for example, got into legal trouble when critics challenged the company's public statements on working conditions in foreign factories. (See

"Legal Considerations" below.) Unocal recently settled a lawsuit brought by Burmese villagers who accused the oil company of complicity with government security forces that used forced labor to clear a pipeline route. A key issue in the case was whether the company knew that Burmese security forces would forcibly displace and enslave local villagers to clear a path for the company's pipeline. During the proceedings, a U.S. federal court found that there was sufficient evidence that Unocal should have known that the Burmese security forces were violating human rights in connection with Unocal's operations.[36] Appropriate due diligence should have shaped both corporate action and communication.

Allegations of corporate irresponsibility often prompt calls for government regulation of corporate conduct. Companies that engage policymakers with reliable information and demonstrate that they are taking an issue seriously can reduce pressure for regulatory action. When U.S. chocolate manufacturer Hershey Foods was confronted with news accounts of child trafficking and slave labor on West African cocoa farms, the company's initial response was one of bewilderment: "[N]o one . . . had ever heard of this. Your instinct is that Hershey should have known. But the fact is we didn't know."[37] Shortly thereafter, under threat of U.S. legislation that would ban cocoa imports from West Africa, chocolate companies and the global cocoa industry mobilized around the issue, commissioned independent research to assess working conditions, and averted legislation or regulatory action by committing to a voluntary, industrywide program to eliminate the worst forms of child labor from cocoa production.[38]

Accurate information is just as important for advocates who seek to improve corporate performance. A common set of facts provides a basis for engagement and collaboration among stakeholders. In 2001, for example, after Mexican police intervened in an apparel factory labor dispute, factory customers Nike and Reebok worked with independent factory monitoring and labor rights organizations to establish common findings on factory conditions, worker sentiments, and applicable law. Agreement on the origins of the dispute allowed the apparel companies and their various stakeholders to work with factory management to reinstate illegally fired workers and protect the right to organize. The collaborative effort based on common facts resulted in the first independent union in the Mexican maquiladora sector and met the expectations of key corporate stakeholders.

Transparency. Transparency—communicating accurate information that is complete, relevant, and meaningful—is a common demand of stakeholders and a feature of the most serious corporate responsibility efforts. As a rule of thumb, more information is better than less when communicating corporate responsibility. Transparency allows stakeholders to make their own assessments of corporate performance. The benefits of transparency include greater credibility with stakeholders and critics, incentives for continuous improvement, and the potential adoption of best practices by others.

Leading companies communicate complete information that provides a full picture of a company's actions and performance. When addressing efforts to enforce minimum labor standards, for example, it is insufficient for a brand that subcontracts most of its manufacturing to communicate only its efforts to enforce standards in its own facilities.

Transparency, however, is not a corporate value that companies embrace readily or without reservation. Every company that implements a compliance program faces the issue of whether, and how, to make public the program and its results. Companies that embrace full disclosure risk becoming a target of critics. No compliance program can eliminate all violations and it only takes one media exposé to damage corporate reputation. Nike opened up its contract factories in Vietnam to independent experts and the result was a very critical report. The risk is substantial for a company that has never disclosed before or a company that has been the focus of intense attention. Companies tend to make public only what is required by law. Often, that is a shortsighted strategy.

> Transparency allows stakeholders to make their own assessments of corporate performance.

In the apparel industry, for example, mounting pressure to eliminate sweatshops in the 1990s created a need for transparency that eventually outweighed corporate concerns over proprietary information and public criticism. At first, apparel brands relied on their own codes of conduct. At the urging of the Clinton administration, a number of well-known brands joined human rights advocates and labor unions in what became the Fair Labor Association (FLA). Another group of less visible brands created an industry-led initiative, the Worldwide Responsible Apparel Production Principles (WRAP). Each initiative features a level of transparency that reflects the objectives of participants. WRAP requires no reporting beyond certification by the WRAP governing board. The FLA provides public reporting that aggregates instances of noncompliance and does not identify individual factories.

During the same period, the most influential brand sourcing its products from independently owned factories worldwide, Wal-Mart, resisted any transparency in its factory monitoring programs and failed to meet the expectations of stakeholders. Confronted with allegations of abusive treatment of workers in a Chinese factory producing handbags for the company, Wal-Mart initially denied any connection to the factory, later conceding it had concealed its relationship with the factory because it was "defensive" about the issue of sweatshops.[39] Consistent with this corporate posture on corporate responsibility, Wal-Mart did not participate in any industrywide or multistakeholder initiatives. Only recently has Wal-Mart begun to publish results of its internal factory certification process and to explore collaborative monitoring initiatives with other companies. Today, Wal-Mart faces intense criticism from corporate responsibility advocates, including a class action lawsuit alleging Wal-Mart has failed to uphold its minimum standards for suppliers.

Despite, or because of, its experience as a target of criticism, Nike ultimately made the business decision to disclose all of its factory locations, having determined that the benefits of full disclosure outweighed the risks of publicizing individual violations.

Leading companies communicate relevant information. Relevance in corporate responsibility communications is analogous to materiality in financial reporting. Companies should address the issues important to their stakeholders. If a reasonable stakeholder would consider certain information to be relevant, companies should seek to disclose it.

External stakeholders want more information from companies than simply a list of corporate charitable donations. The fact that a company has donated money to a children's charity is laudable but irrelevant for the investor assessing whether a company faces human rights exposure for child labor in a particular market. The fact that a pharmaceutical company prices life-saving drugs below cost in developing countries is relevant for investors concerned about the role of the private sector providing access to medicines. Fund managers want to understand corporate positions on global warming and political contributions. Investment analysts for socially responsible investment funds rely on social and environmental performance data to reveal corporate risks, liabilities, and opportunities not revealed through financial disclosures.[40] Government officials want to know how companies are helping to address HIV/AIDS. Nongovernmental organizations (NGOs) seek to expose corporate complicity with corrupt governments and the abusive working conditions.

> Companies must overcome their cultural bias against public disclosure.

Finally, companies should provide meaningful information that is comparable, understandable, and measurable. Again, the objective is to go beyond mere compliance to demonstrate corporate action. Investors and other stakeholders want to be able to compare corporate responsibility efforts over time and to establish a basis for measuring future performance. Metrics for corporate environmental performance are well developed. Companies like BP, Shell, Ford, and GE have begun to report total greenhouse gas emissions, for example. In other areas, metrics are less helpful. It is difficult to quantify human rights risk, though there are now some creative attempts to do so.[41]

The trend is toward greater corporate transparency. Companies must overcome their cultural bias against public disclosure and seek levels of transparency sufficient to establish facts, demonstrate corporate responsibility performance, and earn credibility among stakeholders.

Credibility. Communicating corporate responsibility places a high premium on credibility. Accuracy and transparency earn credibility. Companies also earn credibility by submitting to third-party assessments, adopting widely accepted standards, acknowledging obstacles, and partnering with stakeholders. Whenever possible, companies should demonstrate that their corporate actions are aligned with the goals and expectations of independent stakeholders.

Since much of the corporate responsibility debate stems from skepticism over corporate motives, the most powerful communication of corporate responsibility comes from third parties. The opinions of credible experts and independent stakeholders almost always carry greater weight than corporate assertions. Independent third-party monitoring was one of the first expectations of stakeholders when companies began to adopt voluntary codes of conduct. Self-policing is insufficient. In response to early allegations of poor working conditions, Nike pointed to its code of conduct and said, effectively, trust us to enforce our own standards. Compliance with Nike's code was monitored by Nike itself, or by auditors hired by Nike. What might have met the expectations of stakeholders for a company with a robust reservoir of goodwill, fell short for a company under intense critical scrutiny. Nike's strategy failed in 1997 when a leaked audit report of a Nike supplier in Vietnam revealed significant health and safety violations. Eventually, Nike agreed to allow critics into its subcontracted factories and to submit to monitoring by independent organizations.

> Adopting widely accepted standards earns credibility.

Third-party assessments add little value if stakeholders can reasonably question the independence or credibility of the third party, as when Nike hired Andrew Young to produce a report on working conditions in its factories. Although Young was widely respected for his civil rights experience, he was unfamiliar with local conditions, was unable to communicate with workers directly, and was not a factory monitoring expert. Young's report for Nike was considered cursory and viewed negatively by many of Nike's stakeholders.

Adopting widely accepted standards earns credibility. Voluntary corporate standard setting is often criticized as a self-serving tactic designed to head off stricter government regulation. Companies can counter this argument by adopting standards for corporate conduct that are widely accepted by stakeholders. A recent survey of leading multistakeholder and business codes of conduct reveals an emerging core of global standards for business.[42] On human rights issues, for example, the private sector has found it useful in many instances to reference international legal standards, such as the Universal Declaration of Human Rights and ILO Conventions; voluntary standards such as the OECD Guidelines for Multinationals and the UN Global Compact;[43] and industry codes and best practices.[44]

Acknowledging problems earns credibility. Reasonable stakeholders are able to put corporate responsibility efforts in perspective. There is a limit to corporate influence; a single company cannot solve systemic problems affecting social and environmental conditions wherever they operate. When a company cannot meet the nonfinancial expectations of stakeholders, it should explain why.

Many recent corporate responsibility reports are notable for the candor with which they acknowledge failures and address obstacles to improved performance. In 2003, Gap Inc. issued its first Social Responsibility Report. In addition to describing the company's internal and third-party factory monitoring process, the report detailed the regional distribution and frequency of specific documented violations of Gap's Code of Vendor Conduct found at approved subcontractors. While Gap's reporting prompted media coverage of the poor factory conditions it revealed,[45] Gap's candor earned the company credibility among stakeholders:

> We think this goes far beyond the public relations fluff that other companies put out a lot of the time. By making some very candid admissions, they are taking an important first step toward cleaning up the problems.
>
> – Bob Jeffcott, Maquila Solidarity Network

Acknowledging problems earns credibility.

Failing to acknowledge problems and corporate limitations is more likely to damage corporate credibility than addressing stakeholder concerns directly, even if the corporate record is less than perfect.

Partnering with stakeholders earns credibility. Companies are experimenting with ways to engage stakeholders. Formal and informal processes—group consultations, stakeholder interviews, facilitated workshops, one-on-one meetings, advisory committees—allow a company to identify issues of concern, tap needed expertise, build relationships, and communicate corporate responsibility performance in a highly targeted fashion. Often, the critics and experts companies engage to collect information and improve corporate responsibility performance are the most important audiences for corporate responsibility communications.

From information gathering through program design and implementation, partnerships allow companies to share information, resources, and responsibilities. Nike has worked to restore its credibility by partnering with competitors, labor, government, and experts to improve working conditions in foreign factories. Initiatives like the Fair Labor Association and other sector-specific initiatives draw strength and credibility from the participation of diverse stakeholders.

Tools

Tools for communicating corporate responsibility include all of the traditional communication channels, as well as some unique ones, such as codes of conduct, monitoring and certification initiatives, training and education programs, and corporate responsibility reporting.

Codes of Conduct. A code of conduct is often a company's first step. The past decade has witnessed an explosion of voluntary codes of conduct to guide corporate conduct.[46]

A code of conduct communicates minimum standards for employees, suppliers, or business partners. Codes also convey messages to corporate stakeholders generally. Royal Dutch/Shell's 1997 revision of its Statement of General Business Principles was a first step toward restoring Shell's reputation among customers, the general public, and other stakeholders after the public criticism surrounding Shell's conduct in Nigeria. The changes made by Shell, particularly acknowledging the company's responsibility to "express support for fundamental human rights in line with the legitimate role of business," signaled an important corporate policy change and implicitly acknowledged that Shell had been wrong to insist that the company had no role to play advocating human rights with the governments where Shell operates. The about-face was so abrupt that *The New York Times* editorial page, which two years earlier had excoriated Shell for its failure to intervene on Saro-Wiwa's behalf, applauded Shell's new statement of principles in an editorial titled, "Citizen Shell."[47]

The content of a code communicates a company's priorities and can help define the limits of a company's responsibility. A code also provides an opportunity to reference widely accepted standards. More and more companies, for example, reference the Universal Declaration of Human Rights as the common standard for corporate human rights programs.

While codes are a useful tool, they also create an expectation of a compliance program and can become targets for criticism if companies fail to live up to the standards they set.

Monitoring and Certification. Communicating standards creates an expectation of further communications that demonstrate compliance or progress against stated goals. Companies participating in the UN Global Compact, for example, must communicate annually with stakeholders about progress implementing the Global Compact principles. Companies seek to ensure code compliance by monitoring performance through audits, surveys, inspections, and other means.

A challenge for companies is how to handle monitoring results. Companies are justifiably reluctant to make public the results of internal monitoring. It goes against corporate culture and practice to publicize any internal processes, let alone internal processes that reveal poor corporate performance.

Most companies keep code monitoring results confidential, but a number of companies have begun to share monitoring results with external parties, report instances of noncompliance, or summarize results in public reports. The agricultural importer Chiquita Brands, for example, invited independent observers to participate in the company's internal assessment of its code of conduct and the company's compliance with the multistakeholder workplace code, Social Accountability 8000, at its banana farms in Latin America. The Fair Labor Association (FLA), a multistakeholder initiative to improve working conditions in apparel production, summarizes the findings of independent monitoring visits to factories producing apparel for participating apparel brands. The FLA publishes tracking charts of individual factories that detail noncompliance findings and remediation efforts by participating companies, but identify factories by country only, not by name or address. In its own Social Responsibility Report, Gap published, by region, the number of new supplier factories evaluated and the percentage approved by its internal compliance team.

Independent certification is another way to communicate code compliance. Under the apparel industry Worldwide Responsible Apparel Production (WRAP) program, for example, an independent board certifies factory compliance with published standards without disclosing the results of independent monitoring visits. The certification itself, if issued from a credible source, communicates adherence to minimum standards. Similarly, the FLA accredits the workplace compliance programs of participating companies.

> Companies are devoting more resources to corporate responsibility training and education.

The highest levels of transparency, and the least common, are compliance mechanisms that make all monitoring results public. Since 1999, the U.S. toy maker Mattel has published the results of independent factory audits conducted at its owned and subcontracted factories, primarily in Asia. The public reports identify factories and detail findings of both compliance and noncompliance with Mattel's Global Manufacturing Principles. The mining company Freeport-McMoran has released an independent human rights assessment of its mining operations in Indonesia that found questionable links among company security personnel and the Indonesian military.[48]

Training and Education. Companies are devoting more resources to corporate responsibility training and education. Employees and business partners understand the value of successful initiatives. A key finding of a recent study of global supply chains is that companies need to educate suppliers on the business benefits of investing in higher social and environmental standards.[49] Many of the first companies to adopt codes and monitoring are now investing in building the capacity of suppliers and business partners to improve performance and meet minimum social and environmental standards.

Corporate Responsibility Reporting

"By all indications, nonfinancial reporting is on a trajectory to becoming standard business practice in the early 21st century."[50] To communicate corporate responsibility efforts and results to diverse stakeholders, companies have begun to report publicly on nonfinancial performance. More than 2,000 companies are publishing reports, including three-quarters of the world's one hundred largest companies.[51] Corporate responsibility reports demonstrate actions taken, serve as the basis for third party assurance, and are a means to share results and best practices. Companies view reports as a primary information source for socially responsible investment analysts; a vehicle for communicating with employees; a knowledge management tool; a driver of sustainability strategy; and a tool for improved risk management.[52]

The strongest reports embrace the basic principles of accuracy, transparency, and credibility. Effective corporate responsibility reports:

⇒ Prioritize issues.
⇒ Place a company's efforts in the context of business objectives and strategy.
⇒ Reference best practices and widely accepted standards.
⇒ Provide sufficient detail for stakeholders to make their own assessment of performance.
⇒ Serve as a basis to measure future performance.
⇒ Acknowledge obstacles and challenges, such as issues for which a single company's efforts are insufficient.

Reporting benefits from a management discussion, along the lines of the management discussion and analysis required in corporate financial reports. Nike's most recent corporate responsibility report, for example, includes a section titled "Management Discussion & Strategy" that provides a strategic context for the company's corporate responsibility initiatives.

Efforts are underway to standardize nonfinancial reporting. The Global Reporting Initiative (GRI), launched in 1997, is a multistakeholder process that provides a voluntary reporting framework for economic, environmental, and social issues.[53] The GRI Guidelines help companies to present a balanced picture of their corporate responsibility performance, promote comparability of corporate responsibility reports, serve as an instrument to facilitate stakeholder engagement, encourage incremental reporting, and seek to establish performance indicators for key issues. Hundreds of companies, including BP, Ford, GE, Nike, Shell, and Starbucks reference the Guidelines in their corporate responsibility reports, and many companies have published corporate responsibility reports "in accordance" with the GRI Guidelines.

One way companies have sought to strengthen their corporate responsibility reporting is by convening committees of independent experts to publicly critique their reports. The Gap, Nike, and Ford include statements from independent experts in their most recent reports. Constructive feedback from stakeholder groups can be a valuable resource for companies seeking to better understand the issues, information, and metrics of greatest interest for external stakeholders.

Legal Considerations

Corporate communication was at the center of an important legal case that shapes current thinking about what a U.S. company can and cannot say publicly about its corporate responsibility efforts.[54]

In 1998, Nike was sued for unlawful and unfair business practices under California law. The plaintiff argued that Nike's advertising and public statements about working conditions in its supply chain presented a deceptive image of the company, and that Nike falsely claimed to protect workers through its code of conduct. The communications cited in the lawsuit included corporate advertising, press releases and publications, the CEO's letters to university presidents, athletic directors, and *The New York Times*, and the CEO's remarks at Nike's annual meeting of shareholders. In these communications, Nike responded to criticisms of the working conditions in its foreign supplier factories and made assertions about labor standards and Nike's compliance efforts.

The legal question at the heart of the case, Kasky v. Nike,[55] was whether Nike's public statements about its labor practices and about working conditions in factories making its products should be considered commercial speech, like advertising, which the government can regulate for false or misleading statements; or free speech, which enjoys a higher level of protection under the United States Constitution. Nike argued that its statements were made in response to public criticism and on a public issue, calling for protection as free speech. In a 4–3 decision, the California Supreme Court found that Nike's statements were commercial in nature and intended to induce consumers to buy its products. After the U.S. Supreme Court chose not to decide the company's appeal of the California decision, Nike settled the case. As part of the settlement, Nike agreed to pay $1.5 million to the Fair Labor Association. The underlying facts of the case—whether Nike's statements were indeed false and misleading—never reached a jury.

Initially, Kasky had a chilling effect on the communication of corporate responsibility efforts in the United States. Companies began to reconsider their public statements about working conditions and corporate compliance efforts, particularly communications made in California. After Kasky was filed, Nike suspended its corporate responsibility reporting for four years and declined invitations to speak on corporate responsibility issues in public fora in California.

Most companies active on corporate responsibility issues, however, including Nike, have concluded that the benefits of communicating outweigh the risks of litigation or of not communicating at all. Kasky reinforced the need for accuracy. Companies are more careful to ensure the accuracy of what they say, but they continue to communicate. In 2004, Gap Inc., a California-based apparel brand, issued a corporate responsibility report widely considered to be groundbreaking in its detail and scope.

Kasky highlights the need for standardized corporate reporting. Nonfinancial reporting suffers from the absence of universal, or even widely accepted, standards; no consensus on relevant indicators; and underdeveloped metrics. Nike has taken up this cause in its most recent corporate responsibility report, calling for collaboration among all stakeholders in support of common standards.[56] Defining common reporting standards and how they will be enforced will be near the top of the agenda for the next generation of executives responsible for communicating corporate responsibility.

Best Practices for Communicating Corporate Responsibility

Companies that take corporate responsibility seriously have developed a variety of best practices, including the following:

1. Engage critics and experts
2. Define the company's "sphere of influence"
3. Connect corporate responsibility to business strategy
4. Integrate corporate responsibility efforts throughout the organization
5. Demonstrate responsibility; do not assert it
6. Understand your audiences and tools
7. Communicate internally as well as externally
8. Provide accurate information
9. Be transparent
10. Prioritize issues important to stakeholders
11. Measure performance
12. Earn credibility
13. Submit to third-party assessments
14. Adopt widely-accepted standards

15. Acknowledge challenges and obstacles
16. Partner with stakeholders
17. Adopt common reporting standards, such as the Global Reporting Initiative Guidelines

Resources for Further Study

Further Reading

John Elkington, *Cannibals with Forks: The Triple Bottom Line of 21ˢᵗ Century Business* (1997).

Anthony P. Ewing, *Understanding the Global Compact Human Rights Principles, and Implementing the Global Compact Human Rights Principles*, in United Nations Global Compact and the Office of the High Commissioner for Human Rights, Embedding Human Rights into Business Practice (2004), available at http://www.unglobalcompact.org.

Harvard Business Review, On *Corporate Responsibility* (2003).

Elliot J. Schrage, *Promoting International Worker Rights Through Private Voluntary Initiatives: Public Relations or Public Policy?* (University of Iowa Center for Human Rights, January 2004), available at http://www.uichr.org/content/act/sponsored/gwri_report.pdf.

World Bank, *Strengthening Implementation of Corporate Social Responsibility in Global Supply Chains* (October 2003).

Web sites

Business & Human Rights Resource Centre
http://www.business-humanrights.org
Business for Social Responsibility (USA)
http://www.bsr.org
Global Reporting Initiative
http://www.globalreporting.org
International Business Leaders Forum
http://www.iblf.org
United Nations Global Compact
http://www.unglobalcompact.org

Noteworthy Corporate Responsibility Reports

BP (http://www.bp.com/extendedsectiongenericarticle.do?categoryId=9002276&contentId=7005391)
Chiquita Brands (http://www.chiquita.com/chiquitacr02/default.htm)
Fair Labor Association (http://www.fairlabor.org/2005report/)
Gap (http://www.gapinc.com/public/SocialResponsibility/sr_report.shtml)
General Electric Company (http://www.ge.com/en/citizenship/)

Ford Motor Company[57] (http://www.ford.com/en/company/about/sustainability/default.htm)

International Center for Corporate Accountability (Mattel and Freeport McMorRan reports) (http://www.icca-corporateaccountability.org)

Nike (http://www.nike.com/nikebiz/nikebiz.jhtml?page=29&item=fy04)

Novo Nordisk (http://www.novonordisk.com/sustainability/reports/reports.asp)

Pfizer (http://www.pfizer.com/pfizer/subsites/corporate_citizenship/report/index.jsp)

Shell (http://www.shell.com)

Starbucks (http://www.starbucks.com/aboutus/csrannualreport.asp)

Questions for Further Discussion

1. What is the relationship between corporate responsibility and legal compliance?
2. What is the relationship between corporate responsibility and business ethics?
3. How important is the concept of a company's "sphere of influence" in determining corporate responsibility standards?
4. What are various ways that a company can link corporate responsibility to business strategies?
5. What is the relationship between corporate responsibility and corporate communication?

CHAPTER 14

Challenges and Opportunities in Public Relations and Corporate Communication

> *The greatest challenge of communication is the illusion that it has taken place.*
>
> — George Bernard Shaw

It's not easy, ProCom. But you're on the right road.

An organization's reputation is the sum of how its various stakeholders view it. But all too often companies leave such stakeholder perceptions to chance.

Enlightened companies know that an effective corporate or organizational communication process can both enhance and protect its reputation. And they also know that reputation, while an intangible asset, provides a number of tangible benefits to the company.

Fordham University Business School professor Kevin T. Jackson describes the benefits of a strong reputation in his book Building Reputational Capital: *"A critical mass of credible evidence is showing a link between superior corporate reputations and financial performance … Companies with above-average overall corporate reputation scores demonstrate greater ability to sustain or attain an above-average return on assets."[1]*

Professor Jackson also elaborates some of the benefits such a reputation provides, noting that firms gain sustainable competitive advantage by cultivating intangible and inimitable assets, based on their ability to maintain the confidence of key constituencies: "Companies compete for clients, customers, investors, partners, employees, suppliers, and the support of local communities. A good reputation erects an intangible barrier that rivals stumble to get over. You can cut marketing expenses, command top dollar for your services, erect barriers to competition, and enjoy expanded latitude in decision-making. By itself, this competitive advantage ensures stronger long-run returns to better-reputed firms."[2]

* * * * *

A significant challenge for those who run corporate or organizational communication functions is to manage the ways the organization engages its key constituencies. Because an organization competes for the positive attention of the groups who matter to it, how it engages those constituencies has meaningful bottom-line impact. As Professor Jackson notes, effective engagement with constituencies and a strong reputation create a barrier to competition. But ineffective engagement, and weak reputation, make it easier for competitors to penetrate those barriers.

Chapters 2 through 13 focused on tangible ways to organize and manage the various forms of corporate and organizational communication, including communication intended to engage particular stakeholder audiences.

A further challenge is to make all the functions align with each other and with the operational, legal, financial, and administrative functions that collectively define the work of companies, governmental agencies, and not-for-profits.

A related challenge is for the communication function to be a respected participant in corporate deliberations, not an afterthought. Leaders of enlightened companies include reputational considerations—and the input of those whose primary job is to protect and enhance reputation—at the table when they make decisions. But that does not mean that the communication function is entitled to be at the table. It must earn the right to contribute.

This Chapter Covers

⇒ Earning a seat at the table and defining the professional communicator's role

⇒ Historical perspective: Edward L. Bernays and the roots of applied anthropology

⇒ The future of public relations and corporate communication

⇒ Sidebar: Five challenges facing the public relations practitioner today, by Judy Voss

⇒ Sidebar: Ten patterns of success in public relations, by Bill Heyman

⇒ Becoming truly strategic

Earning a Seat at the Table: Defining the Professional Communicator's Role

> As public relations becomes increasingly important to senior executives, many professional communicators find themselves marginalized as CEOs take advice from lawyers, friends, and others rather than from their chief communication officers. Professional communicators who aspire to work at the top levels of their organizations need the grounding necessary to become trusted advisors to their senior-most executives.

There are several reasons the communication function gets marginalized. Sometimes the marginalization is self-inflicted; often it is imposed by other functions such as corporate law, finance, or even by the CEO. But whether self-inflicted or imposed by others, the marginalization typically is grounded in how the communication function—and hence the leaders of that function—are defined. These reasons include:

⇒ Being cast as an implementor: the head of communication is seen as a doer rather than as a leader.

⇒ Being cast as a tactician: whether the head of communication is implementing or managing the function, communication is seen solely as a tool or tactic, and not as part of the strategic focus of the enterprise.

⇒ Being cast as part of a functional area: the head of communication is seen as a writer, or as a media person, or as a technology person, and not as having enterprise-wide standing to offer advice beyond the narrow functional area.

There are a number of ways to overcome this marginalization. At the very least, professional communicators need to learn the objective and subjective factors that leaders use to choose whom to listen to, and develop the skills and temperaments necessary to become trusted advisors to management. Three skills, or areas of expertise, are especially necessary.

⇒ First, in order to speak for the organization, and to have standing to advise on how the organization should communicate, a communicator must have a thorough knowledge of its operations and of finance, product development, marketing, and human resources.

⇒ Second, the communicator must have a worldview that includes knowledge of issues that affect the company, its industry, the marketplace in general, and emerging social trends.

⇒ And third, the communicator must possess the art of giving advice and of building trust, everything from thinking problems through from the perspective of senior executives to offering insights that would not otherwise occur to a senior management team.

> The top communicator in the company needs to be demonstrably the most gifted communicator in any meeting of senior executives.

But these three approaches, while necessary, are not sufficient. Part of the challenge to be overcome is the very word, communication. Unlike the skill-set needed for nearly every other business function, communication is a skill that every executive thinks he or she possesses. Because noncommunication executives often assume that communicators' key competence is speaking and writing, they assume that the function is something anyone could do well if only he or she had the time. After all, they have been speaking since they were young children, and reading and writing since at least first grade. The same cannot be said of manufacturing, engineering, finance, or law.

As a result, executives who would not dream of micromanaging the work product of the engineering department or the corporate law department have no problem micromanaging the work product of professional communicators. Or of bypassing the professional communicators until it is time to distribute what has been drafted (usually poorly) by others.

There are several ways to overcome this perception. The first is for the professional communicator to model communication excellence in everything he or she does. The top communicator in the company needs to be demonstrably the most gifted communicator in any meeting of senior executives.

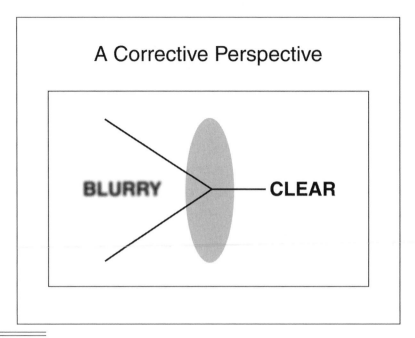

A Corrective Perspective

BLURRY   CLEAR

Figure 14.1

But the bigger challenge is to frame the communication role as something more than words on paper or in electronic format, as more than the simple transmission of information from the company to its audiences. The key is to define the communication role in terms of the constituency groups who matter to executives. The primary value of a senior communication executive is less about transmitting information—the typical definition of "communications"—than about predicting how the constituencies who matter to senior management are likely to behave.

One of the most important roles of the professional communicator is to provide a perspective on constituency behavior that an organization would not otherwise have access to. In this sense, the professional communicator's role is like a lens: to provide a corrective perspective to bring into focus what may be unclear to the executive team.

The corrective perspective works in both directions: the professional communicator helps a management team understand how any given constituency is likely to think, feel, and behave in any given circumstance; the communicator also helps bring a company's desired perception into focus for the constituency.

Doorley and Garcia have long believed that professional communicators are valued not only because of their communication skills, but rather because of their ability to predict how groups who matter to management are likely to behave, and further to predict how to get those groups to behave in more beneficial ways. In this sense professional communicators, doing their best work, function as applied anthropologists.

> The professional communicator helps a management team understand how any given constituency is likely to think, feel.

Like any anthropologist, the best communicators undertake rigorous observation of the behavior of individual groups. Such groups could include any or all of the following:

Customers
Employees
Investors
Regulators
Legislators and federal and state executive branch officials
Business partners
Lenders
Suppliers and vendors
Communities in which a company does business
Competitors
Academics and other thought leaders such as think tanks and industry experts
Industry associations
Contract sales force, such as agents, brokers, and dealers
The news media
Society at large
Any subset of any of the above

The best communicators further diagnose the values systems, social relationships, and power relationships within any given group, and among various groups. They understand what drives behavior within those groups, and understand how particular decisions are triggered and how a group's behavior plays out.

They can advise on how any given action or communication is likely to be interpreted by the group in question and how the behavior of any one group is likely to influence the behavior of the others.

Finally, professional communicators help mobilize the resources of their organizations to affect the behavior of those groups in ways that are more beneficial, that enhance the groups' relationship with the organization and that affirmatively contribute to a better reputation.

So the knowledge base of professional communicators is not just the mechanics of communication, or the industry or sector of the organization. Rather, like any anthropologist, the knowledge base involves understanding how to influence the groups that matter to the organization. Most of the chapters of this book address ways to assure the most effective engagement of these groups for mutual benefit.

In most organizations there are structures to deal with each specific constituency. So the sales force deals with customers; human resources deals with employees; finance deals with bankers and investors; corporate law with regulators and legislators; and so on.

But the only standing structure whose mandate includes understanding all of these constituencies, and the links among them, is the corporate or organizational communication function. Those who preside over corporate or organizational communication need to understand these links, and to be able to harvest the best knowledge about any given constituency. So the professional communicator needs to be able to diagnose behavior and prescribe a response beyond the individual silos that create barriers between functional areas in a company. This cross-silo insight is a core competence, and one of the keys to reversing the marginalization of the function.

The ability to see patterns early, and to help a company influence the way a pattern plays out, can be greatly valued by a company's management team. The ability to engage management with a discussion of patterns and predictions of group behavior allows a professional communicator to argue persuasively in favor of taking difficult business decisions, even decisions that are contrary to the advice of other members of management who have their own expertise, such as lawyers, finance officers, or scientists.

Finally, to overcome the marginalization of the function, and to demonstrate value beyond what is otherwise seen as the tactical practice of communication, the professional communicator should generally avoid discussion of communication tactics and implementation with senior management. Rather, the focus should be more strategic, on the outcomes that are desired among the constituencies who matter: what do we want our customers, employees, investors, communities, and other core constituencies to think, feel, know, and do? What do we need to do or not do, to say or not say, to cause them to think, feel, know, and do these things? Only after reaching agreement on desired end states should the discussion focus on the mechanics of making that happen: on the tactics of communication. (More on being strategic follows at the end of the chapter.)

Historical Perspective: Edward L. Bernays and the Roots of Applied Anthropology

The seminal thinking about public relations as applied anthropology dates to the 1920s. One of the fathers of modern public relations was Edward L. Bernays, who worked on the U.S. government committee that shaped U.S. public opinion during World War I, and who was the first person to call himself a public relations counselor. In 1923 Bernays taught the first university course in public relations—at New York University, where Fred and John now teach. In that year he also published the first book on modern public relations, *Crystallizing Public Opinion*. Bernays described public relations as "the vocation of the social scientist who advises clients on social attitudes and on the actions to take to win support of the public upon whom the viability of the client depends."[3]

Bernays writes, "The public relations counsel is first of all a student … [whose] field of study is the public mind. His textbooks for this study are the facts of life … He brings the talent of his intuitive understanding to the aid of his practical and psychological tests and surveys."[4]

Bernays adds:

The public relations counsel must discover why it is that a public opinion exists independently of church, school, press, lecture platform, and motion picture screen——how far this public opinion affects these institutions and how far these institutions affect public opinion. He must discover what the stimuli are to which public opinion responds most readily. To his understanding of what he actually can measure he must add a thorough knowledge of the principles which govern individual and group action. A fundamental study of group and individual psychology is required before the public relations counsel can determine how readily individuals or groups will accept modifications of viewpoints or policies. [5]

It describes the public relations counselor as a social scientist—essentially 1923 vocabulary for an applied anthropologist.

Bernays' description of public relations has direct bearing on professional communication for many reasons, not the least of which is that it does not mention the mechanics of communication at all. Rather, it focuses on how those who matter to a company think and feel, and how to get them to think and feel differently. It focuses on social attitudes and on the actions a company must take to win support. It describes the public relations counselor as a social scientist—essentially 1923 vocabulary for an applied anthropologist. Even the title of his book, *Crystallizing Public Opinion*, focuses not on the mechanics of communication but on the outcome.

Bernays' description also recognizes that the most effective way to change groups' perceptions is to act in certain ways, and that communication needs to be grounded first in the action a company takes. He says that a public relations practitioner is "as much an advisor on actions as he is the communicator of these actions to the public … He acts in this capacity as a consultant both in interpreting the public to his client and in helping to interpret his client to the public. He helps to mould the action of his client as well as to mould public opinion."[6]

Bernays also recognized that groups—in modern vocabulary constituencies such as those listed above—behave in predictable, if shifting, ways: "The public relations counsel works with public opinion. Public opinion is the product of individual minds. Individual minds make up the group mind. And the established order of things is maintained by the inertia of the group. Three factors make it possible for the public relations counsel to overcome even this inertia. These are, first, the [overlapping] group formation of society; second, the continuous shifting of groups; third, the changed physical conditions to which groups respond. All of these are brought about by the natural inherent flexibility of individual human nature."[7]

And finally, Bernays notes that the interaction between a company and its critical constituencies is not a one-time event, but rather continues over time, and each interaction is shaped by prior interactions and reactions: "Action and interaction are continually going on between the forces projected out to the public and the public itself. The public relations counsel must understand this fact in its broadest and most detailed implications. He must understand not only what these various forces are, but he must be able to evaluate their relative powers with fair accuracy."[8]

Bernays recognizes that the value of the public relations counselor—and today the value of any professional communicator—is the ability to advise on the ongoing engagement between a company and its critical constituencies, and in particular how a company's engagement is likely to influence how that constituency is likely to think, feel, and behave across a number of scenarios.

Bernays' description of public relations—as a vocation applied by a social scientist who advises clients on actions to take to win support of the public on whom the clients' viability depends—is a good way for a professional communicator to see his or her role.

The Future of Public Relations and Corporate Communication

Fortune magazine, drawing on U.S. Bureau of Labor Statistics figures, projects that public relations will be among the ten fastest growing professions in the United States over the next ten years.[9]

This growth is due mainly to three trends, according to John Paluszek, senior counsel to Ketchum Public Relations and past president of the Public Relations Society of America:

⇒ PR is important today to every major institution: for-profits, not-for-profits, governments, and religions.
⇒ Increasingly, institutions recognize that they practice many kinds of communication with many constituencies, and that they must all be coordinated, which is the proper role of public relations or its subset corporate communication.
⇒ Public relations is being practiced around the globe.

Paluszek, at a professional development seminar sponsored by the M.S. degree program in public relations and corporate communications at New York University, said that the profession "is at its pinnacle, in terms of challenges and opportunities," and that his only regret is "that I am not starting out now."

The following sidebars describe how two industry experts view the challenges facing the profession today, and the qualities that make for a successful professional communicator.

Five Challenges Facing the Public Relations Practitioner Today

By Judy Voss, APR,
Director of professional development,
Public Relations Society of America (http://www. prsa.org.)

Successfully conquering today's challenges will give you the experience and perspective you need to secure your organization's reputation, and keep you employed for a long time to come. From my point of view, these five challenges are the most critical:

1. Tell the Truth. Prove It with Action.

Ethics is at the top of my list of challenges. I am quoting two Arthur Page Society* principles in the subhead above. Page, a pioneer in the practice of public relations, served as the first vice president of public relations for AT&T beginning in 1927. He set the standards for the position as it related to strategic public relations in corporate management. He counseled corporations and several U.S. presidents, always managing their reputations supported with ethical conduct. The Page persona is missing today.

I asked a colleague, Tom Vitelli, APR, Fellow PRSA, assistant vice president, public relations and advertising for Intermountain Health Care, Salt Lake City, UT, about challenges he sees in the field. Ethics is also at the top of his list. He comments: "Ethics are a foundation for credibility, and credibility is a foundation of business development. It should be possible for PR firms and professionals to deliver their services on the basis of ethical advocacy as well as effectiveness in the achievement of business goals."

Public relations professionals who aspire to sit at the management table, to develop policy and participate in strategic planning to meet business goals must choose to demonstrate ethical behavior. You must think ethics, feel ethics, communicate ethics. That is your challenge.

Your CEOs and CFOs must be counseled to do the right thing in all cases at all times. Period. Corporate leaders read newspapers and listen to CNN. They see dishonest corporate leaders getting caught and going to jail. So those leaders who dare to think or act without considering ethics should be prepared for a downfall with no sympathy from their publics. Or their public relations counselor after the fact. Period.

* The Arthur Page Society can be found at http://www.awpagesociety.com/.

2. New Communications Technologies

Second on my list of challenges facing the PR practitioner today is how to keep up with changes in the new communications technology field. As a professional, you must pay attention to technology plus experience it yourself in order to learn just how powerful the new tools are. You obviously have to know the media habits of your publics. In 2006's segmented markets you may choose to reach them using blogs, wikis, RSS feeds, or podcasting to get your company's message to them. (After 2006, who knows? But it will be interesting.) After all, in this day of participative journalism, new technology is how your publics are reaching you, talking about your company, offering their opinions about your company's reputation.

Mixing the new technology with the "old fashioned" television and radio broadcasting, print advertising, and direct mail will be the constant challenge. I never thought I would consider faxing as a type of direct mail, but today I do.

3. Globalization

Third on my list is the globalization of companies. The fact that corporations buy and partner with their counterparts in other countries means having to understand language and culture barriers. Certainly technology has shrunk the world. Our friends are closer—so are our enemies.

As much as the practice of public relations emphasizes working things out—solidifying relationships and building a better community—not everyone is listening. Americans are finding out just how much some of the world hates us. The process of globalization is where we have the most to learn and gain. Globalization, in the long run, will impact individuals, jobs, our economy, security, and power base.

4. The Media

Another colleague I turned to for the challenges she faces is Melissa May, APR, public information director for the Population Council, New York, NY. Journalists show up prominently on her list of challenges. She cites such media challenges as journalists' failure to fully explore topics, and their focus on titillating news. She goes on to mention media spinning and says, "I've been troubled by the habit of some journalists to print ideological language and concepts as if they are reality, using the language of extremists and incorporating it into journalistic lexicon ... lending the terms credibility by repeating them."

Her examples include the media "describing a judge whose political leaning is different from yours as a 'judicial activist'" or "the purposeful confusion over . . . emergency contraception and how reporters continue to discuss this medicine as if it were abortion, when the research shows that it prevents pregnancy, thus actually reducing the numbers of abortions."

She points out that "Some terms used by reporters today may have started out as quotes by people on one side of an argument, but they soon were incorporated into coverage as standard language, skewing the perception of these issues by readers, listeners, and viewers. It seems more and more that reporters come into interviews with their minds made up and are simply looking for quotes to reinforce the story they have already written," says May.

5. Survival

The guidance you are receiving while reading this book will help prepare you to meet the challenges listed above. In addition, I see the list of character traits below as "must-haves" for the new millennium public relations professional. To not have them is an additional, very personal challenge.

⇒ Ambition – searching for opportunities to showcase your strengths and move up in the world.
⇒ Knowledge – keeping up with changes, and wanting to participate with the new technology tools and whatever the future holds.
⇒ Energy – eating, sleeping, and staying fit; doing what you have to do to be proactive and responsive at work.
⇒ Joy – liking what you do; enjoying your job while helping others carry out their own job.
⇒ Curiosity – being inquisitive not only about work but also your entire environment; developing your perspective.
⇒ Caring – having integrity and sincerity as a base for coming into the public relations profession in the first place; staying in touch with these feelings as you grow in your career.

Back to the Arthur Page Society for one more principle: "Conduct public relations as if the whole company depends on it." We continue to see from today's headlines and the PR practitioner's capabilities to manage a company's reputation, that indeed, the whole company does depend on it.

Ten Patterns of Success in Public Relations

By Bill Heyman,
President, Heyman Associates

Why is one public relations executive more successful than another? Why do some PR careers derail while others soar? What factors contribute most to success in public relations?

In 2004 Heyman Associates partnered with graduate students from the University of Alabama, who conducted thirty-minute telephone interviews with ninety-seven high-level public relations executives from leading U.S. corporations, agencies, nonprofits, and educational institutions. They were first asked to define success in the field, and then to discuss factors in their own success, favorable tipping points in their careers, potential career derailers, characteristics of "ideal" job candidates, and limitations on their professional power.

Profile of the Executives

The executives interviewed shared two characteristics: They were the highest-level PR leaders in their organizations, and they were seasoned professionals, averaging more than twenty-three years of experience. Beyond these two similarities, the sample was deliberately selected to be diverse.

Our sample of ninety-seven executives included thirty-nine women and fifty-eight men whose educational backgrounds represented eighteen fields of study, though most had studied in one of five areas: public relations or communication (twenty-four executives), business (twenty-one), journalism (fifteen), political science (ten), and English (nine). The executives also represented diverse organizations, including corporations in nine industries (sixty executives), PR agencies (sixteen), nonprofits (nine), educational institutions (six), and professional service firms (six).

The results indicated there is no "Holy Grail of Success," or specific universal characteristics and credentials of successful PR executives.

However, ten themes or patterns of success emerged from the study, which highlight important factors that contribute to success in PR. Although some of the patterns reflect conventional wisdom, the interviews added new dimensions and insights into such themes. There is no other in-depth empirical study that examines success factors in public relations leadership from the perspectives of senior leaders. Thus, this study breaks new ground and makes an important contribution to understanding success in the field.

1. PR Success Is an Individual, Organizational, and Group Achievement.

The executives used more than ninety descriptive words or phrases to define success in public relations; for example, becoming a trusted adviser, meeting objectives, gaining financial rewards, and growing the business. The collective answers, however, suggest that PR leaders see success primarily at three levels: the individual, the organization, and the group or work unit, in that order.

2. Many Pathways May Lead to Success in PR Leadership.

There is not one golden path to success in public relations leadership—there are many. The interviewees possess diverse educational backgrounds and professional experiences across different types of organizations.

The leaders identified more than sixty success factors and tipping points in their own careers. These ranged from particular skill sets or experiences (forty executives), to risk-taking and successful crisis management experiences (thirty-two), to incremental advances over time based on experiences (thirteen), to serendipity, simply being at the right place at the right time (eleven).

3. Performance Lights the Pathway to Success.

The power of performance was the most distinctive pattern, underscoring the idea that excellence on the job—solving problems, meeting objectives, providing valuable counsel and producing results—is a requirement for success.

Performance track record was cited as the second most valuable influencing factor by the executives, while incompetence was identified as a leading career derailer. In addition, successful project or crisis management experiences were career tipping points for nearly one-third of the executives.

But the executives added two other dimensions to this performance pattern. First, a number emphasized that excellent performance means more than being an "order taker." It also means being creative, taking risks and being willing to challenge others.

Second, outstanding performance has short- and long-term benefits. A specific project achievement can enhance recognition and provide new opportunities in the short-term, while consistent high performance over time opens doors to PR leadership positions and to key decision-making circles.

4. Years of Experience Count, But Diverse Experiences Count More.

Experience was also a primary source of influence in decision making, and a number of executives indicated that the accumulation of experiences over time was a favorable tipping point in their careers. Some said the quality and diversity of experiences was a factor in their own success; it was important in hiring others as well.

Working on different projects, in different organizations, in different locations with different people will be increasingly important in our rapidly evolving and globalizing world. These diverse experiences help professionals develop problem-solving and negotiation skills in differing contexts, enhance interpersonal communication skills with a variety of people, and build a reservoir of knowledge—creating experiences to draw from in strategic and tactical decision making.

5. At the Top Level, Communication Skills are More Than Just Writing.

The importance of technical communication skills was also highlighted in the study. But the PR leaders ranged far beyond the requirement for excellent writing skills, indicating a more complex set of communication skills required for success in leadership positions. These skills refer to the analytical, tactical, and strategic thinking that underlie effective communication planning and campaigns.

Executives also said communication encompasses vital interpersonal skills and the ability to build and cultivate effective relationships and coalitions with others. At the highest level, communication skills refer to how persuasive and influential professionals can be with CEOs and other powerful decision makers, both inside and outside organizations.

6. Relationships, Relationships, Relationships.

Public relations is all about developing and nurturing relationships, but we often link such relationships to external audiences, from media to government. The study, however, emphasized the importance of relationships inside the organization. Nearly half of the executives said the most valuable source of influence they possessed was relationships with senior executives, peers, and subordinates.

Overall, the findings hint that relationships may provide more power to professionals than their titles or formal positions in organizations. So who you know does count, according to the interview group, and so does who else you get to know and how you cultivate and nurture enduring relationships.

7. Proactivity and Passion Pay Off.

Call them go-getters, self-starters, risk-takers, opportunity-seekers, or just high energy, curious and committed individuals—a number of successful PR leaders point to the importance of being proactive on the job and passionate about the practice.

They said proactive natures and self-starting capabilities were crucial to success, as well as important characteristics in new hires and valuable qualities for aspiring professionals. A third of the executives also cited a crisis or project management experience, risky opportunities for which they volunteered.

Some also linked passion for work and being proactive in trying to do the right thing. Another agency leader put passion in the context of social responsibility: "PR ... has to do with doing the right thing. You can't just make a contribution to the symphony and then think that's going to make up for the fact that you're polluting the local water supply."

8. Crucial Intangibles are Rooted in Interpersonal, Relationship Skills.

"Intangibles" typically refer to such things as chemistry, likeability, fit, personality and presence. Positive personal character traits were named by eighty-four executives as the single most desired characteristic in job candidates. Developing positive personal characteristics was the second most frequently mentioned piece of advice to young professionals (by forty executives).

These traits largely reflect the intangibles listed above, which appear to have their roots in more visible interpersonal qualities and relationship-building skills. An individual's chemistry, fit, or likeability factor indicates whether the individual interacts comfortably with others, and has the ability to effectively manage well both up and down. The individual is deemed a valuable team member and integrates smoothly into organizational networks and cultures.

9. The Power of PR is Limited by Perceptions of its Role and Value.

Nearly half (45 percent) of those interviewed said the most significant limitation on public relations practice and influence is the inaccurate or incomplete perceptions of the function's role and its value by other executives.

It is significant that top-level PR executives report that their superiors do not fully understand or appreciate what public relations can do for their organizations. This places a high professional priority on eliminating deceptive practices and developing convincing metrics and case studies to better explain and justify the role and value of public relations.

10. Female and Male PR Executives View Success the Same (Almost).

Overall, female and male subjects responded in more or less similar ways. However, several modest differences were noted.

⇒ Female, more than male, executives emphasized the importance of dealing proactively on the job and the power of relationships—mentors, coalitions, and internal and external networks of relationships—in achieving success and gaining influence. Male executives more often credited their success to individual skills and the respect and credibility they gained through performance.

⇒ Male, more than female, executives suggested their influence on the job was limited by the views or (mis)perceptions of PR by other senior executives in the organization. Female executives more often explained limitations on their influence as the result of resource deficiencies or lack of formal authority.

⇒ With respect to skill sets, men highlighted the value of communication and interpersonal skills slightly more often than women, who gave somewhat greater emphasis to overall leadership and team-building skills.

These subtle differences may suggest that women see the journey to success as one accomplished in the company of others, while men may view the trip as an individual venture.

The Profile of a Highly Successful Public Relations Leader

Overall, Heyman's research suggests that a highly successful public relations leader might possess the following portfolio of attributes:

⇒ An outstanding performance record marked by individual achievements and continued high performance over time, linked to group and organizational goals.

⇒ A diverse set of experiences encompassing different types of organizations, projects, issues, skills, people, and cultures.

⇒ A multidimensional set of communication skills that work effectively at the technical, strategic, interpersonal, and persuasion/advocacy levels.

⇒ The ability to develop and nurture internal and external relationships. Professionals with dense networks of relationships appear to have greater influence in decision making and better opportunities for advancement.

⇒ A proactive nature that includes high energy, initiative, and the willingness to take risks and engage passionately in the complex work of helping organizations do the right thing.

⇒ A set of positive intangibles reflected in strong interpersonal and relationship-building skills.

⇒ A commitment to further understanding, at the highest levels, of the role and value of strategic and ethical public relations.

Based on this research, success in PR appears to involve juggling a complex set of roles, possessing excellent communication and leadership skills, gaining wisdom through diverse experiences, and achieving high performance at the individual, group, and organizational levels. The central characteristics include the ability to balance complex roles, conflicting demands, and relationships with diverse publics and tensions among individual, organizational, and societal needs.

> The most enlightened companies see communication as a strategic asset; as what in the military is known as a "force multiplier." Effective communication can help a company meet its business goals faster and better; ineffective communication can be a drag on performance.

Becoming Truly Strategic

One key to success is for those who run the communications function to organize communication strategically: focused on accomplishing defined business and communication goals.

Many communication people default to the tactical—to discussion of press releases, or e-mails, or of other tools of the trade, leading to self-marginalization. But enlightened communicators at all levels default to the strategic—to the goals that communication is intended to accomplish, and the most effective ways to accomplish those goals. Over time this strategic emphasis can become habitual, and can lead to even greater contribution to an organization's success.

Being habitually strategic means making judgments based on the goals to be accomplished, as one's first resort and not as an afterthought. It means conditioning one's behavior to resist the temptation to leap to tactics and instead to consider consequences of various forms of action and communication. And because, as Aristotle taught us (see Chapter 2), we are what we habitually do, we become strategic by deliberately and persistently behaving in goal-oriented ways, and remaining focused on a specific outcome.

Individuals become habitually strategic when they persistently weigh alternative courses of action against desired outcomes, and act on the choices that most clearly lead to those outcomes. Organizations become habitually strategic when their leaders insist that all parts of the organization act strategically as a first resort. This means encouraging strategic thinking by, among other things, rewarding strategic decisions even if they sometimes fail, and discouraging immediate defaults to the tactical even when they sometimes succeed.

Habitually strategic organizations set clear goals and hold managers accountable for reaching those goals; they persistently reinforce those goals. The classic contemporary example of a corporation behaving strategically is General Electric, which, under the tenure of chief executive officer Jack Welch, had very clear goals and strategies and held managers accountable for meeting those goals and fulfilling those strategies. Tactical execution that advanced those strategies was encouraged; tactics that distracted from the fulfillment of the strategies were discouraged, even when they were otherwise incrementally attractive. The best-known General Electric strategy during that period was to be number one or two in each of its areas of business, or to exit that sector.

Jack Welch's successor as General Electric CEO, Jeffrey Immelt, told *Fast Company* magazine the most important lesson he learned from Welch. Immelt said, "Every leader needs to clearly explain the top three things the organization is doing. If you can't, you're not leading well."[10]

Habitually strategic organizations also establish a culture of accountability, insisting that their values be lived and not merely posted on bulletin boards. And, not surprisingly, these companies find it easier to survive significant setbacks with minimal reputational, operational, and financial harm. Because all players in a company know what is expected, they manage to avoid many of the crises and much of the self-inflicted damage that plague organizations that have not developed these habits. And when the inevitable negative event happens, the organization is able to respond quickly and effectively, to take responsible action, and to communicate in ways that restore or maintain the confidence and trust of its core constituencies.

> Being habitually strategic means making judgments based on the goals to be accomplished, as one's first resort and not as an afterthought.

Those who head corporate and organizational communication can contribute to an organization's strategic success in two ways: first, they can use communication as a strategic tool that allows all stakeholders to understand what the organization's mission, vision, and values and intrinsic identity are. Second, they can establish a strategic focus for each of the elements of corporate and organizational communication: employee communication, community relations, media relations, investor relations, and so forth. They assure alignment of the various functions in support of a corporation's larger corporate goals.

What Is Strategy?

The word "strategy" is much-used and misunderstood in business and in communication. Its origins lie in warfare: the skills necessary to command an army. The English word "strategy" comes from the ancient Greek verb στρατηγεω (strategeo), to be a general or to command a military force. That verb, in turn, derives from the noun for army, στρατοσ (stratos), and the verb to lead, αγειν (agein). So the classical meaning of a strategist is a leader of a military force, what we would call a general. The word carried that meaning for much of Western history, from the Greeks to the Romans to the nineteenth Century in Europe.

Not surprisingly, then, the first prominent modern use of the word was by a military officer writing about warfare. It appeared in the classic volume on military affairs, *On War*, by the Prussian general and head of the Prussian War College, Carl von Clausewitz. His 1832 book, ostensibly about the qualities necessary to conduct a military campaign, has become a classic of military strategy, governing much U.S. war planning (except for the Vietnam war). But *On War* is useful not merely as a book about warfare. It is in many ways the seminal book on strategy itself, both military and civilian, and can provide valuable insights into business management and leadership in general and into the leadership of communication in particular.

Indeed, the Strategy Institute of the Boston Consulting Group argues that the principles elaborated upon in *On War* are essential to understanding contemporary business strategy: "Clausewitz' magnum opus … deserves, now more than ever, the full attention of the modern business strategist for accomplishing the unlikely feat of offering new ways to order thinking in disorderly times and provides steadiness in charting strategy in an unstable environment."[11]

In Clausewitz, the Boston Consulting Group finds a kind of thinking that is not restricted to military matters, but rather is an integral part of leadership—leadership that applies to business management, and also leadership as it applies to those who run communication. The key is "ordered thinking"; that is, thinking that proceeds in a certain sequence and is directed toward certain outcomes. In a time of rapid social and technological change, the more unstable the environment, the greater the need for such ordered thinking.

Too often communication is seen as soft: as sentimental, and as intended to make people feel good. But using ordered thinking to help an organization accomplish tangible goals can help change the perception of the communication function internally. A strong leader can cut through the misperception, emotion, and clutter, and can use Clausewitz's principles to guide his or her communication organization to more closely resemble the hard science of management.

The Boston Consulting Group notes: "It is the true strategist ... who can benefit most from the work of Carl von Clausewitz because *On War* is quintessentially a philosophy of strategy that contains the conceptual seeds for its constant rejuvenation. It is a philosophy that fuses logical analysis, historical understanding, psychological insight, and sociological comprehension into an encompassing exposition of strategic thought and behavior. It is a philosophy that effectively prevents strategy from ever degenerating into dogma."[12]

The Boston Consulting Group describes why Clausewitz's way of organizing thinking and courageous behavior is so important: "In its ultimate consequence, the philosophy of Clausewitz demands that commanders and executives not merely think when formulating strategy but that they arrive at a stage where they literally think strategy."[13]

In other words, by following Clausewitz one can learn to become habitually strategic. Over the years coauthor Fred Garcia has stressed that following Clausewitz holds one of the keys to effective stewardship of the organizational communication function. Clausewitz's principles can help professional communicators think clearly and organize their activities in ways that predictably help enhance an organization's reputation, operation, financial performance, and enterprise value. The ordered thinking, and the rigor that it represents, also appeals to executives and begins to neutralize the objection that communication is soft or sentimental.

Among the strategic principles Clausewitz lays out that have particular relevance to the communication function are these three:

Ends and Means: Eyes on the Prize. Clausewitz's most famous utterance is the observation that war is the continuation of policy by other means. It is part of a continuum, a tool in the service of a much broader process. But it is only a tool. Clausewitz writes: "The political object is the goal, war is the means of reaching it, and means can never be considered in isolation from their purpose."[14]

Means can never be considered in isolation from their purpose. This is the essence of habitual strategic thinking. This is Clausewitz's breakthrough concept that informs contemporary business leadership, and that can inform leadership of organizational communication.

The corollary to Clausewitz's famous observation is that organizational communication is merely the continuation of business by other means. The specific ways to communicate with constituencies are tools in a continuum of tools, all in the service of some clearly articulated business goal. And just as war is not the goal but the means, communication is not the goal, but simply the means to some other end. And since means must never be considered in isolation from their purpose, this view sees communication as the continuation of business, not as something separate from business, and in particular not as an afterthought.

The principle of the objective, as Clausewitz's principle is called, helps the habitual strategic thinker to avoid impulsive—and self-indulgent—rushes to the tactical. Rather than doing what feels good, or what has always been done, the enlightened communication leader considers the situation as it presents itself and as it is likely to evolve, identifies a clear goal or end state toward which the resources of the enterprise will be directed, and prescribes the means that are most likely to accomplish the goal or end state.

The test of whether any given tactical response should be taken is its alignment to the goal.

The leader further evaluates tactical options based on the likelihood they will contribute to the achievement of the goal, not because they make the leader feel good, or defer short-term pain or embarrassment. The test of whether any given tactical response should be taken is its alignment to the goal.

So one begins to manage communication by understanding a business goal: either a desired business outcome, or a change in the business environment. This may include enhancing employee productivity, selling more products, changing a regulatory requirement that impairs organizational performance, and so forth.

Communicating effectively, in turn, begins with a clear communication goal: a change in the emotional, intellectual, or behavioral predispositions of target constituencies. This may include improving employee morale, increasing demand for a company's products, changing regulators' minds, and so forth.

Focusing on how those who matter to management—employees, customers, investors, regulators, adversaries—think and feel, and how they are likely to think and feel in the future, is a critical part of habitual strategic thinking in communication.

It is all too common for communication professionals to measure output: the number of employee meetings held, the number of press releases issued, the number of stories published. But these are measures of process, not of goal. They are at best a weak proxy for effectiveness. Rather than focus on process, a more meaningful measure of communication impact is the degree that the communication goals—changes in constituencies' attitudes, opinions, and behavior—have been accomplished.

Action and Reaction: A second Clausewitz concept that informs contemporary business leadership and communication is his observation that war is less like art and more like commerce; he calls it an "act of will directed toward a living entity that reacts."[15] Communication is also an act of will directed toward a living entity that reacts. That living entity is the group of constituencies who matter to management; the reaction is how that group is likely to think and feel and what it is likely to do in any given postcommunication scenario.

The effective communicator grounds all planning and implementation on the desired reaction among critical constituencies. Communication is not merely the transmission of information, but the predictable reaction to that information by the audience to which it is directed.

Building in Flexibility: The third principle of Clausewitz that informs communication is his notion of friction: the innumerable small barriers to effective implementation of a strategy.

Clausewitz takes account of the inevitable distractions that interfere with the implementation of a plan: "Everything in strategy is very simple, but that does not mean that everything is very easy. Once it has been determined, from the political conditions, what a war is meant to achieve and what it can achieve, it is easy to chart the course. But great strength of character, as well as great lucidity and firmness of mind, is required in order to follow through steadily, to carry out the plan, and not to be thrown off course by thousands of diversions."[16]

Similarly, in communication, the important principles are simple. (Many are described in Chapters 1 through 13.)

But implementing the simple principles can be complicated, especially in an environment of instantaneous, linked communication, where all constituencies have near-simultaneous access to information about a company, both positive and negative. It can be difficult to keep the various communication disciplines aligned with each other and with the communication and business goals, especially as each discipline works to respond to issues that arise with the constituency over which it has responsibility.

The "thousands of diversions" Clausewitz speaks about can be a defining part of many communication tasks. For example, in many large corporate media relations departments, a common complaint is that the media rela-

Winston Churchill observed, "You'll never get to your destination if you stop to throw a rock at every dog that barks along the way."

tions staff spends so much of their time fielding incoming press inquiries that they rarely get the opportunity to think strategically and to affirmatively shape stories. One of the challenges for communication leadership in such circumstances is to create structures that are immune from the day-to-day crush of incoming inquiries and to focus intently on self-generated media visibility.

Being strategic in communication involves recognizing that there will always be real internal and external obstacles to implementing any communication plan effectively. But that should not deter one from developing the plan and being diligent in its implementation. Rather, recognizing the likelihood of obstacles allows the leader to plan for the inevitability of distraction, and to build processes to overcome, ignore, prioritize, or otherwise manage through those distractions. To use the Churchill analogy, the leader needs to recognize the likelihood that dogs will bark along the way, and build a plan that permits the organization to not allow the barking dogs to deter it from the most productive course.

Clausewitz's successor in the development of Western military strategy was Helmuth von Moltke, who served as chief of staff of the Prussian (and after unification, the German) General Staff for thirty years in the mid-to-late nineteenth century. He famously observed that no plan survives its initial implementation. Rather, each plan needs to be continuously adapted to take account of individual tactical encounters that modify what is possible and what is likely to be accomplished in the short term. But this observation does not minimize the importance of planning. Rather, it places a premium on having a clear and powerful set of goals and strategies, and recognizes that individual tactics will change as the plan is implemented. The goals and strategies, however, are unlikely to change; only the tactics, which will need to be adapted to reflect the situational reality. But the tactics are merely means, and means must never be considered in isolation from their purpose. So if the planned tactics should become ineffective in accomplishing their goals, they should be discarded in favor of other, more promising tactics.

Moltke writes:

"No plan of operations extends with certainty beyond the first encounter with the enemy's main strength. Certainly the commander in chief will keep his great objective continuously in mind, undisturbed by the vicissitudes of events. But the path on which he hopes to reach it can never be firmly established in advance. Throughout the campaign he must make a series of decisions on the basis of situations that cannot be foreseen. The successive acts of war are thus not premeditated designs, but on the contrary are spontaneous acts guided by military measures. Everything depends on penetrating the uncertainty of veiled situations to evaluate the facts, to clarify the unknown, to make decisions rapidly, and then to carry them out with strength and constancy."[17]

So the communication leader needs to develop a robust plan that clearly manifests the goals and strategies, but remains sufficiently flexible to deal with midcourse corrections based on results of the initial tactical implementation of the plan. He or she needs to develop structures to penetrate the uncertainty of veiled situations, to evaluate facts, and to have procedures to make tactical decisions quickly.

Chapter 1 opened with the observation that "If you don't know where you're going, any road will take you there." The key to successful public relations and corporate communication is to have clarity about the destination—the reputation that will help a company better accomplish its goals—and of the best path by which to get there. That path typically includes assuring that all of the communication functions of an organization are strategically grounded, well managed, and aligned with each other and with the broader activities of the enterprise. When they are, the destination is reached faster and more effectively; and the journey is considerably more enjoyable.

* * * * *

Notes

Chapter 1

1 David W. Guth and Charles Marsh, *Public Relations, A Values-Driven Approach* (Needham Heights, MA: Pearson Education, Allyn and Bacon, 2000), 292–294.
2 Charles J. Fombrun, *Reputation: Realizing Value From The Corporate Brand* (Boston: Harvard Business School Press, 1996), 376.
3 Ibid., p. 9.
4 George Cheney, *Rhetoric in an Organizational Society* (Columbia, SC: University of South Carolina Press, 1991).
5 *The New York Times* advertisement, August 29, 2005.
6 Homily by Archbishop Sean P. O'Malley, July 30, 2003, at: Archdiocese of Boston Web site, http://www.rcab.org/News/homily030730.html.
7 Kurt Eichenwald, *Conspiracy of Fools: A True Story* (New York: Broadway Books, 2005), 590.
8 Hugh Lofting, *The Story of Doctor Doolitle* (A Yearling Book, May 1988), 76.
9 Johnson & Johnson Credo at: http://www.jnj.com/our_company/our_credo/index.htm.
10 "CEO Succession 2004: The World's Most Prominent Temp Workers," by Chuck Lucier, Rob Schuyt, and Edward Tse, *Strategy + Business*, at http://www.strategy-business.com/.
11 Guth and Marsh, *Public Relations: A Values-Driven Approach*, 164.
12 Brent D. Ruben, Linda Lederman, and David W. Gibson, Eds., *Communication Theory: A Casebook Approach* (Dubuque, IA: Kendall Hunt, 2000), 173-201.
13 Watzlawick, Beavin, and Jackson, *Pragmatics of Human Communication* (New York: Norton, 1967).

Chapter 2

1 John R. MacArthur, *Second Front: Censorship and Propaganda in the Gulf War* (n.p.: Hill and Wang, 1992), 49.
2 Jack O'Dwyer, "PR Opinion/Items," *Jack O'Dwyer's Newsletter*, January 22, 1992, 4.
3 *O'Dwyer's PR Services Report*, 6, no. 8, August, 1992, 1.
4 *Public Relations Society of America Member Code of Ethics*, Approved by the PRSA Assembly, October, 2000, 13.
5 Interview with James E. Lukaszewski, APR, Fellow, PRSA, and member of PRSA Board of Ethics and Professional Standards, July 22, 2005.
6 Edward L. Bernays, *Propaganda*, with introduction by Mark Crispin Miller, IG Publishing, 1928 and 2005, 69.
7 "Enforcement and Communication of the IABC Code for Professional Communicators," p. 2 of *International Association of Business Communicators Code of Ethics for Professional Communicators*, http://www.iabc.com/members/joining/code.htm.
8 *International Association of Business Communicators Code of Ethics for Professional Communicators*, http://www.iabc.com/members/joining/code.htm.
9 Lukaszewski interview, ibid.
10 Lukaszewski interview, ibid.

11 "A Message from the PRSA Board of Ethics and Professional Standards," of *PRSA Member Code of Ethics*, ibid., p. 6.
12 *PRSA Member Code of Ethics*, ibid., p. 11.
13 *PRSA Member Code of Ethics*, ibid., p. 11.
14 *PRSA Member Code of Ethics*, ibid., p. 11.
15 John Stauber and Sheldon Rampton, *Toxic Sludge is Good for You: Lies, Damn Lies and the Public Relations Industry* (n.p., Common Courage Press, 1995), 14.
16 *Toxic Sludge is Good for You*, ibid., pp. 203–4.
17 *Toxic Sludge*, ibid., pp. 205-6.
18 *Toxic Sludge*, ibid., p. 4.
19 *Toxic Sludge*, ibid., p. 192.
20 David Barstow and Robin Stein, "Under Bush, A New Age of Prepackaged TV News," *The New York Times*, March 13, 2005, at http://www.nytimes.com/2005/3/13/politics/13covert.html.
21 "FCC Warns Broadcasters on Sourcing Video News Releases," *Reuters*, April 14, 2005, at http://www.nytimes.com/reuters/politics/politics-television-videonews.htm.
22 Quote by Michael Copps, FCC Commissioner, *Reuters*, ibid.
23 Radio-Television News Directors Association, *RTNDA Guidelines for Use of Non-Editorial Video and Audio*, 2005, developed by the RTNDA Ethics Committee, as found on the organization's Web site, http://www.rtnda.org.
24 RTNDA, ibid.
25 Sheldon Rampton, "Fake News? We Told You So, Ten Years Ago," *PR Watch*, published by Center for Media and Democracy, 12, no. 2, at http://www.prwatch.org/prwissues/2005Q2/toldyouso.html.
26 Greg Toppo, "Education Dept. Paid Commentator to Promote the Law," *USA Today*, January 7, 2005, at http://www.usatoday com/news/washington/ 2005-01-06-williams-whitehouse_x.htm.
27 Statement by Tribune Media Services, published in *Poynter Forums*, *PoynterOnline*, by the Poynter Institute, at http://www.poynter.org/forum/view_post.asp?id=8580.
28 Ben Feller, "Senators Probe Administration-Paid Journalist; Pundit Paid By Education Department Calls Move a 'Witchhunt,'" *Associated Press*, January 13, 2005.
29 Howard Kurtz, "Propaganda Wars," *Washington Post*, January 27, 2005.
30 PRSA *Member Code Of Ethics*, ibid., 11.
31 Larry Tye, *The Father of Spin: Edward L. Bernays and the Birth of Public Relations* (np: Owl Books, 1998), 7.
32 *The Father of Spin*, ibid.
33 *The Father of Spin*, ibid.
34 *The Father of Spin*, ibid., p. 58.
35 *Public Relations Society of America Member Code of Ethics*, approved by the PRSA Assembly, October, 13.
36 PRSA *Member Code Of Ethics*, ibid., p. 14.
37 IABC *Code of Ethics for Professional Communicators*, ibid.
38 PRSA *Member Code Of Ethics*, ibid., p. 15.
39 IABC *Code of Ethics for Professional Communicators*, ibid.
40 PRSA *Member Code Of Ethics*, ibid., p. 15.
41 IABC *Code of Ethics for Professional Communicators*, ibid.
42 Unattributed article, "Omnicom Unit Settles on Overbilling Suit," *The New York Times*, April 21, 2005, at http://www.nytimes.com/2005/04/21/business/media/21addes.html. (Full disclosure: At the time of this writing coauthor Helio Fred Garcia held shares of Omnicom Group, the parent company of Fleishman-Hillard.)
43 Ted Rohrlich and Ralph Frammolino, "PR Exec to Plead Guilty in Fraud; Steve Sugerman Will Cooperate in the Probe of Overbilling of DWP by Fleishman-Hillard," *Los Angeles Times*, June 10, 2005, at http://www.latimes.com/news/local/la-me-fleishman10jun10,1,5463756.story?coll=la-headlines-california.
44 Unattributed article, "Former Ogilvy Executives Sentenced for Overbilling," *The New York Times*, July 15, 2005, C5.
45 PRSA *Member Code of Ethics*, ibid., pp. 6 and 7.
46 Bernays, *Propaganda*, ibid.
47 IABC *Code of Ethics for Professional Communicators*, ibid.

48 IPRA *Code of Athens,* ibid.

49 PRSA *Member Code of Ethics,* ibid., p. 15.

50 *The Father of Spin*, ibid., p. 49.

51 *CBS 60 Minutes*, January 19, 1992.

52 MacArthur, *Second Front*, ibid., pp. 51 and 53.

53 *Integrity: The Spirit & Letter of Our Commitment,* General Electric, at http://www.ge.com.

54 *Boeing Code of Conduct*, January 26, 2004, at http://www.boeing.com.

55 Dan Richman, "Analysis: Boeing Conduct Code Worked Properly, Expert Says," *Seattle Post-Intelligencer*, March 8, 2005, at http://www.seattlepi.nwsource.com/business/214916_ethics08.html.

56 Alan Murray, "Citigroup CEO Pursues Culture of Ethics," *The Wall Street Journal*, March 2, 2005, A2.

57 *Enron Corp. Code of Ethics*, July 2000, p. 4, at http://www.thesmokinggun.com.

58 *Enron Corp. Code of Ethics*, ibid., p. 2.

59 Barbara Ley Toffler with Jennifer Reingold, *Final Accounting: Ambition, Greed, and the Fall of Arthur Andersen* (n.p.: Broadway Books, 2003), 7.

60 *Final Accounting*, ibid., p. 124.

61 *Final Accounting*, ibid., pp. 124 to 126.

62 *Final Accounting*, ibid., p. 60.

63 *Final Accounting*, ibid., p. 8.

64 *CBS 60 Minutes*, ibid.

65 *Second Front*, ibid., p. 58.

66 *Second Front*, ibid., p. 61.

67 *Second Front*, ibid., p. 58.

68 *Second Front*, ibid., p. 68.

69 *Second Front*, ibid., p. 65.

70 As recounted in *O'Dwyer's PR Services Report*, 6, no. 2, February 1992, 1, and *Jack O'Dwyer's Newsletter*, February 26, 1992, 1.

71 On September 9, 1992, Helio Fred Garcia contacted Hill & Knowlton about the CFK controversy and was referred to Thomas Ross, head of the media services group. Garcia told Ross that he was about to launch a communication ethics class at New York University; that he was assigning MacArthur's book, and that MacArthur would be a guest speaker in the class. Garcia told Ross that in fairness to H&K, he wanted to give H&K the opportunity to tell its side of the story, and would make available time either before, during, or after MacArthur's talk. Ross said he was not interested in debating MacArthur, whom he described as a self-defeating alarmist. Garcia reiterated that he was inviting H&K to speak before, during, or after MacArthur.

    Ross said that H&K had probably spent too much time addressing MacArthur's views already, and would be reluctant to commit more resources to address the class. Garcia noted that he intended to continue to include MacArthur's allegations in his writing and teaching. H&K was invited to send documents outlining their point of view on the scandal. Ross said that H&K had been vindicated and declined to discuss the matter further. Source: Contemporaneous notes taken after phone call between Helio Fred Garcia and Thomas Ross, September 9, 1992.

72 *Inside PR*, July/August 1992, 30.

73 Edward L. Bernays, *Crystallizing Public Opinion*, 1923, 12, Boni and Liveright, New York.

74 Aristotle, *Rhetoric*, I, 2, 1, in *The "Art" of Rhetoric with English Translation* by John Henry Reese, vol. XXII of *Aristotle in Twenty Three Volumes*, Loeb Classical Library (Cambridge, MA: Harvard University Press, 1982), 15.

75 Aristotle, ibid.

76 Cicero, *Brutus*, xxii, 46, in *Cicero on Oratory and Orators*, translated by J.S. Watson, (Carbondale and Edwardsville: Southern Illinois University Press, 1970), 273.

77 Cicero, ibid, p. 274.

78 Plato, *Gorgias*, 452e, in *Lysis, Symposium, Gorgias with an English Translation* by W.R.M. Lamb, vol. III of *Plato in Twelve Volumes* (Cambridge, MA: Harvard University Press, 1983), 279.

79 Plato, ibid.

80 Plato, ibid., 455a, p. 287.

81 Plato, ibid., 458e to 459c, pp. 299 to 301. Note: the translator alternates his translation of *ho rhetor* between "rhetorician" and "orator." For the sake of consistency, we translate it as "rhetorician" three times in this quotation, and shall do so in all subsequent quotations.

82 Plato, ibid, 463a, p. 313.

83 Plato, ibid, 463d, p. 315.

84 Plato, ibid, 465b, p. 319.

85 Plato, ibid, 465c, p. 321.

Chapter 3

1   2000 Merck & Co. Inc. Annual Report, pp. 22.

2   James E. Grunig and Todd Hunt, *Managing Public Relations* (Orlando, FL: Harcourt Brace Jovanovich College Publishers, 1984), pp. 49, 399.

3   *Business Week*, March 18, 1991. "Merck Needs More Gold From The Whitecoats."

4   Grunig and Hunt, ibid., pp. 13.

5   Gina Kolata, "Pharmacists Help Drug Promotions," *The New York Times*, July 29, 1994.

6   Letter from *The New York Times* news editor William Borders to John Doorley at Merck, August 17, 1994.

7   *The Star Ledger,* "Merck Pays $127,500 In Fines For Cuba Deal." October 25, 1995. Juan Forero.

8   1995 Merck & Co., Inc. Annual Report, pp. 51.

9   Erik Eckholm, "River Blindness: Conquering An Ancient Scourge," *The New York Times Magazine*, January 8, 1989.

10 Herb Schmertz with William Novak, *Good-bye To The Low Profile* (Boston: Little Brown and Company, 1986, 73.

Chapter 4

1   David Kirkpatrick, Daniel Roth, and Reporter Associate Oliver Ryan, Features/Cover Stories: Special Report/Ten Tech Trends, "Why There's No Escaping the Blog, Freewheeling Bloggers Can Boost Your Product—Or Destroy It. Either Way, They've Become a Force Business Can't Afford to Ignore," *Fortune*, U.S. Edition, January 10, 2005.

2   Alan R. Earls, "Winning the Name Game; Technology Tools Are Helping Companies Monitor Their Reputations on the Internet," *Computerworld,* April 5, 2004, p. 19.

3   http://www.instruct-online.com.

4   Adapted from Alice Z. Cuneo, "Marketers Dial in to Messaging; with Success Overseas, Chance to Snag Hip U.S. Consumers More Enticing," *Advertising Age*, November 1, 2004, p. 18.

5   "Left Brain Marketing," Forrester Research, April 6, 2004.

6   Ibid.

7   "The Consumer Advertising Backlash Worsens," Forrester Research Inc. Trends, January 5, 2005, p. 3.

8   "What's Next for TV Advertising?" Forreston Research Inc., December 23, 1994, p. 4.

9   Anthony Bianco with Tom Lowry in New York, Robert Berner and Michael Arndt in Chicago, Special Report, "The Vanishing Mass Market; New Technology, Product Proliferation. Fragmented Media. Get ready: It's a Whole New World," *BusinessWeek,* July 12, 2004, p. 18.

10 *BusinessWeek*, ibid. p. 18.

11 Alan Deutschman, "Commercial Success: Traditional Advertising Is In Deep Trouble. Now Yahoo Is Reinventing the Game Thanks to Ad Boss Wenda Millard. and Her Cooperative Approach Is Winning over Madison Avenue," *Fast Company*, January 1, 2005, p. 74.

Chapter 5

1   Enron video produced by Enron for employee audiences.

2   John Doorley interview with Bill Heyman of Heyman Associates, February 17, 2006.

3   Barry Mike, synthesis from his readings, observations, and presentations to clients.

4   "Connecting Organizational Communication to Financial Performance," Communication ROI, Watson Wyatt Worldwide, 2003–2004.

5   *Fortune* magazine, February 28, 2005.

6 Charles J. Fombrun, *Reputation: Realizing Value from the Corporate Image* (Boston: Harvard Business School Press, 1996), 111.

7 Fraser P. Seitel, *The Practice of Public Relations*, 9th ed. (Upper Saddle River, NJ: Prentice Hall, 2004), 261.

8 *Corporate Reputation Review*, Winter 2005.

9 D.H. Maister, C.H. Green, and R.M. Galford, *Trusted Advisor* (New York: Touchstone, 2000).

10 T.J. Larkin and S. Larkin, *Communicating Change* (New York: McGraw-Hill, 1994), Ch. 1, 1–11.

11 M. Gladwell, *The Tipping Point: How Little Things Can Make a Big Difference* (New York: Little, Brown, 2000), Ch. 2, 30–88.

12 William Zinsser, *On Writing Well, 25th Anniversary: The Classic Guide To Writing Non-Fiction* (New York: Harper Collins, 2001).

Chapter 6

1 The lobbying firm formerly known as Wexler, Reynolds, Fuller, Harrison and Schule, founded in 1981, is now known as Wexler & Walker Public Policy Associates.

2 Ohio Edison is now part of the First Energy Corporation.

3 United States Constitution, First Amendment.

4 Web site of Intercontinental Willard Hotel, http://www.washington.intercontinental.com.

5 Microsoft Encarta Online Encyclopedia, http://www.encarta.com.

6 The Center for Public Integrity, http://www.publicintegrity.org.

7 Bob Burke and Ralph Thompson, *Bryce Harlow, Mr. Integrity*, Oklahoma Heritage Assocation, 2000, Foreword by Dr. Henry Kissinger, p. 14.

8 Speech by Vice President Dick Cheney, given at Bryce Harlow Awards Dinner on March 16, 2005, in Washington, D.C., http://www.bryceharlow.org.

9 Bryce Harlow, "Corporate Representation," published by the Bryce Harlow Foundation, Washington, D.C., 1984, http://www.bryceharlow.org.

10 Jeffrey H. Birnbaum, "Road to Riches is Called K Street," *Washington Post*, June 22, 2005.

11 Debra Mayberry, "37,000? 39,402? 11,500? Just How Many Lobbyists Are There in Washington, Anyway?" *Washington Post,* January 29, 2006.

12 The Center for Public Integrity, http://www.publicintegrity.org.

13 "Code of Ethics," American League of Lobbyists (ALL), http://www.alldc.org.

Chapter 7

1 Notes: Walter "Buzz" Storey, "Uniontown and Fayette County: Another Look," *Herald-Standard* (Uniontown Newspapers, 2001).

2 John Doorley interviews with Mr. Joe Hardy on May 11 and May 25, 2005.

3 Edmund M. Burke, *Corporate Community Relations: The Principle of the Neighbor of Choice* (Westport, CT: Praeger, 1999), 15–16.

4 Ibid., p. 16.

5 Ibid., pp. 17–18.

6 Ibid., p. 10.

7 Ibid., p. 28.

8 Charles J. Fombrun, *Reputation, Realizing Value from the Corporate Image* (Boston: Harvard Business School Press, 1996), 195.

9 Burke, Corporate Community Relations, ibid., p. 25.

10 Ibid., pp. 47–50.

11 Ibid., p. 19.

12 David W. Guth and Charles Marsh, *Public Relations, a Values-Driven Approach* (Needham Heights, MA: Allyn & Bacon, 2000), 424–427.

13 Erik Eckholm, Cover Story, *"River Blindness, Conquering An Ancient Scourge,"* *The New York Times Magazine*, January 8, 1989.

14 2005 Merck Corporate Responsibility Report.

15 John Doorley's old notes verified by Dr. Vagelos in November 2005.

16 Facts via e-mail from Ken Gustavsen, Merck's manager of global product donations, February 1, 2006.
17 Burke, Corporate Community Relations, ibid., p. 54.
18 Ibid., 21–23.

Chapter 8

1 Share price adjusted for later stock splits.
2 See Eugene L. Donati, "The Softer Side of Corporate Reporting," *Investor Relations Update,* a publication of the National Investor Relations Institute, September 2001; and "Street Smoke," the *Daily Deal*, April 18, 2001.
3 TSC Industries v. Northway Inc.
4 *General Rules II under the Securities Exchange Act of 1934* (New York: Bowne & Co., 1987), 9.
5 Securities and Exchange Commission, *Securities Exchange Act Rel. No. 21138*, July 12, 1984.
6 Financial Industrial Fund v. McDonnell Douglas Corp.
7 Financial Industrial Fund v. McDonnell Douglas Corp.; see also SEC v. Texas Gulf Sulpher Co. and Elkind v. Liggett & Meyers Inc.

Chapter 9

1 Morley, 24.
2 Wakefield, 2000.
3 Wilcox Ault Agee, 284.
4 *Newsweek*, June 27, 2005, 39.
5 Seitel, 378.
6 Wilcox, 283.
7 Anthony P. Ewing, *Understanding the Global Compact Human Rights Principles*, and *Implementing the Global Compact Human Rights Principles*, in United Nations Global Compact and the Office of High Commissioner for Human Rights, *Embedding Human Rights Into Business Practice* (2004), available at http://www.unglobalcompact.org).
8 *See, e.g.,* Norms on the Responsibilities of Transnational Corporations and Other Business Enterprises with Regard to Human Rights (Aug. 26, 2003), U.N. Commission on Human Rights, Subcommission on the Promotion and Protection of Human Rights, U.N. doc. E/CN.4/Sub.2/2003/12/Rev.2, preamble (noting that transnational corporations "have the capacity to foster economic well-being . . . and wealth as well as the capacity to cause harmful impacts on the human rights and lives of individuals . . . ").
9 Anderson, 413.
10 Anderson, 413.
11 It is not uncommon for nonprofessional workers around the world to have limited literacy in their native language. Companies must make verbal communication available as needed. Truck drivers, factory workers, maintenance staff, and others may also have limited access to computers. Provision must be made to get these employees the information they need.
12 Trissel, 2005.
13 In many companies, communication and marketing, communication and HR, or communication and investor relations are combined into one department.
14 Bough, 2005.
15 Tactics, 1998.
16 Harris, 2005.
17 Schroeder, 2005.
18 Anderson, 421.
19 Sriramesh, 16.
20 Sriramesh, 16.
21 Burns, 2005.
22 Drobis, 2002.
23 Edelman Public Relations, 2004.
24 Vogl, 2001.
25 Cokefacts, 2005.

26 *The Wall Street Journal,* 2005.
27 *The Wall Street Journal,* 2005.
28 Drobis, 2002.
29 UN Global Compact, 1999.
30 Amery, Turegano, 2001.
31 Starbucks, 2005.
32 Burns, 2005.

Chapter 10

1 Dave Sutton and Tom Klein, 2003, p. 19.
2 Ibid., pp. 20–21.
3 Edelman, 2003.
4 Ibid.
5 Bossidy and Charan, 2004, p. 68.
6 Ibid., p. 79.
7 Schultz, 2005.
8 Tichy and Sherman, 2001, p. 84.
9 Collins, 2001, p. 21.
10 Kouzes and Posner, 2002, p. 13.
11 Kotter and Cohen, 2002, p. 1.
12 Senge, 1999.
13 Pottruck and Pearce, 2001, p. 222.
14 Senge, 1999, p. 10.
15 Schein, 1997, p. 4.
16 Ibid., p. 22.
17 Gill and Whittle, 1992; Higgs and Rowland, 2000; and Miller, 2002.
18 Garvin, 1993.
19 Conger, 1998, p. 87.
20 Deetz, Tracy, and Simpson, 2000, p. 67.
21 Borden, p. 6–7.
22 Borden, p. 13.
23 Kumar, 2004, p. 13.
24 Moser, 2003, p. 15.

Chapter 11

1 M. Taylor et al., *Public Relations Review,* 29 (2003): 257–270.
2 *The Art of War,* by Sun Tzu, translated by Thomas Cleary, Shambhala, 1988, p. 82.
3 "GE's Jeff Immelt on the 10 Keys to Great Leadership," *Fast Company,* April, 2004, 96.

Chapter 12

1 Editorial, "Time for Exxon to Pay," *The New York Times,* January 30, 2004, A24.
2 Todd S. Purdum and Marjorie Connelly, "Support for Bush Continues to Drop, Poll Shows," *The New York Times,* September 15, 2005, at http://www.nytimes.com/2005/09/15/politics/15poll.html.
3 *Time* magazine, September 19, 2005 issue, published online on September 11, 2005, at http://www.time.com/time/magazine.
4 Tamotsu Shibutani, *Improvised News; A Sociological Study of Rumor,* (Indianapolis: Bobbs Merrill, 1966), 172. Note: Shibutani uses the gender-specific words "man" or "men" to refer to people in general. Throughout, I will quote him using the gender-neutral "person" or "people."
5 Steven Fink, *Crisis Management: Planning for the Inevitable* (New York: American Management Association, 1986), 15.
6 Fink, ibid., pp. 15–16.
7 Fink, ibid., p. 16.

8   Ronald J. Alsop, *The 18 Immutable Laws of Corporate Reputation: Creating, Protecting, and Repairing Your Most Valuable Asset, A Wall Street Journal Book* (New York: Free Press, 2004), 220.

9   Alsop, ibid., p. 218.

10 For more on these behaviors, how to recognize them, and how to prevent them, see also *Avoiding Crisis Mis-Steps*, by Helio Fred Garcia (Logos Crisis Monograph Series, 2004), at http://www.logosconsulting. net.

11 For historical roots of the phrase "Golden Hour" in emergency medicine, see "New Techniques Developed for Treatment of the 'Epidemic'" by Robert Locke, the Associated Press, January 18, 1982.

12 Carol Hymowitz and Joanne S. Lublin, "McDonald's CEO Tragedy Holds Lessons" *The Wall Street Journal*, April 20, 2004, p. B1.

13 Hymowitz and Lublin, ibid.

14 Jonathan Harr, *A Civil Action* (New York: Random House, 1995), 295.

15 Shibutani, ibid., p. 62.

16 http://www.ruralfire.qld.gov.au/level2/M06/introduction.htm.

17 Gordon W. Allport and Leo Postman, "An Analysis of Rumor," *Public Opinion Quarterly* 10 (1946):505 and 506., italics in the original.

18 Jean-Noël Kapferer, *Rumors: Uses, Interpretations, & Images* (New Brunswick, NJ: Transaction Publishers, 1990), 12.

19 Kapferer, ibid., p. 108, italics in original.

20 Kapferer, ibid., p. 9.

21 Gordon W. Allport and Leo Postman, *The Psychology of Rumor* (New York: Henry Holt, 1947), p. ix, italics in the original.

22 Allport and Postman, *The Psychology of Rumor*, ibid., p. x.

23 Allport and Postman, *The Psychology of Rumor*, ibid., p 1.

24 Allport and Postman, *The Psychology of Rumor*, ibid., p 44, italics in the original.

25 Allport and Postman, *The Psychology of Rumor*, ibid., p 2.

26 Allport and Postman, *The Psychology of Rumor*, ibid., p. 3.

27 Allport and Postman, *The Psychology of Rumor*, ibid., pp. 33 and 34, italics in the original.

Chapter 13

1   Nike Inc., FY04 Corporate Responsibility Report (2005), p. 11.

2   *Cf.* Milton Friedman, "The Social Responsibility of Business is to Increase its Profits," *The New York Times Magazine*, Sept. 11, 1970; Peter Drucker, "The New Meaning of Corporate Social Responsibility," *California Management Review* (vol. 26, no. 2, Winter 1984).

3   See, for example, Virginia Haufler, *A Public Role for the Private Sector* (2001).

4   The UN Millennium Development Goals, to (1) eradicate extreme poverty and hunger; (2) achieve universal primary education; (3) promote gender equality and empower women; (4) reduce child mortality; (5) improve maternal health; (6) combat HIV/AIDS, malaria, and other diseases; (7) ensure environmental sustainability; and (8) develop a global partnership for development, were adopted by world leaders at the Millennium Summit of the United Nations in 2000. UN General Assembly, UN Millennium Declaration (8 Sept. 2000).

5   General Electric Company, Our Actions: GE 2005 Citizenship Report (2005), p. 4.

6   Communicating financial performance is covered in Chapter 8, Investor Relations.

7   Nike, for example, defines its stakeholders broadly as "anyone affected by, or affecting, our business operations." Nike Inc., FY04 Corporate Responsibility Report (2005), p. 11.

8   Anthony P. Ewing, *Understanding the Global Compact Human Rights Principles*, and *Implementing the Global Compact Human Rights Principles*, in United Nations Global Compact and the Office of High Commissioner for Human Rights, Embedding Human Rights Into Business Practice (2004), available at http://www.unglobalcompact.org.

9   See, for example, UN Sub-Commission on the Promotion and Protection of Human Rights, Norms on the Responsibilities of Transnational Corporations and Other Business Enterprises with Regard to Human Rights (Aug. 26, 2003), U.N. doc. E/CN.4/Sub.2/2003/12/Rev.2.

10 See, for example, Elliot J. Schrage and Anthony P. Ewing, "The Cocoa Industry and Child Labor," *Journal of Corporate Citizenship* (vol. 18, Summer 2005), p. 99.

11 The Coalition for Environmentally Responsible Economies (CERES) Principles address protection of the biosphere, sustainable use of natural resources, reduction and disposal of wastes, energy conservation, and product safety. CERES Principles (1989), available at http://www.ceres.org/coalitionandcompanies/principles.php.

12 See generally Fair Trade Labeling Organizations International, http://www.fairtrade.net.

13 See Publish What You Pay, http://www.publishwhatyoupay.org.

14 See, for example, John Elkington, *Cannibals with Forks: The Triple Bottom Line of 21ˢᵗ Century Business* (1997).

15 "The Case for Social Responsibility," Presentation to the Annual Conference of Business for Social Responsibility, Boston (Nov. 10, 1998).

16 General Electric Company, Our Actions: GE 2005 Citizenship Report (2005), p. 3.

17 World Economic Forum, Values and Value (2004).

18 The Fair Labor Association (FLA) seeks to improve working conditions in apparel and footwear factories in the United States and abroad through an industrywide Workplace Code of Conduct and monitoring system. FLA members include consumer, human and labor rights groups, universities, and leading manufacturers and retailers. See http://www.fairlabor.org.

19 Roger L. Martin, "The Virtue Matrix: Calculating the Return on Corporate Responsibility," *Harvard Business Review* (March 2002), p. 69 (arguing that voluntary corporate responsibility initiatives that provide a clear benefit to shareholders can become industry standards).

20 *The New York Times*, "Shell Game in Nigeria" (Dec. 3, 1995), at E14.

21 Royal Dutch/Shell, "Statement of General Business Principles" (March 17, 1997).

22 Human Rights Watch, "Colombia: Concerns Raised by the Security Arrangements of Transnational Oil Companies" (April 1998).

23 See generally, Bennett Freeman, "Drilling for Common Ground," *Foreign Policy Magazine* (July/August 2001).

24 Amnesty International UK, *Human Rights On the Line* (May 2003), available at http://www.amnesty.org.uk/images/ul/H/Human_Rights_on_the_Line.pdf.

25 Jay Pearson, Regional Coordinator, BP p.l.c., UN Global Compact Learning Forum, Nova Lima, Brazil (December 2003).

26 Human Rights Watch, "Turning a Blind Eye: Hazardous Child Labor in El Salvador's Sugarcane Cultivation" (June 2004).

27 See, for example, Royal Dutch/Shell Group of Companies, "Shell's Approach to Human Rights," available at http://www.shell.com/home.

28 Edwin V. Woodsome, Howrey Simon Arnold & White LLP (Unocal outside counsel in Doe v. Unocal), "Corporate Liability for Conduct of a Foreign Government," presentation to Loyola Law School International Law Symposium (Feb. 8, 2003) ("[T]o invest in a foreign country, private corporations must to a large degree rely on that countries' infrastructure, including its police force and firefighters, to provide a safe working environment for its workers. Under the Ninth Circuit ruling, private corporations could be liable for the conduct of these police forces.")

29 Starbucks, "Green Coffee Purchasing Pilot Program for Preferred Suppliers" (Nov. 12, 2001). The Starbucks Program was developed in partnership with Conservation International's Center for Environmental Leadership in Business.

30 Starbucks, Starbucks Corporate Social Responsibility Report, Fiscal Year 2002 (2003), p. 4. The Starbucks C.A.F.E. (Coffee and Farmer Equity) Practices Program is an "incentive based performance program that provides purchasing preference to coffee suppliers providing green coffee that is grown, processed and traded in an environmentally, socially and economically responsible manner." Scientific Certification Systems, "C.A.F.E. Practices Program Overview, Starbucks Coffee Company Preferred Supplier Program" (March 29, 2004).

31 Elliot Schrage, "Supply and the Brand," *Harvard Business Review* (June 2004). In 2004, Starbucks purchased 43.5 million pounds of coffee from Preferred Suppliers.

32 E-mail from Unocal Director of Information Carol Scott to Unocal Media Contact and Spokesperson David Garcia, cited in Doe I v. Unocal Corp. (9ᵗʰ Cir. Filed Sept. 18, 2002).

33   Examples are Business for Social Responsibility (USA) and the International Business Leaders Forum (UK).

34   Business for Social Responsibility, "Taking the Temperature of CSR Leaders" (January 18, 2005).

35   See Addressing Child Labor in Pakistan's Soccer Ball Production, in Elliot J. Schrage, Promoting International Worker Rights through Private Voluntary Initiatives: Public Relations or Public Policy?, p. 13 (University of Iowa Center for Human Rights, January 2004), available at http://www.uichr.org/content/act/sponsored/gwri_report.pdf.

36   Doe I v. Unocal Corp., 395 F. 3d 932 (9th Cir. Cal. 2002), vacated by Doe I v. Unocal Corp., 395 F.3d 978 (9th Cir. Cal. 2003).

37   Robert M. Reese, Senior Vice President of Hershey Foods, quoted in Bob Fernandez, "Hershey 'Shocked' by Report," *Times Union* (Albany, NY, June 24, 2001), p. A7.

38   See Elliot Schrage and Anthony Ewing, "Business and Human Rights in Africa: The Cocoa Industry and Child Labor," *Journal of Corporate Citizenship* (vol. 18, Summer 2005), p. 99.

39   "A Life of Fines and Beating," *Business Week* (Oct. 2, 2000).

40   "Social Research Analyst Statement on Corporate Sustainability Reporting" (September 2005).

41   The California Public Employees' Retirement System uses an investment analysis for emerging markets that quantifies factors such as civil liberties, political risk, freedom of the press, and productive labor practices. Wilshire Associates, "Permissible Equity Markets: Investment Analysis and Recommendations" (February 2004). See also The Danish Institute for Human Rights, "Country Risk Assessment Reports," available at http://www.humanrightsbusiness.org/070_country_risk.htm.

42   Lynn Paine et al., "Up to Code," *Harvard Business Review* (December 2005).

43   Formally launched in July 2000, the UN Global Compact is a voluntary corporate citizenship initiative that calls on companies to integrate into their core business operations ten principles on human rights, labor rights, environmental protection and transparency. By adopting the Global Compact, companies commit to make the Global Compact principles part of their "strategy, culture and day-to-day operations" and report publicly on their progress. More than 1,600 companies have signed on to the Global Compact, including seventy-nine of the world's 500 largest corporations. See "The Global Compact Database of Participants," available at http://www.unglobalcompact.org.

44   Examples of industry corporate responsibility initiatives include the Fair Labor Association Workplace Code of Conduct, the International Council of Toy Industries Code of Business Practices, the Common Code for the Coffee Community, the Cocoa Industry Protocol, the Electronics Industry Code of Conduct, and the Equator Principles (financial services).

45   See, for example, Michael Liedtke, Associated Press, "Gap Inc. Says Some of its Factories are Sweatshops," *Ventura County Star* (CA) (May 13, 2004).

46   For a brief listing, see Business & Human Rights Resource Centre, http://www.business-humanrights.org/Categories/Companies/Policies/Companieswithhumanrightspolicies.

47   *The New York Times*, "Citizen Shell" (March 31, 1997), at A14.

48   Aaron Bernstein, "Freeport's Hard Look at Itself," *Business Week* (Oct. 24, 2005), p. 108.

49   World Bank, *Strengthening Implementation of Corporate Social Responsibility in Global Supply Chains* (October 2003).

50   Allen L. White, *New Wine, New Bottles: The Rise of Non-Financial Reporting* (Business for Social Responsibility, June 20, 2005).

51   Allen L. White, ibid.

52   Business for Social Responsibility, Reporting as a Process (June 2005), p. 18–19.

53   Global Reporting Initiative, Sustainability Reporting Guidelines (2002).

54   United States courts have provided a forum for efforts to hold transnational companies accountable for business practices abroad. See, for example Elliot J. Schrage, "Judging Corporate Accountability in the Global Economy," 42 *Columbia Journal of Transnational Law* 153 (2003); Elliot Schrage, "Emerging Threat: Human Rights Claims," *Harvard Business Review* (August 2003).

55   Kasky v. Nike Inc. (Cal. S087859, May 2, 2002).

56   Nike Inc., FY04 Corporate Responsibility Report (2005), p. 12.

57   The author served as a member of the independent Report Review Committee for the 2004/5 Ford Sustainability Report.

Chapter 14

1 Kevin T. Jackson, *Building Reputational Capital: Strategies for Integrity and Fair Play That Improve the Bottom Line* (Oxford: Oxford University Press, 2004), 12.

2 Jackson, ibid., p. 12.

3 Glenn Rifkin, "At 100, Public Relations' Pioneer Criticizes Some of His Peers," *The New York Times*, December 30, 1991, D6.

4 Edward L. Bernays, *Crystallizing Public Opinion* (Boni and Liveright, 1923), 52.

5 Bernays, ibid., pp. 96 to 97.

6 Bernays, ibid., p. 57.

7 Bernays, ibid., p. 139.

8 Bernays, ibid, p. 77.

9 *Fortune*, May 21, 2005, at http://www.fortune.com.

10 "GE's Jeff Immelt on the 10 Keys to Great Leadership," *Fast Company*, April 2004, 96.

11 *Clausewitz on Strategy: Inspiration and Insight from a Master on Strategy*, edited and with commentary by Tiha von Ghyczy, Bolko von Oetinger, and Christopher Bassord, a publication of The Strategy Institute of the Boston Consulting Group (New York: John Wiley & Sons, 2001), 2.

12 *Clausewitz on Strategy*, ibid., p. 4.

13 *Clausewitz on Strategy*, ibid., p. 37.

14 *On War*, ibid., p. 87.

15 *On War*, ibid., p. 81, italic in the original.

16 *On War*, ibid., p. 178.

17 *Clausewitz on Strategy*, ibid., p. 55.

Index